PHILOSOPHICAL PERSPECTIVES ON PSYCHIATRIC DIAGNOSTIC CLASSIFICATION

D1121262

The Johns Hopkins Series in Psychiatry and Neuroscience

Consulting Editors:

Paul R. McHugh, M.D.

Richard T. Johnson, M.D.

Also in This Series:

The Prevention of Depression: Research and Practice, Ricardo F. Munoz and Yu-Wen Ying

Depression in Neurologic Disease, edited by Sergio E. Starkstein, M.D., and Robert G. Robinson, M.D.

Psychiatric Epidemiology: Assessment Concepts and Methods, edited by Juan E. Mezzich, M.D., Ph.D., Miguel R. Jorge, M.D., Ph.D., and Ihsan M. Salloum, M.D., M.P.H.

Philosophical Perspectives on Psychiatric Diagnostic Classification

EDITED BY

John Z. Sadler, M.D.
Associate Professor of Psychiatry
University of Texas Southwestern Medical Center
Dallas, Texas

Osborne P. Wiggins, Ph.D.
Associate Professor of Philosophy and
Family and Community Medicine
University of Louisville
Louisville, Kentucky

AND

Michael A. Schwartz, M.D.
Professor and Vice Chairman of Psychiatry
Case Western Reserve University School of Medicine
Cleveland, Ohio

THE JOHNS HOPKINS UNIVERSITY PRESS
Baltimore and London

© 1994 The Johns Hopkins University Press
All rights reserved
Printed in the United States of America on acid-free paper

The Johns Hopkins University Press
2715 North Charles Street
Baltimore, Maryland 21218-4319
The Johns Hopkins Press Ltd., London

Library of Congress Cataloging-in-Publication Data will be found at the end of this book.

A catalog record for this book is available from the British Library.

Contents

Foreword

Our work on DSM-IV stirs up all sorts of conceptual and epistemological questions for which there are often no very clear answers. Since our task in preparing DSM-IV is essentially a pragmatic one (i.e., to develop a classification that will be as useful as possible in the day-to-day work of clinicians, researchers, and educators), we are sometimes prone to an epistemological nearsightedness in the face of conceptual problems that are complex and impossible to resolve. It has, therefore, been a source of pleasure and enlightenment for me to have participated, over the last several years, in the planning and implementation of this work. This effort has provided an opportunity to study the implications of the broader philosophical issues that lurk just behind what must (to the philosophically inclined observer) seem to be our naively positivistic approach to the DSM effort. Drs. Sadler, Wiggins, and Schwartz are to be congratulated for having assembled an especially comprehensive and probing analysis of the theoretical issues that inform psychiatric classification. Their effort should be equally interesting to those who come to the issues from the mental health as well as the philosophical disciplines, and it has greatly enriched my own understanding.

I will take up just one of the problems raised in the book, chosen for discussion here because it is of fundamental importance, is difficult or impossible to deal with, and serves as a theme linking a number of the chapters that follow. DSM-IV is a manual of *mental disorders*, but it is by no means clear just what *is* a mental disorder and whether one can develop a set of definitional criteria to guide inclusionary and exclusionary decisions for the manual. Although many have tried (including the authors of DSM-III-R), no one has ever succeeded in developing a list of infallible criteria to define a mental disorder. A similar problem exists in all of medicine. We treat *diseases* without being able to define precisely just what is a disease. This failure of definition is not a reflection on the skill or ingenuity of the dozens of authors who have attempted to define *mental disorder*, *disease*, and *illness* but rather results from the essentially heterogeneous conceptions captured under the everyday understanding of these terms. Although any definition of *mental disorder* or *disease* which reduces to what *clinicians treat* is tautological (and potentially self-serving), it is probably the best of a bad lot of ways of defining these necessarily imprecise terms.

It must be admitted that the lack of a universally applicable definition of mental disorders results in a manual that has *disorders* at quite different levels of abstraction. It also causes confusion in deciding when one should add a newly suggested disorder or delete one that has already been included. This is an immediate problem, since we have been inundated with suggestions (more than 100 of them) for new mental disorders in DSM-IV. Some of these seem to be on the border of normality (e.g., Minor Depression, Age-Appropriate Memory Impairment); others have been criticized as role behaviors imposed by aspects of our society (e.g., Self-Defeating Personality Disorder); others seem to have been suggested as a way of stigmatizing undesirable behaviors by labeling them as an aspect of mental disorder (e.g., Racist Personality Disorder, Delusional Dominating Disorder). Unfortunately, it seems unlikely that we will ever have a set of definitional criteria for mental disorder which will precisely guide decisions about including entities at the boundaries of the mental disorder concept. Instead, for now and at least until we have a clearer notion of pathogenesis, these decisions must be made in a commonsense way—how frequent and how important is the proposed disorder; is there an empirical literature documenting its descriptive characteristics, course, family loading, biology, and/or treatment response; what are the relative costs of false positives or false negatives if it is included or excluded; what are possible misuses of the diagnosis in other than clinical settings, and so forth. This may not be very satisfying to those who insist on clear algorithms and definitional consistency, but the rough-and-ready application of such guidelines is often the best we can do in a situation lacking clear epistemological definitions and extensive empirical evidence.

The problem with the construct *mental disorders* extends beyond its lack of clear definition to the very nature of the term itself. There could arguably not be a worse term than *mental disorders* to describe the conditions classified in DSM-IV. *Mental* implies a mind-body dichotomy that is becoming increasingly outmoded, considering the accumulating evidence that most if not all such disorders have a biological as well as a psychosocial contribution. Any division between purely mental and purely physical disorders ignores that these conditions result from an interaction that belies the distinction. Unfortunately, we have not been able to devise a substitute term that would not have its own serious disadvantages, and we are therefore reluctantly forced to continue in DSM-IV with the misleading term *mental disorders*.

The book you are about to read goes much more deeply into these and many other issues. It provides a rounded history of psychiatric diagnosis, a discussion of the many philosophical and conceptual issues that have attended this history, and a number of challenging solutions—most of which may be more suitable for DSM-V than for DSM-IV. It is important not to reify our diagnostic system and its mental disorders. This book will help us see the context in which the system has developed and must be used.

Allen J. Frances, M.D.
Professor and Chairman, Department of Psychiatry
Duke University Medical Center
  & Chair, DSM-IV Task Force

Acknowledgments

Practical, spiritual, and conceptual inspiration contributed to the success of this book.

Linda Muncy and her dogs (Monika and Sydney) organized, buffed, polished, and wrapped this book. Thanks for her essential and practical contribution. We are also appreciative of Wendy Harris's forbearance and support.

Our spouses, Abbie, Michele, and Joan, deserve our thanks in all three areas: assistance, discussion, and forbearance. Most of all, their love provides a foundation in spirit for us.

The fellowship of the Association for the Advancement of Philosophy and Psychiatry has been a source of collegial support and inspiration.

Whenever there is talk of the connection between philosophy and psychiatry, pride of place for us always goes to Karl Jaspers. His work exemplifies the importance that ideas on the philosophical plane have for practitioners in psychiatry.

We would also like to mention our longstanding indebtedness to Herbert Spiegelberg, Maurice Natanson, and Richard Zaner. Their achievements have served as guidelines for what we sought.

Our conviction that philosophy and psychiatry are closely and fruitfully akin has been confirmed countless times by Paul R. McHugh and Phillip R. Slavney. These two philosophical psychiatrists embody what is best in this kinship.

Contributors

George J. Agich, Ph.D., Professor of Medical Humanities, Philosophy, and Psychiatry, Southern Illinois University School of Medicine, Springfield, Illinois; and Vice President, Association for the Advancement of Philosophy and Psychiatry

Peter J. Caws, Ph.D., University Professor of Philosophy, George Washington University, Washington, D.C.

K. W. M. Fulford, D.Phil., M.R.C.P., M.R.C.Psych., Research Psychiatrist, Warneford Hospital, University of Oxford, Oxford, England; and President, Philosophy Interest Group of the Royal College of Psychiatrists

Aviel Goodman, M.D., Medical Director and President, Minnesota Institute of Psychiatry, St. Paul, Minnesota

George Graham, Ph.D., Professor and Chair, Department of Philosophy, University of Alabama at Birmingham, Birmingham, Alabama

Carl G. Hempel, Ph.D., Professor Emeritus of Philosophy, Princeton University, Princeton, New Jersey

Yosaf F. Hulgus, Ph.D., Clinical Assistant Professor of Psychiatry, University of Texas Southwestern Medical Center, Dallas, Texas; and private practice, Family Therapy Associates, Plano, Texas

Alfred Kraus, M.D., Professor of Psychiatry and Medical Director, Psychiatrische Klinik und Poliklinik, Ruprecht-Karls-Universität Heidelberg, Heidelberg, Germany

Joseph Margolis, Ph.D., Professor of Philosophy, Temple University, Philadelphia, Pennsylvania

Aaron L. Mishara, Ph.D., studies phenomenological philosophy and psychology at Julius Maximilians Universität Würzburg, Würzburg, Germany

Denise Russell, Ph.D., Professor and Head, General Philosophy, University of Sydney, Sydney, Australia

John Z. Sadler, M.D., Associate Professor of Psychiatry, University of Texas Southwestern Medical Center, Dallas, Texas; and cofounder and Treasurer, Association for the Advancement of Philosophy and Psychiatry

Kenneth F. Schaffner, M.D., Ph.D., University Professor of Medical Humanities, George Washington University, Washington, D.C.

Michael A. Schwartz, M.D., Professor and Vice Chairman of Psychiatry, Case Western Reserve University School of Medicine, Cleveland, Ohio; and cofounder and President, Association for the Advancement of Philosophy and Psychiatry

Manfred Spitzer, M.D., Ph.D., Lecturer in Psychiatry, Psychiatrische Klinik und Poliklinik, Ruprecht-Karls-Universität Heidelberg, Heidelberg, Germany

G. Lynn Stephens, Ph.D., Associate Professor of Philosophy, University of Alabama at Birmingham, Birmingham, Alabama

Edwin R. Wallace, IV, M.D., Professor of Psychiatry, Medical College of Georgia, Augusta, Georgia; Professor of Social Work, University of Georgia, Athens, Georgia; and cofounder, Association for the Advancement of Philosophy and Psychiatry

Osborne P. Wiggins, Ph.D., Associate Professor of Philosophy and Family and Community Medicine, University of Louisville, Louisville, Kentucky; and cofounder, Association for the Advancement of Philosophy and Psychiatry

PHILOSOPHICAL PERSPECTIVES ON PSYCHIATRIC DIAGNOSTIC CLASSIFICATION

Introduction

From the *Malleus Maleficarum* to DSM-III, the Rat Man to Son of Sam, sha-
man to psychopharmacologist, Hippocrates to Frances, and King David to
Senator Eagleton, concepts of mental disorder have fascinated us. It therefore
seems surprising that there has never been an extended monograph on the conceptual groundwork of psychiatric nosology. This book is designed to explore
some of the philosophical assumptions, trade-offs, compromises, omissions,
commissions, possibilities, impossibilities, successes, and failures of contemporary psychiatric classification. As an exploration it cannot claim to be a comprehensive review of psychiatric taxonomies or an exhaustive critique of them.
We hope that it will accomplish a few modest functions, including bringing
some shock of the new. In the Foreword, Allen Frances warns of the danger
of reifying diagnostic concepts——treating mental disorders as concrete things
rather than useful abstractions or constructs. Instead of reifying classification,
we intend this book to expand the conceptual scope of it——to be a long essay
on the many possibilities of psychiatric classification. Indeed, we conceive an
important task of good science to be the uncovering and elaboration of alternative ways of making sense of things, including scientific things themselves.

Part of the inspiration for this book has been a recent revolution in psychiatry: the development, release, and acclaim of the *Diagnostic and Statistical
Manual of Mental Disorders, Third Edition* (American Psychiatric Association,
1980), and the *Third Edition, Revised* (American Psychiatric Association,
1987), heretofore called DSM-III and DSM-III-R, respectively. The accom-
plishments and changes provoked by these DSMs receive much attention here,
as elsewhere (see, e.g., Birley, 1990; Chodoff, 1986; Faust & Miner, 1986;
Freedman, Brotman, Silverman & Hutson, 1986; Kaplan, 1983; Kendler, 1990;
Klerman, Vaillant, Spitzer & Michels, 1984; Mezzich & von Cranach, 1988;
Millon, 1991; Tischler, 1987). Suffice it to say that these latest DSMs have
generated significant transformations in psychiatric diagnostic practice, training, research, record keeping, reimbursement, and world diagnostic unity. The
emphasis of DSM-III/III-R on descriptively oriented, highly reliable, low-

inference diagnosis within a multiaxial system has largely contributed to the success of these manuals.

In our view, however, the innovations of these DSMs are an intellectual outgrowth of Carl G. Hempel's contribution to psychopathology more than 20 years ago. In February 1959 Hempel, then as now a preeminent philosopher of science, presented a paper for the Work Conference on Field Studies in the Mental Disorders in New York, under the auspices of the American Psychopathological Association. He had been invited to assist in conceiving a more scientific classification system for mental disorders. His paper, published in Zubin's *Field Studies in the Mental Disorders* (1961) and in Hempel's *Aspects of Scientific Explanation and Other Essays in the Philosophy of Science* (1965e), emphasized many of the innovations to be borne by DSM-III 20 years later: the importance of taxonomic description with minimal inference, operational definitions, the minimizing of valuational statements, the requirement of testability, even the "multiaxial" diagnosis. Hempel's foresight and influence inspired this book as well. His benchmark essay on psychopathological taxonomy is reproduced in the Appendix.

These close similarities between the DSMs and Hempel's philosophy establish an important point: what philosophers do can be directly relevant to psychiatrists' work. In 1959 Joseph Zubin was quite insightful when he invited Hempel to address psychiatrists and psychologists. Unfortunately, Hempel's address did not reach a wide audience. Consequently, those aspects of Hempel's philosophy which appear in the DSMs entered in a roundabout and limited fashion. It would have been far better, we think, if Hempel had had a wider audience, so that the full import of his well-conceived ideas—as well as those of other philosophers of science—could have directly influenced the DSMs. When psychiatrists confront large-scale statistical problems, they draw on the expertise of established statisticians outside of psychiatry. This is merely good scientific practice. We suggest that it would be equally advantageous to solicit the advice of experts in philosophy when psychiatry confronts a methodological, conceptual, or any other kind of philosophical problem.

Hempel's work and its place in psychiatric history are a classic example of the formative role of philosophical inquiry in psychiatry. Hempel's work discusses the many approaches to science and the variety of ways to divide up clinical reality. It also illustrates some of the critical pragmatic and moral considerations in science and raises some of the many worthwhile, even essential, nonempirical questions to be answered. It shows, in short, that there are important questions that empirical research can never resolve. We aspire to build on Hempel's example in this book—to reveal assumptions, to point to alternatives, to answer nosological questions outside of the domain of empirical research while maintaining a commitment to an empirical psychiatry. As a monograph of the Association for the Advancement of Philosophy and Psychiatry, this book represents an outgrowth of that organization's values and interests.

THE VALUE OF PHILOSOPHY OF PSYCHIATRIC NOSOLOGY

What is the need for a volume on the philosophy of psychiatric nosology? We could summarize the need under five headings: (a) revealing tacit assumptions that shape the clinical worldviews of existing nosologies; (b) revealing the scientific, value, and practical consequences of particular nosologies; (c) clarifying methodological approaches to psychiatric classification for review by the profession; (d) evaluating degrees of success in developing and implementing a particular nosological approach; and (e) generating innovative ideas to stimulate new research.

Revealing Tacit Assumptions

Philosophy is, among other things, an unearthing and questioning of tacit assumptions. What scientists take for granted should be rendered explicit and critically examined by philosophers (Longino, 1990). The essays in this volume are philosophical in this sense. These tacit assumptions function in systems and procedures of psychiatric classification. The reader will find that psychiatric classifications harbor tacit presuppositions of numerous sorts: scientific, sociocultural, evaluative, therapeutic, practical, and others.

Tacit assumptions are an unavoidable precondition for knowledge. Because of the particular limitations these assumptions impose, however, all of our descriptive and explanatory tools in science are limited in their scope and applicability. In psychiatry, portions of clinical reality are omitted; for instance, interviewing individual patients for signs and symptoms of disorder harbors its own assumptions about the parameters of disorders and tends to exclude the gathering of information which shapes a psychodynamic understanding of patients. Moreover, both kinds of data collection, because of their own peculiar assumptions, deemphasize the interactional aspect of the patient and family. In an effort to preserve a holistic approach to the psychiatric patient, clinicians combine scientific approaches in routine practice. Indeed, this scientific pluralism is at once a source of therapeutic power, confusion, and controversy (Mc-Hugh & Slavney, 1983; Sadler & Hulgus, 1991; Schwartz & Wiggins, 1988). Psychiatry's pluralism becomes a particular problem in the face of the classification of psychopathology. The ideal classification would be clear, concise, and comprehensively inclusive of the various scientific approaches in psychiatry. Realizing such a classification is impossible, however.

The consequence of the demand for simplicity combined with the fact of pluralism is necessary compromise. In the case of the DSMs, many of the compromises were acknowledged in the manuals themselves as well as in the literature. Nevertheless, other compromises were (perhaps inadvertently) made through the prevailing attitudes, assumptions, and values of the individuals creating the manuals. A role for philosophy in psychiatric classification is to excavate the conceptual artifacts of our taxonomies, ask what these artifacts teach us, and evaluate whether the artifacts are worth keeping.

Today, for instance, many psychiatric researchers are hoping to disclose the neurobiological and genetic determinants of schizophrenia. Kenneth Schaffner's essay in this book clarifies the assumptions involved in such projects. Schaffner explicates the necessary structure of any etiological account of schizophrenia. He explains that such research assumes the possibility of a reductionistic theory in which a functional psychosis, such as schizophrenia, can be identified and explained ultimately by reference to the terms of neurobiology and molecular genetics. Schaffner alludes to the prototypical structure of such an explanation, a structure he has developed more fully in his prior work. Here he focuses on the logical form of the reductionism, and he illuminates the complexity of analyzing this kind of reduction in psychiatry when he emphasizes the need to account for behavioral and environmental variance in a molecular genetic explanation. Although Schaffner confines himself to schizophrenia, his views, we think, are equally pertinent to any reductionistic explanation in psychiatry.

Several commentators (e.g., Schwartz & Wiggins, 1986) have contended that the classification scheme found in DSM-III and DSM-III-R implicitly presupposes a particular view of scientific methodology, namely, the logical empiricism best delineated by Carl Hempel (see the Appendix). Joseph Margolis's essay clarifies this presupposition and points to the manifold difficulties involved in adopting this particular methodology. Margolis bases his reflections on the more recent philosophy of science, which often focuses on the problems of logical empiricism. Drawing on this literature, Margolis addresses DSM-III and DSM-III-R directly and points to specific problems inherent in their atheoretical approach and use of operational definitions. Like Schaffner, Margolis helps us appreciate the perplexities involved in linking functional disorders to biochemical explanations.

Bill Fulford's essay delineates the evaluative assumptions of psychiatric classifications. Fulford argues that our current science-based approach to disorders necessarily presupposes a value-based experience of illness. His intriguing proposal is to reorient psychiatric classification around these evaluative contents of classification.

George Agich unearths evaluative *and* pragmatic presuppositions in DSM-III and DSM-III-R. His approach supplements Fulford's focus on tacit valuational components in diagnosis (as does Denise Russell's essay). Moreover, earlier critics of DSM-III and DSM-III-R viewed the atheoretical stance of these documents, along with their emphases on operational definitions and reliability, as the results of assuming a particular scientific methodology. Agich, by contrast, sees these methodological commitments as rather evincing "the acceptance of a specifically pragmatic approach to nosology." Agich employs the language of politics instead of science when he describes the writing of the diagnostic manuals as "a collective enterprise governed by consensus and compromise." From this point of view, it is interesting to compare Agich's essay with Margolis's treatment of DSM-III and DSM-III-R as primarily scientific documents. We suspect that Agich and Margolis are equally correct: DSM-III and DSM-III-R have been shaped by both pragmatic and scientific assumptions that require philosophical explication and critical examination. Moreover, we wonder about how scientific methodology could serve practical purposes as well as about how the practical aims move psychiatry toward a particular methodology.

Revealing the Scientific, Value, and Practical Consequences

Just as philosophers are accustomed to seeking out implicit and unnoticed assumptions, so they regularly search for implicit and unnoticed consequences. Philosophers thus examine statements, theories, classifications, attitudes, decisions, and commitments and ask what these, when fully developed, logically imply. Rendering explicit the heretofore implicit consequences of a classification scheme can help us greatly in determining whether we really want to accept such a scheme.

Because they issue from compromises, psychiatric classifications in particular have unique consequences. Classifications can, in part, determine the results of empirical research through means such as selective attention, avoidance of cognitive dissonance, or simply by shaping research questions. They certainly shape practice by shaping the clinician's thinking, as well as that of the third-party payers. The release of a classification for use by the profession can generate social and political repercussions. Consider, for instance, the professional controversy about Self-Defeating Personality Disorder in DSM-III-R (Ritchie, 1989; Walker, 1987). The controversy can reflect ordinary scientific concerns, but it also may reflect a clash of values between the authors of the classification and their critical opponents. Moreover, the classification has everyday, practical consequences outside scientific and value ones. How easy is it to use? Are there too many diagnostic groups? Will the classification be computer friendly? Philosophical inquiry can assist in uncovering, anticipating, or understanding these consequences of classification.

Agich, for example, traces the consequences of a prototypical definition of Antisocial Personality Disorder. Prototypical definitions tend to suppress the varying contexts of the defined category, and yet these contexts can prove crucial in determining differences among the categories. Exemplar definitions, by contrast, retain the various contexts. Because Antisocial Personality Disorder is necessarily defined as deviance from a social context, its meaning would seem to be best captured in an exemplar definition instead of a prototypical one.

Clarifying Methodological Approaches

Methodology consists of the rules that ought to be followed to secure genuine knowledge. Methodology, in other words, helps us distinguish between genuine and specious knowledge. Because methodology consists of rules, it remains a normative discipline, not a factual one. It is thus philosophy and not science.

Because methodology is concerned with establishing the legitimate bases for knowledge-claims, it is concerned with (a) the concepts, categories, and classifications that constitute the elements of these claims, and (b) the larger theories, frameworks, perspectives, and scientific attitudes into which such claims fit. By setting up norms of good science, methodology can also delimit the requirements of good protoscience.

Methodological considerations have occupied much of the time and energy of the DSM-IV Task Force (Frances, 1982; Frances, Pincus, Widiger, Davis & Furst, 1990; Frances, Widiger & Pincus, 1989; Frances et al., 1991; Millon, 1987, 1991; Widiger, Frances, Pincus & Davis, 1990; Widiger, Frances, Pincus, Davis & First, 1991). A few examples of methodological questions in psychiatry include: (a) What role does reliability play in scientific procedure? (b) What are the varieties of correctness, validity, or truth, and how can we assure them? (c) What is the relationship between observable and postulated entities (e.g., how can mental states be inferred on the basis of observation of behavior)? (d) What are the relationships among diagnostic manuals and biological research, psychological tests, clinical treatment, etc.? (e) What criteria should be employed to justify changes in classifications (i.e., what constitutes an improvement in classification)? (f) How can classifications be based on ongoing and incomplete research programs? (g) How can classifications stimulate research?

Many of the essays in this volume concern themselves with methodology as well. The essay by Osborne Wiggins and Michael Schwartz views classification as a tool in choosing a methodological approach to the patient. Their proposal for psychiatric classification has an intrinsic hierarchy that suggests degrees of methodological openness or closure, depending on the level of scientific certainty about a particular category. In contrast, John Sadler and Yosaf Hulgus lament the narrowly descriptive focus of DSM-III-R on symptoms and their courses, and they propose a psychosocial fleshing out of the DSM. Their proposal involves a methodological means for classifying the nebulous, unique properties of the patient: personal history, familial communication, environmental factors affecting the illness, and so forth.

Evaluating Success

An important, perhaps the most important, task in evaluating the value of a taxonomy is its empirical power. In the case of psychiatry, a classification's empirical power could include a variety of assessments, all experientially testable. Are diagnostic categories reliable and valid? Are diagnostic entities relevant to standard (or novel) etiological theories? Are the diagnostic entities actually used by clinicians? administrators? educators? Does the classification lead to new discoveries, whether etiological, epidemiological, or treatment oriented?

On the other hand, there will be other evaluative questions for nosologies which are not so readily answered by empirical data. What kinds of explanation are favored by the terms employed in classification; which are disfavored? How will the descriptive commitments of a nosology be reflected in psychiatric practice? How historically relative will a psychiatric classification be? What clinical needs are met by the classification? What societal needs are met by the classification? Is the classification "good" science? To what degree can a psychiatric classification be scientific, and how scientific are the extant ones?

In these last senses, all of the essays in this volume evaluate current psychiatric classification. The range of discussion is broad—from the degree of descriptive success of psychopathology (Caws, Mishara, Spitzer, Stephens, Graham), to gender concerns (Russell), to the degree of theory neutrality and value neutrality aspired to (Agich, Fulford, Goodman, Margolis), and other dimensions of evaluation as well.

Generating Innovative Ideas

Philosophy possesses no hegemony on good new ideas. Nevertheless, there is a tradition of philosophy's direct and indirect contributions to psychiatry: consider Rene Descartes's writings on mind-body, Edmund Husserl's formative contributions to cognitive science and cognitive therapy, Karl Jaspers's writings on psychopathology (including his direct influence on notions such as delusions and mood-congruent psychosis), Adolf Meyer's philosophical reflections, or Carl Hempel's aforementioned contribution to nosology, to name a few examples. This book intends to build on this tradition of innovation, critical reflection, and discovery. We think the reader looking for new ideas in classification will find a few surprises within these essays.

DESIGN AND GOALS FOR THIS BOOK

We wanted this book to be an exploration of the conceptual foundations of psychiatric diagnosis and classification. We knew that, as an exploration, a summary of the state of the art was impossible (as if such a state exists at all), and we wanted the problems explored to have relevance for contemporary psychiatry. We wished to avoid an ivory-tower approach to psychiatric classification, keeping ourselves and our contributors close to the nitty-gritty of psychiatric practice, research, and education. A simultaneous goal, perhaps posing a paradox with the first, was to minimize the historical relativity of the work; that is, we wanted the book to have relevance not only to the current problems in psychiatric nosology but also to fundamental problems that any nosology might face, in any historical era. Realizing that the latter is an unreachable ideal, we thought aiming for it would provide the focus that would balance practical utility with intellectual rigor.

We puzzled over the means to achieve such complex and contradictory ends. Our solution was to give the contributors a very focused task, guessing that the philosophical bent toward universals and fundamentals would emerge, balancing our perhaps overly concrete instructions. The task we asked was straightforward: to take some (any) aspect or facet of the *Diagnostic and Statistical Manual for Mental Disorders, Third Edition, Revised* (American Psychiatric Association, 1987) and first, criticize it, and second, provide concrete alternative conceptions or suggestions for the problem(s) at hand. Allen Frances, by generously supplying prepublication copies of DSM-IV relevant professional articles or manuscripts, allowed our contributors to consider many of the conceptual issues facing DSM-IV as well. Our hunch was that the contributors would approach DSM-III-R/IV as an *example* of a psychiatric nosology and would use it as an example to illustrate a variety of conceptual problems with psychiatric nosology *which is not limited to the DSMs*. As a discussion of the newest DSMs, the essays would be focused on important issues facing psychiatry today. Using the DSMs as general examples of psychiatric nosology, the essays could address general problems that many psychiatric nosologies share.

Although some essays emphasize particular proposals and others emphasize conceptual analysis, we were gratified to find that the book as a whole strikes the balance we sought. As a consequence, it can be read two ways: as a philosophical inquiry into DSM-III-R and, to a lesser extent, DSM-IV; or as a discussion of philosophical issues in psychiatric nosology, using DSM-III-R/IV as case examples. In the following overview we will bridge these two readings by briefly discussing essays from these two perspectives. In addition, we shall discuss some of the common themes that have emerged from the essays and suggest new directions and questions for psychiatric nosology.

THE TENSION BETWEEN SCIENTIFIC AND PRAGMATIC NEEDS

Of all of the perplexing tasks of psychiatric classification, perhaps none is as piquant to nosologists who represent major national professional organizations as the tensions between scientific and practical needs. The issue floats over the DSM-IV literature like a dark cloud, at any moment ready to burst into lightning and thunder. Indeed, the issue cuts deeply into the philosophy of medicine as a whole: Are the primary goals of medicine (or psychiatric classification) practical (tending to the ill) or scientific (mastery of illness through knowledge)? Which goal should prevail if they come into conflict (as they *do* often in psychiatric classification)?

The authors of DSM-III-R and IV faced a number of practical obligations, most of which forced undesired compromises for an empirical-scientific document. Research into diagnostic groups was patchy and incomplete. Does the manual then respond to research, shape research, or do both (Pincus, Frances, Davis, First & Widiger, 1992)? DSM-IV is obligated by treaty to be compatible with the *International Classification of Diseases*, *Tenth Edition* (ICD-10). How then should new scientific data be incorporated into DSM-IV? A variety of special interest groups advocated a plethora of requests: new diagnostic categories, increasing descriptive detail, more ease of use for insurance companies, and so forth. Indeed, as Ned Wallace makes apparent in his essay, some of the earliest nosologies in American psychiatry were direct responses to needs arising from housing and caring for chronically mentally ill people. Perhaps most important, DSM-IV must be user friendly (i.e., a tool that is specific enough to be authoritative yet brief enough to be manageable).

Some of the contributors' views of DSM-III-R were constructed around this continuum of science-practice. Margolis' essay, as a response to Hempel's historical essay, focuses primarily on DSM-III-R and IV as documents reflecting scientific psychiatry. In contrast, Agich and Goodman approach these manuals as pragmatic guides to (primarily) facilitate practice. Goodman proposes even more overt consideration of the practical consequences of diagnostic categories, and he demonstrates a method for deriving diagnostic categories which more closely reflects clinical needs. Agich argues in favor of the pragmatic approach to classification found in DSM-III-R/IV, but he shows the equally important role of value issues, suggesting that value assumptions are the covert determinant of some diagnostic categories, particularly Antisocial Personality Disorder. This concern for the determinative role of implicit values is more radically stated by Fulford in his essay. Fulford argues that psychiatric disorders are better conceived in primarily evaluative, instead of scientific, terms. He shows how many of the practical difficulties in psychopathology and psychiatric classification can be obviated by conceiving psychiatric disorders as evaluational concepts instead of scientific ones. The approach of Sadler and Hulgus to the problem is to build more context in classification. Their proposal for a nosology of context resolves some of the science-practice tension by adding more theoretically diverse descriptive terms—terms that more closely mirror the fact of psychiatric pluralism. On the other hand, Wiggins and Schwartz emphasize the limits on the ambitions of a diagnostic manual and increase user friendliness by hierarchically ordering classification by degree of scientific knowledge.

CAN PSYCHIATRIC CLASSIFICATIONS BE ATHEORETICAL?

A large number of contributors were skeptical about the claim of DSM-III-R to being atheoretical with regard to etiology. These doubts take different forms.

Some contributors say that classifications cannot be atheoretical because observation statements and even acts of observing are influenced by theoretical commitments or prototheoretical presuppositions. Statements draw on a vocabulary that comes from and therefore expresses some theoretical or commonsensical view of things. Observations are made by observers who have a personal history and who have thus been educated to perceive things a definite way. This carries implications for etiology. If the observer accepts only certain theories or a particular worldview, then only certain predetermined options are considered when that person contemplates possible causes. It is no accident, after all, that some researchers are predisposed to consider solely biological etiologies, whereas others strongly insist on psychological determinants. These predispositions shape the researcher's science, but they issue, at least partially, from deep-seated personal commitments regarding what is truly real.

Other contributors maintain that no classification can be atheoretical because all concepts are abstractions. Scientists and clinicians thus disregard evidence that falls outside the scope of these abstract concepts. By restricting the relevant evidence, classifications prejudge the range of theoretical statements which can be empirically tested.

Still other contributors deny the possibility of value-neutral descriptions and stress instead their value-laden quality. Values, not cognitions, determine what we select as important, crucial, central, decisive, or related. In other words, values lend structure to the field of attention, predefining background and foreground, and clustering disparate items into groups. Consequently, descriptive statements about psychopathology issue from presupposed value stances that conceal their own deeper sources, compatibilities, and incompatibilities.

Finally, other contributors describe how explanatory preferences in DSM-III-R emerge in subtle and not-so-subtle ways. Although, for example, DSM-III-R denies that we possess much knowledge regarding etiology, its classifications abound with mention of factors that could easily be deemed *causes* if one were not predisposed to overlook causes of that sort. Nothing, after all, tells us unfailingly what counts as a *cause* and an *effect*. Therefore, the decision to award the status of *cause* to some realities and to deny it to others arises from particular presuppositions about the causal nature of reality.

THE DEPENDENCE OF CLASSIFICATION ON PSYCHOPATHOLOGY

Several essays in this volume emphasize the close and essential relationship between psychopathology (the descriptive science of mental disorder) and psychiatric nosology. Indeed, it seems obvious that a careful description of psychopathology is essential to classificatory efforts. Two essays directly address descriptive psychopathology in DSM-III-R: Spitzer challenges the DSM notions of hallucinations, delusions, and mood-congruent psychotic symptoms, whereas Stephens and Graham provide convincing philosophical and empirical arguments against the conventional notion of auditory hallucinations.

What these essays indirectly reveal about the DSMs is as vital. Spitzer's essay shows how the DSM-III/III-R definitions of core psychopathological terms actually confuse matters by reaching toward an unreachable goal: homogeneity and nonoverlapping boundaries between psychopathological terms. Spitzer's recast notions of hallucinations and delusions present an apparent paradox: that psychopathological definitions with *more* ambiguity can be *more* precise! The essay by Stephens and Graham exposes DSM-III-R in another way: it illustrates how a narrowly construed sense-perception psychology can infect observation and shape psychopathological description. Their essay is an inadvertent case study in theory-dependent observation and description.

Goodman, Russell, and Caws deal with psychopathology in still different ways. Goodman portrays classification as a practical interpretive task with the development of classification as a conjunction of observation, self-reflection, and empiricism. Psychopathological concepts are practical tools for thematizing clinical experience. For Russell, the linguistic ambiguity of psychopathological concepts is the breeding ground for sociopolitical misuse. She describes how seemingly neutral psychopathological terms in DSM-III/III-R (such as *dysfunction*) perpetuate ideology and conceal social-contextual etiological factors. Caws, on the other hand, upends all through his analysis of subjectivity in psychopathology and psychiatric classification. He, like Spitzer, is not bound by the implicit faculty psychology of the DSMs, and he provides a basis——new to psychiatry——for conceiving the psychopathology of such disorders as schizophrenia, autistic disorder, and borderline personality disorder. In his essay, Mishara provides another set of descriptive options with empirical potential. He shows how consideration of psychopathology as a disturbance of subjective meaning can reveal a new range of descriptive possibilities.

INTERPRETIVE AMBIGUITY IN PSYCHIATRIC CLASSIFICATION

We have already mentioned Russell's essay and its concern for the political uses of ambiguity. Her essay embodies a theme that a number of other contributors share: the problem of interpreting diagnostic criteria and diagnostic categories. Historiographically, Wallace discusses the cognitive habit of interpreting others' experiences in light of one's own and how this can result in a misleading *presentism* (seeing traces of the past with present-day eyes) for the historian. He then discusses some examples of presentism in the history of psychiatry and psychiatric nosology and the influence of this presentism on today's classifications. Margolis discusses a related theme: the relevance of linguistic, cultural, and conceptual conventions for the validity of psychiatric classification. He describes how these conventions shape nosological language and how their referents can change as cultural conventions shift and evolve. For Margolis, a diagnostic category can designate one reality today, but that reality may be a different one tomorrow, even for psychiatric practice as a social institution. For Schaffner, the relationship between diagnostic entities and their neurobiological referents is the main problem of reduction. For Kraus, Mishara, and Spitzer, the very attempt to resolve or eliminate ambiguity poses the risk of misleading the clinician into misunderstanding the patient. In their essay, Wiggins and Schwartz take the interpretive ambiguity of nosology as given. Scientific knowledge, when it is available (and it is not often enough), can help clarify the ambiguities of psychiatry's realities. Short of the precision of established scientific knowledge, they propose that psychiatry's ambiguities be preserved—not eliminated—through the diagnostic use of ideal types as guiding concepts in investigation. Their notion of diagnosis is practice centered, and like Kraus and Mishara, they view the clinical encounter as a Jaspersian process of discovery and understanding (as contrasted with the usual notion of diagnosis as simply a guide to treatment selection and outcome prediction).

CONSIDERATIONS FOR THE FUTURE

Readers of this book will find little consensus and no definitive answers. Instead, they will encounter challenges and questions. At this stage, philosophical discussions of classification must remain tentative, preliminary, and prospective as psychiatric classification itself remains. Perhaps DSM-III, DSM-III-R, and DSM-IV should all be read as attempts at a not-yet-realized future of psychiatry. The true payoff, the real success, then, lies in the future, if anywhere. To the degree that careful thinking and hard work can contribute to success, we hope that this book contributes to the ongoing development and refinement of psychiatric classification.

Looking toward the future, we would like to sketch some areas deserving attention by both philosophers and psychiatrists. This book, we think, points in these directions.

1. The most fundamental question about psychiatric diagnosis and classification, namely, "What are they?" has been frequently treated in the recent psychiatric literature (consider, e.g., Frances et al., 1991; Freedman et al., 1986; Kendler, 1990; McGuire, 1986; and Millon, 1991). This book further elaborates the complex scientific, evaluative, and practical concerns that seem to be inextricably combined in psychiatric classification. What emerges can perhaps be summarized as follows. The scientific concerns: psychiatric classification shares some characteristics of traditional scientific taxa (such as those of biology). The evaluative concerns: psychiatric classification serves the medical goals of patient betterment. The practical concerns: psychiatric classification must be shaped by such pragmatic necessities as utility, reliability, and simplicity. The essays in this book thus disclose the complex and various purposes of classification and call for their systematic clarification.

2. The limits of psychiatry, suggested by the limits of classification, provide a topic for discussion in the future. This topic is of major social and clinical importance. In the current climate of managed care, an ever-expanding health care budget, and increasing demands for accountability to both patients and payers, the scope of mental disorder becomes a conceptual issue that cannot be avoided. The *scope of mental disorder* refers to the boundaries of mental health and mental disorder—boundaries that remain ill defined. As various biopsychosocial disciplines and technologies deepen our understanding of humanity, there develops a tendency to view a person's undesirable predicament as a medical disturbance instead of a problem in living. Focus can thus shift away from other social resources for distressed people to medical or medicalized assistance for them. The implications for the cost of health care, mental or otherwise, are profound. As our scientific understanding of the full range of human distress expands, so does the social impetus for the medical care of these ills. For these pressing reasons, definitions of what does and does not constitute a mental disorder will become essential for the psychiatric classifications in the future. That these decisions are more likely to pivot on values than facts makes our contributors' insistence on greater focus on values in classification even more relevant.

3. Criticisms of the older philosophy of science (logical empiricism), have usually entailed criticisms of older dichotomies and dualisms. The traditional distinctions between the subjective and the objective, overt (outer) behavior

and covert (inner) awareness, fact and value, the observable and the unobservable, and even the distinction between scientific knowledge and nonscientific knowledge have all been repeatedly called into serious question (see, e.g., Agich, 1983; Bernstein, 1983; Dennett, 1987; Feyerabend, 1981a, 1981b; Fulford, 1989; Gadamer, 1960; Hanson, 1958; Heelan, 1983; and Margolis, 1987, 1989). We submit that in the future psychiatry would profit from a philosophical rethinking and redefining of these terms and their relationships. Indeed, perhaps some of these notions will have to be discarded as merely misleading.

4. The multifaceted connection between psychiatry and society is not, of course, a novel topic. However, this connection should remain firmly in view, especially as relatively new modes of thought, such as feminism, challenge our assumptions regarding society and its institutions. The role of psychiatry in informing the public, treating disturbed members of society, and shaping an awareness of the part that values play in health issues can no longer imply that scientists should systematically set aside all values and forge a value-free science. It must instead imply that values, like all other formative forces in psychiatry, are openly and critically debated and not simply taken for granted. The choice, in other words, is not between values and no values. It is instead a choice of which values psychiatry will explicitly endorse as one influential social institution among others.

THE ORGANIZATION OF THE VOLUME

A volume such as this one, using a variety of contributors, risks both redundancy and omissions. The latter are unavoidable in our cross-disciplinary field, in which new territory is being explored. Redundancy is less likely in an area that is relatively new. We think this book covers a lot of territory, but that territory is far from a complete mapping. Most of the essays are quite general in their approach, justifiably so, but in their generality there will be noticeable overlap in themes or problems discussed, but very little overlap in ideas. Although some contributors deal with similar issues or problems, there is great variety in conceptualizing and approaching them. This conceptual variety and flexibility are benefits of philosophy: staid ways of thinking are challenged, and new ways of thinking are offered.

However, a hefty book can be daunting to the reader new to philosophy in psychiatry. For this reason, we have loosely organized the book around four sections: methods, psychopathology, values, and future prospects and alternatives. Although it would be misleading to assert that the essays in each section are wholly encompassed by each of the section themes, the latter can be useful in guiding particular interests or in casually surveying the book. This overview and Wallace's historical chapter provide good starting points for a careful reading. After that, the order of reading the chapters is less critical.

Putting this book together was a conceptual adventure for us. We hope you find it so as well.

1 Psychiatry and Its Nosology: A Historico-philosophical Overview

EDWIN R. WALLACE IV, M.D.

The topic of psychiatric diagnosis and nosology is, of course, an impossibly large one, even for a volume such as this. For one thing, the myriad issues of classification pervade any discipline that would be scientific to any degree, since classification is both a scientific starting point and an arena of ongoing evolution, evaluation, and debate. This, too, is the case even with the discipline of history, although its categories are necessarily ambiguous, open, and carried by ordinary language.

For another thing, classificatory activity demands the usual modes of scientific testing (intradisciplinary, predictive, retrodictive, statistical) as well as consideration of the consequences for clinical and therapeutic activity. These dimensions demand philosophical scrutiny regarding (a) the taxonomy's metaphysical, ontological, and even cosmological commitments; (b) the a priori assumptions about what counts as pertinent data and how these interact with theory- or program-bound interpretations; (c) the logical consistency of the criteria defining each category and the amount of criterial overlap among categories; and (d) the logicoempirical fit between a classificatory system, on the one hand, and the actual levels and range of processes of the phenomena under consideration, on the other.

In addition, ethics and social/political philosophy examine the moral, sociopolitical/economic, professional interest, and popular cultural ramifications. Finally, other disciplines (such as the social and biological sciences in the case of psychiatry) help clarify and evaluate the classification; hence, they too are integral to a broadly philosophical, or critical, attitude toward one's discipline and its functioning. Indeed, Wittgenstein, probably this century's greatest philosopher, saw philosophy more as philosophizing. For Wittgenstein, philosophizing represented certain attitudes and approaches to intellectual and practical problem solving, instead of being an isolated discipline pursued by a specialized cadre of scholars.

When psychiatry attempts to clarify itself, philosophical *and* historical research methods go hand in hand with the explicitly natural and social scientific, clinical, and moral/ethical vantages. Moreover, as many historical and philosophical figures have asserted, the history and philosophy of science/medicine cannot proceed without one another (Kuhn, 1970; Lakatos, 1978; Laudan, 1977; Sarton, 1952, 1959; Sigerist, 1951, 1961; Temkin, 1977). And, as we shall see, history's epistemological issues are important not only in evaluating the psychiatric history writing at our disposal, but because of their pertinence to certain psychiatric conceptual and methodological issues as well.

HISTORIOGRAPHY (PHILOSOPHY AND METHODOLOGY)

Historiography has two contemporary meanings: (a) the history of the historical enterprise, that is, of the published works, points of view, and scholarly findings of historical work (in general or on particular topics) over the years; and (b) the philosophy of history——the critical examination of historical methodologies and the theories and philosophical principles from which they derive. This section looks at both, but primarily at the latter (and, as promised, as it is relevant to *both* history and medicine/psychiatry).

The Persistence of the Past

In general, the past lives on in several related aspects, to be clarified in the following paragraphs. Of course I am not referring to the prior occurrences themselves; those are, indeed, "dead and gone," or tautologically past. Rather, I am alluding to the tracks in, and effects on, the present from those bygone activities and events. Some of these points apply more to the individual with whom the biographer or practicing clinician is primarily concerned, others more to the collectivities with which the historian proper or the medical scientist is preeminently preoccupied, and some to both. Let us turn to them, focusing first on the physician/psychiatrist and then, via transitional considerations, on the academic historian, after which we shall go back and forth between—— or simultaneously examine——them.

To begin with, the momentary present is, importantly, a continuation of the past, even as that instantaneous now is perennially becoming the past of its own future, and so on and so forth. Hence, there is a sense in which *all* of our knowledge, including scientific and medical, is historical, coursing from our continual processing of the present representations of prior events, experiences, and activities (see Wallace, 1985, 1988c, 1989b).

For example, the psychiatric interviewer and nosologist deals with many current traces of historical processes and manifestations with varying lengths of time behind them. Some examples of these traces include: (a) the patient's phenomenology/behavior, communication, and account (verbal and non-verbal) of the development of his or her present clinical problems; (b) the patient's report of his or her experiences and interpretations of previous medical/psychiatric problems; (c) some measure of phenomenologically and biopsychosocially oriented developmental, longitudinal, and premorbid history; (d) the results of physical, neurological, and mental status examinations, which disclose time-bound processes and states; and finally (e) pertinent laboratory, radiological, psychometric, and other auxiliary explorations and their reasonably well-established findings and interpretations which, likewise, reveal and suggest activities with a history and unfolding future. Moreover, the sensitive practitioner will grasp aspects of the doctor-patient relationship which reflect transferential and counter-transferential (i.e., historically-situationally codetermined) processes and manifestations in each of these clinical activities.

Again, it is key to appreciate that all of the aforementioned species of clinical information are not important as indices of time-static states or current cross-sections of personal dysfunction/distress. Rather, they are significant as indicators of prior and ongoing pathophysiological/psychopathological processes, whose histories and time contexts it is the clinician's task to reconstruct. As these latter become more accurately and completely reconstructed and intercorrelated with the help of basic and clinical research, we derive (always tentative, incomplete, and evolving) knowledge of their multifactorial or biopsychosocial causation. It is through this activity that our diagnostic categories will become more etiologically based, rather than being merely syndromal or incompletely pathophysiological/psychopathological.

The collective or institutionalized past, as well as the personal past, persist (quite apart from the medically purposeful quest for knowledge) for each person in several ways. In the present there are conscious, preconscious, and unconscious memory images of it, extricable/inextricable mélanges of "outer" and "inner", or psychical (private) and actual (potentially consensually validatable), reality. These memorials——configurations of earlier apperceptions of self in the world—— are, as implied, in some ways accessible to other people, and in other ways not. In addition, they are not static, but elaborated upon, modified, and associatively connected to subsequent thematically similar representations over time. Be all of this as it may, they are current psychological realities nonetheless; and, as such, they are capable of affecting all interactions with the outside world, whether those of the clinician or historian.

At the social level, whole groups of individuals absorb, through each member's particular lens, the society's and nation's present-day traces and representations of their cultural past. Such enculturation occurs through a variety of social experiences and activities, as well as via a host of cultural documents. The former occur in a spectrum of settings, from family and informal social networks to public educational and indoctrinational systems; the latter range from monuments to museums to books, music, and so forth (Popper & Eccles, 1981).

At the more private, or individual psychological level, these sociocultural traces and representations reflect the intermingling of historical fact and personal motivation, defense, misinterpretation, and mythology (fantasy). Nevertheless, whatever the mixture of these in the individual, such communities constitute sociopsychological realities which, in turn, affect both the local society as well as neighboring ones. The same holds true, at more microlevels, for the sciences and professions. Consider, at the world historical plane, the impact of Germanic/ Nordic *mytho*history on Nazi policy and World War II and, more benevolently, that of Hippocratic legend/history on the evolution of medicine.

In sum, the past lives on in the historian and clinician, in both hidden and potentially self-aware cognitive/affective schemata, perceptual/interpretive modes, patterns of motivation, conflict, and interpersonal relations, and in multifarious styles of acting and adapting (often atavistically) in the on-going world.

Events and Traces

In historical research, the subject matter is not the past as it actually transpired, but its present-day traces. Even though this truth is readily apparent, generations of outstanding scholars have forgotten it, although notable 19th- and 20th-century historians and philosophers of history came progressively to terms with it. Even so, the great early to mid 19th-century savant von Ranke (1821; 1874, p. viii), while knowing better, still aspired to write history "*wie es eigentlich gewesen* [as it actually happened]"! Some of the best classical historians, such as Thucydides and Herodotus, limited their traces to direct and hearsay oral reports, questionable local sources, and their own recollections of events and personal experiences. Centuries of subsequent scholars limited their data to written documents, especially earlier chronicles and histories, whose testimonies and interpretations were accepted uncritically.

From the Renaissance to the 18th-century, historians gradually augmented their repertoire of traces with a widened range of works from historically important periods and figures in the original languages. These works included antiquarian and archaeological discoveries from many cultures, requiring, as did the newly discovered original texts, novel modes of reconstruction and interpretation. At the same time, new theories and philosophies of history (e.g., Herder's and Vico's) stressed hitherto unappreciated modes and aspects of historical development and sectors of civilization.

Moreover, for their part, 19th-century historians increasingly grasped the importance of archival material: official and unofficial government and diplomatic documents, reports of legal proceedings, a wide arc of economic data, extant collections of statistics on myriad matters, letters, diaries, contemporaneous third-party accounts, and so forth. They were less willing to limit themselves to the period's standard chroniclers and to histories by subsequent generations of scholars or secondary sources (tertiary really, since the chronicles, or contemporaneous histories, were themselves largely secondary, based on eyewitness narratives and official and unofficial reports). Furthermore, attitudes toward all of their sources and traces were more searching and critical.

Thus, by the late 19th-century, historians better differentiated between the irrecoverable actual events and their current traces. Simultaneously, there was expanded recognition of the historically pertinent trace. Such extensions did not result simply from purely empirical observation; they also flowed from philosophies and theories of historical interpretation and from newly related disciplines (such as archaeology, numismatics, philosophy, philology, hermeneutics, epigraphy, paleography, statistics, and economics and the social sciences) which, in effect, constituted new objects as historical traces.

Moreover, once deemed a relevant category of traces, the new data did not simply announce their relative significance, but had to be criticized, contextualized, and interpreted. How this last is done depends, in part, on the scholar's presuppositions about what constitutes an intellectually respectable enterprise; the philosophy and methodology of the historical inquiry; cosmological, metaphysical, and moral commitments; as well as the various psychological quiddities of the historian himself or herself. These methodological issues mirror many issues in clinical work as well. Indeed, some historians have underlined important similarities in the historical and medical/psychiatric endeavors.

In the latter 19th-century a number of philosophical and methodological texts on historical research began to appear, the still-useful book by Langlois and Seignebos (1898), for example. The first 5 decades of the present century witnessed a mushrooming of such work, as well as a burgeoning interest by professional philosophers which continues today, for example, Atkinson (1978), Beard (1934, 1935), Becker (1958), Berlin (1954), Bloch (1953), Carr (1961), Collingwood (1940, 1946, 1965), Croce (1921), Danto (1965), P. Gardiner (1961), Mandelbaum (1938, 1977), and Walsh (1958, 1969).

Externalism/Internalism and Epistemology

As already mentioned, late 19th- and early to mid 20th-century innovations in archaeological and philological technique (the latter culminating from its roots in the Renaissance and the 17th-century) brought historians new species of traces, novel dating technologies, and additional cross-validational approaches and findings. Physical anthropology, medicine, and epidemiology awoke scholars to the impact of sanitary, nutritional, and disease factors on the history of civilization (Cartwright, 1972; Rosenberg, 1962; Sigerist, 1943; Zinsser, 1935). Psychiatry and psychology suggested further genres of traces and innovative insights and methodologies, and some abuses of historical inquiry as well (Barzun, 1974; Fischer, 1970; Gay, 1985; Runyan, 1988; Stannard, 1980; Wallace, 1985). Social philosophy and the social sciences have done likewise; adding two whole new subdisciplines, social history and cultural history, to history's traditional subspecialties—political, diplomatic, military, and intellectual.

Social and cultural historians brought their interests in reconstructing the lives and cultural matrices of common folk. They often uncovered appalling working and living conditions that pointed fingers at social, political, and economic structures (e.g., Ladurie, 1966; Thompson, 1963). They saw externalist factors (usually socioeconomic and political institutions, special interests and motives) in the work of historians of ideas and disciplines as well, including, as we shall see, the history of medicine and psychiatry. Darwin's evolutionary theory, for example, was reinterpreted as reflecting and reinforcing his prior social class, political, and economic allegiances (Young, 1985). Indeed, these scholars provided salutary counterbalances to an old-style king and battle, great man history of civilization, and to such a history of ideas and disciplines too (see Himmelfarb, 1987).

Moreover, social and cultural historians have warned enterprises such as science and medicine that they do not develop purely internally, in societal- and value-free vacuums. Instead, they may be unwittingly governed by certain externalist codeterminants; and, at the very least, their theories, research, and applications can have far-reaching (though perhaps unpredicted and unintended) effects on society, culture, morality, and even experiences and concepts of personhood themselves. Nevertheless, it must be acknowledged that social historians often (a) adopt highly moralistic stances, from which historians have taken strenuous centuries to free themselves;   (b) write as if externalist factors dominate the development of ideas and disciplines, and as if their putative internalist determinants are at best disavowing rationalizations of the true externalist causes and hidden disciplinary self-interests; and (c) assume that if a specialty's projects, results, or implications seem to support the political and socioeconomic status quo then, ipso facto, the former must have been intended to do so.

From manifold and proliferating species of traces, and innovative theories of interpretation, historians aspire to ever more comprehensive and veridical reconstructions of civilizations, endeavors, and life-modes. Although never claiming absolute clarity, breadth, depth, and truth, such reconstructions strive to utilize the broadest and best criticized data and methodology.

Contra Popper (1965), historical *interpretations* (which he prefers to *hypotheses*, as if science is not interpretive as well [e.g., Bridgman, 1945b]) are indeed testable in a variety of ways: the canons for historical research and evidence themselves; commonsense and courtroom criteria for cross-examining data and testimony; and modes akin to those of the social, and the natural sciences (e.g., historical geology and paleontology, archaeological data, dating technologies, etc.).

Hence historical investigation, like scientific and clinical investigation (including nosological), is not purely and one-sidedly a priori or a posteriori, deductive or inductive, nomothetic (lawlike and generalizing) or idiographic (involved with totally idiosyncratic features, factors, and developmental lines), idealist or realist.

Instead, historical investigation reflects an ongoing interaction between these opposing viewpoints (Wallace, 1985, 1989b). However, historical testing does utilize a more traditional version of science's familiar, but perhaps simplistic, hypothetico-deductive method. Certain logical consequences of particular historical interpretations are indeed deduced, and their confirmation or disconfirmation is assessed through multiple sources and lines of evidence. Although this is, properly speaking, as in paleontology, a form of *retro-* or *post*diction, rather than *pre*diction, in principle the processes are equivalent; for the historian is searching for supporting or sapping evidence that he or she *has not yet encountered* (see Wallace, 1985, for example). Like any scientist, the scholar knows that better-evidenced historical interpretations and reconstructions or new discoveries may undermine many seemingly well-supported hypotheses. For example, archival findings bearing on the French revolutionary Barère led to the recent refutation of his own contemporaries' and subsequent historians' ostensibly well-grounded reports that he was an egoistic opportunist (Gershoy, 1963). Thus, present-day historians, although they cannot *become* and *enter* the mind- and place-sets of their ancestors, can often form more cogent perspectives on their ancestors' situations than the ancestors themselves did——immersed as the latter were in the unexamined hurly-burly of events. Still, of course, there is an immediate sense in which the historian can never *know* Barère and his times as did even his most obtuse acquaintances.

Although there is some controversy among philosophers of history (e.g., Gay, 1976; Marrou, 1966; Oakeshott, 1933; Wallace, 1985), as recently among psychoanalysts and philosophers of psychoanalysis (e.g., Grünbaum, 1984; Schafer, 1978; Spence, 1982; Wallace, 1985, 1988c, 1989c), about the veridicality and utility of the concept of causation in history, most historical (and psychoanalytic) research and writing have been firmly rooted in causal reasoning or in euphemisms for it (Fischer, 1970). The best historians, like the best psychiatrists and psychoanalysts, appreciate the operation of multiple varieties of causation, such as overlapping and mutually determinative lines of causation or causal nexus (overdetermination). In the history of ideas, two paths for causal reasoning have emerged and subsequently converged to shape our current historical understanding of events: the internalist and externalist. There can be multiple internalist, or intradisciplinary rational/empirical, determinants converging with the historical figure's personal psychological factors. There can also be externalist causes, such as social/political/economic structures and forces within and without the figure's professional enterprise itself. And of course similar points apply to the work of historians themselves.

Finally, just as the past determines the present, so present conceptions and misconceptions of the past can determine the present and future. For example, early American political founders partly justified both the Revolution and its constitutional democracy by reference to the classical Greek concept of democracy. Their actually somewhat distorted view of the Athenian polity was at once a determinant, and a rationalization, of their own rebellion and its particular vision of democracy.

On a related medical note, until the corrective work of McKeown (1979), physicians and physician-historians considered medical microbiological discoveries and doctors' eventual "magic bullets" as the reasons for improvements in late 19th- and early 20th-century morbidity and mortality rates. McKeown (1979), on the contrary, documented that these rates had already been declining, largely because of sanitation and public health reformers' growing knowledge and activism, from the mid 19th-century onward. Bacteriology and antimicrobials played relatively late and minor roles in this whole process. Clearly, this historical misinterpretation had lent doctors additional, ostensibly historically founded, sources of respect and remuneration.

In psychiatry itself, biopsychosocially based practitioners like to justify their positions as recoveries of the long-lost tenets of a hoary, holistic medical tradition (e.g., Lipowski, 1981). Actually, this holistic, or quasi-biopsychosocial, historical mainstream seems mostly myth, as Berrios (in press), Wallace (1988c, 1990a), Weiner (1986), and many others contend. The theories of medicine and for the most part psychiatry were overwhelmingly somatic, as were their understandings of treatments, even when their effects, if beneficent, were often placebo or psychological and relational.

The Hippocratics, despite their conversational and pedagogical approach to patients and concern with diet, natural ambiences, and life-styles, were committed somaticists in theory as well as in aspects of practice. Even the 19th-century moral therapists, for all of their attention to milieu, re-education, and what we would consider psychosocial factors, espoused fundamentally "biological" theories of mental illness.

Clinical Historiography

Some noted historians (e.g., Elton, 1970) have compared historical judgment with the pattern and Gestalt-recognition aspects of medical and psychiatric diagnosis. In his 1935 preface to Zilboorg's *The Medical Man and the Witch during the Renaissance*, America's first preeminent medical historian, Henry Sigerist, remarked perspicaciously on the striking parallels in the procedures of historians and psychiatrists (especially psychodynamic and Meyerian psychobiological ones). In light of this, he wondered why so few psychiatrists had distinguished themselves as historians of their field. Charles Hughes, in his (1964) inaugural presidential address to the American Historical Association, commented on similar analogies between history and psychiatry. Many of these have been touched on or must already be apparent to the reader, especially if his or her orientation includes psychosocial and psychodynamic perspectives. Novey (1968) and Wallace (1985) have demonstrated and elaborated on the relevance of historical investigation and its philosophy to epistemological and methodological issues in psychiatry and psychoanalysis.

In fact, it would be interesting to see a history of the psychiatric case history, as it has manifested both in day-to-day institutional and private work and documentation and in published texts or case reports. Although the case history has always been central to both general medicine and psychiatry, its breadth, depth, format, and the types of information emphasized have changed considerably over time——in tandem with novelties in theoretical orientation and data obtained.

Despite occasional exceptions, such as Esquirol and Kraepelin, 19th-century psychiatric case histories were quite skimpy and narrowly focused by our standards today. Even those of Kraepelin were largely limited to the patient's present and prior episodes of illness and their courses. Little attention was paid to the psychosocial context of each relapse or exacerbation, or to the patient's experience and interpretation of current or previous illnesses. Premorbid history was limited to the scantiest information about social and occupational status; and threadbare childhood histories to descriptions of early manifestations of degeneration, or seeming mental/behavioral dysfunction. Family history was confined to a description of familial illnesses (especially any resembling the patient's apparent one). Although to Kraepelin's credit, his view of psychiatric disorders was not static, but natural historical, his public clinical examinations and demonstrations focused largely on signs, behavioral "observations," and general cognitive states. Affect and mood were described at arm's length, with little attempt to appreciate even superficially the patient's life-world. Even recurrent patterns of psychosocial precipitants or likely codeterminants of illness episodes were overlooked (Kraepelin, 1912).

State hospitals did not have separate patient charts for most of the 19th-century, so that the initial histories and subsequent courses of many individual inmates were scattered through at-large logbooks, making it difficult to track personal patient continuity. Case histories were truncated to the present problem, often couched in a theory-laden or moralistic manner; certain general health history; and a terse note on occupational, social, educational, religious, and ethnic status, and sometimes on home and family milieu.

Psychiatry was sorely lacking in solid case historical approaches until three important physicians established them. Kraepelin's clinical historiography began embracing a natural historical (of present and prior illness) and not merely a cross-sectional descriptive approach. Freud developed his detailed and ongoing clinical biographical method. Meyer introduced his longitudinal psychobiological orientation. Even among the three figures cited, the genres of information, although partly overlapping, were quite divergent and partly theoretically determined as well.

Kraepelin, as mentioned, was behaviorally and sign/symptom oriented, with phenomenological (i.e., patient experiential and interpretational) data limited to a few aspects in which he took great interest. Thus, his organic and constitutional interpretive commitments strongly influenced his descriptive nosology and its data base. By contrast, Freud's history gathering was less organically focused and more phenomenological and private, even though embracing external (or consensually validatable) events and aspects of interpersonal relations too. Meyer paid more attention to biological and social factors than did Freud, and his histories were more actual event oriented than phenomenological and intra-psychic. Meyer's stressor/reaction life chart approach reflected little cognizance that the patient's historically-constitutionally determined private experience and interpretation determines both the meaning and stimulus value of the actual event, as well as *parri passu* its degree of stressfulness and the patient's reaction to the event (an event that, moreover, the patient may have unwittingly coengineered [see Wallace, 1985, 1988a, 1989b on intersectional causation and historical determinism]). Similarly, among current psychiatrists, the format, length, and sort of information obtained can vary greatly, depending on: the professional's theoretical and therapeutic slant, the demands of the institution or facility, the sorts of patients seen, the clinical objectives of patient encounters, the time available, and many other factors. That all of this impinges on nosology is of course obvious.

In general, I fear that in present-day medicine and psychiatry, history gathering is becoming downplayed, narrower, and less longitudinal; and that diagnoses, and the awareness of multicausality and of health- and illness-promoting factors, are being missed because of it. Overreliance on laboratory- and technology-derived data and on verbatim, DSM-III-R-derived interviewing manuals, is diminishing the doctor's appreciation of the importance of the establishment of rapport and the therapeutic alliance and of humane *and scientific*, multicat-egorical history taking. Certain aspects of DSM-III and III-R may be further abetting this, with their emphasis on canonical and limited constellations of discrete signs, symptoms, and behaviors (as if these can be understood apart from their meaning to the particular patient and his or her motivation). Consider also their concomitant short-shrift to phenomenological and interpersonal infor-mation, and to developmental/longitudinal biopsychosocial histories (apart from constricted chronicles of present and prior psychiatric episodes). If clinical "historying" is actually losing ground, this is most unfortunate; for internists still tell me that adequate histories take them farthest toward accurate diagnoses and differentials, with physical examination assuming second place, and laboratory and procedures often limited to ancillary roles.

The "Utility" of History

To leave clinical historiography and return to its academic counterpart, I wish to stress that historical scholarship is most pertinent to present-day psychiatric concerns when that history is *first reconstructed in its own right*. Quite apart from its potential impact on the doctor's sense of vocation, professional identity, and sense of continuity with a great theoretical and healing tradition, history is relevant to the psychiatrist in a number of additional ways.

Consider the movement to legalize heroin for American addicts in the 1960s and 1970s, and its "justification" by pointing to Great Britain's 1930 Dangerous Drugs Act, permitting the distribution of heroin to registered addicts. The "hu-manitarian" British stance, with its low number of addicts, was then contrasted to the "reactionary" American juridical one. In fact, reminds psychiatrist-historian David Musto (1973; 1978, p. 25), "there were very few heroin addicts, hundreds at most, in Great Britain in the 1920s, but . . . the policy of giving some of these addicts legal heroin was believed, *in another country and in a later generation*, as being the reason for the low number of addicts rather than the reason for allowing some maintenance." This spurious history was then used to argue for making heroin easily available to a U.S. population of more than 250,000 addicts!

History is useful not because the past clones itself or because historical analysis will necessarily dictate our response to current dilemmas, but because, as Musto (1978) says, it provides a broadened context for decision making. Historical knowledge may protect us from simplistic solutions and headlong rushes, and this applies to nosology as elsewhere.

The best of intentions can go awry. At times this occurred because there was no way the agents could have forecast the consequences, as when the mental hygiene movement led to the unintended, eventual neglect of the chronic patient and mental hospital, and when Dorothea Dix's asylum building program eventuated in custodial patient warehousing. But there are instances in which malignant consequences ensue because we acted in ignorance of available information about the relevant historical context and background. For example, appreciation of the far-reaching changes in societal attitudes toward the mentally ill after the small country asylums of the moral treatment era (see Grob, 1978; and next section), might have influenced recent decisions on deinstitutionalization and stemmed the tide of the many homeless and vulnerable psychiatrically ill left in its wake. Finally, the history of American forensic psychiatry suggests that psycho-diagnostic imperialism, in legal and criminal matters, has been poorly tolerated by the law and public at large (Tighe, in press). This is surely pertinent to determining the current aims and approaches of that subspecialty, as well as perhaps to aspects of the general psychiatric nosological enterprise itself.

In sum, both historians and psychiatrists (as classifiers, investigators, and explicators) must walk a difficult interpretive tightrope between nihilistic skepticism on the one side, and dogmatic certainty on the other. In this endeavor each can help the other, and both can be assisted by philosophy.

PSYCHIATRY: ITS HISTORIOGRAPHY AND HISTORY

Historiographic Considerations

The history of psychiatry and its nosology cannot be understood without an appreciation of the broader and deeper matrix of the history of medicine from which it grew. Since both histories were penned by historians, whether physicians or not, we are back in the philosophical and methodological considerations of the previous section. Understanding these general issues, as manifested in historical writings on medicine and psychiatry, is of course key for anyone who would read this literature critically——for, among other things, the light it might cast on current classificatory quandaries. Moreover, historians of psychiatric nosology, such as Karl Menninger (in Menninger, Mayman & Pruyser, 1963, appendix), begin with philosophical nosological biases (in his case, a unitary and gradational theory of mental disorder) that inevitably affect their writing of history.

It is not surprising that for centuries the history of medicine was done mostly by medical men, with the same king and battle bent of their contemporary academic historians, who concentrated mainly on political, diplomatic, and military history. Generally, such medical histories (usually parts of treatises on medical diagnosis, prognosis, and practice) were compendia of the lives of great theorists and practitioners, and the stories of any schools or systems that they founded. They were usually written with a close eye on the present, each generation of doctors needing to place itself at the current culmination of a continuous tradition of "anticipators" and precursors. Doubtless, this helped to integrate physician identities, establish medicine's claims to an ancient lineage and justified prestige, and bolster medical self-esteem in the face of public opinion and daily practice.

On the other hand, such history, coupled with its worship of tradition and authority, could be invoked against would-be innovators and unwittingly retard medical progress. Finally, from the point of view of historical methodology, it exemplified the academic sin of "presentism"——seeing one's ancestors too much through the lens of present-day interests (Mora & Brand, 1970; Stocking, 1968). This precluded *first* utilizing the pertinent historical traces to accomplish several goals: (a) approximating the earlier sociocultural and professional climates, and probable prior points of view and perceived problems; (b) comprehending past concepts and usages of terms that might only superficially relate to current terms; and (c) imagining how a Hippocratic, medieval Galenic, 17th-century iatromechanical, Romantic, or even Victorian, physician might have conceived of his enterprise.

Otherwise, as has commonly occurred in even early to mid 20th-century medical historical writing, we find pictures and evaluations (clinical, scientific, and moral) of ancestral theories and therapies with our present attainments, challenges, and options too much in mind. Or else we "discover" hosts of forerunners of our own heroes and favorite orientations. To be sure, prior lines of continuity and points of reorientation, as well as important figures, helped shape the medicine of today. Nevertheless, history is best written in large measure "forward", not backward; first understanding earlier periods and workers in light of their particular perspectives, modes of thought and action, and perplexities and attempted solutions, *before* attempting to assess possible direct or indirect impact on later physicians and approaches.

It is in this avoidance of presentism that history was referred to by Hughes (1964) as "retrospective ethnography." The ethnographer's subject matter is a temporally equivalent but geographically, institutionally, culturally, and psychologically distinct society. He or she must expend considerable effort not only in adapting to different modes of life, but in suspending certain filters, biases, and Western assumptions sufficiently to "enter into" the mind- and sociocultural-sets of his or her hosts; a task not dissimilar to that of the psychiatrist vis-à-vis each new patient, with the latter's unique patterning of universals and particulars. The effort to appreciate this life-world and vantage point——be it that of the patient, a contemporary nonliterate culturalist ("primitive"), or an early German-Romantic psychiatrist——is known as the *emic* perspective. It provides important information and pointers for the *etic*, or explanatory, standpoint. This latter allows the historian, anthropologist, and psychiatrist to bring to bear theories, procedures, information, and interventions that need not presuppose the subject's, informant's, or patient's awareness and comprehension of them. The relevance of this distinction to the history of clinical investigation and nosology is patent, but nonetheless insufficiently practiced.

In the history of psychiatry, mostly written by clinician-historians, this lack has been quite apparent. Many books and articles refer to ancient, medieval, or Renaissance "psychiatrists"——when there was no such organized specialty until the dawn of the 19th-century, and few if any "mad doctors" until the 18th-century. Throughout the 1800s many, if not most, "psychiatrists" did not envision their discipline and tasks in anything like that of their present-day counterparts, whatever the latters' professed orientations. Although Reil, primarily a practicing internist and *theorist* of psychotherapy, coined the term *psychiatrist* in 1801, the briefest perusal of his writings points up the differences in his concept and ours (1803). Most of that century's "psychiatrists" called themselves *medical superintendents, asylum physicians, alienists*, and finally *medical psychologists* before the term *psychiatrist* became current.

Similarly, volume-length histories of *psychiatry* came relatively late, Semelaigne's 1869 treatise being one of the earliest (and best). Standard 20th-century historical texts, such as those by the pioneer Russo-American psychiatrist/psychoanalyst-historian, Gregory Zilboorg (*The Medical Man and the Witch during the Renaissance*, 1935; *A History of Medical Psychology*, 1941), are laced with presentistic misinterpretations (see also Kraepelin's [1917] *One Hundred Years of Psychiatry*).

For example, Zilboorg exalted the Renaissance Weyer as the first "psychiatrist" and then, like Weyer, glibly diagnosed all witches as mad or hysterical, when the best historical, anthropological, and social psychological evidence suggests otherwise. Zilboorg's latter (1941) book, still one of the most utilized and referenced texts in psychiatric training programs (when they touch on history or the medical/psychiatric humanities at all), exhibits similar presentism in many other areas. This is especially true when treating his preferred psychoanalytic stance, where generations of seers supposedly groped slowly and strenuously toward Freudian theory. Alexander and Selesnick's (1966) text, quite popular in its paperback edition, also demonstrates a psychoanalytically biased presentism, although in certain other sections the book is perhaps better than Zilboorg's. In many features (e.g., balance of topics) clinician-historian Bromberg's (1954) book, despite pitfalls of its own, is superior to both of the above.

On the topic of physician-historians, one must mention the recently deceased general medical historian Erwin Ackerknecht. A nonpsychiatric physician and noted scholar, he (1968) penned what is still one of the best, although regrettably one of the shortest, volumes on the history of psychiatry (and of medicine [1982] too). However, his organicist and antipsychotherapeutic biases were an obvious weakness, particularly apparent when he turned to the romantics and to psychoanalysis. (For bibliographies, texts, and anthologies, considerably less problematic in their given purviews, see the American Psychiatric Association [APA] Committee on History and Library, 1979; Goshen, 1967; Hall, Zilboorg & Bunker, 1944; Howells, 1975; Hunter & Macalpine, 1982; Mora & Brand, 1970; Wallace & Pressley, 1980.)

So far, these particular physician-historians have one thing in common: the tendency to write the history of medicine and psychiatry in an internalist vein, as did most historians of science until recently. Certainly this bore on their nosologic histories as well, which interpreted the development of nosology as purely a reflection of changes in medical theory, practice, and modes of observation. All of this began to change——and in all of these disciplines——with the aforementioned late 20th-century influx of social historians. This immigration resulted from the influences of social/political philosophy and activism; social science theories, methodologies, and findings; relatively few academic openings for young historians in the more traditional historical sub-specialties; and histories of science and medicine crying for externalist perspectives. Thus, this new breed of scholar began penetrating the hitherto private preserves of science, medical, and psychiatric historians.

These invaders (as they often seemed to the more traditional practitioner-historians and historians of ideas) deserve credit for many important developments. These include emphasizing the mutual impact of scientific, medical, and other sociocultural developments; the possibility of science and medicine's unwitting subservience to self-interests and inequitable political, legal, and socioeconomic trends; and, once more, the witting or unwitting consequences of scientific and medical theories, taxonomies, investigations, and applications for society/culture, public morality, and views of personhood.

However, as mentioned, these new historians often seemed zealous to explain virtually all scientific and medical/psychiatric developments by reference to externalist factors and forces, and to professional motives for prestige, power, and income. Hence, not surprisingly, social history developed an antimedicine/antipsychiatry wing (e.g., Rawlinson, 1987; Sedgwick, 1973; Starr, 1982), at times joining forces with social philosophers and social scientists of similar persuasion (e.g., Goffman, 1961; Ingleby, 1980; Rosenhan, 1973; Szasz, 1961). They approached psychiatry with a strong antinosological bias, with an exclusive focus on presumed external or professional determinants of diagnostic categories and on the potential of such categories for sociopolitical misuse. A cadre of these scholars, influenced by the famous French philosopher/activist/historian Foucault (1962, 1970), viewed psychiatry, its institutions, and diagnoses as arising to sequester and incarcerate the socially and economically deviant and those threatening modern Western norms of rationality, power, and commerce. Foucault's (1965) historical documentation is thought questionable by many experts (e.g., Weiner, 1990), although his points on the relations among power, knowledge, and specialized "truths", and on the normative aspects of psychiatric theory and practice, merit pondering (see Foucault, 1980; Hyer & Wallace, in press).

In any event, Foucault and disciples share with antipsychiatric psychiatrists (Szasz ,1961; Torrey, 1973, 1975) the view that the discipline is a reactionary enemy of civil liberties. Similarly, many feminist historians (see below) see only psychiatry's negatively discriminatory stereotypes of women and women's alleged overrepresentation in certain stigmatized diagnostic categories (e.g., Hysteria, Histrionic Personality Disorder). Among psychiatrists themselves, there is a similarly based DSM-III-R debate over diagnoses such as Late Luteal Phase Dysphoric Disorder, Masochistic Personality Disorder, and Self-Defeating Personality Disorder (APA, 1987). Freud and psychoanalysis have been particular targets for such writers (e.g., Bernheimer & Kahane, 1985; Lerman, 1986; Masson, 1985; Mitchell, 1974), who turn nuggets of possible truth into boulders of incomplete apprehension and one-sided judgment.

Be this as it may, it is certainly correct that external (including political), and not merely scientific and clinical, factors have determined the fate of certain diagnoses, such as the DSM-III/III-R exclusion of the DSM-II category of Homosexuality. Hence, such perspectives are not without relevance and corrective balance for a self-styled "purely" scientific psychiatry. Nevertheless, when carried to an extreme, and ignoring or negating internalist determinants, the new historical perspectives amount, again, to an old-style, unicausal, and moralizing history not seen in years (Wallace, 1985).

Fortunately, there seems to be growing realization among social historians of the internal, scientific, and applied problems and possibilities of medical enterprises. Albert Deutsch, a psychiatric and historical layman, exemplified this as early as 1937 in his classic, *The Mentally Ill in America*; as did the late, great physician-historian George Rosen (self-taught medical, psychiatric, public health, and social historian), with his brilliant *Madness in Society* (1968). Psychiatrist-historian Henri Ellenberger melds internalist and some externalist approaches in his magnum opus, *The Discovery of the Unconscious* (1970). Finally, notable contemporary professional historians such as Norman Dain (1964), Gerald Grob (1978, 1983), and Charles Rosenberg (1967) represent the sort of social/intellectual historical balance here advocated.

If the history of psychiatry, like that of science, is going to assume its place as integral to the history of civilization, then it cannot dispense with sociocultural, economic, and political historical orientations; any more than any adequate psychiatry and psychiatric nosology can ignore the sociocultural, economic, and moral philosophical factors in itself and its patients' disorders.

American Psychiatry: A Historical Sketch

We turn now to the history of American psychiatry, as organized around the theme of its alleged dialectic between *psychical*, or psychosocial, and *"somatic*," or neurobiological/biomedical, approaches. As we shall see, historical treatments of this have often fallen into presentism.

This subsection not only gives the reader general historical background, but also deals with mind-body stances crucial to the psychiatric diagnostic endeavor. That such issues, and the place of psychosocial and neurobiological/biomedical perspectives, are fundamental to a nosology such as DSM-III-R (which ultimately seeks etiological and process-based diagnostic categories) is apparent from its editors' (1989) recent attempt to devise (equally dualistic!) alternatives such as "*physical*" and "*mental*" for disorders allegedly either "organic" or "non-organic" (see Wallace, 1988a, 1988c, 1989b, 1990a). Otherwise, we shall mostly withhold our specific treatment of American psychiatric nosology until a later section.

The Purely Asylum Phase: Early to Late 1800s

The formation of a nosologically sophisticated American psychiatry lagged much behind its European counterparts (especially French and German). Benjamin Rush, the first systematic American psychiatric writer, was primarily an internist, the mad being but one of his concerns. His *Medical Inquiries and Observations upon the Diseases of the Mind* (1812) espoused an overwhelmingly somatic theory of mental disorder. This centered on notions of the constriction or dilatation of blood vessels and the effect of altered cerebral blood flow on brain functioning itself (aspects of such ideas, though with a much richer empirical base, appear today!)—a sort of vascular version of Cullen's (1769) and Brown's (1795) neural constriction/laxity and nerve force theory (to which Rush would have been exposed when studying at Edinburgh). Rush's treatments were mainly the traditional somatic ones as well, including medication, bleeding, purging, and so forth. Had his book been written by a European, it probably would have attracted considerably less notice here and abroad.

Less presentistic psychiatric history suggests that the so-called psychical and somatic orientations—insofar as they can be accurately compared with our current concepts of *psychosocial, neurobiological,* and *biomedical*—have tended to coexist, in various forms, throughout the history of the specialty. Although this history is limited to American psychiatry, much the same point could be made about the ostensible conflicts between the Psychikers and Somatikers in

19th-century Germany (see Ackerknecht, 1968). There, brain psychiatry often included psychological approaches (e.g., Griesinger, 1845, 1867). Alternatively, Romantic "psychotherapists" based their theories on a philosophy of man's continuity with the rest of nature and its fundamental forces (such as magnetism—another resurgence in psychiatric theory today—and others); their treatments incorporated somatic modalities as well.

Let us begin with the American moral therapists. We score an additional point against presentism by noting that then the very word *moral*, in the United States and for the most part abroad, combined concepts that are more clearly separated today. It referred to a vague amalgam of what would now be differentiated into the psychological, social, moral/ethical, and even spiritual (in both its broader, and more strictly religious, sense). Their managerial and milieu therapies reflected the multiple meanings of this concept *moral* (see Bockhoven, 1963; Grob, 1983, 1983).

At the same time, because asylum doctors clung to a theology sharply separating brain/body from the supposedly immaterial soul or mind, they averred that only the former could become diseased (Bockhoven, 1963; Earle, 1887; Grob, 1983; Rosenberg, 1967). Therefore, it was the diseased brain (the mortal and material medium of the operations of this avowedly immortal and immaterial mind) that presented the mind with the peculiarity that manifested in madness. However, just as the functioning of the spiritual mind could be affected by its material brain, so the reverse as well. The soul's free violation of God-ordained natural laws (inclining, but not necessitating) could produce sickness in the mind's mortal medium, the brain/body. The diseased brain could then subsequently interfere with the mind's implementation of its rationality and free choice. Other factors promoting violation of the natural laws included the effects on vulnerable constitutions of improper family, living, and social conditions, as well as the breakneck pace and stress of modern life. Hence their psychopathology was thoroughly somatic, with individual moral/behavioral or social/environmental precipitants, whereas their reeducative and resocializing treatment was directed toward ambience and mind itself. Still, moral treatment hardly abandoned pharmaceutical and somatic therapies, and its interactional metaphysical dualism continues to characterize many physicians today.

The mid to late 19th-century U.S. psychiatric reaction against moral therapy and against its milieu-based reeducational approach to the individual patient did not occur for primarily theoretical or scientific reasons. These succeeding asylum doctors adopted, for the most part, similar theologically based notions of mind, ascribing pathology to the brain or body per se. However, their move to more custodial and somatically based symptomatic therapies resulted from a number of factors. These included the exponential crowding of mental hospitals caused by the larger and more mobile U.S. population; massive immigration and lack of community acceptance of the foreign mentally ill; a growing number of elderly, increasingly confined in such facilities, though often neither demented nor otherwise mentally ill; the growing percentage of chronic patients (resulting from the discharge of more benign moral therapy-type cases); growing proportions of serious organic mental syndromes secondary to syphilis (general paresis), nutritional deficiency (pellagra and beriberi), toxins (drugs, alcohol, endotoxic and endocrine diseases), and so on; and, finally, an insufficient increase in physicians and staff.

Whereas these later, more therapeutically nihilistic, alienists demonstrated that there had been some "doctoring" of treatment results by their moral therapy predecessors (e.g., Earle, 1887), more objective historical scrutiny indicates that the earlier lengths of stay and outcomes were in fact much superior to those of the late 19th-century (as Earle [1887] himself admitted) —indeed, in some respects, not terribly inferior to our own (e.g., Bockhoven, 1963). However, one must remember the much better staff/patient ratios and general asylum conditions of the moral therapy age, the more acute and ethnically similar class of patients, the fewer elderly and chronic organically and functionally disturbed, and the more homogeneous communities more likely to receive their discharged mentally ill back home.

In any event, it is correct that middle to late 19th-century U.S. alienists jettisoned much of what we would, only partly correctly, term the *psychosocial* orientation of the earlier moral therapy. Alienists more consistently emphasized and elaborated upon the organic psychopathology of their predecessors. However, this reorientation resulted, in part, *because of the larger percentage of patients with actual organic mental disease*: Alzheimer's and arteriosclerotic dementias; general paresis and other symptomatic constellations of neurosyphilis; central nervous system sequelae of other acute or chronic infectious diseases; tumors; post-head trauma syndromes; and nutritionally or toxically based syndromes. Moreover, functional mental disorders, such as schizophrenia, melancholia, and mania, were thought (then as now) to have brain structural, systemic, or endotoxic pathologies as well.

Still, try as they might, these more neuroanatomically oriented doctors could not find the clinical/pathological correlations that were increasingly discovered in their medical colleagues' domains. This further decreased the prestige of the once rather arrogant U.S. "psychiatrists" (whose specialty organization antedated the American Medical Association, which they repeatedly declined to join); isolated them, with their larger percentage of organic and chronic functionally psychotic patients; and left them with more custodial and therapeutically nihilistic attitudes.

American psychiatry was born and grew up with the mental hospital. Hence, it was defined by, as much as defined, the ambience and requirements of the institution itself (and by traditional social mores, beliefs, and pressures), as Grob (1983) brilliantly documented. Nor was there, as already implied, a 19th-century U.S. academic psychiatry, as was enjoyed, notably, by contemporary France and Germany. The reputation of American psychiatry rose and fell with that of its asylums. By the late 19th-century, this had reached a nadir. Moreover, a young specialty began attacking the alienists: the neurologists, who received their first impetus from the peripheral and central nervous system injuries of the Civil War. In the last decades of the 19th-century, a healthy contingent of these would enter the then-existing vacuum now known as *outpatient psychiatry*.

The Growth and Consolidation of American Psychiatry: 1890s–1930s

Like Freud and many other contemporary European neurologists, their American counterparts encountered many patients with vague and diffuse, nonpathoanatomically consistent or demonstrable, nervous system complaints. These included paralyses, anesthesias, pains, blindnesses, seizures, faints, and so forth; as well as manifold manifestations of chronic fatigue, anxiety, and mild to moderate depression. Such patients defined themselves as suffering from "nerves," as did their somatically oriented neurological doctors——though with, of course, more sophisticated theories and nosologies than their clients. This, by the way, is an excellent example of how medical conceptions (Cullen's and Brown's *nervous excitability* or *exhaustion*) affect popular idioms and thinking, which then further reinforce medical viewpoints (e.g., Beard, below), and vice versa (see also Carlson, 1980; Cayleff, 1988; Davis & Whitten, 1988; Montagne, 1988). Mushrooming insurance compensations for the "somatic", but often actually hysterical, sequelae of train accidents lent additional economic impetus to "neurologizing" approaches.

Neurologists, and George Beard (1838–1883) was a notable American one, often sought explanations in terms of generalized or specific nerve force or energy. Changes in nervous energy were also said to result from the impact of external precipitating causes (including the speeding up of modern living, excessive studying, etc.) on constitutionally vulnerable nervous systems. Generally, patients were conceived as deficient in this nerve force or energy, for example, Beard's (1869, 1880, 1881, 1884) *neurasthenia*, which made him the most internationally known American physician of his time. A variety of treatments were applied to ameliorate this energic, or functional neurological, disorder, including tonics, electrotherapy and electrotherapeutic massage, dietary and sleep regimens (such as those of Silas Weir Mitchell [1877]) and, eventually, hypnosis by some. In France, Charcot felt that only those with certain neuropathological conditions and predispositions were hypnotizable at all, whereas Bernheim vigorously opposed this point of view.

Today, many of their treatment measures would be considered as having psychotherapeutic elements: physician suggestion, patient faith and expectations (i.e., transference), placebo effects, the sufferer's ready acceptance of such an organic explanation for his or her disabilities, and positive effects of the doctor-patient relationship. With a conviction in the neurological basis of these therapeutic successes, and bolstered by European neurology's bewildering advances in pathoanatomical-clinical correlation, these doctors progressively attacked U.S. psychiatry as scientifically and clinically backward and static.

This is well instanced by neurologist S. Weir Mitchell's formal 1894 address to the American Medicopsychological Association, formerly (1844–1892) the Association of Medical Superintendents of American Institutions for the Insane (and later [1921], of course, the American Psychiatric Association). Reminding them of the early establishment of their discipline (1844, the first American medical specialty organization), he chided psychiatrists for failing to measure up to the progressively scientific standards of U.S. medicine. By then, American medicine was solidly influenced by, if hardly equal to, the German and French pathoanatomically and bacteriologically based medicine and statistical/experimental research.

Although many alienists resented Mitchell's chastisement, others took it to heart. Interest developed in a neuropathologically and scientifically based psychiatry, as illustrated by a number of institutional commitments. These included the founding of the New York State Psychiatric Institute (1897); the establishment of the Henry Phipps Clinic and Psychiatry Department (1913) of the relatively new, European-modeled Johns Hopkins Medical School; and the generally enhanced scientific consciousness and ambitions of the leaders of American psychiatry.

The outpatient neurologists and the asylum doctors would gradually fuse, *forming at the turn of this century the prototype and springboard for the development of the broader, and eventually more scientific, psychiatry that we know today.* There was increasing involvement in ambulatory psychiatry and the formation of acute psychiatric wards in general hospitals. The latter became associated with a broad new nosological category of patients——the "psychopathic"—— not to be confused with the later (e.g., Cleckley, 1941), antisocial-connoting term and concept.

Nevertheless, the vast majority of psychiatrists would remain in mental hospital employment for decades to come. However, their therapeutic nihilism and former nosological laxity were dampened by a number of factors, among them the discovery of the bacterial cause of syphilis and more specific treatments for its neuropsychiatric sequelae, such as Wagner von Jauregg's 1917 malarial treatment; ascertainment of the vitamin deficiencies causing pellagra and beriberi (two major causes of organic mental syndromes, especially in the South); the progressive neuroanatomical localization of lesions associated with certain neuropsychiatric syndromes; the introduction of prefrontal lobotomy; and the development of a number of convulsive therapies in the early to mid 1930s.

Consequently, organically based theories and diagnostic categories predominated in state hospitals. In contrast, theories and nosologies with larger psychosocial components would characterize ambulatory clinics, general hospital acute psychiatric (psychopathic) wards, and many private mental hospitals. Adolf

Meyer, head of the New York Psychiatric Institute before coming to Johns Hopkins as director of the Phipps Clinic in 1913, fostered a psychobiological approach, aiming to bridge and integrate psychiatry's coexisting organic and psychosocial purviews (e.g., Meyer, 1950). Over the years Meyerian psychobiology, which included a detailed patient biography in both psychosocial and neurobiological/biomedical spheres, as well as comprehensive therapeutic approaches, shaped many American psychiatrists who later assumed academic, public health, and American Psychiatric Association leadership positions. It was, of course, a direct precursor of Engel's (1977, 1980) widely endorsed biopsychosocial model. Moreover, the biographical and psychosocial aspects of psychobiology contributed to the eventual popularity of psychoanalysis and dynamic psychiatry.

At the same time, by 1910 numerous forces began augmenting the outpatient and acute/intermediate inpatient wings of American psychiatry. A growing lay activist push for a larger and more social scientifically based welfare system led to a focus on the prevention and early treatment of mental disorders, and on the identification of pathogenic family, community, social, and economic factors. The lay/medical Mental Hygiene Committee was founded that year (1910) by former mental patient Clifford Beers and Harvard psychiatrist E.E. Southard. Although formed in the interests of the chronic and severely mentally ill, ironically it assumed a progressively outpatient, acute inpatient, and social/community stance and indirectly contributed to the increasing neglect of its original charge: the asylums and chronically mad.

Associated with all of this was the eventual formation of a novel psychiatric subspecialty, child psychiatry, arising from interactions between pediatricians and social welfare workers. It overcame the longstanding myth that mental illness does not occur in children (as was still thought, until quite recently, with regard to childhood depression!) and established a number of clinics, often associated with juvenile and family courts. Soon it became an integral, though somewhat distinct, part of American psychiatry. Its different patient population, and its peculiar route of origin, presumably help account for still-existing problems in child psychiatric classification systems vis-à-vis those of general adult psychiatry. As the new century's teens and twenties approached, middle-class parents progressively interpreted their children's and adolescents' behavioral problems as difficulties amenable to psychiatric approaches. This was hardly discouraged by child guidance clinics and child psychiatrists, and added yet another significantly different diagnostic and therapeutic twist to the subspecialty (Jones, 1972, in press).

The Flowering of American Psychiatry: World War II Onward

In addition to the early 20th-century flowering of a science-aspiring social welfare activism, a subsequent factor contributed to both psychiatric prestige and the social/community, preventive, and acute treatment orientation. This was World War II, with its huge number of rejected recruits for neuropsychiatric reasons and its high incidence of battlefield and postwar psychiatric casualties. Psychiatrists' role in the treatment and rapid return to action of many of these soldiers was founded on the therapeutic principles of proximity, immediacy, and expectancy (Grinker & Spiegel, 1945). This provided additional support for the social/ community, ambulatory, and acute inpatient treatment sides of psychiatry (Glass, 1972).

Indeed, postwar military psychiatry applied these same principles. It attempted to identify likely psychiatric casualties and then treat mental disorders early in an outpatient or short-term hospitalization setting, as close to the patient's neighborhood (i.e., battlefront!) as feasible. In short, the expectation was transmitted that treatment would be brief and efficient, enabling rapid resumption of regular responsibilities.

The nation's wartime experience with psychiatric and neuropsychiatric issues led to an astronomical growth in the size of the specialty and in the number of its residencies and university departments (still relatively rare well into the 1920s and 1930s). Federal subsidy of psychiatric education facilitated the entry of medical graduates, with 12.5% of graduating physicians entering residencies in 1954 (compared with 3 to 5% in recent years)! There was an accompanying shift away from state hospital work to private practice, community work, and activity in public or university-based outpatient clinics and acute/intermediate care hospital wards. Similarly, more and more of the new psychiatrists, especially the university-trained, embraced psychoanalytic/psychodynamic and/or social/community psychiatric orientations (Grob, 1983, 1991).

By 1956, only 17% of the 10,000 American psychiatrists were state hospital doctors, leaving a static number of physicians for ever-growing chronic inpatient censuses. The rest turned increasingly toward neurotic and personality disorders and away from the severe organic and functional mental syndromes. Finally, as we shall see in a later section, the two groups of psychiatrists adopted diverging attitudes about the role of diagnosis, favoring different classification systems. This was based partly on theoretical disagreements and also on actual differences in the patient populations served.

The rest of the story, in terms of the status of the psychosocial and neurobiological vantages, and the general development of American psychiatry, is too well known to need extensive elaboration. Moreover, in many respects it is too contemporary for a genuinely historical perspective.

Since then, as previously, American psychiatry has not been characterized by either a unitarily psychosocial or a neurobiological/biomedical stance. It is true that the 1940s, 1950s, 1960s, and early 1970s saw greatly strengthened social/ community and psychodynamic orientations and their dominance of academic psychiatry. This was also reflected, though perhaps less so, in federal and National Institutes of Mental Health (NIMH) support of psychosocially inclined training, treatment, and investigation.

Still, during those years there were important active organic orientations (pharmacotherapeutic, convulsive, and psychosurgical), a Meyerian holism promoting the importance of both psychosocial and somatic viewpoints, and significant psychodynamic and biomedical collaboration in the psychosomatic move-ment. Moreover, we must consider that the psychiatric profession has comprised several sectors. Academic centers differed in predominant orientation and patient population, as did public/community ambulatory and short-term inpatient arenas, private offices, private mental hospitals, state institutions, and even geographic locales. Consider that in 1950 Frieda Fromm-Reichmann could deem the psy-chodynamic orientation sufficiently unfamiliar to rank-and-file psychiatrists to write an introductory text specifically for them.

Similar remarks apply to the apparent hegemony of neurobiological and pharmacological psychiatry since the mid 1970s, exemplified by NIMH and funding agencies' blatant preference for neurobiological and psychopharmaco-logical research over psychosocial projects, when the former already receives substantial corporate pharmaceutical funding. Although the neuroscience/pharm-acological approach now predominates in American academic departments, many still carry faculty with other emphases, and a few are still psychosocially or psychodynamically oriented.

For their part, private or community residencies and state mental health train-ing programs have various flavors and accents. Training/accreditation bodies still require the teaching of social/community, psychotherapeutic, and psychodynam-ic theories and methods. Private practitioners cannot be monolithically character-ized; their approaches are often eclectic, if not outright pluralistic and pragmatic. Many psychiatrically espoused and utilized systems of individual, group, and family psychotherapy abound. Psychoanalytic institutes and societies remain ac-tive, with analysts often serving as part-time university clinical faculty. In gener-al, psychoanalysis and dynamic psychiatry are responding better to criticisms of their scientific and therapeutic status, and a variety of empirical and scientifical-ly rigorous intraclinical and extraclinical tests are being applied (see Dahl, 1972; Edelson, 1984, 1990; Kline, 1981; Luborsky, 1984; Masling, 1983, 1986; Wal-lace, 1985, 1986, 1988c, 1989b; Wallerstein, 1986a, 1986b; Weiss & Sampson, 1986). Engel's biopsychosocial enrichment of Meyer's psychobiological attitude and framework is espoused and actually practiced by many American psychia-trists.

If there are two overriding characteristics of this country's psychiatry, they are its breadth and richness, historically and currently. Even when limited to a literal handful of asylum superintendents (13 in the original organization of 1844), their collective orientation was neither biologically nor psychosocially exclusivistic. Although I applaud plural reductionisms no more than mindless syncretisms, I find it reassuring that, overall, American psychiatry has been and still is best characterized as eclectic and practical, while striving for the best possible science and for open and evolving theoretical/therapeutic syntheses (such as psy-chobiology and the biopsychosocial model) (Wallace, 1991). By contrast, much of the rest of the (at least mid- to late-20th-century) world has adopted a purely descriptive and "organic" psychiatry, with psychosocial perspectives gladly ceded to clinical psychologists, social workers, and a few psychoanalysts. For example, Heinz Häfner (1982), a distinguished contemporary German psychiatrist, sees this as preeminently responsible for European psychiatry's loss of "important ground" to clinical psychology (p. 47).

Finally, a growing literature, such as this volume, attests to the development of a conceptual wing within American psychiatry, a philosophically and ethically self-critical, analytical, and synthetic perspective on its current assumptions, theories, investigations, nosological standpoints, and therapeutic practices. This mode of inquiry, instead of dogmatic claims to fixed, final, clear, and certain truths (or the misguided search for them), will hopefully continue to distinguish our developing specialty.

PSYCHIATRIC NOSOLOGY: HISTORY, HISTORIOGRAPHY AND PHILOSOPHY

Preliminary Considerations

Guideposts

From the historiographical and historical background, let us move explicitly to the history and philosophy of psychiatric nosology itself, bearing in mind the following historiographical points.

1. As there was no psychiatric medical subspecialty before the late Enlightenment and the turn of the 19th-century, the history of *what we now consider to be* psychiatric classification begins with the history of general medicine, as well as with that of enterprises outside medicine itself, such as magic and mythology, theology and religion, the law, and philosophy.

2. It is generally held (e.g., Sigerist, 1951) that medicine originated in an undifferentiated matrix of animism and magic and then religion. This confronts us with grave difficulty determining when social deviance, or peculiar or bizarre behavior, began to be viewed under a category even so diffuse, evolving, and time/place bound as *madness* itself. Consider also the many magical, religious, or folk medicine approaches to such issues today.

3. More or less secular medicine was schoolbound for much of its history. As we have seen, retrospectively denoting a medical mainstream is as much an act of interpretation as of discovery, with all of the related consequences for concepts and categorizations of madness. Moreover, in limiting our purview to mostly Western medicine, we are ignoring great Eastern traditions still flourishing today (e.g., Ayurvedic medicine, recently making inroads to the West itself), as well as certain long-lived currents within our home culture (e.g., homeopathy) (Kaufman, 1971; McKee, 1988).

4. Until the modern centuries (e.g., 17th to present), there was little general medical concern with present-day neurotic and characterological disorders, or

with anything resembling a host of more prominent DSM-III and III-R categories. Whether, or how much, this was because of medical indifference to all but the most blatant mental dysfunction or the lack of descriptive concepts for a broad range of behaviors, or even because of the dismissal of mental disorder as nonmedical (i.e., as religious, moral, political, or legal), or simply because such syndromes were then mostly nonexistent, is difficult to determine.

5. Throughout time and place, there has been a subtly mutual shaping of major presenting syndromes by doctors, patients, and society/culture.

6. Acknowledged or implicit mind-body positions have been perennially relevant to diagnostic categories and whole classificatory systems.

7. Asylums, with few exceptions, were dominated by lay administrators, with medical presence limited to occasional consultants, if that, until the late 18th- and early 19th-centuries. This denied physicians crucial pools of information about the nature and course of forms of madness.

8. There is a complex relationship among psychiatric philosophies, theories, nosologies, and therapies, on the one side, and time/place-linked modes of personal and collective experience and even concepts of personhood, on the other. All of this is patently relevant to any evaluation of prior nosologies, diagnostic categories, and processes of diagnosis (our own included), and to point 9 below.

9. The question of the *ontological status* of diagnostic categories (i.e., concepts) persists unabated: that is, the degree to which diagnoses correspond to well-delineated collective facts, and to which psychiatric categories refer to *diseases, syndromes, symptom complexes,* or even so-called *problems in living.* Some current psychiatrists—Colby and Spar (1983), for example, in their fascinating overview of the philosophical, scientific, and clinical perspectives on nosological issues—even suggested that disturbed *individuals,* rather than putative and perhaps reified disorders, should be (probabilistically) classified. Patients would then be subgrouped by their degree of conformity to interrater-reliable, statistically cluster-related constellations of multicategorical properties (i.e., ideational, behavioral, psychometric, and psychophysiological patterns). In pondering their argument, consider the potentially embarrassing problem of the same patient carrying multiple Axis I or Axis II diagnoses. For example, clinically, and to some degree statistically, we know that many depressed patients experience and exhibit considerable degrees of anxiety (there being recent neurobiological evidence for such overlap also), as well as any other range of symptoms from social phobias to obsessive-compulsive behaviors. Furthermore, despite DSM-III/III-R criteria for relative mood constancy in major depressives and melancholics, the moods of these patients may actually show significant fluctuation over the course of a week or even a day. Such observations suggest that disability in general affect and mood regulation should be added to the set of polythetic criteria for Major Depression. Both of these points perhaps suggest that a dimensional approach to Axis I disorders (such as Millon & Klerman [1986] advocate for Axis II, where it is particularly discomfiting to have *one and the same person* laden with two, three, or more *personality disorders*) may be more

correct *and clinically useful* than the current categorical one. The latter might be falsely reifying the various aspects of the single patient's pattern of distress and dysfunction into multiple diagnostic entities. In any event, psychiatry has yet to demonstrate that even its most apparently universalizable categories (e.g., schizophrenia) comprise diseases in the general medical sense of specifiable pathophysiologies; and its pathological/nosological criteria include concepts such as "maladaptation."

10. There is the related problem of what society allows to be recognized as disease or illness. This problem may manifest in terms of societal belief/action systems and whether the disorder is so modal that it cannot be indigenously construed as abnormal (like yawes in certain areas of Africa).

11. Finally, lest our list overtake us, there is of course the necessity to evaluate nosologies from metaphysical/epistemological, social/moral philosophical, historical, social scientific and transcultural, natural scientific, demographic/epidemiological, clinical, and patient vantages.

Cross-Cultural Issues

Before beginning our brief historical-philosophical sketch of psychiatric nosology, let us reconsider the crucial message that human experience, individual and collective, and concepts of normative personhood have varied immensely across time and space. Consequently, so have conceptualizations of deviation from the norms, whether such deviations are considered sickness, sin, sorcery, or possession. Moreover, deviant or pathological presentations are themselves shaped to some degree by the culture's prevailing schemata and categories for abnormal experiences, cognitions, and behaviors. Official healers played both mediating and creative roles in this process. For example, Bennett Simon (1978) pointed to certain codified and relatively fixed cultural templates in ancient Greece for how to be mad: hearing animal sounds and the music of flutes and cymbals, the conviction that one is Atlas with the world on one's shoulders, or that one is a giant piece of pottery or glass; with, of course, accompanying sets of experiences and actions consistent with such hallucinations and bizarre beliefs.

In line with the recent historical and philosophical accent on the shaping of scientific and medical thought by metaphors and images, a number of articles in *The Anatomy of Madness* (Bynum, Porter & Shepherd, 1985) demonstrate their impact on psychiatric diagnosis and clinical thinking. Montagne (1988) applied this perspective to the history of addictions, an area of centuries-long controversy between moral and medical/psychiatric purviews. Davis and Whitten (1988) surveyed the relation between popular and medical concepts of "nerves" and their influence on physicalist psychiatric perspectives among both laymen and doctors. Cayleff (1988) argued that nervous and gender metaphors have fused to associate many such disorders more closely with women; Gilman's (1982) magisterial *Images of Madness* is a beautiful iconographical study of history's images and metaphors of madness.

Hence, throughout the history of medicine and psychiatry there have been culturally, professionally, and individually coconstituted themes, metaphors, and categories for organizing, experiencing, and expressing one's mental disorder. Speaking to the medical factors in this, the psychiatrist-sociologist team of Stanton and Schwartz (1954) was among the first to underline the role of professional and hospital needs, expectations, and institutions in molding important aspects of mental patients' preoccupations, behavior, and communications on the ward. They did not contend that these persons were not actually mentally ill, but rather that the administration, physicians, staff, and milieu culture and social structure impinged importantly on the manifestations, courses, and severities of patient illnesses.

The aforementioned Goffman (1961) and colleagues argued still more strongly for the patient-sculpting role of institutional factors and physicians' theoretical/nosological commitments and expectations. The psychiatrist-anthropologist Barrett, in two provocative articles (1988a, 1988b), analyzed possible professional and institutional determinants of both the schizophrenia diagnosis and its patients' actual behaviors, including the enculturation of patients into the schizophrenic role, the influence of Western concepts and perspectives on what doctors perceive (even among "Third World" psychiatrists), the impact of selective and patient-shaping interviews and documentary writing, and the socioeconomic and political functions of the schizophrenia diagnosis and psychiatric interventions. In line with certain facets of his argument, consider American psychiatrists' own recent decision (reflected in the DSM-III-R), from studying differences in Anglo-American diagnostic styles, that Americans had been overdiagnosing schizophrenia and underdiagnosing syndromes such as bipolar disorder. Fabrega (1989), a noted American transcultural psychiatrist, and Hahn and Gaines (1985) continue a growing tradition of looking at Western biomedicine and psychiatry themselves as ethnomedicines. Kleinman and Good's (1985) anthology on culture and depression includes much about sociocultural influences on the form, content, and manifestations of affective disorders (see also Kleinman, 1988).

Such historical, social science, and transcultural investigations foster nosological humility, more phenomenological approaches, better appreciation of the multifactorial nature of psychiatric dysfunctions, and consideration of institutional contexts, adaptational issues, and culture-specific conceptualizations of mental illness. They add idiographic leaven to nomothetic nosological aspirations that cause us to overlook not only cultural, but also individual particularities. By alerting us to these intra- and extradisciplinary determinants of our perception and interpretation, they broaden our concept of countertransference and further remind us of the interactional, mutually determinative nature of psychiatric investigation, nosological or otherwise (see Wallace, 1985; 1988a; 1989b).

Nevertheless, some of these positions and insights, carried to the extreme, are hard to defend. First, many overlook important historical and transcultural continuities and commonalities among the differences in certain symptoms, symptom complexes, and even syndromes (Jackson, 1986; Roth & Kroll, 1968; World Health Organization [WHO], 1973). Second, antipsychiatric social scientists and historians, such as Goffman (1961) and Rothman (1971), fail to appreciate the reality of mental suffering and dysfunction, and the extent to which these manifestations have preceded and are independent of psychiatric intervention. Moreover, if the labeling theory and institutional factors of Goffman and others were the sole necessary and sufficient conditions for major mental disorders such as schizophrenia and bipolar disorder, then outlawing diagnosis and closing facilities should eliminate such problems——a hypothesis already apparently falsified by the results of deinstitutionalization! Third, social science and social historical viewpoints can be unidimensional and reductive; they do not approach psychiatric theories, classifications, and methodologies as if extrinsic factors and forces and unacknowledged professional motives may play a role in the determination of these medical activities, but instead operate as if such elements tell the whole tale. Finally, those arguing for the radical historical/cultural relativism of mental disorders, concepts of mental illness, and psychiatric theories and perspectives upon them, actually undermine themselves; for logic entails that their own positions are no less relative, and hence as transitory and nonobjective, as those of the psychiatrists allegedly constructing what they then study and treat.

Culture, Experience, and Personhood

In continuing our consideration of the evolving concepts of mental disorder, we must examine apparent changes in *experiences* of self or, better, of life-world (for *self* is never experienced in a representational or actual interpersonal vacuum), as well as alterations in *conceptions* of personhood. Their relevance to mental disorders is clear (see the chapters by Caws and Mishara), as well as to the classifying of them. Let us begin with current notions of *self*, *life-world*, and *personhood* and move backward from there.

Western, postindustrial concepts and experiences of personhood or self are more individualized and less community governed than those in more traditional, socially cohesive, and communally oriented societies. The postindustrial person and his or her most recent version, Rieff's (1959, 1968) "psychological man" or "therapeutic", appears considerably more introspective, causally self-attributional, autonomous, and self-determining. Social structures and cultural institutions are less compelling, and more open and evolving. Physical architecture and less crowded living conditions allow for forms of privacy unknown in earlier times. Undoubtedly, this has also affected types and incidence rates of what we deem psychopathology; and has given rise to personality traits and constellations hitherto rare or absent, and hence unconsiderable, in the past.

Many of the DSM-III Axis II disorders are probably cases in point. It has been suggested that some of them, to the extent that they are actual syndromal entities (such as the Borderline Personality Disorder), are specific to the recent West or even America. There is both historical and cross-cultural evidence that, to the limited degree that we can compare present-day syndromal concepts with past ones, some of the major psychiatric disorders (such as Schizophrenia, Melancholia, Major Depression, Mania, *and even Delirium and Dementia*) are so multifactorially (i.e., biopsychosocially) shaped that the underlying syndromes themselves, and not merely their manifestations and sociocultural particulars, have changed significantly over time (Berrios, 1987; Wallace, 1990b). Synchronically, for instance, much contemporary anthropology suggests that phenomena as diverse as patterns of response to alcoholic intoxication and psychotropic medication, and psychotic syndromes, can show fundamental differences cross-culturally (see Kleinman, 1988; Lithman, 1983; Wallace, 1990a).

Genetics, constitution, temperament/personality, and micro- and macrosociocultural structures, institutions, and folkways all converge to pattern modes of human being in health and sickness. In this respect, there is no hard and fast line between the so-called biological and sociocultural factors in normality, deviance, and disorder or disease. There is a sense in which the psychosocial sciences are *part* of human biology, that is, its physiology, ethology, and ecology (Wallace, 1990a, in press-b). Thus, they are integral perspectives in pathophysiology/psychopathology as well. Throughout history and across cultures, medicine has had to deal with combinations and permutations of both flux and continuity, and it will continue to do so.

In response to the flux, novel forms of healing have arisen to treat new modes of mild to moderate distress and dysfunction. In the past Western world, somewhat similar disturbances and dysphorias were usually conceptualized—by sufferers, healers, and society alike—as spiritual and moral malaise. The "patient" then experienced and comprehended his or her distress and dysfunction in more homogeneous socialized forms. In line with this, the curing or amelioration of conditions approximating (our contemporary concept of) neurosis or character disorder was effected by the sufferer's confession and participation in socially sanctioned healing rituals and reintegration into the socially normative group (Rieff, 1968). Most commonly these rituals embodied magical/animistic or religious convictions, activities, and institutions.

Such cohesive communities and their supernatural belief/action systems have gradually eroded. At least in the current Western world, they have been replaced by a pluralistic society/culture with fewer binding beliefs and mores, a popular faith in science and medicine, and secularized conceptions of cosmos, personhood, and personal distress. Hence, most Westernized mental sufferers now turn to family physicians, psychiatrists, psychoanalysts, and other mental health professionals rather than, as before, to shrines, sorcerers, temples, and priests (although a significant segment still consults clergy [Wallace, 1983b]). For such persons, it is as impossible to experience and interpret their problems in traditional spiritual and moral terms as it is for them to be helped in that manner (Rieff, 1968; Wallace, 1984, 1991). However, it would be remiss to overlook the growing Western interest in broadly spiritual concerns and perspectives on life-modes in health and sickness. This manifests in a plethora of ways: from the self-help movements, popular fascination with Eastern religions and philosophies, resurgences in faith healing, infatuation with the occult and parapsychology, the holistic health movement and a number of religiomedical collaborations and enterprises, and transpersonal psychology, to the 12-step programs of Alcoholics Anonymous and related recovery organizations.

It is of course impossible to enter the mind-set of, say, a Middle Kingdom Egyptian, a second-millennium B.C. Babylonian, or a medieval noble, cleric, or peasant. Nevertheless, there is ample historical and archaeological evidence that there was less social heterogeneity and individualism. Apparently, in earlier times there was considerably less demarcation between (a heavily enculturated) individual and collective experience and behavior. Moreover, there seems to have been a much less "interiorized" and expansive sense of self, over and against that of society and the natural milieu, than presently (Auerbach, 1946; Dodds, 1951; Rohde, 1925; Simon, 1978). Again, something as mundane as the compactness and closeness of family dwellings probably codetermined this. Ethnologists in such public, nonprivate living conditions have themselves reported their pull into the group mentality and the concomitant and disturbing sense of the incipient loss of their own autonomies and self-identities (e.g., Bohannon, 1954; Read, 1965, 1986).

It is likely that there was also some variation across socioeconomic classes, between, for instance, the Pharaoh's sense of individuality and that of his peasants, although it is hard to tell because of Egypt's highly stereotyped and relatively timeless modes of individual and collective representation. Still, even the Pharaoh's personal identity was inextricably bound up with his "divinity," his ancestors, the gods, and the nation; and his experience and behavior were so shaped by the hoary ritualistic requirements of his role that he probably had a less autonomous experience and concept of self than did even a factory laborer in early industrial England. In any event, any psychiatric historian who does not realize that it is a mind-stretching exercise to attempt to "approximate" the mental sets and self-concepts of a British, French, or German Enlightenment physician——or of the German Romantics——had best stay out of the field altogether.

In returning to Greece before the Hippocratics, it is well evidenced that pre- and early Homerics were similarly less self-circumscribed and possessed a far less integrated experience of personhood than modern Westerners. Thoughts and passions were often experienced as externally implanted or inserted, whether by a deity or by a divinized nature itself (Dodds, 1951). Motivation was first experienced and conceptualized as originating extra-bodily as well, from deities, spirits, or actual inhalations of the ambient air (Dodds, 1951). Initial "internalizations" or privatizations of the experience and concept of motivation localized it to an autonomously operative region of the diaphragm, or *phthumos*.

Personal qualities or excellences (*areté*) were thought to be gifts from without, from a god or whatever. Latter-day phenomenological distinctions between somatic sensations and mental/emotional feelings were then barely experienced or entertained. Such considerations demand that we ponder the impact of concretizing figures of speech—as manifested then and now—on both personal experience and mind-body conceptualizations and theorizing (Wallace, 1988a, 1990a, 1992a). It is far from clear that somatizing metaphors tell us anything whatsoever about the actual ontology of *mind*, much less about that of the so-called *mind-body relation* (Wallace, in press).

It was apparently in democratic Athens that experiences and concepts of selfhood more like ours first emerged, although theirs were still more closely merged with community and the sense of surrounding divinity or divinized nature than we could imagine. Nor were they an industrialized people or anything remotely resembling Rieff's (1959, 1968) "therapeutic" or "psychological man". Moreover, for all its rationality (in our contemporary sense of the term), Dodds (1951) and others (e.g., Rohde, 1925; Simon, 1978) have documented the coexistence in classical Greek culture of deeply irrational undercurrents. For changes in the literary representation of self over the centuries from Homeric Greece onward see, again, Dodds (1951), Laìn Entralgo (1970), Rosenthal (1971), Simon (1978), and especially Auerbach (1946).

The issues surrounding personal mental distress and dysfunction, with their variability across time and space, are patently pertinent to the age-old question of the ontological (i.e., existential) status of disease. This is also part of the perennial philosophical argument about the reality status of particulars and universals. Whence comes the justification for taking a universal (such as a diagnostic category) to be something as concretely given as the actual particulars (i.e., persons in distress and dysfunction) to which that universal refers? No two cells of the same tissue are identical, much less two similarly diagnosed human syndromes or even diseases. Ponder the DSM-III-R classification of Personality Disorders in this light, or in the light of distinctions between psychiatric diagnostic categories as ideal versus real, or artificial versus natural, respectively (see the chapters by Hempel, Russell, Agich, Wiggins & Schwartz, Sadler & Hulgus, and Margolis, in this book).

Still, there can be no science without classification, however rough and preliminary. Histocytological advances came not from those who stopped with the fact that no cell is exactly like any other, but rather from those who recognized that each cell is in some respects like all others and in some respects like only certain others. However, we must not let our nosologies obscure the myriad facets and features of the unique human beings to whom our universalizing concepts are attached. Hence, the best nomothetic comprehensions must be combined with the best idiographic ones, for each influences, refines, and checks the other. Furthermore, we treat never-replicable individual patients and patient situations in the context of equally nonreplicable doctor-patient dialogues and collaborative exploratory and therapeutic activities (see Peterfreund, 1983; Wallace, 1983c, 1985, 1989c). Historical and transcultural studies reinforce this, and suggest that although there are elements of temporal and geographic continuity in some of our major psychiatric presentations (e.g., schizophrenia and the major affective disorders), and in a few of our minor ones (e.g., hysteria), there are more differences than similarities in many (e.g., borderline personality organization) (Kleinman, 1988; Kleinman & Good, 1985).

Historico-Philosophical Sketch of Psychiatric Nosology

Antiquity

Let us turn now to a historical/historiographical overview of actual psychiatric classification and nosologies. Although medical historians have often begun their narratives with the beliefs and practices of 19th- and 20th-century nonliterate societies, as if these resemble actual prehistoric medicine, this cultural evolutionist equation is hazardous on both anthropological and historiographical grounds (Wallace, 1980b, 1983a). Our overview of the history of medical diagnosis (in which psychiatric classifying was enmeshed until much later in its development) thus begins with the earliest literate civilizations, Egypt and Mesopotamia.

The best available documentary and archaeological evidence persuades that everything that is now considered internal medicine was then conceptualized and practiced in the magicoreligious framework that permeated the cultures and institutions of these societies. Sickness was deemed divine or demonic. If the former, it might follow some immoral act, such as breaking a key taboo or omitting an important tithe or aspect of religious ritual. If the latter, it could ensue directly or via the curse or incantation of a maleficent human being. Even the most ostensibly empirical- or medical theory-based Egyptian interventions occurred in the context of prayers, petitions, rites, charms, and so forth. Such more purely empirical healing was enacted by either surgeons or lower-status leeches (healers) and folk herbalists, whose theories and ministrations invariably retained elements of the supernatural. Preventive medicine amounted to prayer, petition, and the wearing and usage of charms, amulets, and apotropaics of all sorts (A. Gardiner, 1961).

Conditions were similar in Mesopotamia (Sumer, Babylonia, and Assyria) as well. The recognized and systematic physicians (our equivalent of scientific doctors) worked from a magicoreligious foundation, and were especially famed for their diagnoses through astrological and hepatoscopic divination. As in Egypt, there was a similarly less prestigious class of leeches or empirical folk healers (Oppenheim, 1977). The situations in ancient India (which had, perhaps, antiquity's best surgeons) and preclassical Greece were comparable (although Ackerknecht [1982] maintained that archaic Greece did have a long and important strain of extrareligious healing craftsmen). The Bible is laced with many examples of disease as divine punishment or demonic possession (recall Nebuchadnezzer's madness and Christ's exorcisms).

Some historians have suggested that Empedoclean and Hippocratic humoral pathology itself was a secularized outgrowth of earlier beliefs on soul loss, demonic possession, and exorcism. The closest archaic and Homeric version of anything resembling our psychotherapy relied heavily on the use of charmed words and phrases (Dodds, 1951; Laìn Entralgo, 1969; Simon, 1978). In any event, the Hippocratic and most other early classical schools of medicine were hardly antireligious; they were not averse to referring patients for temple cures, some early cadres of Greek physicians themselves probably emerged from Aesculapian shrines. Even the famous Hippocratic (1978, pp. 237–251) *Treatise on the Sacred Disease*, often misinterpreted as a purely secular tract, was actually designed to argue that epilepsy was no more sacred than any other disease— for most classical Greeks nature itself being either divinized or seen as a manifestation of divinity (Laìn Entralgo, 1969). The Hippocratic Oath itself was laced with quasireligious, Pythagorean influences (Edelstein, 1967). Simon (1978) demonstrated that the classical Greeks and their Hellenistic and Roman successors, when self-identified as ill, had access to a variety of medical schools with different diagnostic schemata and modes of practice, as well as to hordes of magical, religious, and folk healers. All of this jibes with both Dodds's (1951) depiction of classical Greece's irrationalist undercurrents and Cornford's (1912) and Harrison's (1992) emphasis on classical rationality's continuities with preclassical mythical and magico-religious motifs.

Although our discussion of Greek medical conceptualizations of madness will focus on the Hippocratics, it is important to recall, again: (a) that there were numerous other Greek systems of medical thinking, diagnosis, and practice too (such as that of Cnidos); (b) that brief nosological schemata of madness, therapeutic claims on this domain, and speculations on the mind-body problem were current among philosophers such as the dualistic Plato and the more monistic Aristotle; and (c) that frankly magical or religious nosological codifications, etiological explanations, and treatments abounded, in addition to those of the aforementioned leeches or folk doctors. Plato, for example, divided madness into natural, originating in physical disease, and into four subcategories of divine etiology: prophetic (given by Apollo), religious or enthusiastic (given by Dionysius), poetic (inspired by the Muses), and erotic (infused by Eros or Aphrodite).

The Hippocratics (ca. 460 B.C. onward) parceled madness into three major forms: phrenitis (acute mental disturbance with fever), mania (acute mental disturbance without fever), and melancholia (all forms of chronic mental disturbance). In addition, there were epilepsy and hysteria (the latter characterized more by convulsions and extravagant motor and choreiform movements than by the more modern anesthesias, paralyses, pain syndromes, etc.). Clearly, we cannot equate their "psychiatric" terms and syndromes with ours. From what we can gather, it is unlikely that all phrenitis was actually febrile; plainly, their melancholia probably included conditions ranging from those resembling our major depression and schizophrenia, to any number of organic brain syndromes and other severe disorders as well; and similar comments apply to their mania, hysteria, and even epilepsy.

Moreover, we must remember that the Hippocratic orientation was not primarily diagnostic, in the sense of identifying discrete disease categories—as was, for example, that of their contemporaries at Cnidos. The former focused more on prognosis, holistic etiology, and prevention. Prognosis encouraged some interest in the natural history of sickness, but also seemed significantly motivated by the desire to protect one's medical reputation—knowing when to refuse a likely terminal or incurable case. The Hippocratic concept of medical illness, which of course included our psychiatric disorder, was a more unitary one, as were Griesinger's (1845) and Menninger's (1963) psychiatric ones in much later days.

The Hippocratic theoretical etiology and clinical evaluational process involved imbalances among the four humors (blood, phlegm, yellow bile, and black bile), and between these and (a) certain natural environmental, climatic, and seasonal factors, and (b) the patient's diet and way of life. Imbalances among the humors could manifest in a variety of symptoms and symptom complexes, depending on which were in excess or deficiency, and depending on the structural/ functional systems most affected. Hence, the Hippocratic pathology was, again, a unitary and physiological/environmental/spiritual/behavioral one, emphasizing organismic imbalances or *dyskrasias* among the humors. It was not the pathoanatomical system of specific organ-based diseases which has dominated so much of 19th- and 20th-century medicine—and which, contended Foucault (1975), produced the unempathically objectifying (and, I would add, epistemologically problematic and incomplete) "clinical gaze," with its unself-acknowledged sociopolitical, economic, and moral/ethical dimensions.

Therefore, Hippocratic therapy was more holistic, keyed toward those bodily humors that were in relative excess or deficiency, and toward the relationship between these and life mode and environment. Humoral excesses were targeted by laxatives, purgatives, astringents, emetics, bleeding, and so forth; humoral deficiencies by dietary supplementation, among other measures. However, *dyskrasias* were generally approached through the side of excess, and dietetics were more often used by way of restricting certain foods believed to contain abundant precursors of the particular humor in overplus. Thus Greek medicine was not only therapeutic, but prophylactic and preventive as well. Ironically, this prophylactic orientation was pervasive at times when life-style changes were able to play a much less significant role in reducing morbidity and promoting longevity than they can at present; and yet, for all of our present knowledge of the impact of environment and behavior on the more chronic, less acute and infectious disease patterns of today, modern Western medicine has lagged behind its Hippocratic precursors in endorsing more holistic and preventive orientations.

Hippocratic *dietetics* included conversations with the patient about a number of aspects of what we would call "life-style" and suggestions about appropriate modifications thereof (in diet, exercise, work, recreation, environment, etc.). Just as the Hippocratic exploratory and treatment effort was individual centered, it incorporated dialogue with the patient about the likely etiology of his or her condition. This integrated humoral, environmental, educational, life-style, and therapeutic/preventive approach to the diseased individual (rather than individual disease categories) ensured the centrality of the doctor-patient relationship, something perhaps becoming part of the medicine we have lost.

Whatever the problems with the absence of a *specific disease*-oriented nosology, the Hippocratic concept of disease as a *process in time*, with a *course* or *history*, was an invaluable legacy to all subsequent nosographical efforts. Moreover, its humoral theory of personality types——sanguine, melancholic, phlegmatic, and choleric——bequeathed us a physiological psychology, a precursor to temperament/personality typology, a concept of constitutional predisposition to certain pathologies, and a notion of continuity between normality and illness.

Another historical message for the contemporary psychiatric nosologist is the theory boundedness of the Greek approach to disease. Although some aspects of their humoral pathology may have been influenced by observing certain accumulations, neoplasms, excretions, and local infectious swellings and discharges; most of it seems to have been a priori, whether influenced by earlier magico-religious theories, armchair natural philosophies such as that of Empedocles, or whatever. The subsequent history of medical/psychiatric diagnosis further points up the role of metaphysical and theoretical presuppositions in classificatory schemata. Again, the tenability of the DSM-III and III-R claims to atheoreticism is undermined on both historical and philosophical grounds. The great Kurt Schneider (1959), of current nuclear schizophrenia interest, himself denied the possibility of theory-free nosography.

In addition, we shall see that philosophers (who claimed "psychology" as their private domain until well into the 19th-century) continued to offer nosologies of madness competing with, or influencing, medical approaches to the same (e.g., Plato and Kant). The Catholic and Orthodox churches, and a host of medical traditions outside the allopathic mainstream, had and have their own nosologies as well. Regarding cultural issues in psychiatric diagnosis, Eisenberg (1977) and Kleinman (1979) have drawn distinctions between patient illness behavior, and disease or disorder from our current Western medical/psychiatric point of view. The question of whether modern Western psychiatrists can correctly diagnose culture-syntonic, and locally adaptive individual and even group behaviors, by our psychopathological categories will again be illuminated by our examination of the Medieval and Renaissance protopsychiatrists and the witchcraft trials.

Unfortunately, we must move swiftly through the rest of antiquity and thence to the Middle Ages and the Renaissance. In the Hellenistic period, a number of rival medical sects existed. Let us look briefly at the most prominent. The Dogmatics, exemplified by the great neuroanatomists Erasistratos and Herophilus, searched for the hidden causes of disease. The Empiricists took up arms against such hidden causes. The Methodists emphasized the commonality in all diseases, such as the laxity or tension of the body as a whole, or in its parts, which they treated with astringents and laxatives. Their approach is reminiscent of aspects of the much later nervous constriction/laxity theories of Cullen and Brown. All of these Greek schools had, of course, their representatives in Rome as well.

Much more historiographically and psychiatrically problematic is the place of philosophical groups such as the Stoics and Epicureans, considered by many latter-day psychiatric historians (e.g., Alexander & Selesnick, 1966) to have espoused early systems of psychotherapy. Nevertheless, although unacknowledged psychotherapeutic maneuvers and psychological mechanisms probably played a role in much medical and philosophical healing, it would definitely be anachronistic to deem the Stoics and Epicureans as anything like a present-day Freudian or other psychotherapeutic school. Whatever the psychologically meliorative effects of their philosophies, they saw themselves as philosophers living in consonance with their metaphysical and moral codes. They were certainly not "psychological men" or "therapeutics" in any way remotely resembling Rieff's terms. Nor were they professional cadres of psychotherapists although, it is true, philosophers since Plato (e.g., Wittgenstein) have spoken of the "physicianly" strain in philosophizing, and some Sophists were said to have "treated" people. Of course, the issue of the so-called Stoic and Epicurean psychotherapy is itself a philosophical as well as an historiographical and psychiatric one, involving the concept, nature, and boundaries of psychotherapy itself; as well as the relations between the notions of *psychological* and *spiritual/moral*, and between the *wholeness-sickness-healing* categories of each (Wallace, 1990b, 1992b).

In the Roman Celsus (1935), a 1st-century A.D. medical writer (though perhaps not himself a physician), we find the first known instance of what would become the typical medical nosological pattern: the classification of diseases from head to heel (*a capite ad calcem*). Other than a few important 1st- and 2nd-century nosological figures for psychiatry (such as Aretaeus, and Soranus the "gynecologist," who described the recurrences of, and relationship between, mania and depression), Galen (A.D. 130–201) is our key figure for the next 1,300 years.

It is historiographically interesting that Galen is significantly responsible for the historical and philosophical accent on the Hippocratics from then until now. There is some evidence (e.g., Switz, 1978) that Galen elevated Hippocrates, who may never actually have existed (see Edelstein, 1967), to the latter's fatherly status, in part to support *presentistically* some of his own thinking. In any event, Galen solidified and refined the humoral pathology that would dominate for centuries to come. He ranked his concepts of the six nonnaturals—air, exercise and rest, sleep and wakefulness, food and drink, excretion or retention of superfluities, and the passions or perturbations of the soul—as pathogenic co-factors alongside the humors themselves. Among the *nonnaturals*, as with the humors, proportion (*eukrasia*) was equated with health, and disproportion (*dyskrasia*) with disease. The Greek and Hellenistic infatuation with balance, present in Platonic and Aristotelian philosophy and ethics as well, has affected general medicine and psychiatry to the present day as, for example, in the concept of homeostasis and in many of the concepts of dynamic and neurobiological psychiatry (see Temkin, 1973, for a masterful study of Galen and Galenism).

Like that of Celsus, the nosology of Galen was head to heel, and his great authority helped perpetuate this mode until well into the 16th-century. What we consider mental disorders fell, not surprisingly, almost invariably under diseases of the *caput* (head/brain); although brain pathology was often deemed secondary, as in Galen's hypochondriacal melancholy, in which the spleen fails to filter out the black bile from the liver adequately, hence allowing the bile to rise to the brain. (See Jackson, 1986, for a thorough discussion of etiological and symptomatic notions of hypochondriasis and its relation to depression or melancholia over the years.)

Whereas in some of his case histories, Galen seemed to have some grasp of psychological factors in general medical presentations (Siegel, 1973), his psychopathology was overwhelmingly somatic. His systematics of what we now consider psychiatric disorder did not go much beyond the typical tripartite division (i.e., mania, melancholia, and phrenitis), with hysteria (an ever-present hanger-on) still thought to be caused by a wandering uterus.

As the centuries wore on, concepts of madness, and even milder mental disorders, became better clarified and classified. Environmental events, and even personality/temperament (usually conceived of as more physiological than psychophysiological), were given precipitant or even coetiological roles along with more classical somatic determinants. Still, mental pathologies, and the psychiatric nosologies influenced by such theories, remained predominantly organic throughout most of history.

The Middle Ages and the Renaissance

In moving from Galen through the decline of Rome and the early centuries of Byzantium, the tripartite classification remained prepotent, although occasionally with considerable elaboration. Much of this elaboration was provided by Alexander of Tralles (A.D. 6th century), Caelius Aurelianus, and Paul of Aegina. Aurelianus translated important conceptualizations of mania and melancholia into concepts more congenial to ours, the latter characterized by anguish and distress, with dejection, silence, animosity, suspicion, weeping, and longing for death. From various sources, Paul of Aegina (A.D. 625—700) compiled a number of ancillary categories of diseases of the head (Ackerknecht, 1968; Jackson, 1986).

In Northern Europe and the Europe of the old Roman Empire Galenic medicine dominated the field, from the foundation of the first formal Western medical faculties in the dawning universities of the 11th—13th-centuries, to the end of the Middle Ages and well beyond. In the Arabic world it was Galen, too, with a tincture of Aristotle (e.g., Avicenna, A.D. 980—1037). Mora (in press-a) points out the paucity of detailed and reliable medieval descriptions of mental illness. Indeed, it is historiographically important to know where our current scholarly limitations lie (see also Finley, 1975).

This period, like parts of the Renaissance, seems to have been characterized by occasional mass epidemics of apparent, time-limited madness or psychopathology (choreiform dancing and all manner of unusual group phenomena, including ostensible delusions and hallucinations). Theories about these involve etiologies from toxins (e.g., ergot) to psychological contagion (mass hysteria, group psychosis, or dissociation, etc.). This touches on the knotty question mentioned earlier: that of applying categories of individual psychopathology to groups or whole societies and cultures, in which unusual behaviors are institutionalized within the norm and therefore are more socially tolerated. Freud, of course, and some of his followers have been fond of such group diagnoses. Ackerknecht (1971), an ethnologist as well as a physician-historian, charged that such psychodiagnostic practice turned the world into a giant mental hospital and made "pathography" the universal science. Examining recent psychiatric nosologies (e.g., *trichotillomania* of DSM-III-R) and epidemiological reports on the incidence and prevalence of mental disorders, both U.S. and worldwide, one begins to wonder if what Ackerknecht feared has already transpired. Some, such as Spiro (1965) and Wallace (1983b), take a middle position, pointing out the pros and cons of each perspective and offering revised alternatives. The same issues arise in psychiatric and psychoanalytic approaches to history in general (Wallace, 1980a, 1980b, 1985).

One cannot examine Medieval psychiatric nosology (of course never systemized as such in our current sense) without taking account of the pervasive intellectual and cultural influence of the Church. Apart from sanctioning traditional Galenic medicine, its attitudes toward the mad or mentally disturbed centrally determined those of society and to some extent the attitudes of medicine as well. Moreover, many Christian theologians wrote about psychological and psychiatric topics. Augustine (A.D. 345—430), and later Thomas Aquinas (1225—1274), reintroduced Aristotle's three souls (vegetative, animal, and rational), with their respective faculties or powers. Aquinas emphasized the absence of free will as a decisive criterion for madness and developed a bipartite psychiatric nosology, parsing madness into conditions of natural versus supernatural origin. Mora (1980) described a medieval ambivalence toward madness institutionalized in the Church and elsewhere. The characteristic stylistic depiction of the mad person as an unholy wild man such as Nebuchadnezzar, or with bells, staff, mismatched colors, and so forth, doubtless reflected and shaped Catholic as well as lay influences, both of which affected medicine and medical images too. (Later we shall discuss the iconographical impact on diagnosticians such as Kraepelin and Bleuler.)

The medieval period, although not noted for its innovative theorists and nosologists, is at least remarkable for the establishment of secular and religious psychiatric hospitals, and general hospitals with separate wards for the insane. The Arabic world was particularly advanced in this respect, and Islam seemed to promote a less ambivalent attitude toward the mentally ill than that in contemporary Europe (Mora, in press-a). With a few exceptions (e.g., Juan Vives, in Spain at the end of the Middle Ages), European medical men were not generally in control of such wards and asylums. Medieval Europe also had a number of such units or hospitals then, further attesting to some changes in practice vis-à-vis the mentally ill.

From the earliest medieval monasteries (4th-5th-centuries A.D.), in places such as the Sinai and Egypt, religious concepts and nosologies of madness (as well as of what we would consider lesser mental disorders) abounded. One of the most noted of these was *accedia* (whose spelling has changed kaleidoscopically over the centuries, e.g., *accedie*, etc.). It originally denoted a certain apathy and laxity in a previously diligent monk; it sounds somewhat like the modern category of asthenia or neurasthenia. Depressive phenomenology and signs were apparently not pronounced in such persons in the earliest phase of the concept, and ambiguity and ambivalence existed as to whether the persons were sick, simply lazy and sinful, or influenced by demonic or satanic forces. The concept, or rather the term and related terms, remained and evolved for centuries, influencing both mainline medical taxonomy and popular lay opinion (see Jackson, 1986). The category appears to have moved toward emphasizing conditions remotely akin to the DSM-III Dysthymia and thence to take in, at times, states resembling contemporary Major Depression or Melancholia.

The term, with its various spellings and referents, was still common in the 17th-century (see Burton's *Anatomy of Melancholy* [1621]). I am told, by good authority, that it is still extant in certain rural areas of mountainous Kentucky (e.g., *acidie*, with the accent on the first syllable), to refer to states ranging from the passing blues to severe and chronic dejection, much as the American public now uses *depressed* and *depression*. In this context, it is notable that suicide became socially abhorrent only during the Christian era, anger and despair over salvation believed to be its major cause (Mora, in press-a).

We must note also the Church's impact on the resurgence of supernaturalist explanations in the Middle Ages, and its continuing support of Galenic medical theory. Galenic theories and the *caput* classification of *mental disorder* continued through the Renaissance, with a few important exceptions to be touched on directly. Fernel (1497–1558), "the French Galen," combined humoralism with brain structure to produce a fairly elaborate *caput* nosology, with the following major categories: diseases of the brain envelopes, diseases of the brain substance, and diseases of the ventricles (Menninger, 1963). Johannes Schenck (1530–1598) developed a contemporaneous German example of this humoral-brain structuralist, *caput* nosology (Menninger, 1963, pp. 4–26).

The Renaissance is noteworthy for its medically related science of *physiognomy*, claiming to divine important temperamental, as well as pathological, features from facial signs and the face's overall structure. However direct its lines of subsequent influence, it can be seen as prototypical for a much later variety of medical readings of surface anatomy. The traditions emerging from physiognomy could include Gall's (1815) phrenology, through Sheldon and Tucker's (1940) and Kretschmer's (1925) constitutional/temperamental/disease-prone classes, Lombroso's (1911) criminal types, to widespread mid 19th- to early 20th-century emphasis on hysterical, schizophrenic, and other pathological or degenerative signs and stigmata (discussed later).

The Renaissance, including its physicians, began attending more to passions and the irrational. *Imaginatio*, or imagination, was for them an almost catch-all psychological concept for everything from what we consider imagination to phenomena such as suggestion, hallucinations, delusions, and so forth (Mora, in press-b). Moreover, Renaissance faculty psychology localized each faculty (generally imagination, memory, and will) to a separate ventricle of the brain. Renaissance thinking about *caput* pathology was, in short, basically organic.

Timothy Bright, widely considered the author of the best English Renaissance book on psychiatry (*A Treatise on Melancholie*, 1586), exemplified how, by then, the word *melancholy* had taken on a most vague and broad medical and lay meaning. Although his book has some important phenomenological and psychological contributions, most of its pathology and nosology were clearly traditional, derived from the three forms of melancholia attributed to Galen. For Bright, general, brain, and hypochondriacal melancholia depended on the presence of whole-body black bile excess, brain excess, or secondary brain effects from abdominal (hypochondrial or splenic) defects in filtering and clearing the dark humor. Bright also spoke of melancholia caused by alterations of black bile, yellow bile, blood, and phlegm, respectively. The semblances of these varieties of melancholia run the gamut from major depression through dysthymia, to depressive personality, to mere sullenness and irritability, to schizophrenia, and to psychotic forms of depression and schizoaffective disorder.

During the Renaissance, we encounter the first major rebels against Galen. Paracelsus (1493–1541), for all of his personal and intellectual oddities, must be deemed the father of this revolt. He rejected the humoral and other aspects of Galenic pathology, and substituted his own emphasis on chemical factors, magnetic forces deriving from the lunar phases and astral movements and, finally, his vital spirits. Ackerknecht (1968, p. 25) likened Paracelsus' conception of the body to an alchemist's kitchen, whose caustic fumes rose to the brain to cause mental illness. His famous *Diseases which Deprive Men of their Reason* (1520) has, not surprisingly, a consistently organic orientation; although it is not without certain psychological insights, for example the sexual elements in group chorea lascivia and, some maintain, a primitive idea of the unconscious. Rejecting Galenic head-to-heel nosology, his own classificatory system grouped apparently related diseases into families, hence diseases leading to the loss of reason.

In general, Paracelsus supported humane attitudes toward witches, although on the basis of his own sensitivities, instead of psychiatric diagnoses as with Weyer. Indeed, his pluralism and syncretism were such that in his 1531 treatise on mental illness, *The Invisible Diseases*, he reverted from his secular, chemical theories to supernatural, satanic, and demonological ones. Nevertheless, even though his general and inconsistent dismissals of tradition proved a dead end, his less idiosyncratic side offered a non-Galenic general medical and psychiatric pathology, nosology, and therapeusis. Furthermore, he did the first important work on occupational diseases, introduced a number of metals and chemicals to the European pharmacopoeia, founded the important iatrochemical school of medicine (Pagel, 1958), and even adumbrated current psychophysiological theories and practices regarding the impact of imagination and state of mind on both the causation and treatment of certain general medical disorders.

Felix Plater (1536–1614), like Paracelsus from Basel, also rejected Galenic medicine and its head-to-heel nosology. Like Paracelsus, he included a category of mental diseases of supernatural etiology. Plater was an early advocate of autopsy for clinicopathological correlation in madness; and he was part of a growing interest in alcoholism, much on the rise since the medieval discovery of distilling processes—medical claims on the addictions being hardly a recent phenomenon! His four broadest psychiatric categories, each with a number of subtypes, were mostly conceived as organically caused: (a) mental deficiency and dementia; (b) disturbances of consciousness; (c) psychosis; and (d) mental exhaustion. Melancholia, under psychosis, was further partitioned into hypochondriasis, lycanthropy, and misanthropy. If space permitted enumerating subcategories in the other three classes, the great difficulty comparing them with our current diagnostic concepts would become immediately apparent: some categories and subcategories seem to contain many, or parts of many, of ours; others seem to overlap or be wholly redundant by present-day standards.

Before turning to Johannes Weyer, whom Zilboorg and Henry (1941, p. 180) called the "father of the first psychiatric revolution," and to the related witchcraft story, let me mention an orienting comment by Ackerknecht (1968, p. 80). The 17th-century was the beginning of attention to forms of psychiatric disorder akin to what we now call the *neuroses* (especially hysteria and hypochondriasis). (*Neurosis* was later coined by Cullen [1769] and originally carried a literal, neurological meaning.) As early as 1600, Mercuriali complained about the increase of hypochondriasis in his practice. Sydenham, whom we shall turn to shortly, believed that one-sixth of his patients were hysterical. Such percentages would rise to Cheyne's (1733) one-third hysterical or hypochondriacal, and Trotter's (1807) two-thirds, as the years wore on. Such estimates remind one of current statistics on psychiatric problems in medicine and family practice clinics!

Now we must turn to the great Weyer, whose medical and antiinquisitorial treatise on witchcraft, *De Praestigius Daemonicum* (*On the Trickery of Demons*, 1563), made him famous for all time. Moreover, he was a hero to psychiatric historians such as Zilboorg (1935, 1941), who hailed him as more evidence for psychiatry's beneficent impact against regressive and sadistic supernaturalist explanations of psychopathology. In hands such as Zilboorg's and other psychiatrist-historians (e.g., Bromberg, 1954), Weyer was depicted as recognizing Kramer and Sprenger's (1484) *Malleus Maleficarum* (*Witches' Hammer*), the inquisitor's Bible, for what it "actually" was: a psychiatric case-book, not a roster of satanically inspired careers. Weyer saved witches by diagnosing them, and by persuading others of their mental illness (schizophrenia or hysteria, so this particular school of modern psychiatrist-historians most frequently believed).

The matter of forensic and humanitarian importance was Weyer's contention that witches and the possessed were mad, and hence they were in the doctor's purview, not the priest's or inquisitor's. He believed the phenomena described by witches not to be real, but instead sick fantasies, somehow implanted in them by the Devil. His explanation and diagnosis were hence clinico*theological*, and not purely psychiatric (as so many moderns have mistakenly declared them). Moreover, his argument was merely the most sophisticated in a long train of such Renaissance medicotheological ones from Paracelsus through Agrippa, Cardano, and others.

It is interesting that so acute a medical and psychiatric historian as Erwin Ackerknecht (1968) seemed to buy much of this story. Although recognizing that Weyer's impact on the later development of psychiatry was not particularly strong, continuous, or direct, he did not seem to realize that Weyer's importance was primarily because of two latter-day students. The first, Pinel, used Weyer to bolster the reputation of, and find a history for, the nascent psychiatric profession. The second, Charcot, sought historical precursors and justifiers for the legitimacy of his own work on hysteria (Spanos, 1978; Weiner, 1990). Of course every profession needs its mythology. Another example is the "fact" that it was Pinel, rather than his lay administrator Pussin (the *actual* liberator), who initially broke the chains on the mentally ill (Weiner, 1979). Benjamin Rush is yet one more instance, to be elaborated on shortly.

In any event, Weyer's diagnosis of witches was read as courageous and unassailably correct by generations of psychiatrists and psychiatric historians. It remained for outsiders—especially general and social historians, social scientists, and certain segments of the antipsychiatric wing—to point up the difficulties in such nosographies of witches *then*, and of shamans, sorcerers, and medicine men *now* (see Ackerknecht, 1971; Boyer, 1962; Boyer & Nissenbaum, 1974; Macfarlane, 1970; Spanos, 1978, 1985). Closer scrutiny of the actual records and traces of the period's ambience suggest that the accusers, or those thinking themselves hexed or otherwise spellbound, were probably more often psychopathological than the accused witches themselves. For instance, self-alleged victims would often fall hysterically ill in the presence of the accused.

Moreover, consider the likely general operation of the psychological mechanism of projection, in which accusers and inquisitional witch torturers and executioners could quite easily attribute their own disavowed hostile, sexual, egoistical, and other impulses to the accused. The late, great physician and historian of medicine and public health, George Rosen (1968), documented that in the days of witchcraft belief, the mentally ill were far more often considered to be victims of the alleged witches, rather than witches themselves. Except for a handful of Renaissance and late Renaissance physicians such as Weyer, there was no widespread contemporary feeling that witches were mostly mad.

Although undoubtedly some of the accused were mentally ill, as Weyer, Zilboorg, and others contended, the majority appear to have been economically dependent social deviants; especially, in England at least, alms-seeking old widows and other economically noncontributory persons (Macfarlane, 1970). Furthermore, although both accusers and accused included members of both sexes, most alleged witches were female, suggesting to social historians and to Zilboorg (1935) himself the operation of a certain institutionalized misogyny as well, whatever its determinants. One must also bear in mind that witchcraft and demonology were part of the world-view of the time and, as such, were ready incentives and vehicles for both individual and group-wide projections. Were that overlooked, one could facilely diagnose that entire population as mad!

In addition, as social psychologist Spanos (1978) pointed out, many factors operated in the admissions of the alleged witches. Some of these factors included the suspect's isolation from those who might support his or her resistance to confession; strong and sustained pressure from the authorities to confess, and perhaps even pressure from his or her own family members too; false promises and leading questions; and torture, brainwashing, and suggestion. Too, there were definite institutional and economic incentives for accusations. For example, accusations assisted in removing the socially dependent, alms-seeking poor; thereby alleviating Christians' guilt over the refusal to succor the poor, and accruing profits for various sectors from confiscations of the holdings of those successfully convicted (Macfarlane, 1970). Patently, there are many functional parallels between the normatively compelling and repressive Renaissance concepts of "Christian faithfulness," and many similarly pressing modern notions of "mental health;" as between the cosmologically and sociopolitically-economically motivated witch hunters, and the similarly determined misuse of psychiatric diagnosis in Communist Russia and McCarthy-era America (recall e.g., Foucault, 1980).

Finally, anthropological studies of witches, shamans, sorcerers, and medicine men, in current nonliterate societies or in certain subcultures of both "Third World" and industrialized nations, not only fail to find them mad or hysterical:

but often superior and particularly well-adjusted by the standards of their own culture, and often by those of ours as well (Boyer, Klopfer, Brauer & Kawai, 1964). Once more, it must be remembered that such persons operate out of culturally sanctioned belief/action systems subscribed to by their community and society, and not out of individual psychopathology.

Historiographically, the Weyer-Zilboorg witchcraft nosologies remind us how long the mistaken opinions of authoritative physicians and their historians can hold sway. Moreover, in this particular case as in many others, it was not simply better scrutiny of already extant data or discovery of new ones that were sufficient to revise the erroneous opinions. Rather, it required the application of different historiographical perspectives and techniques (i.e., social historical), as well as those borrowed from ancillary disciplines (i.e., anthropology and social psychology), and culturally broadened concepts of psychopathology and nosology within psychiatry itself. Obviously, this contains another message for psychiatrists working within present nosologies, as well as for those striving for new and better ones, a message that cannot be heard if diagnosis is taken to be purely "empirical."

Before closing our treatment of a Renaissance which, in some ways, our story has already passed; let us touch again on the contribution of stylistic, literary, and iconographical studies, important to all periods of psychiatry, including our own. Mora (in press-a, in press-b), among others, has written on the complicated relation, in Medieval and Renaissance times, between folly and madness; and on literary forms as shapers of both the experiences and actions of the mad, and of their doctors' descriptions of them. There was, he argues, an increased valuing of feeling, and even of the irrational, in the Renaissance. Mora drew on a number of sources: historical, anthropological, literary, social psychiatric, and the study of schizophrenic art of the 19th- and 20th-centuries. He bolstered his hypothesis that certain Renaissance artists (such as Bosch and Brueghel) were schizophrenic by comparing their work to the art of known schizophrenics. He relied on similar perspectives in examining the Renaissance's explicit iconographical representations of madness. Mora used Warburg historiographical notions in alleging that our next period, the 17th-century with its scientific revolution, was a reaction to the Renaissance openness to madness, feeling, and the irrational, because of that later century's fear of the chaos unleashed by its own scientific idea of an infinite universe.

The 17th- to Mid 18th-Centuries

Moving squarely into that century of reason and science (see e.g., Cohen, 1985), the defection from Galen was well under way. Earlier, iatrochemical forms of contesting the Greco-Roman master were becoming supplemented and to some degree replaced by iatrophysical or iatromechanical ones, inspired by Galileo's and Newton's revolutionary reorientation of 17th-century physics and by medical discoveries such as Harvey's (1628) circulation of the blood. Iatrophysics, or iatromechanism, seems even farther from humoralism than was iatrochemistry. The former would, with a few exceptions such as the neo-Paracelsian Van Helmont (1577–1644), eventuate in more and more solidistic pathologies of disease: Morgagni's (1761) gross pathological anatomy, Bichat's (1801) tissue pathology, and Virchow's (1859) cellular pathology. Indeed, this reached the point that the brilliant mid 19th-century Viennese endocrinological pathophysiologist, Rokitansky, was suspected as a closet resurrector of humoralism! Still, such otherwise sharp 17th-century psychiatric thinkers as the great neuroanatomist and neurophysiologist Thomas Willis (1662–1675) (*De Morbis Convulsivis*, 1667; *De Anima Brutorum*, 1672), the "father of neurology," were influenced, pathologically and nosologically, by their lingering Galenism. Significantly, though, Willis saw hysteria as an illness of the brain, not of the uterus (as had been perennially maintained).

The previously cited clergyman Sir Robert Burton (1577–1640), a nonphysician Galenist, will be mentioned only in passing for his widely read *Anatomy of Melancholy* (1621). His book is a fascinating potpourri of descriptions of, and thoughts about, melancholia by a variety of physicians, clerics, philosophers, literary men, and first-hand sufferers themselves. Laced among Burton's hackneyed Galenisms and somaticisms, were some worthwhile psychological insights on constellations with family resemblances to our affective disorder subcategories today. Alongside his humeroanatomical pathology and nosology of depression was a psychological one (i.e., love melancholy, scholar's melancholy, and religious melancholy) (see also Jackson, 1986).

Paolo Zacchias (1584–1659), the pioneer of forensic medicine, strongly insisted, in the face of philosophers and other dissenters, that only physicians were competent to judge a person's mental state. Zacchias is important less for his psychiatric nosology than for his careful examination of the accused's behavior, language, emotional state, and ability to exercise sound judgment. He was a firm believer in the exculpatory status of certain diagnoses.

Given the many theoretical systematizers of this period (and indeed the next), the great Thomas Sydenham's (1624–1689) rejection of expansive theorizing and emphasis on careful observation were refreshing. Although this doctor was a firm believer in the concept of multiple disease entities, with their singularly characteristic etiologies and pathologies (as opposed to the Hippocratic/Galenic idea of a unicausal humoral pathology, manifesting in different ways), he had not totally rid himself of humoralism. However, he leaned more closely toward solidism, and clearly advocated specificity and pluralism in the conceptualization of diseases. He was, moreover, painfully aware of then-contemporary medicine's lack of sufficient knowledge for an etiologically and pathologically based taxonomy of diseases. Hence, he limited his role to close observations and classifications of syndromes (e.g., angina, dropsy, the various fevers, hysteria, etc.) and their courses. Eventually, he felt, all diseases would be reduced to definite species based on a knowledge of their underlying causes and pathological processes.

Otherwise, Sydenham's specifically psychiatric contributions lay in the realm of hysteria and of what would become the neuroses. Although, curiously enough, he held to the ancient idea of the uterine pathology of hysteria, he knew that it could occur in men as well (although it was until then usually termed *hypochondriasis* in males); he made many important psychological observations about it. For Sydenham, the main features of hysteria were its protean nature and its ability to simulate a variety of bodily syndromes. He also noted certain affective and behavioral characteristics—from mood lability and depressions to boisterousness. He seemed to be struggling with the inadequate concepts of the day, and therefore explained the illness as neither purely physical nor psychical (Ackerknecht, 1968, p. 31). His treatments of hysteria were simple and, as was often (and sometimes still is) the case, *they were seldom the logical consequence of his theoretical beliefs.* For example, he used phlebotomy and purgation (less than customarily), and iron preparations, milk diets, horse riding, evil-smelling drugs, and opium quite liberally.

Boissier de Sauvages, physician and botanist, took eagerly to Sydenham's suggestions about classifying extant syndromes and diseases into definite species, just as with plants. His *Traité des Classes des Maladies* (1731) grouped disorders into classes, orders, and genera. Eventually, his nosology included 2,400 diseases under 10 classes! What we now consider mental disorders (as well as neurological ones) were scattered through a number of classes, although class 8 comprised the bulk of Boissier's nearest equivalents to psychiatric *syndromes*—itself divided into 4 orders and 23 species! The 14 species of melancholia revealed, for example, the vague and diffuse nature of his disease concepts; the former including, for instance, monodelusional states (such as the belief that one has been transformed into a horse, or from a man into a woman).

Linné, or Linnaeus, the famous botanist and taxonomist, was so charmed by Boissier's nosology that he published his own similar, but somewhat altered and elaborated one, with 11 classes and 325 genera, to Boissier's 10 and 295, respectively. Neither man's taxonomy represented a move toward the sorts of preliminary or eventual classifications which Sydenham envisioned. Their alleged diseases were often single symptoms rather than symptom complexes or syndromes, and they were certainly not pathologically and etiologically based. It is no wonder that Lester King (1958) termed the 18th-century "the great age of systems in medicine."

A third great taxonomist to give mental disorders their fair share of the tree was William Cullen (1712–1790), a pioneer neuropathologist and coiner of the term *neurosis* (injury of sense and motion, without idiopathic pyrexia or local affection). Insofar as his *neuroses* bore any resemblance to our current conceptions, they fetched a group of patients, among them hysterics, formerly said to suffer from the *vapors* (produced by decaying bodily humors, affecting bodily organs and often rising to the brain).

Cullen's general explanation of disease, and not purely of its psychiatric varieties, was based on the physiologist von Haller's (1752) distinction between the *sensitivity* of the nerves and the *irritability* of the muscles. Cullen's theory, and its subsequent development and popularization by his pupil the alcoholic John Brown (1735–1788), conceptualized psychopathology as secondary to imbalances in nervous energy. These were related, in part, to states of laxity (understimulation) or constriction (overstimulation) of the nerves. Benjamin Rush's psychiatric pathophysiology would be influenced by this, as we shall see, with the addition of the idea that it was vascular hyperemia, or its opposite, that themselves caused the Cullen/Brown postulated changes in nervous energy. This provided Rush with yet another theoretical justification for extending his beloved bloodletting to cases of madness as well. A subsequent mid 19th-century American, Charles Beard, would become internationally famous for his diagnosis of neurasthenia and for his ostensibly neurostimulatory therapies of it——wittingly or unwittingly also indebted to the Cullen/Brown theories.

Transition to the Psychiatric Specialty: Late 18th-Century

In the late 18th-century, lay humanists and philosophers such as the French *Encyclopédistes* and Immanuel Kant entered the psychiatric theorizing and nosological act. This is a further reminder of the extent to which we have always shared our domain with a variety of mental health and other disciplines—nowadays the clergy, alternative healing traditions, occultists, syncretistic therapeutic movements, newspaper columnists, and self-help books and movements galore.

In psychological medicine itself, predictably, there was some backlash to the prior splitters, or proliferators of disease classifications. Arnold's (1782) *Observation on the Nature, Kinds, Causes and Prevention of Insanity* (Carpenter, 1989) was the product of a prototypical *lumper*, or unitary mental disorder theorist, again like Griesinger (1845–1867) and Menninger (1963) after him. Arnold declared that there was only one genus in psychiatry——Insanity——divided into that with hallucinations and illusions, and that without.

Whereas most nosologies and theories of "mental disorders" were overwhelmingly somatic from the Hippocratics forward, psychiatric subnosologies began to reflect psychological thinking as well. This was perhaps partly a result of the influence of the vitalistic German chemist George Ernst Stahl (1660–1734), who divided mental disorders into *sympathetic* (i.e., secondary to organ disease) and *pathetic* or *functional* (i.e., without apparent organic basis). Of course, explicit subscription to an ontological dualism such as that of Plato, Descartes, or Stahl, was (and is) not necessary for psychological theory and nosology (see Wallace, 1988c, 1990a, 1992a).

Many, such as Cabanis (1757–1808), began to combine psychological and somatic perspectives within a materialist/physiological ontology. Again, psychological theorizing and therapy were logically possible within such a purely organic vision of man, provided that the *psychological* refers to a set of organismic brain functions which can be addressed either at their level of emergence or at the levels of their underlying, constituent physiological processes (Wallace, 1990a, in press-b). Discovery of the nervous system, and the theorizing and psychiatric nosologies based on it by Cullen and others, allowed, somewhat surprisingly, for the growing recognition of the importance of the passions; whereas previous psychiatric theory and classification had focused almost exclusively on disorders of reason, perception, and behavior.

It became conceptualized that the passions could even cause systemic disease itself. (Recall earlier in this chapter the treatment of the psychosocial and neurobiological/biomedical perspectives in psychiatry, and the aforementioned regarding Cabanis.) This functionalist approach allowed for both the assertion of a material/energic ontology, and a conception of the reality of mentation as the body/brain's highest and most integrated plane of activity. Such a philosophy would come to ground more and more of the theoretical and practical approaches in psychiatry, such as Adolf Meyer's psychobiology (Meyer, 1950; see also Engel, 1981; Lidz, 1966; Wallace, 1990a) and even Freud's psychoanalysis (Wallace, 1992a) and, much later, Engel's (1980) biopsychosocial model. Still, its message has been lost on the curious combinations of reductionism and metaphysical dualism characterizing the DSMs (Wallace, 1990a, in press-b).

Chiarugi (1759–1829), an early moral therapist, was, like many in this movement, not interested in producing expansive psychiatric taxonomies. His diagnostic system was limited to three classes: *melancholia* (partial distortion of reality in regard to one or a few ideas); *mania* (general insanity with violence and impetuous actions, disconnected speech, disorganized sequence of ideas, poor judgment, abnormal actions); and *amentia* (general insanity without emotional manifestations, with deficiency of both intelligence and volition).

When one reads Chiarugi's categories or stages of each of these one grasps, again, the folly of overreading our concepts into those of the physicians and psychiatrists of the past. For example, his *mania* sounds suspiciously similar to ours, especially when it may turn into *amentia*, which might tempt one to equate it with "paralytic" depression or melancholia. However, one is then surprised to find, under Chiarugi's *melancholia* itself, a class resembling our *mania* as well (imaginary happiness or elation, due to erroneous ideas). Moreover, as if things are not already complicated enough, we encounter one that smacks more of our *melancholia* than does Chiarugi's *melancholia* itself——his aforementioned *amentia* (constant depression of spirit, restlessness, impatience)! Let us refrain, then, from declaring him the "*anticipator*" of Falret's (1854) *Folet Circulaire*, which did in fact more closely simulate our *bipolar disorder*. Finally, in other aspects of Chiarugi's codification of *amentia*, it would perhaps better correspond to what we consider *schizophrenia* than to our *melancholia*, with which we have just compared it! But this, too, is hard to know.

Meanwhile, across the channel in England, several notable physicians with strong psychiatric leanings were at work. Cullen has already been mentioned regarding his theories. Influenced by Boissier and Linné, his nosology, including its psychiatric aspects, was copious, like theirs. Discussion and analysis of it would compel an essay the length of this one itself. Other important 18th-century British figures, only the last of whom is discussed here, include: William Battie (1703–1776), John Munro (1715–1791), William Perfect (1737–1809), William Pargeter (1760–1810), Andrew Harper (d. 1790), the aforementioned Thomas Arnold (1742–1816), and finally, Alexander Crichton (1763–1856).

Doubtless Crichton, a Scot, was one of the most influential of all British psychiatric physicians. Among others, both Pinel and Reil acknowledged their debts to him. Knowledgeable about the major foreign psychiatries, he knew and incorporated organic and psychological perspectives and theories (the latter including the associationist psychology of Locke and Scottish common-sense philosophical psychology, as well as the expansive antimetaphysical mental philosophy of Sir Thomas Reid). On matters clinical and nosological, Crichton was a keen observer and natural historian. He also emphasized the physician's self-analysis as an important prerequisite to clinical and theoretical work. He supplemented the traditional medical accent on reason with detailed attention to, and close analysis of, the emotions. This latter included a psychosomatic point of view. His impact on nosology came less from any classificatory work of his own and more from his psychophysiological philosophy, general clinical theory and methodology, and his rigorous observation and analysis of affects (along with reason and other aspects of mental functioning).

Birth of the Psychiatric Specialty: Post-Revolutionary France

Pinel (1745–1826) is so important, and yet so well known for his many psychiatric contributions (being perhaps the first psychiatric specialist in any form relatable to ours), that I shall treat his nosological work sketchily. Moving to psychiatry from internal medicine, he began as a Linnaean-type classifier, with a system so large (*Nosographie Philosophique*, 1798) that it dwarfed even those of his botanical predecessors. Nevertheless, as Pinel matured and garnered experience, he turned from the disease entity model of Sydenham and trimmed his diagnostic schema to only four clinical types: *mania* (all conditions with excitement or fury), *melancholia* (depressive conditions, delusions with limited topics), *dementia* (lack of cohesion among ideas), and *idiotism* (including idiocy and organic dementia).

Integral to Pinel's intent was the development of a nosology permitting flexible concepts and emphasizing clinical description. His classifications were put forward as functional categories, to be modified through subsequently accumulated knowledge. Moreover, Pinel was a strong proponent of psychological thinking and therapies. He recognized, as did very few of his recent predecessors, that emotional life could be disturbed with reasoning left relatively intact. That this had not been generally appreciated for centuries drives home the power of theoretically determined blind spots, over even the most patent aspects of clinical reality. Pinel's hospital administration and treatment reflected his accent on the *disturbed individual*, rather than upon his or her alleged disease entity (Pinel, 1801).

He sounds so modern and prudent, especially given the state of psychiatric knowledge at that time, and the consequent impossibility (then, as now) of any rigorous and systematic etiologically based nosology. Yet, he embraced certain contemporaneous tenets that we would deem quite erroneous, if not fantastic and laughable, such as the gastrointestinal localization of mania (especially were we to forget our own recent enteropathic and vitamin deficiency theories of schizophrenia, and our treatments of that disorder with renal dialysis and other equally peculiar means). Furthermore, in regard to Pinel's clinical reports, as to those of most of his contemporaries, we would be appalled by their lack of what we would consider essential categories of the case history.

Esquirol, Pinel's successor at the Salpêtrière, was the true founder of the important French clinical psychiatric school, French clinical internal medicine having already established a reputation as Europe's finest in the first half of the 19th-century (see Ackerknecht, 1966). Although adopting Gall's theory of cerebral localization of mental functioning and of disorders thereof, Esquirol was still as (or more than) psychologically observant and psychotherapeutically minded as his teacher. He also considered the role of social upheaval, and of growing individualism or social isolation, in the causation of mental disorder.

Esquirol's (1845) approach was a longitudinal, natural historical one, bent on closely following the course of the illness or syndrome. It would be hard to overemphasize the centrality of this, both for the subsequent development of the French school and for psychiatry in general. He made the important distinction between hallucinations and illusions, and pursued the careful phenomenological and behavioral observation and analysis so crucial to the science of psychopathology, the ground for any adequate psychiatric nosology. With few exceptions, such work is insufficiently prosecuted today, the aim being much more to establish pathophysiological correlations with descriptive, insufficiently phenomenological diagnoses (many of which have dubious statistical descriptive, much less construct, validity). Furthermore, as mentioned, without sufficient attention to the historical and present contexts of the ostensibly purely observable behavior or sign, and without knowledge of the phenomenology ("feel," meaning, and, if possible, motivation) of the *individual patient's particular behavior*, one has truncated and perhaps erroneously inferential knowledge.

In the light of the need for a basic science of psychopathology, and Esquirol's innovations, consider the psychopathology of today's DSM-III (p. 356) and the III-R (p. 395) conception of *delusion* (a *false* personal belief). To hinge such a definition on *truth criteria* is philosophically scientifically, and clinically quite hazardous (see Spitzer's chapter in this book). In large measure, we have not ourselves observed the situations about which we deem the patient believing falsely, and we too often lack access to reliable third-party testimony on the matter. Few so-called delusions are so bizarre as to be prima facie unbelievable; many paranoid ones, for example, often have some degree of apparent plausibility, particularly given our ignorance of the activities of those with whom the patient associates in the situations in question. Furthermore, there is frequently a metaphorical, psychical, and interpersonal communicational truth value in certain otherwise seemingly totally false beliefs. Because of these and other factors, Spitzer (Spitzer, Uehlein & Oepen, 1988, pp. 128—142) proffers an alternative conception, not based on the impossible implicit requirement to establish the absolute truth value (i.e., falsity) of the content of the delusion. He finds more pertinent an alternative consideration: Is the patient's unusual belief presented in a preponderantly *autistic and self-referential manner*, with a quality of unshakable conviction which needs no further evidence, and which feels no requirement to give good reasons to another attempting to engage him or her in dialogue upon it.

Hence, better definitions of our basic psychopathological concepts, and not merely of diagnostic categories themselves, are key to the psychiatric nosological enterprise (see Spitzer et al., 1988; Spitzer & Maher, 1990; and the Spitzer chapter in this book for scrutiny of other basic psychopathological concepts). Another important example of brilliant work in the basic science of psychopathology is Strauss's (1969) and Strauss and Carpenter's (1981) natural historical/ phenomenological studies of stages in the formation of hallucinations and delusions, and of other aspects of the evolution of the schizophrenic process in numerous individuals. Without such information, we cannot begin to establish etiologically relevant statistical correlations between sufficiently validated syndromes, and the biomedical/neurological and psychosocial factors most commonly accompanying them.

Nevertheless, let us return directly to Esquirol. Surprisingly, he rejected Pinel's concept of what became known as *moral insanity* (emotional disturbance with relatively intact reasoning), thus reverting to the centuries-old predominant opinion. Among Esquirol's many important students and successors, we have already referred to Falret (1794—1870). Bayle (1799—1858), although eventually leaving the Paris school, was notable for demonstrating (1822) the organic basis of the then-most prevalent mental disease, general paresis. Thus began the replacement of the description of the purely symptomatic states of a psychiatric syndrome with the natural history and (at least partial) etiology that Sydenham had called for.

The Infant Grows Up: Psychiatric Nosology circa 1840–1920 and Beyond

The easy earlier 19th-century French relationship between the psychological and organic orientations began to be replaced by accentuation of the latter in the next half-century. It came in the form of the soon-to-be influential *degeneration theory*. First formulated by Moreau de Tours (1804—1884) at mid-century, its true propagator and elaborator was Benedict Morel (1809—1873), credited with the first description of schizophrenia, which he termed *démence précoce*. It was, ironically, his very imbuement with Esquirol's natural historical and longitudinal approach which strengthened his conviction that so many disorders end in degeneration. Insofar as there was sufficient empirical justification for his far-ranging extension of such ideas, one must recall the percentage of serious organic cases, such as general paresis, in the psychiatrist's practice of that day.

Curiously enough, Morel combined degeneration theory with his own passionately held Christian beliefs. He posited a variety of causes from toxins (including alcohol), through the social milieu and psychological factors, to congenital and hereditary determinants. Degeneration was subject to the law of progression: typically nervousness in the first generation, neurosis in the second, psychosis in the third, and idiocy and then extinction in the fourth. His claim to have found degenerative stigmata in a variety of cases influenced prominent psychiatrists all over Europe, including Griesinger (1817—1869), Krafft-Ebing (1840—1902), and the criminologist Lombroso (1836—1909). The latter viewed the criminal type, which he believed to be based on physiognomy and other stigmata, as an atavism or a lingering remnant of an earlier phylogenetic phase in the evolution of humanity. Here John Hughlings Jackson (1834—1911), with his neurological theories of evolution and devolution, was doubtless important, as he was to Freud's phylogenetic interpretations of psychopathology and views on primitive culture (e.g., Breuer & Freud, 1895; Freud, 1913; see Wallace, 1983a, 1992a). Currently, evolutionary perspectives are returning to general medical and psychiatric pathology/nosology (see e.g., Williams and Nesse, 1991).

In any event, Magnan (1833—1916), Morel's succeeding theoretician, disavowed his mentor's religious beliefs for a purely secular vision of degeneration as Darwinian regression. Magnan's prestige helped this theory flourish in France for years to come. Morel and disciples left a particularly lasting legacy in their conviction that dementia praecox, or schizophrenia, inevitably progresses to deterioration and dementia. This influenced Kraepelin and Bleuler, and set up a long-enduring therapeutic nihilism toward such patients.

On a more positive note, the French degenerationists, by including alcohol and alcoholism as an important pathogen and syndrome, respectively, shaped what was to become a central concern for many contemporaneous European psychiatric physicians and asylum heads, among them Forel, Bleuler, Kraepelin, and Jung. Despite such attention by some of our most prominent predecessors, it has been only recently that psychiatrists have more adequately appreciated the importance of addiction as an independent syndrome, as a mimicker or masker of any number of other psychiatric conditions, and as an integral component of many so-called dual-diagnosis cases. Indeed, alcoholism and the addictive disorders provide a splendid forum for pondering the disease concept in general medicine, its applicability to psychiatry in particular, and the possible physicochemical environmental, genetic/biomedical, cultural/historical, psychosocial/ family systemic, moral, and (dare I use the word?) broadly *spiritual* (e.g., A.A.) parameters involved.

The degeneration hypothesis enjoyed broad and longstanding popularity in scientific *and* lay circles. In regard to possible externalist determinants of this theory, social historians, social scientists, and social philosophers could have a field day. To begin with, such a hypothesis accorded with the growing popularity of social Darwinism, itself quite supportive of conservative political, social, and economic thinking. Moreover, the degeneration hypothesis was attractive for the growing French reaction to the radical liberalism of the prior revolution. The France of that day, and that following the Franco-Prussian War, also witnessed an upsurge in racist and eugenic thinking such as that of the notorious Gobineau.

It is difficult to determine the extent to which such extrinsic forces actually motivated individual degeneration theorists; but their theories, insufficiently scientifically supported from the outset, were especially convenient for certain sociopolitical, ethnic, and economic orientations. Given Morel's devout Christianity, who knows what moralistic, apocalyptic, and eschatological elements may have influenced his prediction that extinction lay at the end of progressive degeneration? On a different note, Jan Goldstein (1987) has supported the impact of late 19th-century French anticlericalism on French psychiatric thinking on hysteria, that is, on its reinterpretation of aspects of historical and then-current Catholic spirituality as just so much hysteria or other more severe psychiatric disorder.

Be all this as it may, by the end of the century degeneration theory began losing adherents. Kraepelin was already expressing reservations, and the stigmata, insofar as they were identifiable at all, came to be taken as normal variations without pathological significance. This is yet another instance of how theory or world-views can dominate perception in the nosological enterprise. Nevertheless, the erroneous degeneration hypothesis, for all of its unfortunate effects, may have, as Ackerknecht (1968, p. 59) suggested, laid the foundation for eventual interest in psychiatric genetics.

Much of 19th-century German psychiatry, including important aspects of its nosology, were discussed in the preceding section. The nosological work of both the early 19th-century German Romantic and more purely organicist schools were equally speculative and bore little fruit. This was in marked contrast to German nosological research and theory in the latter 19th-century. Before examining these more thoughtful and rigorous central European nosologists, we must mention the group that carved out psychiatry's crucial concept of functional disorders.

The aforementioned cadre developed a whole sphere of mid to late 19th-century psychiatric theorizing, research, and practice: *sexology*; their thinking helped expand psychiatric nosology and practice. These psychiatrists' (Krafft-Ebing and Havelock Ellis being but two of many noteworthy ones) disease conceptions of homosexuality and the perversions (Paraphilias in DSM-III-R) were difficult to square with a solidistic, pathoanatomically/histologically oriented general medicine and (at that time) psychiatry. The persistent failure to find a genital pathological seat seriously compromised their nosological status. With only a few exceptions, such as Magnan (who posited a cerebrospinal lesion), psychiatrists characterized the defect as one in the functioning of the sexual instinct. Before the French alienist Le Grain (1869), it had been held that *instinct* and *function*, too, must have an anatomical seat. By contrast, Le Grain declared the sexual instinct a physiological function, "whose seat is everywhere and nowhere," thereby medically legitimating it with physiology, not anatomy. Freud, similarly, took a physiological route to his functionalist psychology and sexology (see Wallace, 1992a). The possible role of professional, political, economic, and cultural, as well as scientific and clinical, factors in this extension of psychiatry's boundaries need hardly be questioned. In any case, these physicians furnished psychiatry a general and pathological/nosological tenet that it has felt itself unable to do without.

We can move now to late 19th-, early 20th-century central European psychiatric nosology. Regrettably, apart from just touching on Bleuler (and Schneider, a much later fixture) and merely citing some nosological systems otherwise ignored altogether, we shall examine only one other European figure. However, this figure is a giant: Emil Kraepelin (1856–1926). In so doing, we are overlooking important nosological laborers such as Kahlbaum (1828–1899), Hecker (1843–1899), Meynert (1833–1892), Wernicke (1848–1905), and the great psychopathologist-philosopher Karl Jaspers (1883–1964).

After pursuing neuroanatomy with Flechsig and physiological psychology with Wundt, Kraepelin moved into clinical psychiatry through a passionate interest in alcoholism. Eventually, of course, he would become the premier European, if not international, psychiatric nosologist; most noted for his slow and painstaking codifications of dementia praecox and manic-depressive insanity, which are the foci of this brief treatment.

Whatever Kraepelin's reputed powers of observation, they hardly operated without theoretical preconceptions, many of them initially associated with the work of the French hereditary degenerationists on what was known as *adolescent dementia*, a concept current throughout the 19th-century (and much broader than that of our schizophrenia). The idea of terminal dementia, associated with this adolescent syndrome, colored much subsequent thinking on dementia praecox (later called schizophrenia), as did the then-widespread concept of adolescent masturbatory insanity. The latter, especially its emphasis on early onset and inevitably progressive deterioration, formed a matrix for all succeeding 19th-century considerations of the subject, a matrix cemented by Pick's (1989) 1891 codification of dementia praecox. Incidentally, it was Pick's, and later Kraepelin's, need to historicize their notions which led to their retrospective resurrection of Morel to his current historical plane.

Sander Gilman (1982), once more, is instrumental in underlining the role of pervasive images and metaphors in shaping theorizing about psychiatric syndromes. He points, for example, to the word/image *bizarre*, which hardly originated as a specifically psychiatric term, although it subsequently underwent various vicissitudes in reference to madness. In psychiatric circles, it was gradually delimited to characterizing schizophrenic thinking, perception, and behavior. Moreover, the graphic German language readily supplied words such as *Zerstreuung*, *Zerbrechung*, and *Zerrüttung* (denoting a violent destruction, shattering, or breaking up) to descriptions of the schizophrenic fragmentation of thought processes and sense of self. Such terms, taken partly from the German Romantic psychiatrists (along with some of their psychological insights), codetermined what later alienists saw, looked for, and emphasized diagnostically, as we shall see with Bleuler.

Kahlbaum's earlier (1874) delineations of catatonia furnished a keystone for Kraepelin's *dementia praecox* (Kraepelin, 1912, p. 22): its "peculiar and fundamental want of any strong feelings of the impressions of life," and its disturbances of "the acts of volition which stand in closest relation to those [emotional] impulses" (p. 26). Besides Kahlbaum, Hecker's (1871) formulation of *hebephrenia* affected Kraepelin's descriptions as well, another demonstration of how predecessors' categories and codifications influence one's observations which, to repeat, are never assumptionless or free of theory and interpretation (contra DSM-III and III-R) (Faust & Miner, 1986; Wallace, 1988a).

Although Kraepelin himself focused more on the nosography instead of the etiology of dementia praecox, he (1912, p. 221) generally assumed that "there is a definite disease process in the brain, involving cortical neurones," whether resulting from constitutional anomaly, autointoxication, metabolic derangement, or whatever. As time went on, however, he put less accent on the French concept of inevitable degeneration, although he remained pessimistic about the syndrome's course and outcome.

For severe depression, which he believed usually alternated with mania or else presented as a mixed picture of both, he (1912) stressed not the absence of volition as with dementia praecox; but rather the "*impediment of volition*, in the sense that the transformation of the impulses of the will into action meets with obstacles which cannot be overcome without difficulty, and often not at all by the patient's own strength" (p. 12; my italics). This, along with an "impediment of cognition" (p. 15) and a number of vegetative signs, was accentuated, with little attention to the patient's actual phenomenology or emotional status. Such overly nomothetic descriptive concepts (even those regarding volition and emotion) were derived, by and large, from preconception-conditioned inferences from observation instead of from eliciting each patient's lived experience of illness.

Kraepelin's third great, although less important, diagnostic codification was *paranoia*, or *progressive systematized insanity* (Paranoia Vera in DSM-II). Un-

like the pervasive disturbances of affect, attention, volition, reasoning and judgment, and the fragmented bizarre speech, behavior, hallucinations, and delusions
of dementia praecox; paranoia exhibited a more circumscribed picture, distinguished by "delusions of being wronged and of over-self-esteem," with a *relatively demarcated* "weakness of judgment" (Kraepelin, 1912, pp. 146–147).

In sum, Kraepelin introduced a more natural historical, less merely cross-sectional, perspective on mental illness, and he emphasized the practical clinical importance of *prognosis* as part of diagnosis. Nevertheless, as mentioned in the preceding section, his case histories were largely limited to the current illness and
its prior episodes and, again, to its signs and behavioral symptoms. There was
little if any developmental and longitudinal premorbid history or consideration
of the patient's family and social matrix. Even when a pattern of potential and
thematically related psychosocial stressors preceded an illness episode (as
limned in some of Kraepelin's own case reports), he simply ignored them. It was
only toward the end of his career, in the eighth edition (1927) of his by-then gar-
gantuan text, that he belatedly recognized his psychological, social environmental, and phenomenological oversights and attempted to rectify them. In this manner he was, in a sense, personally recapitulating the history of psychiatric nosography which, with a few exceptions, accented so-called *observables*——such as
signs, stigmata, and symptomatic behaviors——and apparently organic factors.
Could Kraepelin have known of the eventual near-disappearance, in the West,
of two of the pillars of his nosological theorizing——*catatonia* and *hebephrenia*——
he might have appreciated the likely biopsychosocial (including cultural/histor-
ical) *multi*causality of his universalized *dementia praecox*.

Still, Kraepelin bequeathed us our basic nosological templates for: (a) *schizophrenia* (dementia praecox); (b) *bipolar affective disorder* and, to a lesser degree, *major depression* or *unipolar disorder* (manic-depressive insanity); and (c)
paranoia vera (paranoia). Furthermore, he established *schizophrenia* as the par-
adigmatic psychiatric diagnostic concept of our century, although recently the
major affective disorders have been bidding to supplant it.

From a host of subsequently important European psychonosologists and their
perspectives, I shall mention but three——Eugen Bleuler (1857–1939) and the
more recent Kurt Schneider and Karl Leonhard——and then allude to the nosological issues between ideal and natural types and to related concepts. In so doing,
we are again ignoring a number of important European diagnostic systems and
vantages on the role or importance of diagnosis and psychopathology, including
Wernicke's (1900) and Meynert's (1892), the phenomenologists' (e.g., Ey, 1969,
1975; Minkowski, 1970; Straus, 1966; see Spiegelberg, 1972); the existentialists'
(e.g., Binswanger, 1963; Boss, 1963; Sartre, 1956; see May, Angel & Ellenberger, 1958); the 20th-century French rationalist tradition (see Kroll, 1979);
and, to repeat, the preeminent phenomenological psychopathologist-philosopher
Karl Jaspers (1963). Nor shall we attend sufficiently to the antipsychiatrists (e.g.,
Ingleby, 1980).

Eugen Bleuler, director of the preeminent Burghölzli Mental Hospital and professor of psychiatry at the University of Zurich (1897–1927), attained fame by coining the term *schizophrenia*. In so doing, he (1911) gave us a categorical concept rather different from Kraepelin's dementia praecox and generally elided the latter's criterion of inevitable deterioration to a demented state. Certainly, his concept was more psychological than Kraepelin's, perhaps reflecting the influence of Jung (*The Psychology of Dementia Praecox* [1907]) and Freud (earlier writings and the 1911 Schreber case).

Instead of "purely" [sic] behavioral signs, Bleuler (1911) emphasized disordered thought (loosening of associations, etc.), language, and communication; affect (flat, ambivalent, or grossly inappropriate to thought content or situation); and autism (self-referential and bizarre, often repetitive, and seemingly unintelligible and noncommunicative words, phrases, behaviors, mannerisms, and gestures). Overarching all of these was Bleuler's concept of the schizophrenic process as a loss of the integration and cohesion of mind, self, and personality, a sort of "shattering of the ego" as his psychiatrist-son Manfred put it. Curiously enough, Bleuler placed less importance on hallucinations and delusions, unlike Kraepelin and Schneider (Kraepelin, 1917) as well as Freud (1911) (who deemed these symptoms to be the schizophrenic's attempt to rebuild a world from which he or she had previously autistically withdrawn).

Much more than Kraepelin, Bleuler (1911, 1924) considered aspects of the schizophrenic's thinking, behavior, and communication as motivated and potentially meaningful within the patient's historical and current life-context. In short, once more, his orientation was more phenomenological and psychological than Kraepelin's. For a time Bleuler was an avid aficionado of psychoanalysis, and he encouraged Jung's researches and practices from this vantage, although Bleuler soon became disenchanted by what he viewed as dogmatic features in the movement and theory.

Despite his psychological leanings, Bleuler attributed the primary causation of schizophrenia to brain disease, itself secondary to some sort of metabolic dyscrasia or autointoxication. Moreover, he abandoned Kraepelin's pessimistic prognoses less than is commonly imagined; both men, on this score, continuing to color public and professional expectations about the outcome of the syndrome. As most readers know, Bleuler's four As (*autism*, loose *associations*, *ambivalence*, and blunted or inappropriate *affect*) governed the codifications of schizophrenia in America and many other nations until relatively recently. Among other things, the 1973 World Health Organization (WHO) cross-cultural studies and the DSM-III field trials demonstrated the subjectivity, ambiguity, and low interrater reliability of some of Bleuler's criteria. These and other factors contributed to the decline of Bleuler's impact, and to the rise of Schneider's criteria for schizophrenia (examined below).

Kurt Schneider (1959), a decades-long close observer of the mental states and natural histories of thousands of German schizophrenics, came to accentuate what for Bleuler had been but secondary criteria: hallucinations and delusions. Schneider emphasized certain varieties of hallucinations and delusions in his criteria for what has become known as *nuclear schizophrenia*. These include two or more voices discussing the individual as a third party; voices speaking directly to the patient or continually commenting on his or her behavior; command hallucinations; delusions of thought broadcasting, or of external control, insertion, or withdrawal of one's thoughts. His third major criterion, cognitive derailment, subsumed Bleuler's criterion of loosening of associations. As mentioned previously, Schneider, noted for his observational gifts, himself denied the possibility of theory-free diagnosis, nosological categories, and classificatory systems. As a student of Jaspers, he appreciated the conceptual or ideal aspect of psychiatric classifications. In this vein, he acknowledged the image/metaphor/idea of psychic permeability as an important codeterminant of his own notion of schizophrenia.

Similarly, with reference to manic-depressive insanity, Leonhard's great predecessor, Kraepelin, had been dependent on his knowledge of prior codifications of *la folie circulaire* and *la folie à double forme* by Falret (1854) and Baillarger (1854), respectively (who were themselves influenced by a unitary and gradational theorem of mental illness). As Berrios (in press) cogently remarked, the data supporting such categories had been there for centuries, as evidenced by independent reports by Soranus and Aretaeus of similar cases in antiquity. Thus, Kraepelin's *manic-depressive insanity* could not have been sufficiently appreciated, much less codified into a coherent syndrome, without prior knowledge and nosological precommitments favoring the apperception *and* accentuation of certain features demonstrated by some patients. The same holds for Leonhard's (1959) recodification of *manic-depressive insanity* into *unipolar* (depressive) and *bipolar* (manic, or alternatingly manic and depressive) *affective disorders*, and for Manfred Bleuler's (1978) further epidemiological support and refinement of Leonhard's concepts.

In short, the classificatory concept of *bipolar disorder*, to take only one of the aforementioned, was neither purely a posteriori nor purely a priori, neither wholly theoretical nor empirical (see Wallace, 1985, 1986, 1988c on intersectional causation and perspectival realism). Hence, construed as a syndrome (whether polythetically categorical or multidimensional), *bipolar disorder* is *neither* a so-called ideal or artificial type *nor* an ostensibly real or natural one. It is not the former because (a) it corresponds, in some measure (absolute identity being hardly necessary among its members), to certain consensually validatable characteristics of a pool of actually existing human individuals, and (b) it has probabilistic predictive value in terms of subsequent course and natural history, prognosis, and response to treatment.

However, it is not a purely natural type either (even if ultimately proved to be a single disease). This is because people with the diagnosis differ not only empirically from one another in respects independent of the illness, but for a number of other reasons as well. Few, if any, "bipolars" ever exhibit *all* of the possible criteria and subcriteria—much less in identical form, content, and intensity—for the category as codified, say, in DSM-III-R. The concept encounters people at its margins or in gray zones, whose actual phenomenological/behavioral constellations fall neither squarely within nor without it. Although meeting sufficient criteria for the category does yield *partial* and *probable* treatment algorithms, especially pharmacological ones, there are massive individual differences here as well. Furthermore, the differing tapestries of the syndromes, personality structures, cognitive/interpretive sets, motivational and conflictual patterns, and histories and transference predispositions among all bipolar patients, argue against "cookbook" total treatment plans (see Wallace, 1983c, 1985, 1988c, 1989b, 1989c, 1990a, 1990b on the nomothetic and idiographic aspects of psychiatric theorizing, investigation, and treatment). The significance of such issues is highlighted further by those offering data opposing Leonhard's and DSM-III's splitting of Kraepelin's manic-depressive category (e.g., Angst, 1980; Goodwin and Jamison, 1990).

Psychiatric Nosology in the United States

Pre-DSMs

Important aspects of this final subsection have, of course, already been treated earlier. As mentioned, American psychiatry, like the rest of U.S. medicine, lagged behind Europe until after the turn of the 20th-century. During the 19th-century many, if not most, American medical schools were proprietary, and the courses of instruction were limited to two, or later three, roughly 4-month terms. The students, if fortunate, spent the rest of the year in apprenticeship with a more or less competent practicing physician. For the most part, no baccalaureate degree was required for entry. Even by the end of the 19th-century, science instruction was inadequate and antiquated, barring a handful of schools such as Johns Hopkins, Harvard, Yale, and the University of Michigan (Duffy, 1979; Ludmerer, 1985).

Students who could afford it, from precolonial days, took their degrees or at least further education at the European schools dominating the various periods. It is significant that one of the first great homegrown and internationally noted American psychiatrists, Harry Stack Sullivan, graduated from a typical proprietary college (Perry, 1982).

For information on 19th-century American psychiatric nosology, one should turn to the early state asylum annual reports to the legislatures or to several useful histories of asylums such as that at Williamsburg (Dain, 1964). These yearly reports included breakdowns of censuses, admissions, and discharges by diagnosis and often etiology. The diagnoses themselves were hashes of what we would consider symptoms, precipitants, putative etiologies or pathological processes, and morally frowned-upon, but rather ordinary, behaviors such as masturbation. Some were as curious and valuational, even humorous as, for example, the diagnoses of *vagabond*, *volitional old maid*, and *noisy and idle*. A few of these diagnoses were rather universal for particular spreads of 19th-century America: *religious melancholy*, *idiocy*, *dementia*, and *epilepsy* (see, e.g., the 1853 *Report of the Regents of the Lunatic Asylum to the Legislature of South Carolina*). One of these latter, more universal diagnoses, was *insanity*. Usually followed by a descriptive adjective such as *indolent*, *boisterous*, or *industrious*, and occasionally preceded by an alleged cause or precipitant, such as mastur-bation, overwork, excessive study, political excitement, or intemperance, these tell us essentially nothing. *Insanity*, now a purely legal or popular term, was, well through the 19th-century, a rather loose medical term as well.

During and after the Civil War, *nostalgia* became a popular diagnosis, to re-appear for a time in the recent Persian Gulf War! Others would become much more longlasting, for example Beard's term *neurasthenia*, introduced and popularized in the mid 19th-century, adopted around the world, and present in official U.S. psychiatric nomenclatures until 1980 (DSM-III).

Otherwise, as many of the leaders of middle and later 19th-century American psychiatry recognized, it was virtually impossible for one state hospital to com-municate diagnostically with another, much less to obtain any meaningful national statistics. However, as the century wore on and, for reasons discussed earlier, hospital patient censuses became larger, more chronic, and increasingly organic, more accurate and meaningful diagnoses emerged: (general paresis, or paralysis of the insane), pellagra, beriberi, senile dementia, vascular brain disease, brain tumor, and so forth. Kraepelin's term *dementia praecox* had entered many asylum reports by end-century, and diagnoses of *mania*, *depression*, and *manic-depression* were seen more commonly. Indeed, in many areas of the country, Kraepelin's *dementia praecox* remained current long after Bleuler's concept of schizophrenia made its debut.

As early as 1869, the national organization of U.S. psychiatrists began officially considering their nosological quagmire. Impressed by efforts of the 1867 International Congress of Alienists (Paris), the former (the Association of Medical Superintendents of American Institutions for the Insane) adopted its categories and formulated some statistical tables that were, however, never official and were only used by a few places for several years. In any event, the Paris proposal contained but eight categories, all of them extraordinarily diffuse and inclusive, of which three fourths were probable organic brain syndromes (Menninger et al., 1963, pp. 464–465).

In 1886, the American Association adopted the classification of the British Medico-Psychological Association, with the exception of *moral insanity* (yet another instance of psychiatry's long-time difficulty acknowledging profound affective disturbance with relatively intact cognition) and with the addition of *toxic insanity*. But new proposals and nosologies continued, such as the one at the Hartford Retreat (now the Institute of Living) and the New York State Commission in Lunacy (1909), the latter spearheaded by psychiatrist-neuropathologist Adolf Meyer who, along with August Hoch, popularized Kraepelinian teachings in the United States (Meyer, 1950).

Still, the state of psychiatric diagnostic classification remained chaotic in this country, as reported by the Committee on Statistics of the by-then (1917) American Medico-Psychological Association (name changed in 1892) (Grob, 1983). The committee pointed out that, at best, only a few states had uniform classification systems for their mental hospitals, whereas in the remainder diagnostic slates varied across facilities. The National Association adopted the report that very year, and it was published with the support of the National Committee for Mental Hygiene in 1918 (*Statistical Manual for the Use of Institutions for the Insane*).

Largely Kraepelinian, it consisted of categories of psychoses from *organic*, *toxic*, *infectious*, and *nutritional*, to *functional* (dementia praecox and manic-depressive insanity), except for a slot devoted to *psychoneurosis or neurosis*. The *Statistical Manual* would undergo 10 editions by 1942, all of them, except in some respects the last, reflecting overwhelmingly somatic theoretical orientations.

The social/institutional historian of American psychiatry, Gerald Grob (1991, pp. 424–425), pointed to external determinants of the profession's concern with improving and standardizing its nosology. The earlier thrust began with mid 19th-century statistically oriented social welfare activists, who wanted a scientific foundation for efforts to improve the lot of the socioeconomically disadvantaged. Because their target populations included the mentally ill, they naturally sought more scientifically based and organized information about their numbers and plight.

After the turn of the 20th-century, partly out of eugenic concerns precipitated by massive immigration, the U.S. census sought better data on the ethnic and diagnostic status of mental patients. Psychiatrists' dawning move to the community (as depicted earlier), partly in response to the aforementioned social activism and to Beers' 1909 Committee for Mental Hygiene, both exposed them to additional outside pressure and showed them increased opportunities for a profession hitherto confined within asylum walls. It was this segment of the specialty, represented by those such as Thomas Salmon, which became most active on the 1914–1917 and later association diagnostic committees. Still, Grob (1991, p. 427) maintains, the 10 editions of the *Statistical Manual* were used primarily to facilitate the collection of institutional data. These goals were of little more than marginal concern for psychiatrists and their patients. Hence, "Psychiatric therapies between the World Wars . . . were for the most part eclectic and nonspecific, and diagnosis only of peripheral significance" (Grob, 1991).

Harvard's Southard (Grob, 1991) took issue with what he viewed as the etiological pretensions of many of the new categories. Others, too, were not infatuated with the association's new official nosology. Among those with alternative visions was Adolf Meyer (1866–1950), called to the Hopkins Phipps Clinic in 1913, where he established himself as the dean of American academic psychiatry. There he popularized Kraepelin's work, partly because of Kraepelin's prognostic emphasis, which was quite a practical matter for Meyer and any hospital psychiatrist. However, Meyer felt that Kraepelin's nosological approach and classification system (revised a good deal in the eight editions of Kraepelin's textbook) implied that many of its categories were disease entities far in advance of any sustaining scientific evidence.

Consequently, Meyer developed his own six-fold classification in terms of energy distributions (*ergasias*) or reaction types. His psychobiological, individual biographical/biomedical approach was, in part, a reaction to Kraepelin's corresponding lack of focus on the patient's social ambience, developmental and longitudinal history, and phenomenology or subjective world. As discussed previously, Meyer became well known for his life charts, with their correlations between the patient's life events and his or her psychological and biological reactions to them (see Meyer, 1950–1954, four volumes).

On the mind-body issue Meyer was a monist, but not a neurobiological or a psychosocial reductionist; he viewed the *symbolic* as simply the most integrated level and manifestation of the human organism's functioning in its particular environment (Meyer, 1950). His patient charts contained a wealth of general medical, neurological, and phenomenological/psychosocial data. He saw himself as treating the entire organism, from meaningful and motivated patterns of energy utilization and reaction to indices of bodily function such as Kraepelin's famous attention to weight changes. It was said by those who knew Meyer that none equaled his capacity to weave diverse strands of data into clinically useful information, formulations, and multimodal treatment plans (Jerome Frank, personal communication, 1978).

In the early years of the American psychoanalytic movement, Meyer played an important receptive role, although increasingly he came to view Freudianism as dogmatic and metaphysical. Nevertheless, his indirect positive influence on the growth of American analysis and the new "dynamic psychiatry" (as opposed to Meyer's original one in terms of reactions and energy types) continued, through his many students who would become prominent in the movement.

In any event, it seems that Meyer's system held to a few core values. It intended to combat categories and nosologies in advance of the requisite scientific data. Meyer wanted to prevent individual patients from becoming treated as merely disease entities or cyphers in nosological codes. He also wanted to emphasize a thorough and holistic perspective on each patient, while also promoting the search for more precise and generalizable multifactorial etiologies. Surprisingly, some (e.g., Menninger et al., 1963) have denied Meyer any substantial impact on American psychiatry, even arguing that his ideas were better received overseas. However, like Lidz (1966) and many others, I credit him for the comprehensive attitude and orientation espoused by many American psychiatrists up to this day, despite the recent political/academic hegemony of reductive neuro-biological and pharmacological perspectives. Engel's (1977, 1980) biopsycho-social model is itself a more sophisticated version of Meyerian psychobiology. Like the latter, it is an integrating force in a period of centrifugal psychosocial and neurobiological reductionistic forces.

Nevertheless, it can be charged that Meyer (the quondam neuropathologist!) went overboard in his relative lack of concern with biomedical and neurobio-logical perspectives and research; in his distrust of classification which is, after all, a necessary preliminary and ongoing task for any science; and finally, in his epistemologically naive belief in the possibility of theory-free, purely empirical observation (perhaps partly reactive to psychiatry's many evidentially premature systems and nosologies).

As mentioned, the profession's multiedition *Statistical Manual* displayed an overwhelmingly somatically determined classificatory system. This particular theoretical and nosological orientation would lose ground as a result of World War II psychiatric activity. As remarked earlier, a number of factors shaped this change: wartime experience with acute battlefield neurosis and other mental health casualties (e.g., Grinker & Spiegel, 1945); increased national awareness of psychiatric problems; greatly enhanced numbers and importance of the specialty; spawning of the community mental health movement; and the tran-sition of psychiatrists to practice outside public hospitals.

Psychiatry heightened its attention to acute psychological reactions, symptom and character neuroses, and personality disorders. The community mental health movement and declining public concern with state hospital patients furthered professional interest in psychosocial approaches, especially psychoanalytic, broadly psychodynamic (i.e., neo-Freudian), and social psychiatric ones. The director of the division of neuropsychiatry of the wartime U.S. Army, Brigadier General William Menninger, was himself a well-known psychoanalyst. Per-suaded that there was a continuum between mental health and illness (as, incidentally, was Kraepelin himself), he focused away from the psychoses to the above-mentioned and related disorders. Thereby, he hoped to prevent their pro-gression to more serious, chronic, and disabling conditions. Under such in-fluence, the U.S. Army adopted its own psychiatric classification system in 1945, and the Veterans Administration followed suit a year later.

The DSMs

Hence American psychiatry had three competing official nosologies by 1946, none of them in line with the International Statistical Classification (later the *International Classification of Diseases* or ICD). Consequently, the American Psychiatric Association's Special Committee on Reorganization was formed none too soon (1944). Fearful that this committee might enforce a predominantly somatic, hospital-oriented classification system, William Menninger and a cadre of like-minded psychiatrists formed the Group for the Advancement of Psychiatry (GAP) to ensure that extramural, psychodynamic, and social psychiatric concerns would prevail over traditional psychiatric ones. For a time, it has been said, it appeared as if American psychiatry might split, but the GAP and its fellow travelers carried the day. The dominance of American psychiatry and its nomenclature passed to the psychoanalytic/psychodynamic and social psychiatric contingents.

Thus, DSM-I (completed in 1950, published by the American Psychiatric Association [APA] in 1952) reflected several decades of outside social, political, and economic currents, wartime experience, professional economics and prestige, and the rise of psychoanalytic and social/community vistas (Grob, 1991). The clout of these latter vistas permeated DSM-I, especially the part devoted to the functional or nonorganic disorders. This is patent in the incorporation of psychoanalytic etiological theories into its very definitions and criteria for such disorders. Its frequent use of the term *reaction* reflected the influence of Meyer and his students as well. As opposed to the *Statistical Manuals* (1918–1942), DSM-I, whatever its scientific, statistical, and clinical deficiencies from our current perspective, enhanced the role of diagnosis in American psychiatry. It would reign until 1968, when a variety of forces had necessitated a revised edition (DSM-II).

There were a number of important causes for the revision of DSM-I. It was not accepted by relevant national organizations, such as the American Medical Association. There were difficulties translating its categories into those of the ICD. There was discontent with its classification of organic brain syndromes, including its failure to specify whether they were psychotic or nonpsychotic. There was dissatisfaction with its approach to mental deficiency and its ignoring of childhood mental disorders. Many viewed the tendency to *lump* as a problem— rather than to *split* when appropriate (e.g., Chronic Brain Syndrome Associated with Intoxification, instead of differentiation into Korsakoff's Psychosis, Alcoholic Hallucinosis, and Alcoholic Paranoia). There was criticism about its categorical separation of the two subtypes of Hysterical Neurosis into separate Dissociative and Conversion Reactions. There were certain logical inconsistencies and out-and-out clinical errors, such as putting Compulsive Personality with its "chronic, excessive . . . concern," under Personality Disorders (said to be characterized by "minimal subjective anxiety, and little or no sense of distress"). The inclusion of Sexual Deviations and Addictions under Antisocial Reactions was also problematic (DSM-II, 1968; Grob, 1991; Jenkins, 1968; Kramer, 1968). Moreover, an immediate impetus for a new manual (DSM-II) came from U.S. psychiatric collaboration in the mental disorders section of the ICD-8—completed in 1965, adopted by the 19th World Health Organization Assembly in 1966, and becoming effective in all WHO member states in 1968.

During those years APA leaders, some of whom worked on both the DSM-II and ICD-8 projects, were redrawing the old manual (DSM-I) with a close eye on international events. Furthermore, the widespread American and foreign discontent with the psychiatric section of the former ICD was not present with this one (ICD-8). Simultaneously with ICD-8, DSM-II became official in 1968. Apart from redressing the aforementioned problems and a few others, it dropped the Meyerian term *reaction*.

Although not claiming to be atheoretical, as did its DSM successors (III and III-R), it (1968, p. viii) did claim to "avoid terms which carry with them *implications* regarding either the *nature* of a disorder [hence, its change of DSM-I's Schizophrenic *Reaction* to Schizophrenia] or its *causes*" (first italics DSM-II's, latter mine). On the other hand, when etiological presuppositions were integral to a diagnostic concept (such as, for example, with various Organic Brain Syndromes), it was explicit about them (American Psychiatric Association, 1968).

In sum, however, the displacement of DSM-I by DSM-II did not reflect, as did the formulations of DSM-I and DSM-III, a major transformation in the predominant theoretical orientation of American psychiatry. The leadership of the profession, its academic and training centers, and probably the bulk of its nonpublic hospital cadre, retained psychodynamic and/or social/community leanings. This remained so until the middle 1970s, with the passing of the mantle to more descriptive/nosological, statistical, and neurobiological vantages.

Like DSM-I, the formulation of DSM-III (1974–1979) reflected both external factors (the imminence of ICD-9) and changes in theoretical, investigative, and therapeutic purviews within the American profession. In mentioning the latter, I am not necessarily contending that DSM-III presupposed neurobiologically comprehensible etiologies and pathological processes, and purely pharmacological treatments, for most or all of its divisions and categories. Rather, I argue that a decline in the hitherto predominant psychodynamic and social/community orientations was necessary, but not in itself sufficient, for the development of DSM-III. This is evidenced by the attempt in DSM-III and III-R to avoid psychoanalytic theories of unconscious meaning, motivation, conflict, defense, and perceptual/interpretive sets, except in the sections on Conversion Disorders and Psychological Factors Affecting Physical Conditions. Moreover, there is no emphasis on sociocultural, political/economic, developmental/longitudinal, and phenomenological information essential to the social psychiatric and psychodynamic approaches. Among other reasons, the decline in the psychodynamic and social/community perspectives was inevitable because, although not indifferent to nosology, they gave less priority to it.

Apart from the factors alluded to, and a few to be treated below, it is not my intent to "history" DSM-III and III-R. For one thing, most of our readership have themselves practiced or trained through the passage from II to III to III-R, and it is hence part of their personal and collective professional histories. Moreover, it is historiographically questionable whether one——or this writer at least——could apply a truly historical stance and methodology toward this work, still ongoing as it is, and with DSM-IV in the offing. In any event, most are familiar with the salient changes from DSM-III to III-R, which are outlined in the editor's introduction to the latter. Rather, the bulk of these last few pages will comprise a limited philosophical (and, to some extent, scientific and clinical) critique of our latest diagnostic manuals.

But first, two important historical items deserve mention. First, although the early work toward DSM-III was motivated by knowledge of the forthcoming ICD-9, as the latter emerged it was felt by the fashioners of DSM-III that it was both questionable and unserviceable to an American audience; hence less effort was expended to square DSM-III with it. Second, whatever the externalist and intraprofessional/theoretical motivators for the replacement of DSM-II, the sheer mass of new nosologically relevant data, from a host of directions and disciplines, would seem to have necessitated the new volume.

Perusal of letters and articles in the *American Journal of Psychiatry* in the immediate aftermath of DSM-I through III-R, and of *The Psychiatric News* (for periods shortly before and after DSM-II through III-R), reveals strongly emotional debates and hardly purely intellectual dialogues. Given what we have already seen regarding the yet-to-appear DSM-IV (see Frances et al., 1991, on the work for the new edition), there is every reason to expect similar reactions, generating as much heat as light.

Before turning specifically to a critique of DSM-III and III-R, let me emphasize that one item for which they have been reproached particularly is also true of their predecessor (DSM-II), that is the claim to atheoreticism and etiological agnosticism. Hence, whereas DSM-III and III-R may have accented this more strongly than DSM-II, all three have felt it to be fairly true of themselves. DSM-I, although chock-full of theoretical and etiological presuppositions, did not claim to have escaped them. This century's most respected philosophers of science (e.g., Chalmers, 1982; Harré, 1972; Mayr, 1982; Popper, 1968) have held this to be logically and empirically impossible for any classificatory system in any field of the basic natural sciences, much less for the value-laden and extraordinarily multivariable-burdened psychosocial and clinical sciences. Needless to say, this would apply for an ultimately pragmatic and incredibly broad-based art/science such as medicine and its psychiatric subspecialty (see also Faust & Miner, 1986; Wallace, 1988a, 1989a, 1990a, 1990b). Our history of medical and psychiatric nosologies has supported what the philosophers say, and what I believe *is likely to remain the case*. Any taxonomic system, whatever the science, is influenced by the purposes and aims of the classifiers (Colby & Spar, 1983, pp. 159–161; Hempel, 1965b; Mayr, 1988).

No scientific or clinical discipline can dispense with a number of presuppositions about reality or methodological assumptions. Examples of this abound: certain transempirical, untestable axioms; varying degrees of theoretical commitments; inferences and interpretations; and a priori factors in the generation and testing of scientific clinical hypotheses, classificatory or otherwise. Moreover, it is not merely scientific and clinical assumptions and theories that we cannot escape; it is social, political, and moral philosophical ones as well. Consider the nature of debates around such current, former, or recently proposed diagnoses as: Homosexuality, Late Luteal Phase Dysphoric Disorder, Self-Defeating Personality Disorder, Masochistic Personality Disorder, and Sadistic Personality Disorder (e.g., Bayer, 1981; Rivera-Tovar & Frank, 1990). Would anyone claim that these are purely scientific or medical issues, or that the DSMs have decided on them as such? Indeed, can anyone pretend that psychiatric (or *any*) classification is a purely scientific endeavor? Could there be such a thing, without acknowledged and unacknowledged, conscious and unconscious, metaphysical/valuational presuppositions and consequences?

Let me exemplify this with DSM-I and DSM-III/III-R. The former's primarily psychoanalytic/psychodynamic, and secondarily social/community, theoretical orientations are particularly obvious in its nonorganic, functional categories. Moreover, I see its organic section as largely a rule-out roster. In addition, the theoretical orientation of DSM-I is further clarified by the omissions, not merely the commissions——that is, its indifference to possible biomedical/neurobiological parameters in its functional categories. This cannot be explained away by the then-relative paucity of patient-pertinent biomedical/neurobiological data and theories compared with the times of DSM-III, III-R, and today; such theories, with their presumed supporting data, were present then as well.

The theoretical commitments (including etiological) of DSM-III and III-R may be less obvious than those of DSM-I, but they are there nonetheless, as was impinged on earlier in this chapter. For one thing, some of the syndromes followed, not preceded, certain *apparently* specific and exclusive pharmacological and other somatic treatments of particular presumed symptomatic constellations. A good example of this is the Melancholic Type of Major Depression, in which DSM-III-R (1987, p. 224) explicitly states the following diagnostic criterion: "previous good response to specific and adequate somatic antidepressant therapy, e.g., tricyclics, ECT, MAOI, lithium." It has long been a philosophical and scientific tenet that response to treatment is not a valid criterion for the codification or confirmation of a diagnosis. A minority of the DSM-III-R subcommittee on melancholia opposed its inclusion on the accurate grounds that the therapeutic criterion made it tautological (see Zimmerman & Spitzer, 1989). In any event, we now appreciate that there is less syndromal/pharmaceutical specificity than was thought before.

Such is the case even in infectious disease, whose diagnoses are the most pathophysiologically and etiologically based in all medicine, and whose therapeutic agents are likewise the most diagnosis specific. The variability in response to treatment of infectious disease is evidenced by (a) that the same microbial infestation may not respond to the identical antibiotic or antiviral in two different patients, and (b) that divergent microorganismic infections may respond to the same chemotherapeutic. The former is in part a matter of host factors, covering a plethora of biopsychosocial codetermining factors influencing both course of illness and specific antimicrobial response. How much truer is all of this for psychiatric syndromes and treatments!

Etiological presuppositions have also prefigured in many DSM-III and III-R categories. An excellent instance is, again, the Melancholic Type of Major Depression, whose descriptive criteria, the DSM-III/III-R Senior Editor Spitzer (Zimmerman & Spitzer, 1989, pp. 20–21) makes plain, were taken from the etiologically theory-laden *Research Diagnostic Criteria* concept of *endogenous depression*. Such is even more problematic, considering that many of our most cherished neurobiological etiological theories were themselves derived by reasoning and researching "backward" from the posited mechanisms of pharmaceutical agents.

Consider also omissions or relative inattentions that betray the DSM-III and III-R allegiances as much, or more than, their positive declarations, such as their short shrift to phenomenology (i.e., meaning and subjective experience) and developmental, longitudinal, and premorbid history. This is coupled with the earlier criticized infatuation with allegedly purely observable behaviors. These last are conceptualized and treated as if they exist independently of the particular patient's antecedent and concurrent phenomenology, and as if meaning and motivation are not intrinsic to them. It is common sense, and not only general clinical and psychodynamic wisdom, that generically similar observable behaviors in different patients can (a) feel and mean quite different things to each, and (b) reflect quite divergent determinants, to say nothing of the psychical and actual realities of the specific doctor-patient relationship. Moreover, the phenomenology preceding and accompanying behaviors and behavioral constellations can be communicated (as *mediated through* language and noverbal expression) by the patient, and hence is as potentially "observable" (i.e., perceivable/interpretable [Wallace, 1988b, 1989b, 1989d]) as the bare "externals" emphasized by the latest DSMs. Their focus merely on the latter may reflect their preoccupation with interrater reliability; but if this is achieved at the expense of the phenomena themselves, then what sort of reliability is it, and what kind of validity does it return?

Given the above caveat, it is at least helpful that DSM-III-R includes an Axis IV, Severity of Stressors. Nevertheless, this is undercut by its (1987, p. xxi) announcement that proposed diagnoses associated with psychosocial stress were considered premature for DSM-III-R, and more properly within the scope of DSM-IV, in which they would have to be deliberated upon as a whole new diagnostic class, Disorders Associated with Psychosocial Stress. When one ponders the overwhelming clinical and scientific evidence supporting or suggesting the important role of psychosocial stressors in general medical and psychiatric illnesses, this is perplexing. Moreover, the idea of a separate nosological niche seems to implicitly minimize the role of psychosocial stressors in other psychiatric disorders, as well as to imply falsely that such factors operate unicausally in the proposed class of syndromes. This could also help foster a metaphysical and clinical mind-brain/body split or, at best, a higher cortical/environmental one, both of which are contrary to the allegedly comprehensive stance of DSM-III-R (American Psychiatric Association, 1987, p. xxvi).

Furthermore, why is there not an Axis IVa, Prior or Overall Life Stressors? It is well known that particular patterns and genres of prior stressful experiences may both affect vulnerability to later life and current stressors and co-determine what constitutes a stressor——and a pathogenic one (i.e., precipitant)——for any specific individual (see, again, Wallace, 1985, 1986, 1988c, 1989b, 1989d on intersectional causation). And finally, stressors do not sit totally outside the person, but in the interface between his or her mental/interpretive set and the ambience. Their occurrence may also, of course, be unwittingly and often repetitively arranged by the patient himself or herself. Both points support suggestions that some sort of psychogenetic/dynamic axis be incorporated into DSM-IV as well. Without some such cuing, the recent and future DSMs will likely promote truncated information gathering that favors simplistic explanations for sparsely defined symptoms and unidimensionally behavioral complexes or putative disease entities.

A self-fulfilling unicausal and pathophysiological prophecy would then be realizable, simply because inconvenient perspectives, classes of data, and whole genera of possible or likely determinative variables would have been ignored, or barely attended to, by the DSM-derived interviewing manuals. Consider the *SCID: Structured Clinical Interview for DSM-III-R* (Spitzer, Williams, Gillon & First, 1990). A series of verbatim questions are *read* to the patient, as if this ensures the identity of the "stimulus values" across multiple clinician-patient dyads! If algorithmic treatment manuals are based on such stereotyped interviewing, and on diagnoses whose descriptive codifications were based partly on a priori assumptions such as apparent pharmacotherapeutic specificity and *uni*-genetic/neurobiological etiological assumptions (e.g., melancholia), then such therapies will amount to tautologies laid on tautologies. Need we even consider the possible impact of both interviewing and treatment manuals on the doctor-patient relationship, including the therapeutic alliance and the patient's sense of being understood, empathized with, and treated as an incredibly complex and in many ways unique individual? This determines treatment adherence and therapeutic outcome as much, if not more than, the most unimaginably specific and pharmacologically effective therapeutic (in which placebo psychophysiological factors always play some role) (Brody, 1977; Spiro, 1986; Wallace 1990a). Read novelist William Styron's (1990) response to such evaluation and treatment of *his* melancholia.

I hope I am wrong about the apparent trajectories of our most recent DSMs, and that their introductory disclaimers of these (e.g., DSM-III-R, portions of pp. xxii–xxvi) will prevail. But, as I said, many such disclaimers are seriously undercut by the manuals themselves. It remains to be seen whether DSM-IV will not only contain such caveats, but demonstrate them as well (see Frances et al., 1989, 1991).

In any event, I do not want my criticisms of DSM-III and III-R to be taken as wholly negative, or to imply that DSM-I and II were superior. In their own ways, reductive psychoanalytic or social psychiatric orientations, such as those from which the earlier manuals flowed, do violence to large arcs of the person and ignore or deride theoretical purviews and therapeutic modalities that can be necessary or lifesaving.

On the credit side, DSM-III and III-R demonstrate important advances. They pay better attention to the indispensable descriptive part of the patient's presentation, that is, the enumeration and clustering of signs and symptoms whose frequent simultaneous occurrence was hitherto less recognized. The concern with interrater reliability (a necessary first step toward any eventual validities), and with taking account of better controlled, large-N clinical, laboratory, epidemiological, and medical basic science studies, is essential as well. These nosologies have supplied much-improved diagnostic criteria for schizophrenia and clearer demarcation of it (considering its likely syndromal and etiological heterogeneity) from major affective disorders and other syndromes (many of which will probably eventually prove similarly heterogeneous); and the same could be said for certain other diagnoses as well. Most importantly, the aim for a more open, self-critical, and developing stance is important, as is acknowledgment of the road yet to be traveled toward more veridical *and* processually/etiologically based nosologies.

For the rest, the reader will find ample philosophical scrutiny of our recent, current, and ongoing classificatory enterprise in the chapters of this book. There is a host of historical/philosophical issues that this overlong paper has not addressed. Jaspers (1963) and others (e.g., Lipowski, 1966; Spitzer et al., 1988) raise issues on the constitution of, and need for a science of psychopathology (examining, among other things, concepts basic to all modern nosological systems, such as delusion, hallucination, etc.). Especially, there are knotty questions on concepts of mental health and mental illness and their potential boundary straddling with areas traditionally moral, valuational, metaphysical, and religious——issues unclear for health and disease/illness in the rest of medicine as well (see Canguilhem, 1989; Culver & Gert, 1982; Engelhardt, 1976; Pellegrino & Thomasma, 1981; Temkin, 1977; Toulmin, 1977; Wallace, 1990b, 1991, in press-b, in press-c; White, 1988). Finally, much pertinent philosophical ore is yet to be mined, such as Wittgenstein's (1958) thinking on mind and cost/benefit analysis of language (see Drury [1973], his psychiatric pupil; and von Wright [1987] for an extensive bibliography of Wittgenstein's writings).

CONCLUSIONS

What is the purpose of this essay and the collection in which it is embedded? Is it to punish or paralyze the psychiatrist as practicing or investigative nosologist? No, and their points will do neither to those psychiatrists deeming both medicine and their subspecialty a preeminently and ultimately practical and moral endeavor——a vocation or calling to the care, assistance and, where possible, amelioration and enablement of the distressed and disabled. Such a profession consumes and cross-checks itself with the best-available basic and clinical science; struggles for the most rigorous and self-reflective clinical judgment; applies it to the unique patient phenomenologically and empathically; and seeks more coherently comprehensive and evidenced, although always tentative and evolving, theories and formulations (Wallace, 1988a, 1992b).

The nosologist searching for universal features and factors in otherwise highly particularized fabrics of disordered personhood is laying essential foundations for a more moral *and scientific* psychiatric humanism. But the one who never really sees the patient and his or her actual problems and possibilities because of nomothetic commitments to the presumed disease or disorder is neither physician nor scientist (see Engel, 1988; Wallace, 1992b, in press-b; White, 1988).

I METHODS

2 The Limits of Psychiatric Knowledge and the Problem of Classification

OSBORNE P. WIGGINS, Ph.D.
and MICHAEL A. SCHWARTZ, M.D.

DIVERSITY IN PSYCHIATRIC CLASSIFICATIONS

Classifications, we have recognized recently, come in diverse kinds. Gone are the days when we could assume that all classificatory concepts, if truly scientific, must specify necessary and sufficient conditions for including an individual in a general class. Such "classical" categories are now called *monothetic concepts* and not only are contrasted with the quite different "polythetic" classifications of DSM-III and DSM-III-R but also stand opposed to the "fuzzy concepts," "family resemblances," "prototypes," and "dimensional concepts" that other writers advocate (Cantor and Genero, 1986; Frances and Widiger, 1986; Kendell, 1983). We now seem to suffer from an embarrassment of riches in which we have to choose from among all of the available options the kind of classification scheme a psychiatric manual should adopt without the benefit of any viable standard to guide such a choice.

In this chapter we shall attempt to provide the elements of such a standard. By reflecting on the requirements of a manual of classification at the present juncture of the development of psychiatry, we shall offer some ideas that, we hope, will delimit and clarify the task. The approaches afforded by prototypes, dimensions, polythetic concepts, and so on do not lead us into a quandary in which we confront merely an unmanageable diversity. We shall maintain that all of these approaches implicitly embody a recognition that at the present time the classification of psychiatric disorders must contend with certain intractable and unavoidable limitations. We shall try to explicate these limitations and develop their implications for a manual that would classify psychiatric illnesses, an imaginary manual we shall call simply *Mental Disorders*. This path leads us to develop further the notion of *ideal types* which we have treated in previous essays (Schwartz & Wiggins, 1987a; Schwartz, Wiggins &

Norko, 1989; Wiggins & Schwartz, 1991). Ideal types, if properly understood, contain the unifying insight that underlies prototypes, dimensions, and the other contenders for the field of classification. The structure of the manual we are imagining grows more definite when we realize that both the medical notion of *disease* and unnoticed evaluations guide psychiatrists in their categorizations of disorders.

Much of what we say here recalls the work of Karl Jaspers. We hope to make evident just how contemporary this classical work is.

A CLASSIFICATORY MANUAL AND THE LARGER CONTEXT OF PSYCHIATRIC PRACTICE

Although we focus here on the requirements of a scheme of classification for a psychiatric manual, we would like to note at the outset one of the unavoidable limitations of such a manual. Any psychiatric manual that classifies the various mental illnesses can play only a restricted role in psychiatric practice. The psychiatrist, both clinician and researcher, must utilize far more information, skills, conceptual frameworks, and techniques than can possibly be contained in any such manual. Indeed, if the physician attempts to limit his or her understanding of patients to what is conveyed in the manual, this understanding would remain inexcusably shortsighted, reductionistic, and prejudicial. At best a manual of classification can depict only a few of the manifold factors that should be taken into account when examining and treating a patient. The broader context, the intellectual and practical context that no manual can possibly supply, should always be kept firmly in mind; and information conveyed by a manual should be comprehended and utilized only within this more encompassing context.

THE PURPOSES OF PSYCHIATRIC CLASSIFICATIONS

To approach our own suggestions regarding psychiatric classification, we would like to pose and address some elementary questions regarding such classification. First, why is there a need for a single, unified set of psychiatric categories common to all psychiatrists? Second, granted that there is a need, why does the discipline of psychiatry confront especially difficult problems in arriving at a single, unified set of categories—problems that apparently do not plague other branches of medicine?

For the past 20 years American psychiatry has been propelled by the need to develop a system of classification which operates in the same way as classification systems in medicine. Psychiatric classifications, like medical classifications, should achieve the following goals:

1. They should provide a relatively concise, clear, and rational list of psychiatric illnesses.
2. They should furnish concepts and criteria that guarantee the reliability of communication; that is, these concepts should ensure that a psychiatric term, when used, always conveys the same meaning and refers to the same state of affairs.
3. Psychiatric categories should prove equally useful to all practitioners in the field, for example, for clinicians, researchers, and administrators.

If these are the needs that a system of classification must meet, why has psychiatry encountered special difficulties in doing so? Most psychiatric illnesses have proven resistant to concise, clear, and rational description. Moreover, the nature of psychiatric illnesses is such that classifications that work well for clinicians may not be fruitful for administrators, and classifications that serve the purposes of researchers may not be useful for administrators, and classifications that suit administrators may not prove helpful to clinicians. In the past this problem prompted some writers, notably, Joseph Zubin (1977), to recommend that different classification systems be tailored to the purposes of different groups. Such a recommendation seems unsatisfactory, however, because other areas within medicine have succeeded in developing single, unified systems. Consequently, the conviction remains that psychiatry should strive for the same exemplary unity.

The classification scheme embodied in DSM-III-R does furnish this unity, and it therefore serves the purposes of the medicalization of psychiatry and communication. Because these two purposes remain paramount, almost all clinicians, researchers, and administrators, after voicing some displeasure with it, find DSM-III-R acceptable.

Contributing to these peculiar circumstances are the two following problems. At present psychiatry lacks much knowledge about mental illnesses. Moreover, the field of psychiatry remains divided among different "orientations" whose adherents disagree over the conceptualization and treatment of mental disorders (McHugh and Slavney, 1983). Because no particular orientation or limited subgroup of schools has established its credentials as the sole *scientific* approach, there remains no *scientific* criterion for officially adopting one orientation over the others (Schwartz and Wiggins, 1988). Thus the field of psychiatry must somehow accommodate all of the divergent schools and yet arrive at a single classification scheme that all agree to use. How then to reach agreement amid such unyielding disagreement?

The authors of DSM-III sought to achieve this agreement by separating psychiatric observation from psychiatric theory. The common classification scheme would consist of categories whose meanings could be defined as far as possible through direct observation. In this way the adherents of different schools could nonetheless agree on basic terminology because disputes regarding definitions could be settled by appeal to what all could observe and could not reasonably deny. To base definitions on what can be observed is to devise "operational definitions." This entails, of course, that what cannot be observed is excluded from the definitions. What cannot be observed are the "theoretical" entities that the different schools use to account for the observations, and it is these theoretical entities about which there is so much irresolvable dispute. Agreement over terminology requires, then, that the definitions of the terms remain operational and atheoretical. Exceptions are admitted only when theories are very well confirmed by the evidence, that is, only when "the etiology or pathophysiologic processes are known" (American Psychiatric Association, 1987, p. xxiii).

This distinction between observation and theory can be seriously challenged, however. If the *observable* is taken to mean "overt behavior" exclusively, psychiatry cannot restrict itself to the observable. Psychiatry, as the science of *mental* disorders, must refer regularly to mental events. A mere glance at DSM-III-R discloses countless terms that refer to mental realities: *delusion, hallucination, anxiety, low self-esteem, feelings of hopelessness, ideas of reference, neither enjoys nor desires close relationships, unusual perceptual experiences, paranoid ideation*, and so on. Of course, the mental occurrences of patients are frequently expressed through their overt behavior, such as bodily gestures and speech. But one person's mental processes are never directly observable by another person, and it thus remains necessary for the observer to interpret the meaning of the overt behavior to decide which mental events are correlated with it. Even at the level of the clinical syndrome, therefore, a hermeneutical or interpretive element unavoidably permeates the methodology (Spitzer, 1988, pp. 3–18).

Nevertheless, to develop a unified classification scheme for the entire field of psychiatry, it would appear necessary, we think, to distinguish that about which psychiatrists agree from that about which psychiatrists persistently disagree. We suggest that the official manual of psychiatry do precisely that. We propose that psychiatry abandon the indefensible distinctions between the observable and the theoretical. The required distinctions here seem to us to be simpler and more straightforward. We need to distinguish simply between that concerning which psychiatrists agree and that about which psychiatrists differ. We therefore propose that any manual that is to serve as the official document of the discipline of psychiatry should contain the following information: *all information concerning the nature of mental disorders on which psychiatrists generally agree*. We shall henceforth entitle this manual we are imagining simply, *Mental Disorders*.

To determine the contents of *Mental Disorders*, the authors must distinguish, then, between those claims in psychiatry concerning which there is general agreement and those claims concerning which there is substantial dispute. The claims concerning which there remains substantial disagreement could be left to their advocates to develop, refine, and support.

Thomas Kuhn's (1970) writings on scientific revolutions suggested that scientific views, views that present themselves as scientific knowledge, can attain dominance in a field, not because they are in fact proven knowledge, but instead because they are widely accepted by practitioners in the field and subsequently transmitted as *the truth* to subsequent generations. What Kuhn delineated in this regard is, we think, a genuine danger if some particular school does possess a monopoly on research, funding, publication, and education. One view dominates the field, not because of its scientific power, but rather because of its political power. The only possible remedy for this kind of blindness lies in opening the field up to competing points of view, that is, in giving all points of view access to research, funding, publication, and education; and this in turn requires a demanding scientific conscience on the part of all psychiatrists so that they are willing to admit the tentative and hypothetical status of many of their claims.

It is crucial, therefore, that at the present stage of the development of psychiatry no one research program determine the contents of *Mental Disorders* such that this research program comes to be viewed as *the* paradigm for psychiatry. At present there exists no *scientific* basis for the dominance of one research program. Consequently, the only way that a single research program could dominate the field is through political, economic, or educational influences. The stifling of other research programs which this would produce would merely block avenues of inquiry which may eventually prove fruitful and informative.

Scientific work cannot proceed, of course, without guiding hypotheses and theoretical frameworks (Lakatos, 1978; Popper, 1965). It is necessary, then, for psychiatrists to construct, refine, and test such hypotheses and frameworks. While this labor of theoretical elaboration and testing proceeds, no particular approach can be viewed as the only genuinely scientific one. As long as no particular approach has satisfactorily answered the major questions of the field, no particular approach can claim sovereignty. Hence the field must remain open to all views that can reasonably respond to the criticisms and objections aimed at them.

The information published in *Mental Disorders* should therefore be formulated in a neutral language that does not favor the technical vocabulary of any particular research program. In other words, the language used in *Mental Disorders* should also be a language concerning which psychiatrists can generally agree.

We must address, however, the problem of what it means to say, in the midst of a multitude of different research programs, that psychiatrists *agree* to include certain information in the manual.

In the ideal case psychiatrists would agree to include the information because it had been proven in accordance with the methods of empirical science. In this ideal case psychiatrists would agree to this information because it had been established as sound *scientific knowledge*. If this were the basis upon which one were to decide what would be included and what excluded from the psychiatric manual, then the authors would need merely to distinguish between the known and the unknown. The scientifically known would be included, and the unknown excluded. Unfortunately, however, as we mentioned earlier, there exists little information in psychiatry which qualifies as established scientific knowledge. There is some, and it should definitely be included in the manual. But if this were the only material contained in the manual, the volume would fail to serve the basic purposes described above.

IDEAL TYPES AND PSYCHIATRIC CLASSIFICATION

Fortunately, the purposes outlined above can be served by means other than established scientific knowledge. To achieve these four purposes, what psychiatrists require are concepts that are merely *helpful*; psychiatrists need concepts that function as *heuristic devices*. Concepts can fruitfully guide and inform treatment and research without having been proven.

A concept such as *antisocial personality disorder*, for example, can guide the clinician as he or she examines and treats a patient even if some features of the concept do not apply to that particular patient. Suppose that the concept stipulates, among other things, that a patient with antisocial personality disorder "is irritable and aggressive" (American Psychiatric Association, 1987, p. 345). Further suppose that the psychiatrist determines that this particular patient does not exhibit this feature although he does more or less exhibit other features enumerated in the concept. The concept could still prove to be useful in the examination and treatment of this patient precisely because some of its features do apply. Indeed, it might also prove fruitful for the psychiatrist to wonder why this patient, while manifesting other features of antisocial personality disorder, does not appear to be irritable and aggressive.

Similarly, the researcher may find the same concept of antisocial personality disorder to be useful although some of its features did not apply to all patients. If there were a significant number of patients who exhibited certain features of the concept but at the same time were not irritable and aggressive, the researcher might wish to study precisely those patients to determine what in the patients' social histories, laboratory findings, or personality structures might account for that variation.

We propose that such heuristic concepts can take the form of what Karl Jaspers, following Max Weber, called *ideal types* (Burger, 1987; Weber, 1949). In other papers we have explicated ideal types as developed and used by Weber in sociology and Jaspers in psychiatry (Schwartz & Wiggins, 1987a; Schwartz, Wiggins & Norko, 1989; Wiggins & Schwartz, 1991). Here we would like to try to clarify the basic nature of conceptualization and concept formation which underlies the notion of ideal types. To do so, we must ask the reader to engage in a thought experiment.

Suppose that the inherent structure of reality is unknown to us. We would then not be able to define any concepts that captured the invariable relationships among events or objects. Our concepts could not then mirror nature. Consequently, any definition of concepts would be arbitrary and purely conventional. If reality, whose structure is unknown, is to present any structure to our minds, we must impose that structure on it by defining our concepts however we choose and then conceiving of reality through our arbitrarily created concepts. Reality is then ordered, but it is ordered only through the imposition of an arbitrarily defined conceptual order on it. Let us call such concepts *nominalistic* ones (Scaff, 1989, pp. 50–59).

Now suppose that, on the contrary, we know the inherent structure of reality. In that case our concepts could specify the invariant features of events and things. Our concepts could then "carve nature at the joints." Let us label such concepts *naturalistic* ones (Scaff, 1989, pp. 50–59).

In our scientific endeavors we, of course, aim at arriving at naturalistic concepts. To undertake scientific work, however, we must employ nominalistic notions. Now, of course, we cannot in our scientific inquiries permit our concepts to be purely nominalistic; they cannot be defined entirely arbitrarily. Our categories must bear *some* resemblance to the inherent features of reality; our scientific terms must be *partially* naturalistic. We should remain cognizant that the order we conceive in reality is an order determined largely by our concepts and not by reality itself.[1] If we remain conscious of the arbitrary character of our concepts, we can see that different sets of concepts can serve different scientific purposes. No set of terms is privileged because no set has a claim to truth. We may define our concepts in one way, but for the sake of pursuing a different scientific goal we may choose to define them differently.

Let us cite some specific examples. For some research purposes in psychiatry it might be more helpful to classify mental illnesses using prototypes. A prototype would allow us to investigate particular cases of an illness in terms of how they approximate the best exemplar of the type. In pursuit of other research purposes, however, it might be more fruitful to conceive of the same mental illnesses along dimensional lines. By using dimensions investigators might study the gradations that separate one type of illness from another. Neither prototypes nor dimensions "carve nature at the joints." Both are nominalistic approaches: they impose a conceptual order on reality which may prove helpful in the scientific investigation of it.

The ideal types endorsed by Weber and Jaspers embody a nominalist approach to classification (Scaff, 1989, pp. 50–59). Ideal types, as developed by Weber, create a conceptual order that, when imposed on reality, merely permits inquiry to begin. Ideal types delineate in reality a certain pattern that may not actually exist in reality but which can at least orient and structure scientific inquiry into it. As the inquiry proceeds, however, the ideal type will likely require modification and redefinition to conform to the investigator's findings. As Lawrence Scaff wrote about Weberian ideal types, "at their best, types

serve an orienting function and suggest questions, hypotheses, and relationships for investigation" (Scaff, 1989, p. 55).

The arbitrariness involved in defining an ideal type allows us to choose the
features we wish to contain. It allows us to focus selectively on certain aspects
of reality and to ignore other aspects. In constructing ideal types we focus on
those aspects of reality which interest us, and we ignore those features that do
not. Because in defining ideal types we are guided by our psychiatric interests
and values, our ideal types are necessarily perspectival and one-sided. The
same reality, if approached with different values in mind, could be defined
from a different point of view; and this other point of view would yield a different set of concepts. Jaspers explicitly recognized that any given set of types
provides only one limited perspective on reality. He wrote that types "aim at
points of view [*Gesichtspunkte*] for understanding; they do not capture the
substance of reality" (1949, p. 362, translation ours).

Weber (1949) characterized the process of defining an ideal type in the following way. "An ideal type is formed by the one-sided accentuation of one or
more points of view and by the synthesis of a great many diffuse, discrete,
more or less present, and occasionally absent concrete individual phenomena,
which are arranged according to those one-sidedly emphasized viewpoints into
a unified thought-construct" (p. 90).

Ideal types focus on reality from a particular point of view. This point of
view is determined by our psychiatric values. From this point of view we develop an *idealized* description of the reality under study. To call the description *idealized* is to say that it provides a clearer and more precise picture of
reality than reality itself sometimes exhibits. The features of reality itself may
prove difficult to distinguish from one another; their boundaries may remain
fuzzy, fluid, indefinite, and vague. In defining the ideal type, however, we
draw clear and precise boundaries around these features of things. We imagi-
natively set aside the real indistinctness and ambiguity, and we conceive of a
"pure" kind in which the features are distinct and definite. Furthermore, in real
cases the features may vary so widely that each individual seems unique and
incomparable with others. The ideal type, however, specifies many features all
of which are not found in each actual case. The features contained in the ideal
type are, as Weber phrases it, "more or less present and occasionally absent"
in real individual cases (Burger, 1987, pp. 154–167).

We suggest that mental disorders can be best defined using ideal types. Because they make no claim to truth, psychiatrists should be able to agree on
their merely *heuristic* value. Because ideal types are more or less arbitrary
nominalistic concepts and not fixed naturalistic ones, they can be adapted
easily to accord with different research goals. For instance, an ideal type could
be changed readily into a prototype or dimension to suit various research purposes.

Ideal types, therefore, should not be viewed as an *alternative* to dimension-
ism, prototypes, or polythetic concepts. Ideal types do not represent one kind

of categorical approach which may be contrasted, for instance, with a dimensional approach. Ideal types rather represent the way in which we should think about all such approaches to classification at this juncture in the development of psychiatry. First, all approaches to psychiatric classification—whether dimensional, prototypical, polythetic, or whatever—should be conceived as *nominalistic*: all classifications fail to "carve nature at the joints" and thus provide merely a more or less arbitrarily constructed guide to further investigation. Second, all classifications have only a *heuristic value*: they are only *helpful* in guiding inquiry; they must undergo change and adaptation to serve better the purposes of any particular inquiry. Third, all psychiatric classifications are *one-sided* and *perspectival*: all depict only selected features of reality and consequently ignore other features of the same reality; these other features can be captured only by devising other concepts. Fourth, all classifications specify features that in any given case may not exist at all or may exist only partially or slightly.

We propose the following four criteria for deciding which ideal types should be included in the manual:

1. Does this classification help secure the uniformity, simplicity, and definiteness required for effective communication among different groups, for example, psychiatrists, social workers, physicians, lawyers, and hospital personnel?
2. Does this classification help clinicians with the understanding and treatment of patients?
3. Does this classification help researchers in the understanding and empirical investigation of patients with disorders?
4. Does this classification help establish the uniformity, simplicity, and definiteness of categories required for administrative purposes, for example, hospital, clinic, and insurance record keeping?

DISEASES AND DISORDERS

Any discussion of the questions surrounding psychiatric classification must account for the modeling of psychiatric classification on classifications in the larger field of medicine. The very fact that the main classificatory manual, DSM-III-R, is a *diagnostic* and statistical manual that consists of sets of diagnostic criteria implies that psychiatric classification plays a role in *diagnosis* just as classification in medicine functions in diagnosis. Diagnosis of what? The obvious medical answer would appear to be diseases. But that is not the answer of DSM-III-R. In DSM-III-R it is mental *disorders* that are diagnosed.

Viewing psychiatric problems as disorders generates difficulties, however. Alzheimer's disease, for instance, must be listed in two places, Axis I and Axis III. On Axis I it is viewed as a clinical syndrome and a mental disorder;

there it is called Primary Degenerative Dementia of the Alzheimer Type (American Psychiatric Association, 1987, pp. 119–122). On Axis III Alzheimer's disease is considered a physical disorder. Notice that on Axis III Alzheimer's disease is called a physical *disorder* and not a physical *disease*. The same holds for a variety of other conditions when mental changes are associated with physical illnesses, such as delirium and infection, or anxiety and hyperthyroidism. It would appear that the only reason for labeling Alzheimer's or Huntington's physical *disorders* rather than physical *diseases* is to create the impression that there are physical disorders that are analogous to mental disorders. In other words, the label is intended to create the notion that medicine treats disorders rather than diseases and that psychiatry closely resembles medicine by also treating disorders. The only difference between medicine and psychiatry thus lies in the fact that, whereas medicine is concerned with *physical* disorders, psychiatry is concerned with *mental* ones.

This line of reasoning is misleading, however.

First, medical doctors rarely speak of disorders; they refer instead to diseases. When physicians discuss a disease, they are referring to a particular destructive process that has a specified etiology in the patient. The process also has characteristic symptomatology and host resistance factors. Because they possess such a concept of disease, doctors have less use for the notion of disorder. Physicians do employ the term *disorder* to express the idea that the patient has a functional rather than a structural problem. Psychiatrists, however, encounter difficulties when trying to conceive of mental disorders as diseases. (See the chapters by Agich, Fulford, Russell, Sadler and Hulgus, and Schaffner for more discussion of this issue.)

Second, the distinction between *physical* disorders and *mental* disorders perpetuates the assumption of a clear mind-body dualism. In fact it seems that the dualism is so clear cut that mental disorders must be listed on one axis and physical disorders on a different axis. We believe, however, that there are numerous psychiatric and medical reasons for questioning such a mind-body dualism.

Added to these difficulties in the notion of mental disorders are those criticisms of the concept which point to its value ladenness. Even such a neutral observer as R. E. Kendell (1986, pp. 23–45) argued that the entire concept of a mental disorder rests primarily on evaluative assumptions. After surveying the numerous ways in which *disease* has been conceived in the history of medicine, Kendell noted that all of these ways continue to be employed even today. He then turned to this other term, *disorder*, and to mental disorders in particular. Kendell (1986) offered four alternatives for defining *disorder*:

1. The approach of the World Health Organization. Ignore the problem; provide no definition of disease or disorder.

2. The approach of DSM-III-R. Provide a definition that is vaguely worded so as to allow any category with medical connotations to be either included or excluded in conformity with current medical opinion.
3. A conceivable approach not yet employed. Furnish an operational definition of disease or disorder which provides unambiguous rules of application and then abide by the unsatisfactory constraints that result from that definition.
4. The approach Kendell himself prefers. Concede openly that psychiatric classifications are not classifications of diseases or disorders. Such classifications consist simply of problems about which psychiatrists are currently consulted. Kendell's approach admits the evaluative or normative status of classifications of disorders. It concedes that they are social constructs as well as scientific constructs (pp. 41–44).

We agree with Kendell that the classification of certain conditions as *disorders* involves value judgments. We even concur with his stronger claim that the designation of certain conditions as *diseases* also involves social and evaluative conventions. We think that Kendell goes too far, however, by implying that all mental disorders are simply *problems* which, by virtue of widely accepted value judgments, fall within the expertise of psychiatrists. We propose an approach to psychiatric classification developed years ago by Karl Jaspers in his *General Psychopathology*.

KARL JASPERS' GROUPS OF MENTAL ILLNESSES

Jaspers' (1963) proposal delineates a middle ground between Kendell's position and the stance of DSM-III-R. Jaspers applied the notion of disease to one major group of mental disorders. This is important, we think, because it firmly links psychiatry to medical science. With respect to a second group of mental disorders, however, Jaspers still employed the notion of disease but in a novel way. With this group the medical notion of disease continues nonetheless to inform psychiatric research and practice. With regard to the third and last group of mental disorders, Jaspers set aside the concept of disease and claimed that these disorders could be conceived only as *types*.

Here are Jaspers's three groups (Jaspers, 1963, pp. 605–607):

Group I

a. Cerebral illnesses such as trauma, tumor, infection, vascular disease, hereditary atrophic system diseases, and organic deterioration associated with age.

b. Systemic diseases with symptomatic psychoses, such as infections, endocrine disorders, uremia, eclampsia, and so on.

c. Poisons: alcohol, morphine, cocaine, and other drugs; carbon monoxide and other toxins.

Group II. The major psychoses.

a. Schizophrenia and manic-depressive illness. (Jaspers also included epilepsy. Today this would be omitted.)

Group III. Personality disorders (in German the term is *Psychopathies*, a broader notion than *personality disorders*).

a. Isolated abnormal reactions that do not arise on the basis of illnesses belonging to Groups I and II.

b. Neuroses and neurotic syndromes.

c. Abnormal personalities and their developments.

Jaspers (1963) claimed that "*The three main groups are essentially different from each other.* They have no single unifying and comprehensive viewpoint from which any systematic ordering of these three illness groups [*Krankheitsgruppen*] could emerge. With each group we have a different point of view" (p. 610).

Let us note the main distinctions among these three groups. To the disorders in Group I the concept of *disease* fully applies. These disorders have well-defined causes in known bodily events. Such disorders can be categorized by monothetic concepts; that is to say, necessary and sufficient criteria define the different classes. For this reason, distinct boundaries separate the categories from one another. Consequently, an individual disorder, as Jaspers says, "either does or does not belong" to one of these categories. Therefore, an exact diagnosis is possible. Moreover, there are no transitions between illness and health (Jaspers, 1963, pp. 610–611).

Although in one crucial respect the disorders in Group II resemble those in Group I, in another important way they are entirely different. When we consider schizophrenia and manic-depressive illness, according to Jaspers, "We have classes of disease in mind although their definite causes and nature are not known, but in fact one is always confined to types" (Jaspers, 1963, p. 611). For the Group II disorders, then, the concept of disease applies only within significant limits. Within these limits, however, this notion can function nevertheless as a guiding idea[2] with reference to which we can study and treat these disorders. The notion of disease can tell us what to look for as we investigate these disorders further; the notion can delineate concrete research and treatment programs. If further research should uncover specifiable etiologies, then the concept of disease will come to apply to these disorders fully. In other words, disorders in Group II will then be reassigned to Group I. We wish to emphasize, however, that the notion of disease remains at this point only a guiding idea for the disorders in Group II; as Jaspers stressed, we are "always confined to types."

How can we affirm with Jaspers, however, that with schizophrenia and manic-depressive illness "we have classes of disease in mind?" If we do not yet know their definite causes and nature, how can we suppose that they are diseases? Although Jaspers addressed this point, we may respond as follows.

First, many patients with schizophrenia and manic-depressive illness look diseased. This is particularly true in the obviously severe morbid states, which appear acutely in most cases as well as chronically in the more profound forms of these illnesses. Second, the illnesses often occur unexpectedly in a life break as a pathological process that then drastically alters the patient's previously understandable course of development. Third, the features of each of these illnesses are stereotypical and spare across a range of individuals. The basic features of the illness do not vary greatly from individual to individual. Thomas Sydenham characterized *disease* in the following manner. "Nature, in the production of disease, is uniform and consistent; so much so, that for the same disease in different persons the symptoms are for the most part the same; and the self-same phenomena that you would observe in the sickness of a Socrates you would observe in the sickness of a simpleton" (Kendell, 1986, p. 27).

Schizophrenia and manic-depressive illness are like this. Finally, a vast literature reveals findings in the brain, the nervous system, and other biological systems in schizophrenic and manic-depressive patients.

On the other hand, there remain important distinctions between Group II and Group I illnesses. For example, the morbid psychopathological findings in schizophrenia and manic-depressive illness are different in their form from the crude organic destructiveness seen in other psychiatric diseases, such as AIDS dementia and syphilitic general paresis. Furthermore, the more flamboyant features of Group II illnesses often ameliorate and sometimes even cease entirely as the patient ages (Bleuler, 1978). Finally, the research findings in Group II illnesses, although impressive, are not universal, and they have not disclosed causal mechanisms of illness.

Jaspers drew other important distinctions between Groups I and II, however. With Group II, although we can usually draw definite boundaries between health and illness, we cannot delineate the differences between the psychoses definitely. Moreover, basic concepts regarding the extent and limit of the psychoses vary. And although the majority of individual cases fall by consensus of opinion into one of the two classes, differential diagnosis remains unsatisfactory. Consequently, either the diagnosis of the case is clear from the start, or in the discussion over details regarding a differential diagnosis nothing is decided.

Classification grows even more difficult for the disorders in Group III. There is neither a sharp line separating illness from health, nor are there definite boundaries between the different types of disorders. For both of these reasons some researchers have suggested that disorders in this group should be conceived along dimensional scales. Moreover, this absence of sharp boundaries renders diagnosis extremely difficult. All too often, multiple diagnoses apply to the same case.

The concept of a disease may prove to be a helpful guiding idea even with Group III disorders. Obsessive-compulsive disorders, for example, are beginning to reveal some disease-like characteristics (Zohar and Insel, 1987). For most of the Group III disorders, however, the concept of disease helps very little. The features of these disorders are rich and diverse and vary greatly from individual to individual. Group III disorders, a sizable group of disorders currently thought by public consensus to be problems that psychiatrists should treat, are the disorders that we believe are best illuminated through the guiding idea of ideal types.

Jaspers claimed that for the Group III disorders we should employ types to carry out an extensive analysis of each individual case. These analyses would investigate the phenomenological, meaningful, and causal aspects of the case so as to illuminate the precise features of the patient's personality, its reactions, and life history.

In conclusion, we submit that at present psychiatrists can make the following claims. (a) Some psychiatric disorders, the Group I disorders, are definitely diseases. (b) Schizophrenia and manic-depressive illness look like diseases to most investigators, but we must remember that they remain types. Only future research will determine their true nature. In the meantime, psychiatrists should investigate them from a variety of theoretical perspectives. (c) Some human problems are currently thought by public consensus to be problems that psychiatrists should treat because in important respects these problems resemble disorders in Groups I and II. At present, however, there are no clear-cut boundaries between these psychiatric problems and other nonpsychiatric problems; for this reason, psychiatrists who treat and study these problems should remain open to manifold points of view on them.

In closing, we would like to indicate briefly our view of the role of value judgments in delimiting the field of psychiatric disorders.

At the outset it must be said that many different values play many different roles in medicine and psychiatry. This fact has received attention in a growing number of books and articles on medical ethics, bioethics, nursing ethics, and psychiatric ethics (Fulford, 1989). Furthermore, even these numerous books, we suspect, only begin to illuminate the extent of evaluations in the health care professions.

More specifically, however, we would like to claim that value judgments do play a role in actually delimiting what counts as a mental disorder (Fulford,

1989). They play some role when illnesses in Group I are deemed human problems worthy of medical or psychiatric treatment. Evaluations play a larger role in determining that schizophrenia and manic-depressive illness are problems that fall within the province of psychiatry. Evaluations play their largest role in decisions to include the many problems in Group III in the field of psychiatry. Thus the three groups we have distinguished above, following Jaspers, help to explain why the disorders in Group III are those whose genuinely psychiatric status is most often disputed. Of course, some critics would even dispute the legitimacy of viewing what is called *schizophrenia* and *manic- depressive* illness as psychiatric illnesses. The intractable nature of this dispute indicates, we think, that value judgments are indeed at work here in shaping the opposing attitudes.

UNITY IN THE DIVERSE FIELD OF PSYCHIATRY

We have maintained that, even though value judgments influence psychiatric categorization, the concept of disease can aid in structuring the field of classuffocation. Some psychiatric illnesses, for example Alzheimer's disease, definitely are diseases. Furthermore, the concept of disease can function as a guiding idea in investigating schizophrenia, manic-depressive illness, and many other mental disorders. But at least at the present time we cannot actually characterize schizophrenia and manic-depressive illness as diseases. When we attempt to formulate what we do know about such illnesses, we must conceive them, as well as almost all other mental disorders, as ideal types.

We have explained what it means to speak of psychiatric classifications as ideal types. By using ideal types we honestly concede our partial ignorance and partial knowledge of mental disorders. Ideal types lie halfway between the arbitrariness of nominalistic concepts and the validity of naturalistic concepts. Because of the arbitrariness of ideal types, they can be employed as polythetic concepts, prototypes, or dimensions, depending on one's psychiatric purposes.

Conceding our partial ignorance of almost all mental disorders also entails an openness to a wide variety of research programs in present-day psychiatry. Since no research program has proven its superiority by resolving the major questions that confront psychiatrists, no research program can claim the right to monopolize the field. A multiplicity of diverse research projects can thrive while the field nevertheless achieves its systematic unity in a manual that classifies most mental disorders as ideal types.

3   Taxonomic Puzzles

JOSEPH MARGOLIS, Ph.D.

There is, in professional psychiatry, a distinctly optimistic sense, looking forward to the completion of DSM-IV, which holds that DSM-III (1980) and DSM-III-R (1987) marked a large advance over DSM-II (1968) in the scientific taxonomy of mental disorders. Moreover, precisely in admitting the need for further revision, elimination of inconsistency, improvement along the lines of diagnostic reliability, increase in systematic unity, incorporation of new data, and the like, the new *Manual* might have been counted on to add to that improvement. Nevertheless, there are grounds for serious doubts about what those achievements were and what those now being projected actually signify. These doubts originate in the wider questioning of the scientific process which has taken place over the same time period that produced the various DSMs. Serious questions arise regarding scientific methodology, the nature of science, scientific laws and explanations, natural-kind and functional classifications, operational definitions—questions also arise about, among other things, the relation between the mental and the physical, the historical dimension of human behavior, and the analysis of cognitive states.

These matters are not adequately reflected in the taxonomic discussions looking beyond DSM-III. They do, however, bear in an important, even potentially radical, way on the orientation and reception of DSM-IV.

This is not to say that the current DSM conceptual orientation could not, if relatively unchanged, still be counted on to legitimate the improvement of IV as well. Rather, it is only that the seeming progress of the DSMs cannot fail to appear more an artifact of a model of science which once prevailed during (but which has been increasingly challenged since) the interval from II to III (and even III-R). In a word: the theory of science, we now realize, has a quite dramatic history of its own; recent changes in that history have very seriously challenged the largest, most fundamental assumptions of the general model of the physical sciences belonging to the unity-of-science program. This latter program both set the norm and paradigm for every genuine science (a fortiori, psychiatry) during the second and third quarters of this century and was actually consulted in the formation of the taxonomy of DSM-III (see the Appendix). Were the most daring of those changes to be permitted now to influence the recasting of DSM-IV, the taxonomy that would result would be very different with respect to certain diagnostic categories (e.g., Schizophrenia); might well be very differently interpreted, even if they were not very differently defined operationally (e.g., the Anxiety and Sexual Disorders); and might well be seen *not* to form anything like the increasingly unified scientific taxonomy that the work on III and III-R (and, now, IV) has generally been thought to yield.

These are matters serious enough to invite a pause and a moment's reflection. They have always been at least incipiently threatening in discussions about mental disorders—largely polarized between medically and culturally oriented conceptions that have tried to interpret behavioral manifestations more or less congruently with the exclusive use of their own particular models. (The pertinent literature has plainly exasperated both sides.) However, now, the very presumption of an ideally adequate model of science, itself transhistorically constant and fitted with equal felicity to physics and psychiatry, has been judged, on conceptual grounds, to be far more uncertain than was once supposed. The principal (pertinent) casualty that would result from actually favoring the more radical views being hinted at would, of course, be the prevailing sense (in psychiatric circles) of the very meaning of a scientific taxonomy.

This is not likely to be readily admitted. Also, the improvements anticipated in preparing for DSM-IV are not likely to reflect, at the deepest conceptual level, the wholesale revision of the idea of a scientific taxonomy reflected in the interval from II to III-R. It may even be that resistance to the most radical revisionism would actually serve the best (clinical) diagnostic and therapeutic objectives of psychiatry, although at the price of not being entirely up to date on the philosophy of science which the earlier *Manuals* had favored. It may also be that the theory of science itself may now need to fall back from a confident account of the essentials of every bona fide science. Instead, science may be turning to an informal heuristic regulative vision that introduces irregularities in actual scientific practices just at the point of securing a measure of conceptual economy. Still, these concessions recommend a detour from proceeding with an improved taxonomy, toward describing the meaning of making a revision (hence, improving) the extant scientific taxonomy.

It may be useful to summarize the principal themes of the model of science favored by the so-called unity-of-science program which prevailed during the DSM-III–DSM-III-R interval. The authors of the *Manuals* did not explicitly subscribe to this model, but they clearly favored its general themes. They included at least the following: (a) explanation under covering law; that is, the deducibility of explananda from exceptionless laws of nature and initial conditions (or, where necessary, probabilized laws approximating some exception-less limit of variation); (b) physicalism, that is, the reducibility of scientific discourse to terms suited to physics or biology, in terms of which pertinent laws may be formulated (or, where currently impossible, the preference for terms promising such a reduction); and (c) extensionalism, that is, constraints on the logical features of scientific discourse so as to eliminate all idioms that do not conform with the formal requirements of the canons of deductive logic (e.g., so-called first-order predicate logic or, where currently impossible, the preference of idioms promising such conformity). These conditions describe only a minimal sense of the unity model that once nearly monopolized the theory of science—and, even today, continues to exert a strong claim on the theorizing loyalties of all scientists.

ETIOLOGICAL MUDDLE IN APPROACHING THE REVISIONS

The taxonomic considerations governing DSM-III are mixed and muddied. They may well have had to be. Indeed, such considerations may still have to be muddied—looking ahead to DSM-IV. There may not be a viable alternative.

DSM-III-R introduced a number of substantial taxonomic changes, but the arguments in support of them are unsatisfactory when viewed in terms of prevailing notions of what a scientific taxonomy ought to be like. III, it is often said, both by its critics and its champions, was deliberately atheoretical—which is to say, naive about the conditions under which a systematic taxonomy could be attempted and confessedly ignorant about a great many of the etiological conditions such a taxonomy ought (eventually) to capture in its details. The sense of this is already plain in Spitzer's introduction to DSM-III (American Psychiatric Association, 1980). In fact, the principal complaints against III are rather openly conceded by Spitzer himself. They are worth reviewing because they identify the persisting taxonomic difficulties of the entire undertaking now advancing toward IV.

In a recent review of DSM-III, Spitzer (Spitzer & Williams, 1988a) explicitly said (once again) that DSM-III "takes an atheoretical approach with respect to etiology" (p. 84). He justifies the policy on the following grounds: "given our present state of ignorance about etiology, we should avoid including etiological assumptions in the definitions of the various mental disorders, so that people who have different theories about etiology can at least agree on the features of the various disorders without having to agree on how those disorders came about . . . the diagnosis [of, say, a phobia or panic disorder with agoraphobia] is made on the basis of descriptive features and not on the basis of any particular etiologic theory" (p. 84). The same point appears in Spitzer's introduction to DSM-III (American Psychiatric Association, 1980, pp. 6–7). It is also quite clear, there, that a good deal of the work of II as well as of III was guided by the need to remain as consistent as possible with the classification of *The International Classification of Diseases* (ICD-8 and ICD-9, respectively, for DSM-II and DSM-III), while recognizing an unmanageable variety of theoretical orientations at work in American clinical psychiatry. The concession, however, incorporates its own penalty. Whatever the charm of its candor, it cannot be convincingly argued that an atheoretical approach to taxonomy is inherently also theoretically neutral to the development of an adequate taxonomy. The matter cannot be assessed without examining just the detailed classificatory tendencies that the older classifications have favored—and DSM-IV seems disposed to favor.

Certainly, the master theme guiding III is this: to maximize descriptive consensus on the diagnostic categories ranging over all admissible clinical practices and pertinent theoretical orientations, without risking an explicit linkage to any particular such orientation and without sustained attention to the theoretical rationales of the particular practices canvassed. (The candor of this deliberate policy is quite bracing.) Nevertheless, Spitzer was entirely frank to admit that Adolf Meyer's reactive model of mental disorders, which was reflected in DSM-I (American Psychiatric Association, 1952), was specifically retired in favor of "a decision . . . to base" the classification of II on ICD-8, to which the American Psychiatric Association "had provided consultation" (p. 7). In preparing III, the Task Force on Nomenclature and Statistics (which Spitzer led as chairperson) canvassed American clinical practices, with some consultation (chiefly) from Britain and Germany, with an eye to making an American consensus at the descriptive level—without deep theoretical agreement, without a primary emphasis on etiology, and largely in terms of an empirical sense of diagnostic practice.

In Spitzer's own view (Spitzer & Williams, 1988b), DSM-III-R is more "Kraepelinian" than DSM-III (p. 269), offers a "reorganization" of Axes I and II and a "revision" of Axes IV and V, worries about the "clinical utility" of Axis IV (concerned with the severity of psychosocial stressors), favors the overall "consistency" of the "format" of the taxonomy both in terms of the "index of items" among the diagnostic criteria collected and regarding "the way clinicians tend to think of the taxonomy." (The last feature is admittedly specified in the narrower context of personality disorders, but it accords with the general disposition of DSM-III-R.) Nevertheless, DSM-III-R is recommended as "more useful [than III] to clinicians and researchers," without attention to the theoretically implicated changes and constancies that III-R actually introduces (p. 272).

More recently still, Spitzer (Spitzer, Williams, First & Kendler, 1989) took due notice of "advances in knowledge about the etiology of mental disorders" (p. 126), which (he believed) enabled him (now) to offer a resolution of the so-called *organic/nonorganic* problem that has dogged both III and III-R, which entails a closer use of Axis III (concerning physical disorders and conditions) than had previously been possible, and which had occasioned a considerable theoretical worry (see, e.g., Taylor, 1987) regarding DSM-III. The admission of the puzzle and its line of resolution betray the tacit but deep theoretical presumptions underlying the shifting work of all of the *Manuals*. Moreover, the approach to resolving the etiology puzzle reveals the considerable threat that the new taxonomy might well remain just as mixed and muddied as before, if the pertinent methodological questions are not confronted.

TAXONOMIC CONSENSUS AND DESCRIPTIVE "DRIFT"

There are several quite elementary but extraordinarily powerful conceptual difficulties built into the structure of DSM-III. At least three are explicitly featured in Spitzer's introduction (American Psychiatric Association, 1980) under the heading of "Basic Concepts." They cannot be removed by faulting Spitzer's formulation; they appear to be quite fundamental to the taxonomic orientation of III and betray elements of a large conceptual commitment. As we shall see, this bears instructively on the supposedly operational definition of diagnostic categories and the underlying anticipation of an improved approximation to a scientific taxonomy——one that corresponds to natural-kind mental disorders; that is, a taxonomy that collects mental disorders in accord with pertinently specified covering laws (hence, the pertinence of the unity-of-science model). Here, we may anticipate that Hempel's well-known account of scientific taxonomy (Hempel, 1965b; Appendix, this book), originally presented at the Work Conference on Field Studies in the Mental Disorders, in 1959, and first published in 1961 (Zubin, 1961), either clearly influenced the taxonomic orientation of DSM-III or conformed very closely with the kind of thinking which must have provided the theorizing orientation favored by the original task force. (This is not to say that Hempel's views were ever explicitly adopted in the taxonomies. It is only that Hempel's formulation is very likely the best-known version of the unity model.)

Begin, then, with the following. "A common misconception is that a classification of mental disorders classifies individuals, when actually what are being classified are disorders that individuals have. For this reason, the text of DSM-III avoids the use of such phrases as 'a schizophrenic' or 'an alcoholic,' and instead uses the more accurate, but admittedly more wordy 'an individual with Schizophrenia' or 'an individual with Alcohol Dependence'" (American Psychiatric Association, 1980, p. 6).

It is certainly possible to define predicables or categories independent of their extension or scope, that is, independent of any mention of the individual examples of their defining features. It is well known that this cannot be done universally, particularly in empirical contexts. Where it is done locally (with respect to this or that taxonomic category) the prospect of effectively disjoining the relatively unchanging definition of such categories from any (in this case, clinical) field study of cases depends on the reliability with which such predicates conform (in some significant measure) to the invariant exceptionless covering laws to which (at least implicitly and ideally) they are supposed to correspond. In other words, classification, the use of general predicables (or predicates) depends on two different sorts of systematic consideration. With one, we extend given predicates to new cases by judging (rather informally) the resemblance between new candidate cases and the generally admitted exemplars of the categories to be employed. With the other, we extend given predicates to phenomena that are thought to fall under universal covering laws, which in their turn govern the extension of the predicates in question. One sees, therefore, the potential theoretical impact of accommodating an informal taxonomy of resemblances (without covering laws).

Deny strict nomological invariance, or approximate conformity to same, and at least two methodological difficulties arise which cannot be overcome in principle: one, that the *operational* meaning of the categories thus defined cannot be relied on to be constant or nearly constant under actual use; the other, that the very *definition* of the categories in question cannot be disjoined from a strongly *consensual* agreement on the *exemplars* (paradigms, prototypes, core instances) *of* those same categories.

These two difficulties go hand and hand. (They are, of course, difficulties only for those who suppose that the practice of science requires constancy of use regarding descriptive or diagnostic categories comparable to what, in principle, would obtain *if* a psychiatric taxonomy did fall under a discernible set of covering laws or did collect natural kinds that fell under covering laws.) The first corresponds to the well-known philosophical problem of universals— regarding just what is similar (or the same) in applying the same predicate to different particular things. The second corresponds to the equally well-known problem of the historically changing nature of empirical practice (for instance, the practice of the sciences). Here the empirical work inevitably involves a gradual (even an unperceived) shift in the selection and weighting of exemplary instances—that thereby change the theoretical import of independently evolving descriptions and classifications as well as the meaning of the operational categories thus employed (see Putnam, 1975a, 1975b).

So seen, the consensual emphasis of DSM-III actually *ensures* a slippage in the constancy of diagnostic categories (also, the relative imperceptibility of that slippage). For one thing, the very plan of the *Manual* was to reach diagnostic consensus—for a given initial interval, on the condition of a certain general etiological ignorance. Given that, it is impossible that the resulting taxonomy *could* remain constant or could be shown to be constant over its continued empirical life; that is, it already builds in, already obscures, the *divergence* of exemplars *in* the practice of all those consulted. For another thing, the *Manual* deliberately avoids specifying in any way just *which* individual cases could be regarded by all practitioners as working exemplars (and *why*), so that the drift of the categories employed could be effectively slowed. In short, Spitzer's scruple ensures just the reverse of what it sets out to strengthen. In doing that, the very use of the *Manual* creates the false, altogether misleading, completely artifactual, impression of the strict constancy of the *Manual*'s diagnostic categories. In a word, the perceived constancy of the taxonomy cannot but be an artifact of historically changing professional perception. Its apparent constancy cannot be justifiably anticipated to remain hospitable to the progressive discovery of pertinent lawlike regularities.

There are of course all sorts of consequences which follow from this naiveté: legal complications involving expert diagnostic judgment; the very portability of diagnostic judgment itself; unperceived misunderstanding within the profession which masquerades as continuing consensus. It is no accident that Andreasen (1987), reviewing the Bleulerian emphasis in the DSM-III account of schizophrenia, remarked that "current evidence suggests that delusions and hallucinations are not necessarily more reliable than other types of symptoms and that they may have . . . undue prominence in the criteria for schizophrenia" (p. 107); but even the alternatives she reviewed are not likely to be systematically more reliable *in the regard at stake here*.

Of course, one could argue that the *Manual* (DSM-III) *is* clinically, diagnostically, reliable. That would now mean something altogether different from the positivistic naiveté that supposed: (a) that the original consensus could be counted on to ensure taxonomic constancy, and (b) that constancy could, without substantial theoretical legitimation, be assumed to conform, along descriptive lines, to an etiologically obscure taxonomy that (still) managed to play a minimal role in directing the correction of the descriptive categories. If it were to succeed, it would be by sheer methodological magic. The general criticism that applies here is this: description and classification are never theory neutral. Even the explicit avoidance of a premature etiology cannot be protected against the unperceived skewing (theoretical or ideological) of the subsequent clinical perception of individual cases.

DESCRIPTIVE BOUNDARIES AND CLINICAL PRACTICE

A similar (and related) difficulty appears in some remarks (introduction, DSM-III) just before those already cited:

> In DSM-III there is no assumption that each mental disorder is a discrete entity with sharp boundaries (discontinuity) between it and other mental disorders, as well as between it and No Mental Disorder. For example, there has been a continuing controversy as to whether or not severe depressive disorder and mild depressive disorder differ from each other qualitatively (discontinuity between diagnostic entities) or quantitatively (a difference on a severity continuum). The inclusion of Major Depression With and Without Melancholia as separate categories in DSM-III

is justified by the clinical usefulness of the distinction. This does not imply a resolution of the controversy as to whether or not these conditions are in fact quantitatively or qualitatively different. (American Psychiatric Association, 1980, p. 6)

The significance of this considerable informality may be missed entirely. (It reappears, virtually unchanged, in DSM-III-R.) The fact is that the question of whether severe and mild depressive disorders are or are not separate categories *does not arise at all*: it is not merely provisionally unresolved. Even the question of whether depression and no depression (No Mental Disorder) are, diagnostically, different categories does not really arise in any strict sense, and that is astonishing. There are a number of taxonomic essentials ignored here: (a) no anchoring etiology for the set of categories contested; (b) no formally agreed-on exemplars, or exemplars by which to guide the extension, case by case, of descriptive terms to new candidate instances; and (c) no overarching theory informing the taxonomy that includes the contested categories. There *was* obviously *some* initial empirical consensus on the use of the diagnostic and descriptive categories, taken abstractly——that is, taken either without reference to any constant well-articulated exemplars or else supported (consensually) only by reference to whatever local specimen cases the diverse clinical practitioners happened to favor. Thus, the unpleasant truth stares us in the face: given the same diagnostic categories, given the different exemplars favored by different practitioners and not typically favored by all, given all of the different ways of extending the use of the same categories to new cases not shared by all practitioners, it is entirely possible (even likely) that what, on one practice, is counted as mild depressive disorder is, on another, counted as no mental disorder at all——*legitimately*. (In a related vein, see Dr. Russell's chapter for a detailed discussion about some sample categories.)

Now, the goal of DSM-III expressly included reducing idiosyncratic diagnosis (Skodol & Spitzer, 1982); but, clearly, it has gone about it in an impossible way. Short of reaching dramatic etiological gains——nomologically exceptionless regularities, for example——it may even be the case (say, regarding mild depression) that there *is* no conceivable way of bringing idiosyncratic practice down below a very high tolerance for such idiosyncrasy. On the other hand, it may be that the implicated model of scientific taxonomy is entirely unrealistic for psychiatry.

THE MULTIAXIAL SYSTEM: OPERATIONALISM IN OPPOSITION

Finally, along related but more troublesome lines, Spitzer's introduction reported accurately the following (which nearly repeats the definition of *mental disorder* in the glossary):

In DSM-III each of the mental disorders is conceptualized as a clinically significant behavioral or psychological syndrome or pattern that occurs in an individual and that is typically associated with either a painful symptom (distress) or impairment in one or more important areas of functioning (disability). In addition, there is an inference that there is a behavioral, psychological, or biological dysfunction, and that the disturbance is not only in the relationship between the individual and society. (When the disturbance is *limited* to a conflict between an individual and society, this may represent social deviance, which may or may not be commendable, but is not by itself a mental disorder.) (American Psychiatric Association, 1980, p. 6)

The guiding conception here is taxonomically quite perplexing. For one thing, there is no systematic treatment of the distinction intended by "behavioral, psychological, or biological dysfunction." There is, in fact, no serious account of the meaning of *psychological* dysfunction, by the psychologically *functional* and *dysfunctional* (in a clinical sense), or by *mental* in speaking of *mental disorder*. What, after all, is a clinically significant *impairment* in a behavioral or psychological mode of functioning? What is the relationship between behavioral and psychological modes of functioning? What, operationally, is the difference between a behavioral or psychological dysfunction and a mere disturbance . . . *limited* to a conflict between an individual and society?

In context, these are all gratuitous questions. There is absolutely nothing in the construction of the taxonomy which would permit us to provide a measured control or a reduction of the idiosyncratic use of these clinical categories. In fact, without a developed etiology, there could be no principled demarcation between psychological dysfunction and conflict between individual and society. Any such functional distinction, consensually fixed, lacking etiological foundation——lacking an etiology that was not itself grounded in one or another of the parameters of intrasocietal conflict——also lacking theoretical justification, could be little more than an artifact of idiosyncratic clinical practice. As it stands, the distinction is entirely ideal, though its intent is clear enough.

Furthermore, there is no reason supplied for supposing that any increased clinical consensus at the descriptive or diagnostic level would bear on systematizing our conception of distinct behavioral and psychological modes of functioning or their eventual reconciliation with an etiology conformable with covering laws or the strong disjunction between such modes of functioning and mere conflict limited as between individual and society. The point seems clear enough if we bear in mind the DSM-III inclusion of Sexual Sadism and Sexual Masochism (or the DSM-III-R inclusion of Sadistic Personality Disorder and Self-Defeating Personality Disorder). For one thing, if functional disorders (*however* specified) are not linked, directly or indirectly, to known lawlike regularities, then their fixity remains at the mercy of consensual (interclinician) factors. Furthermore, those same disorders, as already remarked, are bound to diverge and vary with the history of the way in which diagnostic categories are effectively extended. For another, there is no obvious alternative to distinguishing between the functioning intended and considerations regarding social conflict; *and* none is actually offered.

Again, the full relevance, for the taxonomy, of Axes III, IV, and V is unclear. Both Axes IV and V specifically address potential psychosocial "conflict" factors. In Chapter 2 of the *Manual* ("Use of This Manual"), Axes I and II are said to "comprise the entire classification of mental disorders" (American Psychiatric Association, 1980, p. 23); yet Axis IV is also said to provide "a coding of the overall severity of a stressor judged to have been a significant contributor to the development or exacerbation of the current disorder" (p. 29). In context, this surely challenges any clear disjunction between the onset of a mental disorder aggravated by a psychosocial conflict and a mental disorder due, partly due, or due in some significant part, to such a conflict. Again, Sadistic Personality Disorder (DSM-III-R) affords a fair test case. In DSM-III, psychosocial stressors are admitted to be etiologically significant (p. 27), but there is no operational criterion provided for determining when a behavioral or psychological disturbance is strictly limited to a psychosocial conflict; the very idea of such a precision seems altogether out of line with the generally relaxed consensual orientation of DSM-III under the conditions already outlined. We simply do not know, operationally, the relationship between the use of Axes I and II and Axis IV. By the same argument, we cannot be sure about the bearing of Axis V, both because Axis V includes clinically relevant psychosocial relations (construed in terms of a prior year's adaptive functioning) and because, though the axis is expressly marked for its "great prognostic significance" (p. 28), no reason is supplied for not supposing that such significance is also diagnostically linked to Axis IV and thence to Axes I and II, which, of course, were never satisfactorily disjoined from Axis IV in the first place.

Furthermore, in the introduction to DSM-III-R (American Psychiatric Association, 1987), Spitzer (who also served as chairperson of the work group to revise DSM-III) specifically mentioned the possibility, looking ahead to DSM-IV, of entertaining "a proposal for a new diagnostic class of disorders associated with psychosocial stress"——one said to have been "premature for consideration in DSM-III-R, and [which would fall] more properly within the scope of DSM-IV" (p. xxi). The implication that such a category would have been operationally ruled out by DSM-III-R would, however, be too sanguine. (The glossary entry actually does allow for the possibility of a bonafide *mental disorder* involving but not limited to psychosocial stress.)

Spitzer expressly indicated (introduction, DSM-III) that "Axes I and II include all of the mental disorders" (American Psychiatric Association, p. 8). (*Mental*, by the way, is meant to range over *behavioral* and *psychological*.) There is a telling concession offered in this context which eventually complicates the new distinctions of DSM-III-R:

Axis III is for physical disorders and conditions. The separation of this axis from the mental disorders axes, is based on the tradition of separating those disorders whose manifestations are primarily behavioral or psychological (i.e., mental disorders) from those whose manifestations are not. It is necessary to have a term that can be applied to all of the disorders that are not considered "mental disorders." The phrase "organic disorder" would incorrectly imply the absence of physical factors in "mental" disorders. Hence, this manual uses the term "physical disorder," recognizing that the boundaries for these two classes of disorder ("mental" and "physical" disorders) change as our understanding of the psychophysiology of these disorders increases. (American Psychiatric Association, 1980, p. 8)

Spitzer suggested here that it is an etiological question open to new findings as to whether disorders now classified as *mental* may not prove to be *physical* (or, presumably, vice versa). However, he failed to supply——the whole DSM-III failed to supply——a working distinction between the *mental* and the *physical*. It is not even clear what Spitzer means in warning us that *organic disorder* "would incorrectly imply the absence of physical factors in mental disorders." For, it could mean that the mental and the physical are not, as such, disjunctive categories at all——which of course is true, on any view that would avoid the classical forms of dualism (Margolis, 1989). It could also mean that conceding a taxonomic distinction between *mental disorder* and *physical disorder*, there may be contributing physical factors regularly implicated in disorders correctly diagnosed as mental——which is what Spitzer apparently did mean. But it could also mean that there is *no* operational demarcation between *mental disorder* and *physical disorder* within the taxonomy itself, simply because there is no mental factor that is not so complex as not to include, intrinsically, factors that, on any familiar view, would also be characterized as physical. On this view, for instance, thinking itself could not be separated in principle from the underlying neurophysiological processes from which it is supposed to be abstracted or without specific reference to which it may be phenomenologically recognized (reflexively or in some way mediated by behavior). Finally, in DSM-III-R, *physical disorder* serves "merely as a shorthand" for "referring" to all of those conditions and disorders which are listed outside the mental disorders section of the ICD (American Psychiatric Association, 1987, p. xxv). The point may be put succinctly. If (e.g., to avoid theoretical dualisms between mind and body) *mental* phenomena already incorporate physical elements (as in the characterization *of* emotions in terms of changes in pulse, body temperature, perspiration, etc.), then the taxonomic distinction between the mental and the physical cannot fail to become problematic. On the other hand, there are no satisfactorily reliable lawlike connections involving the mental wherever the mental is strongly disjoined from the physical, and the fixity of mental predicates is notoriously unreliable.

The matter is notoriously difficult. But the entire rationale of Axes I–V clearly depends on what DSM-III simply fails to supply, namely, an operational distinction between *mental disorder* and physical disorder which is etiologically focused (even if not yet altogether satisfactorily). It is plain that any useful distinction here (looking forward to DSM-IV) would have to identify, and differentially weight, *certain* etiological factors (or certain diagnostic features strongly favoring the pertinent etiology) that would *count* as mental rather than as physical, without regard to the eventual (metaphysical) resolution of the famous mind-body problem. However, no reform of this sort could possibly be introduced as an improvement of the sort wanted, without resolving the puzzles regarding descriptive categories and attributions to particulars, as mentioned above. We may, in fact, now claim, with considerable justice, that the very meaning of our diagnostic categories is, inseparably, a function of their use in making attributions to the paradigm cases that we (somehow) do fix in the diverse clinical practices we support. Stated more conventionally: in the empirical order of things, and in the absence of any reliable nomological universals (psychological, psychophysical, psychiatric, psychoneurological laws), there is no way to treat the connotation and denotation, or the intension and extension, of terms disjointly. The opposing view is a fiction that dies hard, but it is just the fiction that informs DSM-III. Furthermore, the lesson still holds——whether or not our paradigms are constant and whether or not they are diverse. The fact remains that the reliability of our categories depends on the fixity of our paradigms *and* on the reliable consensual convergence of continuing, *independent* extension to new cases of the pertinent predicates, on the strength of some initial agreement on how to apply the taxonomy. Without intervening laws, this confidence, as we have seen, cannot be robustly confirmed. The relative constancy of the diagnostic vocabulary that now obtains cannot be greater than that of a relatively homogeneous family of dialects within a common natural language. Also, if we add here the bare possibility that our descriptive powers have a distinctive and freely evolving history and are (also) tacitly preformed by the local cultural orientation of the different societies to which we belong, then the encompassing naiveté of the theme of descriptive consensus the *Manuals* favor is at once much easier to grasp. The theme, of course, is strongly featured in late 20th-century thought.

HEMPEL'S UNITY-OF-SCIENCE MODEL AND PSYCHIATRIC CLASSIFICATION

The adjustments made in DSM-III-R were strongly influenced by a desire for a more disciplined consensus within the American Psychiatric Association, a reliance on accelerating empirical discoveries, an attention to challenges to DSM-III itself, a concern for the continued usefulness of the taxonomy in clinical and research contexts, a resistance to any reliance on particular psychodynamic or related theories, the ensuring of compatibility with ICD-9, and, above all, a preference for *operationalized* diagnostic criteria (American Psychiatric Association, 1987, p. xxi).

These are very plausible objectives. However, the scrupulous pursuit of any or all of them—particularly the last—cannot, by itself reliably lead in the direction of a scientific taxonomy as envisaged, for instance, by the unity-of-science program. (Also, of course, any more informal conception of a scientific taxonomy will have to accommodate the possibility of an increased informality on taxonomic consensus.) In fact, we may suppose that the strong empirical enthusiasm with which the reforms pursued from III to III-R (and, now, on to IV) could never lead to a fully scientific taxonomy unless we could be sure of the validity of a strong inductivism—something close to the spirit of Mill's canons (Mill, 1974). Such an empiricism now seems hopelessly outmoded, although inductivism of course continues to be disputed. In any case, the progress made through III-R focuses attention on several important conceptual puzzles regarding taxonomies: for one, the relation between operationalized terms and a scientific taxonomy informed by the unity-of-science program; for a second, the relation between operationalized diagnostic terms and functional categories, in which nomologically favored constraints may or may not obtain. (By *operationalized* we mean no more than that criteria of application are in place. The trouble is that such criteria are hardly more reliable than the disorders that they operationalize. Hence, in principle, the criteria would have to be operationalized in turn. There is no prospect of such a practice leading to *increased* consensual conformity or, for that matter, to such conformity's anticipating pertinent lawlike regularities. By *functional categories* no more is meant than what the *Manuals* themselves propose. It is also helpful to bear in mind that DSM-III-R modifies the notion of a mental disorder so that even deviant behavior involving psychosocial conflict could be construed as such a disorder, provided only that such deviance [or conflict] were [also] "a symptom of a dysfunction in the person" [as defined in DSM-III] [American Psychiatric Association, 1980, p. xxii].) These issues lead directly and inexorably to the argument of Hempel's well-known account of taxonomy (Hempel, 1965b; Appendix, this book), which, it is reasonable to suppose, has had a strong and continuing influence on the optimistic thinking of the task force for DSM-III and the work group for DSM-III-R. Certainly, if Hempel's own views have not been explicitly followed, the presumption of a reliable taxonomic consensus must incline toward something very much like his view or else, under the conditions of decentralized professional practice, it must risk the serious threat of an unmanageable taxonomy.

Hempel's account is entirely straightforward—dismayingly so, one may say, given the unlikelihood that the classification featuring *mental disorders* could be expected to move reliably in the direction that Hempel favors:

> The vocabulary of science [he said] has two basic functions: first, to permit an adequate *description* of the things and events that are the objects of scientific investigation; second, to permit the establishment of general laws or theories by

means of which particular events may be *explained* and *predicted* and thus *scientifically understood*; for to understand a phenomenon scientifically is to show that it occurs in accordance with general laws or theoretical principles. (Hempel, 1965b, p. 139)

DSM-III and DSM-III-R are neither scientific taxonomies of Hempel's sort nor promisingly directed to evolving into such taxonomies. Descriptive consensus in diagnostic (and/or research) terms has very little to do with conforming to the strong covering-law model of explanation Hempel favored (Hempel, 1965c, 1965d). This is particularly true given that the *Manuals* have been expressly constructed on the assumption of considerable ignorance about etiological factors, with the intention of avoiding all strenuous theoretical disagreements, and without possessing any strong or exceptionless psychiatric laws.

In fact, on Hempel's view (doubtless, on the view of those who intend to operationalize the *Manual*), a scientifically satisfactory classification "may be thought of as defined by the specification of necessary and sufficient conditions of membership in it [that is, its subclasses], i.e., by stating certain characteristics which all and only the members of the class possess" (Hempel, 1965b, p. 138). Without a strong physicalism (which Hempel favored), it would be quite impossible for the descriptive consensus the recent DSMs claim to be able to satisfy (or even approximate in any measure) this very severe condition. The informality of the consensus is against it; ignorance of etiology adds to its unlikelihood; but, most of all, the strong intentionality of the descriptive terms themselves—the very emphasis on psychological, behavioral, psychosocial symptoms, and the unlikelihood of conceptually reducing such descriptive terms to mere physical descriptions of any kind—confirm the alien nature of Hempel's model. This is not to insist on Hempel's model (or other versions of the unity-of-science model). There may well be a benefit in the informal consensus of the psychiatric categories. However, it is difficult to argue that such informality also contributes to a scientific taxonomy.

It is simply false to hold (e.g., with Hempel) that, under current conditions, we are temporally restricted to an explanation sketch in which, at the end of inquiry, we should have arrived *at* a fully scientific explanation: one that would place *mental disorders* uncompromisingly under universal covering laws—from which they could then be formally deduced. Hempel's tolerance of explanation sketches signifies an unshakable conviction in physical reduction, exceptionless laws of nature, the provisionality of intentionally complex terms (distinctions of thought, mood, affect) and the like, and the merely inessential contingencies of current scientific data. (By an *explanation sketch* Hempel means no more than an informal explanation that, for lack of scientific knowledge, cannot yet be a full-fledged explanation under the covering-law model, but is promisingly in accord with that ideal.) It is true enough that some adherents of the unity model have attempted to avoid the strong reductionism of Hempel's own model (e.g., Grünbaum, 1984), but they have not been able to demonstrate that the intentional complexity of clinically pertinent descriptions (e.g., in psychoanalysis) can be made to behave in anything like the extensionally reliable way the observational terms of the physical sciences do. In fact, it is (also) one of the most troubling consequences of recent radical shifts in the philosophy of science ushered in largely by Kuhn's work (1970). Kuhn demonstrated that the methodology of science could not be disjoined from the history of its actual practice—that even the meaning of the terms of the strongest physical sciences are affected (intentionally) by the tacit history of their use, in particular by the shifting theories in accord with which they are actually used. All of this is almost completely neglected by those who prepared DSM-III and DSM-III-R. The taxonomy itself, however, cannot but be profoundly affected by such changes in our picture of science. Put very simply: the best prospects for a scientific taxonomy appear to depend on the adequacy of something like the unity-of-science model. We have already seen that the *Manuals* are not easily reconciled with that model. The new history and philosophy of science now emphasize the inherently historical nature of scientific theory and description. However, *that* was just what threatened the consensual convergence of the various taxonomies the *Manuals* proposed. Under these altered circumstances, we can only expect an acceleration in the relatively undetected slippage of the diagnostic categories.

Hempel's model is too sanguine. Hempel interpreted our failure to approximate to that model as a sign of temporary scientific ignorance, *not* as a mark of the conceptual inappropriateness of the model itself. Moreover, a strong inductivism construed (naively) along empirical lines is just the orientation that would have led the authors of the *Manuals* to suppose that their own emphasis on diagnostic consensus *would*, if extended, eventually lead to realizing the objectives of Hempel's model. In a word, if scientific laws are not strictly exceptionless, or if statistical laws do not tend, in the long run, to approximate to a fixed limit, then an inductivism of the sort favored could not—on any principle, however generous—be counted on to lead in the direction of a lawlike etiology (even if there were such an etiology to be discovered). Hempel himself, as we have said, invariably treated the failure to discover exceptionless laws as a sign of the temporary cognitive limitation of the pertinent sciences (e.g., Hempel, 1965c, p. 238; 1965d, p. 263). More recently, the very idea of exceptionless laws of nature has been compellingly challenged as a distorting fiction or as empirically unsupportable, excessive, even unnecessary as a characterization of the real world (van Fraassen, 1989). This may surprise psychiatrists who have held to a model of science very much like Hempel's. Precisely because DSM-III and DSM-III-R were constructed with a careful methodology detached from a companion inquiry into an adequate explanatory theory and etiology of *mental disorder*, increasingly radical challenges to the plausibility of the unity model (Hempel's), that had once seemed so reliable and incontestable, cannot fail to raise serious questions about the rationales of III and III-R. It is, frankly, difficult to imagine a model that, if correct, would be more unfavorable to the informality of diagnostic practices. We shall have to confine ourselves, however, to the two questions broached earlier.

ON OPERATIONALISM AND THE HEMPELIAN IMPERATIVE

Turn, then, to the first of these: the relationship between operationalized terms and a scientific taxonomy. It is one of the great ironies of the scientific scruple of DSM-III and III-R that, whereas they sought to operationalize diagnostic criteria, Hempel himself (Hempel, 1965a) firmly believed that operationalism "would [actually] eliminate the psychologistic notion of mental operations in favor of a specification of the logico-mathematical concepts and procedures to be permitted in the context of operational definition"——no matter how much broadened beyond Bridgman's original conception (p. 127). No doubt a sort of operationalism could still be formulated which would favor the intention of the *Manuals*. However, there is no evidence that their construction actually reflects the conceptual difficulties involved in ensuring the reliability of the diagnostic consensus supposed, the constancy of the meaning of the terms involved, or the progress on new empirical findings which would lead diagnostic categories in the direction of the covering-law model.

The sense in which the *Manuals* do approximate a scientific taxonomy is simply unclear, except in aspiration. Hempel himself was quite explicit about the importance of adhering to "the [strict] observational vocabulary of science" (1965b, p. 127). What he meant was, precisely, that mental operations (hence, mental disorders) *are themselves theoretical notions in need of being operationalized*. He took Bridgman to have failed in this regard (Bridgman, 1927, 1945a, 1945b, 1950–1951). He took the difficulty to be endemic to the use of theoretical terms, and he was prepared to retreat to a "partial specification of meaning" in observational terms (1927, p. 130). That very admission profoundly affects the notion of the linkage between consensual agreement and a nomologically governed taxonomy.

In the taxonomy paper, Hempel (1965b) explicitly said:

> In medical science, the development from a predominantly descriptive to an increasingly theoretical emphasis is reflected . . . in the transition from a largely symptomatological to a more and more etiological point of view. Etiology [however] should not be conceived as dealing with the "causes" of disease in a narrow sense of the term [but should, rather, be "replaced by a search of explanatory laws and theories"]. (p. 141)

However, in just these terms, the intention and practice of the methodological scruple of DSM-III and DSM-III-R diverge and produce an unbridgeable gap.

At the very least, the puzzle requires a methodologically pertinent response. (We need to bear in mind first, that the operationalizing practice of the *Manuals* is considerably more informal than anything Hempel would countenance; second, that Hempel's notion of operationalizing is fairly standard, even if the authors of the *Manuals* would not be willing to subscribe to them; and third, operationalizing concepts, without *some* reliance on nomological regularity, cannot fail to increase the informality with which the *Manuals* are applied.)

Now, apart from his own conceptual bias (his logical empiricism), Hempel was most instructive about the limitations and dangers of operational definitions. For our purposes, the most important qualification he mentioned is this: that "the operational criteria of application available for a term often amount to less than a full definition" (1965b, p. 143). What he meant, quite simply, is that, even granting that not all terms can be operationalized (without risking an infinite regress), granting that observation itself should count as a form of operationalizing a term, granting that theoretical terms probably cannot be all fully operationalized, it remains true nevertheless that operationalized definitions tend to yield no more than a *partial definition* or a *partial criterion of application* (1965b, p. 143). This means, first of all, that operationalizing terms in a merely consensual way has nothing to do with progressing toward a scientific taxonomy (i.e., on anything like the unity model). Second, Hempel himself drew attention to the use of *criteria with valuational overtones* in the original DSM-I (as evidence of *partial definition*——the example is the category of Inadequate Personality). Such practice constitutes, he said, a subjective factor; and, in a scientific taxonomy, we should, he said, "aim at a gradual reduction in [the] influence [of such factors]" (1965b, p. 146). There is, however, no evidence at all (in the *Manuals*) of ever abandoning the use of criteria with valuational overtones for the greater part of the mental disorders. (This influx of covert value commitments is discussed further in the chapters by Russell, Fulford, and Agich in this book.)

The mere retirement of certain (prejudiced) diagnostic categories regarding homosexuality and neurosis (but see DSM-III-R on Dysthymia, Anxiety Disorders, and on Sexual Disorder Not Otherwise Specified) and recent concerns about the antifeminist implications of such categories as Sexual Masochism and Self-Defeating Personality Disorder (when applied to women) show more an inclination to abandon certain diagnostic categories altogether than an inclination to revise their criteria in nonvaluational terms. Here, of course, the conceptual role of Axes IV and V are quite decisive——hence, the pointed importance of the questions we raised earlier about their conceptual (diagnostic) relationship to Axes I and II.

The decisive factor in Hempel's account lies in another quarter, however. For Hempel, no operationalizing of any sort contributes to a scientific taxonomy unless it "lend[s] itself to the formulation of general laws or theoretical principles which reflect uniformities in the subject matter under study, and which thus provide a basis for explanation, prediction, and generally scientific understanding" (1965b, p. 146). Operationalizing terms must contribute to their systematic import. DSM-III and DSM-III-R do not do that; do not even attempt to do that; certainly do not give evidence of being able to be made increasingly conformable with that. (In fact, the original notion [Bridgman, 1927] featured the significative rather than the nomological.) In a word, operationalizing *terms* or *concepts* must be brought into line with regimenting *statements* in accord with a genuinely scientific methodology——that of logical empiricism or the unity-of-science program, in Hempel's sense. Failing that, those who mean to revise the *Manual* to yield an improved DSM-IV along increasingly *operationalized* lines need to explain what *they* actually mean by *operationalizing* and what the sense is in which doing that strengthens our grip on a scientific taxonomy. Thus far, the methodological scruples of the *Manuals* appear to be unclear as well as unsatisfactory.

This brings us directly to the second of our questions: the relationship between operationalized terms and functional categories (in the sense the *Manuals* intend). Essentially, the DSMs are, as already remarked, functionally oriented. Some diagnostic categories (for instance, Dyspareunia) may appear relatively unproblematic. Others are more problematic. For instance, in DSM-III, "the essential feature [of the Psychosexual Dysfunctions] is inhibition in the appetitive or psychophysiological changes that characterize the complete sexual response cycle [divided along the lines of 'appetitive,' 'excitement,' 'orgasm,' and 'resolution']" (American Psychiatric Association, 1980, pp. 275– 276). However, we have also seen that III and III-R introduce more global forms of functional and dysfunctional considerations which cannot be centered in anything like the functioning of an organ or related response cycle, however attenuated. In fact, this is just the point of worry about the conceptual role of Axes IV and V. In Spitzer's introduction to DSM-III-R, we may note the following:

> In DSM-III-R each of the mental disorders is conceptualized as a clinically significant behavioral or psychological syndrome or pattern that occurs in a person and that is associated with present distress (a painful symptom) or disability (impairment in one or more important areas of functioning) or with a significantly increased risk of suffering death, pain, disability, or an important loss of freedom. In addition, this syndrome or pattern must not be merely an expectable response to a particular event, e.g., the death of a loved one. Whatever its original cause, it must currently be considered a manifestation of a behavioral, psychological, or biological dysfunction in the person. (American Psychiatric Association, 1987, p. xxii)

Clearly, we have here a potentially expanding series of functional and dysfunctional distinctions: pain (perhaps associated with the functioning of an organ or response cycle) and distress or disability associated with some more global psychological or behavioral mode of functioning, distress or risk to functional freedom and the like. The more global notions are nowhere theoretically defined or defended; they are most obviously connected with the intrusion (seemingly ineliminable) of criteria of valuational tone, and they cannot fail to affect the entire program of diagnostic consensus on which the *Manuals* depend. (Dr. Russell examines more closely the ambiguity of *distress* and other terms in her chapter in this book.)

Hempel's point in this regard (Hempel, 1965e) was simply that, as with operationalizing terms in general, functional categories or "functional analysis has to rely on general laws" (p. 309). He claimed that functional accounts favor statistical laws; and, in the context of the discussion of functionalism, he clearly indicated that this is a stopgap for analyses that genuinely invoke universal laws. Elsewhere (Hempel, 1965e), Hempel had second thoughts about the relationship between universal and statistical laws; and, as we have already suggested, current thinking about the realist interpretation of laws (particularly, of theoretical laws: exceptionless nomic universals) has rendered the entire issue somewhat moot. It seems reasonable, also, to suppose that Hempel had functional complications in mind in his account of operationalizing a taxonomy in psychological and sociological contexts, but the actual term does not seem to appear in the taxonomy paper.

In any case, the conceptual problem is a double one. First, what are we to make of *functional* categories that are *not* clearly linked to laws, whether general or statistical? Second, what are we to make of functional categories that exhibit relatively weak statistical lawlike regularities which we cannot be sure are actual approximations to strong, genuine lawful regularities? Certainly, in the face of the *Manuals'* deliberate avoidance of reaching a consensus on psychodynamic theory and the admitted weakness of psychiatry's command of etiology, we may conclude that it would be very difficult to operationalize the difference between these two possibilities. Functional regularities of a relatively global psychological or behavioral sort are, in fact, more in search of a nomic link than actually based on one. Hempel himself (1965e) was extremely skeptical about functional explanations, tending to treat them as usually guilty of a logical mistake; that is largely because of his strenuous commitment to a deductive/nomological model of explanation. So, for instance, the problem, he felt, could be resolved by shifting from strictly universal to statistical laws (1965e, p. 313); and, in general, functional explanations are said to depend on "a (general) hypothesis of self-regulation" (p. 317). Hempel also felt that, particularly "in psychology, sociology, and anthropology," the pertinent functional terms tended not to be used in an acceptably disciplined (empirical) way (pp. 321–322), which, if true, would lodge a serious complaint against the operationalizing habits of the *Manuals*.

What is more interesting, however, is this: neither Hempel nor the authors of the *Manual* provided a satisfactorily clear account of the conceptual features of functional terms in psychological (and, where analogous, in other) contexts. The charge is serious because, as we have already seen, the *Manual* is basically committed to functionally organized diagnoses. Under the circumstances, we cannot be sure what it means to say that the pertinent categories *are* empirically disciplined, operational, consensually supported, or promisingly oriented toward achieving a scientific taxonomy. Admittedly, the issue of functional categories is a strenuous one across all of the sciences.

The most important conceptual features of psychological terms are these: (a) they are cross-category—that is, not natural-kind or nomologically governed terms at all, terms (e.g., behavioral terms) that, deliberately or ad hoc, mix distinctions that might otherwise yield to lawlike regularities; (b) the empirical reliability with which they may be used need not, typically does not, support in any evidentiary way the presumption that they can, as such, be reconciled with covering laws of any sort; and (c) their use is not in any familiar sense systematically linked with whatever descriptive terms can be directly included in the vocabulary of covering-law explanations (so-called *homonomic* terms). Psychological terms in use in DSM-III and III-R are, admittedly (though not necessarily), *folk psychological* terms—terms that presuppose the existence of persons or selves, cognizing agents, subjects capable of complex intentional states (Davidson, 1980; Fodor, 1975; Stich, 1983), relative to which functional and dysfunctional distinctions are first assigned. In a word, nearly all *cross-category* terms—terms in general use in practical life—are reliable for reasons *not* primarily concerned with subsumption under covering laws. They may, for instance, favor effective piecemeal causal intervention by humans. (Dr. Schaffner discusses an alternative [to Hempel's] reductive model for psychiatry in his chapter in this book.)

The critical question confronting the completion of DSM-IV concerns whether and in what sense working with such functional categories, bracketing theory and theoretical explanations, conceding a distinct weakness in etiology (particularly affecting functional questions), confining methodology to descriptive consensus in the clinical setting, we *can* say that the *Manual* strengthens our command of a scientific taxonomy. At the very least, the model of science would have to be very different from the unity model; and, in any case, it is nowhere supplied.

We need to bear in mind that, relative to distinctions (a)–(c) just offered, psychological (folk psychological) terms *are* functional in two quite distinct senses. In one (the one just aired), we assign a function to particular syndromes, patterns, response cycles and the like that are to be treated as the functioning subsystems of the complex unified functioning of molar persons. This is surely the sense in which, in the introduction to DSM-III-R, Spitzer uncomplicatedly remarked that "each of the mental disorders is conceptualized as a clinically significant behavioral or psychological syndrome or pattern that occurs in a person" (1987, p. xxii). It is, also, in this sense that Hempel (1965e) said that "functional analysis is a modification of teleological explanation" (p. 303). In the other, psychological attributes are (said to be) *functionally* defined even where no explicit set of functions in the first sense constrains their ascription. It is hard to suppose that there are no such functional models (models of the first sort) that actually guide the use of terms of the second sort. For instance, surely a model of the rational or normal interfunctioning of belief, desire, and affect influences our ascription of mental states (thinking, wondering, supposing, fearing, hoping, etc.); some of the DSM-III diagnostic categories presuppose just such a model (e.g., the Developmental Disorders). However, apart from that, psychological attributes in the second sense are functional in that they are intentionally, informationally, or propositionally specified (e.g., fearing horses, searching for the Fountain of Youth) in a way that is (or may be) entirely abstracted from any physical incarnation, even though (on the proposal made much earlier on— against dualism) they cannot have failed to be incarnated in *some* physical, neurophysiological, biochemical or related way (Margolis, 1978, 1984, 1987, 1989). (This simply returns us to the very large mind-body puzzles we noted earlier. They are clearly beyond the scope of this discussion.) The first notion of function is also the site of criteria with valuational overtones; and the second escapes the stigma (if stigma it be) only if, in principle, it may be conceptually disjoined from the first. Certainly, in the context of clinical consensus, that is more than unlikely. If so, then the entire methodological neutrality of the *Manuals* is dubious indeed.

NATURALISTIC KNOWLEDGE AND INTERLEVEL EXPLANATION

We may conclude these remarks with three final distinctions. For one, some of the diagnostic categories—Schizophrenia, in particular (Margolis, 1991)— are, intrinsically, cognitively defined. Unlike the developmental disorders (such as Mental Retardation or Pervasive Developmental Disorder), that are not defined in terms of a favored picture of reality, Schizophrenia and others are defined in terms that, in principle, cannot be freed from a favored conception of reality. Delusions, hallucinations, odd beliefs, magical thinking, loosening of associations and so on are remarkably difficult to specify operationally or in any way that does not entail a reliable grasp of how the world actually is or ought to be conceived or addressed. Even those promising attempts in recent years to determine a somatic etiology must remain hostage to the phenomenologically salient functional features of Schizophrenia: where the diagnosis tends to be analogized to the diagnostic logic of such disorders as Down syndrome or Alzheimer's disease (Primary Degenerative Dementia of the Alzheimer Type). Here, one senses that the disorder has been conceptually slighted; and where it remains central and distinctive (cognitional in the sense given), it introduces classificatory problems of an extraordinarily difficult sort—for, at the present time, nearly the whole of late 20th-century philosophy (including the philosophy of science) is quite unable to provide any principled criteria for reality testing which are not obviously theoretically, historically, ideologically, culturally, and locally skewed. To put the point in too spare a way: *knowledge* is not in any obvious sense a *natural* state (although philosophers have attempted to characterize it thus). The reason is that it depends on the condition of *truth*. Hence, *if* Schizophrenia (but not Dementia of the Alzheimer Type) implicates norms of knowledge, then the theory of Schizophrenia will involve factors that are not readily assimilated either to the covering-law model or to any consensual diagnostic agreement that can be counted on, either intra- or intersocietally. Cognition factors simply are not factors of a sort that can, in principle, be directly assigned a somatic etiology even though, of course, somatic considerations are becoming increasingly important in the etiology of Schizophrenia—particularly, neurochemical abnormalities (Andreasen, 1987). The logic of the argument is such that the increased role of Axis III factors would entail either (a) the replacement of (what we are calling) cognition factors (phenomenologically: Bleulerian factors) in favor of more abstractly conceived cognitive and affective factors relatively detached from any favored picture of how the world should be conceived or addressed or (b) the construction of a ramified explanatory theory that would link these disparate elements together in a plausible way (see Gray, Feldon, Rawlins, Hemsley & Smith, 1991). At the moment, neither strategy is likely to be developed; the entire methodology of the *Manuals* is against it. Yet, it hardly makes sense here to increase biological explanations without the required companion theories. The truth is that the salience of cognition factors among the Schizophrenic, Schizophreniform and allied disorders is simply the least avoidable of the scenarios featuring the intentionality of psychological states. It may be argued that there *are* no cognitive or affective states that are entirely divorced from (what we are privileging as) cognition factors (at least implicitly). Therefore, *some* theoretical position is required to reconcile particular taxonomic idealizations with the conceptual constraints here mentioned. Furthermore, *if* the developmental structure of persons or selves were construed in strongly historicized or constructionist terms so that the entire taxonomy could not fail to be relativized to divergent, somewhat transient cultures (see, e.g., Foucault, 1978a, 1978b, 1984), it would prove quite impossible to eliminate cognition factors from playing a salient diagnostic role, and it would of course prove impossible to reconcile the resulting psychiatric taxonomy with the unity model of science. There is, in fact, a cursory admission of the problem in the Introduction to DSM-III-R (pp. xxvi–xxvii); but there is no discussion regarding whether, if a certain range of psychopathology is unique to a given culture, that signifies that we simply lack the requisite research among non-Western populations or that our taxonomy is in principle regularized for populations the inherent psychodynamics of which is, in essential regards, historically variable, not definable entirely in transhistorical or ahistorical terms. There is every reason to think that this question will become more and more important in 21st-century psychological theory.

This is not perhaps as serious, diagnostically, as it may appear. It *is* serious for the ambitions of a scientific taxonomy, and it draws attention once again to the extreme naiveté of the methodology of III and III-R. There is no recognition of this family of problems in the rationale offered for the diagnostic categories in question. The narrower charge may be put more bluntly. Attributions of knowledge are not in any familiar sense purely descriptive or psychological—although they do of course entail such attributions. On any informed view, ascribing knowledge concerns ascribing a certain valuationally favored status to pertinent psychological states—one in fact which may vary in a profound way from culture to culture and from historical period to historical period. There are indeed some undeveloped efforts to construe knowledge *as* a natural psychological state (e.g., Quine, 1969), but they are not compellingly successful. The matter is, plainly, a vexed one.

A second consideration concerns the interlevel nature of psychological attributions of both the first and second sort of functional state. (An example of an interlevel theory is afforded by evolutionary theory; i.e., it combines at least genetic factors and factors concerning the molar responsiveness of individual organisms and populations of organisms to their environments, without being able to eliminate either in favor of the other. Clearly, medicine, and psychiatry in particular, are oriented in terms of interlevel theories.) The entire idea of interlevel distinctions is already (at least in terms of the history of the pertinent theories) influenced by the unity-of-science model (Schaffner, 1967, 1974a, 1974b, 1984, and this book). Of course, it does also present itself intuitively. Thus, any mental disorder that cannot be diagnosed without reference to genetic factors as well as to the molar functioning of persons (Down syndrome, for instance) is clearly interlevel. Between such extremes, functional attributes (as characterized above) are also clearly interlevel.

The admission of such diagnostic categories raises two important considerations. The first is that such disorders may not always be so regularized as Down syndrome, as an example, that reductive biological explanations *can* be made without close attention to their interlevel functioning as such. Considering the currently strong challenge to the adequacy of the unity model, such ascriptions may not be able to be supported without a strong (quite debatable) theoretical input. The second is that the very introduction of interlevel categories requires a strong consensus on the structure of the enveloping science (psychiatry) so that diagnostic consensus is coherent. Once again, neither of these difficulties is adequately addressed in DSM-III and DSM-III-R.

Finally, DSM-III-R has, unwittingly, generated considerable confusion involving the use of the terms *organic* (*nonorganic*) and *physical* (*mental*). In a relatively recent editorial, Spitzer and his associates (Spitzer et al., 1989) proposed dropping "the organic/nonorganic distinction in psychiatric classification" (p. 126). They argued, for instance, that biological findings encourage the belief that Schizophrenia and the Bipolar Disorders will eventually be reclassified as organic mental disorders. In particular, they conceded that "the implication that the nonorganic mental disorders have no significant biological component to their etiology is inconsistent with current knowledge of these conditions" (p. 128).

The fault is indeed theirs, but it cannot be corrected by the strategy they favor: they have, actually, been confused by their own equivocation. They have not adequately realized that physical and organic considerations arise *both* in the very analysis of what it is to be a *mental state* and of what it is to be a *mental disorder*. The linkage between the opposed terms, as far as mental states are concerned, addresses such metaphysical considerations as that of avoiding dualism and either favoring or disfavoring some form of (reductive) physicalism; whereas their linkage, as far as mental disorders are concerned, addressed the diagnostic, explanatory, and therapeutic aspects of etiology.

The failure to give due attention to at least a minimal theory of mental states and mental disorders is likely to generate further conceptual embarrassment in DSM-IV. The fact is that there is no clarification of the decisive terms *mental, physical, organic, nonorganic* anywhere in the *Manuals*. This accounts for the utterly pointless distinction between organic *mental syndromes* and organic *mental disorders* in DSM-III-R (American Psychiatric Association, 1987, p. 97), where what is intended is merely the difference between lack of reference to etiology and reference to a known Axis III physical disorder or condition. The authors are obliged, therefore, to reassure us that the "differentiation of Organic Mental Disorders as a separate class does not imply that nonorganic ('functional') mental disorders are somehow independent of brain processes. On the contrary, it is assumed that all psychological processes, normal and abnormal, depend on brain function" (p. 98).

However, by the same token, Spitzer and his associates do not seem to have considered seriously enough that *the very nature of Axis III and allied factors remains conceptually unclear*. For, *if* the *mental* or *psychological* is complex enough to include *physical* or *organic* features, then there cannot be an a priori assurance that Axis III etiological factors will not include "a recognized . . . disorder or condition" that is similarly complex——or even an associated condition that is not strictly etiologically organic (what may result, e.g., "from taking a psychoactive substance" [p. 126])——factors in which the mental (nonorganic?) may still play an essential part. The matter can hardly be resolved by way of diagnostic consensus. We touch here on an enormous conceptual problem. It is hardly possible to resolve it here. Our concern has been solely with the difficulty that its *not* being resolved occasions regarding the very rigor of the *Manuals*. The confusion we have noted among the categories mentioned simply cannot be counted on to ensure taxonomic reliability. That's all.

One intuitive clarification is this (regardless of the final diagnostic vocabulary of DSM-IV): *organic*, used in the psychiatric setting in which (with Spitzer) we mean to deny that the *mental* is *not* part of the organic, must then include, must make room for, the specifically *mental*. If that is so, then it is improbable that Axis III could be helpfully confined to physical disorders and conditions unless, indeed, we were already committed in theory to reductionism. The etiological picture must be much more complicated than III and III-R let on. Thus, one group (Popkin, Tucker, Caine, Folstein & Grant, 1989), commenting on the potential problems linked to the new proposal just considered, observed quite sensibly "that psychiatric disturbances may be intrinsic features of many medical illnesses" (p. 441). If so, then if Axis III factors are incorporated into Axis I (as opposed to instances in which they are not), etiological considerations would force us once again to provide an adequate theory regarding the relationship between the mental and the physical. There is no escape.

4 A Phenomenological Critique of Commonsensical Assumptions in DSM-III-R

The Avoidance of the Patient's Subjectivity

AARON L. MISHARA, Ph.D.

THE AVOIDANCE OF "SUBJECTIVITY" IN DSM-III-R

In their recent book, *Manic-Depressive Illness*, Goodwin and Jamison made the following complaint concerning the shortcomings of the classification systems introduced by DSM-III and DSM-III-R:

> The requirements of sound research have produced operational criteria for selecting homogeneous groups of clinical subjects. Extended into clinical diagnostic systems, the criteria as noted have made diagnoses more objective and reliable. Commendable as they are, these achievements haven been purchased at a price. Rarely does one encounter discussions of mental illness in current journal articles that fully represent the varieties and texture of experience. Traditional psychiatric literature is filled with descriptions that make today's accounts seem arid. (1990, p. 14)

To take into account the patient's "subjective"[1] experience of the disorder, these authors employed manic-depressive patients' written and spoken self-reports in their analysis. They also advocated a return to the descriptive style of classical, especially German, psychiatry.

The above work is one of many examples of an increasing effort to take into account the subjectivity of the patient's experience in the classification and investigation of mental disorders. Such scattered developments may anticipate a paradigm shift first indicated, albeit sketchily, by the emphasis on subjective "representation" in cognitive psychology and neuroscience.[2] These attempts are not radical enough, however, in that they do not attempt to inquire systematically into what *subjectivity* means (see also Caws' chapter in this book). This requires addressing the following problems: (a) the systematic clarification of the concept *subjectivity*; (b) of how it can be methodically studied.

In keeping with contemporary trends, current literature on mental disorder emphasizes scientific methodology. This tendency appears to compensate for a lack in conceptual precision about the patient's subjectivity. Subjectivity is generally conceived as the converse of the research notion of "objectively observable and measurable," that is, *behavioral* variables. The concern of the researcher has been the operationalization of subjectivity and not the more philosophical question of what subjectivity is. Despite relatively early stages of research, there is a precipitant optimism concerning recent advances in molecular genetics, laboratory, and family studies in the search for "causal" explanations for mental disorders. The unwarranted optimism and the assumption that very different kinds of disorder will yield to the same research methodology betray a concealed but, nevertheless, increasing discomfort with what to do with the patient's subjective experiencing. Subjectivity had been neglected for so long in the description and research promoted by the prevailing paradigm that the development of adequate instrumentation for its research had been impeded. The study of subjectivity was simply unable to measure up to the sophistication and promise of other areas of psychopathological research.

Current attempts to classify and research mental disorder, however, will not fully attain their goal of discovering the etiology and appropriate treatment of different disorders until the problem of subjectivity is addressed systematically. The *descriptive* approach of DSM-III-R has concealed loyalties to a largely behavioral viewpoint. For DSM-III-R, it is preferable to minimize inferences about the patient's subjectivity. This assumption actually dampens vanguard efforts to study the patient's subjectivity. The authors of the *DSM-III Training Guide* stated that DSM-III is "phenomenologically descriptive" (Webb, DiClemente, Johnstone, Sanders & Perley, 1981, p. 29). This claim is philosophically inaccurate. The descriptive approach of DSM-III and DSM-III-R is more appropriately called *behavioral*. As such, it harbors an array of concealed theoretical assumptions about the nature of mental disorder and its classification.

The writings by Michael Schwartz and Osborne Wiggins have demonstrated how a phenomenological[3] viewpoint can be applied to the study and clarification of diagnosis as a preconceptual process of typification (1987a, 1987b). The present paper attempts to apply the insight of Schwartz and Wiggins concerning the typification process of the clinician to the corresponding subjective experience of the patient. The latter involves a disturbance of the *patient's* typification process of perceptual and experiential meaning of objects and states of affairs in the world (as the concept has been developed by Husserl, Gurwitsch, and Schutz)(Schwartz & Wiggins, 1987a, 1987b). For Husserl, there can be no perception of a particular object without the *simultaneous* accompanying anticipation of its meaning as failing under a certain type (Husserl, 1973). The disturbance of the patient's experience of meaning produces subtle changes or variations in everyday interaction. It may *atmospherically* (Tellenbach, 1987b) bring into play and engage the clinician's corresponding typification underlying the diagnosis.

Although some authors admit a subjective source to the experience of meaning, there is a danger that it is reduced to "raw" feelings (Feigl, 1958) or mystified as tacit knowledge (Weimer, 1977). As a result, the potential of the phenomenological approach to formalize the subjective structuring of meaning is ignored. Then we find ourselves raising old unanswered questions that oppose objective versus subjective, cognitive versus feeling, higher versus lower sources of knowledge. These are residual categories from our Western tradition of metaphysics. As such, they hinder our contemporary understanding of science and the role of subjectivity in mental disorder.

Phenomenological and empirical approaches to psychopathology have been traditionally opposed. This is true for a number of reasons, some of which are historical. Phenomenological authors have criticized reductionist approaches to mental disorder, approaches overconfident in the realism of their explanatory constructs. The phenomenologists (Gurwitsch, 1974; Husserl, 1970a) referred to this naive realism as the *natural attitude*[4] For example, Lee Robins and James Barrett saw the validity of psychiatric diagnosis as a problem of matching clinical entities with "real" processes of nature (1989, p. v). Such reductions of human experiential meaning and its disturbance in disorder to natural/biological categories are problematic from the phenomenological point of view because a step-by-step account of the transition from human meaning to a preferred explanatory realm (e.g., biological, psychodynamic/cognitive, or behavioral/social) is missing.[5] (For a discussion of the problems of reductionism, see Schaffner's chapter in this book.)

With the exception of the writings of Binswanger (1955a, 1955b, 1960, 1963), Blankenburg (1969, 1971), Kraus (this book), Sadler (1992), Schwartz and Wiggins (this book), and a few others, the contributions of phenomenology to the scientific basis of the classification, research, and treatment of mental disorders have largely been overlooked. Phenomenology is in a unique position to do so precisely because (a) it requires a step-by-step account of how abstractions are obtained from everyday clinical experience and encounters; (b) it accounts for the development of these abstractions into formalized entities, providing the basis for the classification and taxonomy of mental disorders; (c) it furnishes a theoretically neutral access to the description of the patient's subjective experience as meaningful structure; (d) meaningful structure can be formalized and arranged into a typology according to basic phenomenological categories of the subjective experience of time, space, embodiment, and the relationship to others and self; (e) the phenomenological approach delimits the points in the genesis of subjective meaning where disturbance may enter, according to these basic categories of experience. The categories can be abstractly studied in isolation but are seen as interdependent in the fabric or embedded structure of the patient's subjective experience. This does not commit the clinician or researcher precipitously to statements concerning the "real" nature of the structure.

Although basic philosophical problems are sometimes admitted in the literature concerning the classification of mental disorder, they are often given merely verbal solutions rather than being seen as fundamental to the discipline itself. For example, Goodwin and Guze (1979) gave token acknowledgment to the philosophical problem of the subject's free will versus determinism in diagnostic classification. They dismissed the problem with the pseudosolution that the "question of 'free will'. . . may be avoided if it is recognized that disease is a convention, and may be defined independently of cause or mechanism" (p. 216).

Similarly, Blashfield pointed to a logical problem in the DSM-III and DSM-III-R classificational system. The introduction to DSM-III-R clearly states that it is disorders and not patients which are being classified (American Psychiatric Association, 1987, p. xxiii). "To state that DSM-III is a classification of disorders is tautological. . . [it] is simply to avoid defining the entities in this system" (Blashfield, 1986, p. 372). Blashfield's solution is to reintroduce the concept of *diseases* as the classified entities. *Disease* would then have conceptual force in psychiatric classification which would be comparable to that of *species* in the taxonomic classification resulting from evolutionary theory.

From the phenomenological point of view, Blashfield's solution is unacceptable. The phenomenological approach to meaning disturbance in the subjective experiencing of the patient requires a different concept of *disease*. It provides a link between the scientific study of subjective experience of meaning disturbance in mental disorder and the phenomenological concept of *illness*. As will be explained below, *illness* involves a shifting threshold between voluntary and involuntary experiences, depending on the level and scope of the meaning disturbance. In addition, illness, in whatever form, has biographical meaning for the subject. It is incidental to the results of the phenomenological study of mental disorder whether the individual researcher wants to categorize the meaning disturbance subsequently as first "caused" by biological anomaly, psychodynamic past, learning history, or cognition, for example.

By selecting a descriptive approach based on behaviorist assumptions in which behaviors are described and classified as clinical features of disorders, DSM-III-R inadvertently compromises not only the preconceptual aspects of the clinician's diagnosis, but also the future research into the causes of mental disorder. A phenomenological approach ameliorates this problem by providing categories for the description and conceptualization of the genesis of the subjective structure of experiential meaning. It introduces new categories for describing the subjective experience of the patient and directing the clinician's focus to pertinent data for diagnosis and therapy. Phenomenology provides a means for formalizing hypotheses resulting from these categories for reliability studies and future research into the classification, causes, and treatment of mental disorders.

THE COMMONSENSE OPPOSITIONS OF DSM-III-R: A PHENOMENOLOGICAL CRITIQUE

According to the introductory chapters of DSM-III and DSM-III-R, both manuals employ a descriptive approach with respect to the classification of mental disorders. With the exception of a few disorders with clear causes (organic, adjustment, post-traumatic stress, and conversion disorders), this is stated to be largely atheoretical with regard to the etiology of mental disorders (American Psychiatric Association, 1987, p. xxiii; R.L. Spitzer, 1989, p. 32). In this way it can be used by a wide range of clinicians with varying backgrounds and theoretical positions for reliable diagnoses and research. The descriptions of the clinical features of the disorders are for the most part made in ordinary language, or, at best, a melange between technical and everyday language.Technical terminology deriving from clinical practice or theory is used only when necessary; for example, Narcissistic Personality Disorder is based on the writings of Kohut and Kernberg (Goldstein, 1985, p. 123; Kernberg, 1975; Kohut, 1971).

Ordinary language, however, does not in itself guarantee that a description is free from unjustified theoretical assumptions or prejudices that issue from commonsense. Language is not a transparent medium that pliantly shapes itself to whatever matter at hand is under discussion. Ordinary language and consensual technical expressions are supposed to do the job of transparently conveying the meaning of the criteria. However, ordinary language and technical terms are made on the basis of presupposed, commonsense distinctions. The implicit theoretical orientation is *behavioral* in that the "descriptions of the clinical features of the disorders . . . are described at the lowest order of inference necessary to describe the characteristic features of the disorder" (American Psychiatric Association, 1980, p. 7; 1987, pp. xxiii–xxiv).

It is not only a desiDeratum to keep subjective impressions of the diagnostician to a minimum, but also to make as few inferences about the patient's subjectivity as possible. This is not to say that DSM-III-R does not require inferences about the patient's subjective experiencing. The manual is full of such references, for example, "depressed mood" in Major Depressive Episode. DSM-III-R theoretically misunderstands itself, however, in several ways when it makes the following assumptions or actions: (a) explicitly prefers a minimum of inferences about the patient's subjectivity; (b) offers a unsystematic melange of ordinary and technical language without inquiring into the relation-ship among descriptive language, clinical experience, and the requirements of a formalized language in scientific method; (c) presupposes that what is "nor-mal" is a constant given in common sense, more or less evenly distributed across clinicians, and can serve as a reliable basis for clinical judgment about what is abnormal; (d) assumes that the diagnostic process for the seasoned clinician can function as a checklist (Kraus, 1987, 1991, and this book) in which isolated behaviors and inferences about the patient's subjective ex-periencing are individually matched against a list of criteria, rather than deriving *atmospherically* from the structure of the interaction with the patient.

DSM-III and DSM-III-R were written with a view to current research methodology and instruments, for example, the celebrated descriptive bio-medical method of Robins and Guze (197). From a phenomenological point of view, however, there are methodological problems with this approach. These problems do not first emerge on the level of research into the etiology of mental disorders, but are already present in their classification according to largely behavioral criteria. The justification for such an approach is to be found in the common sense assumptions that are specific to our culture and period of intellectual history. (See Margolis' chapter in this book for other scientific implications of this fact.)

The phenomenological social scientist Alfred Schutz (1962) wrote that "the so-called facts of common sense perception . . . already involve abstractions of a highly complicated nature." Overlooking this leads to a "fallacy of mis-placed concreteness" (pp. 3–4). Despite its importance, the problem of com-mon sense remains a neglected theme in the discussion and empirical research concerning classification. Blankenburg (1969) considered the reasons for this neglect to be inherent in both the nature of empirical research methods and the phenomenon of common sense itself. *Common sense* is a slippery concept because it conceals its own structure in its very obviousness.

Husserl's method of phenomenological reduction[6] enables conceptual thought to escape the paradoxes of common sense to study their structure. He thereby questioned the apparent obviousness that common sense offers as a basis for scientific judgments, the so-called "*taken-for granted obviousness of the obvious.*" For Husserl, phenomenology is the true positivism because it is not satisfied with the givens or prejudices of common sense, which only *seem* evident. It rather seeks to uncover what really can be taken as evident to methodological and rigorous thought.

Various mental disorders can be viewed as involving the loss or disturb-ance of the normalizing function of common sense. Blankenburg (1969) suggested that a typology of disturbances of common sense in different disorders could furnish criteria for differential diagnosis. "In precisely those areas of life in which mere opinion should prevail, obsessive compulsives demand absolute certainty." On the other hand, "the premorbid personality structure of depressives is overly attached to common sense. . . . The preserving of this ability in cyclothymic disorder is an important criterion for differential diagnosis over against schizophrenics. . . . Not only the feeling for what is fitting or suitable is lost in schizophrenics, but also for what the other thinks, what the situation requires . . . i.e., a feeling for those things which are obvious in themselves . . . (Entirely different is the loss of tact in organic disturbances.) . . . The above disorders in one way or another involve common sense." (pp. 148–149; my translation).

Science presupposes common sense as the beginning point for its abstractions. Aron Gurwitsch, the phenomenological philosopher, wrote about the "abstractive reduction which leads from the world of primordial experience to nature" in the natural sciences.

> The goal of objective science is to disclose nature as it is in itself, independent of and beyond all subjective appearances and interpretations, stripped of all subjective admixture, severed from all reference and relatedness to persons and personal groups. . . . The physicist abstracts from whatever is "subjective," including his own conscious life. Still . . . he depends on his perceptual consciousness and whatever other intellectual functions, among them the mentioned abstractions, are required for and involved in his scientific activity. (1974, pp. 109–111)

All scientific efforts begin with some kind of abstractive idealization in which certain features are excluded to focus on others.

The behaviorist approach attempts to isolate describable behaviors that are presumed to be objectively observable and measurable in themselves. It does so by means of a stripping away of all subjective attributes or predicates that are found in our concrete experience of other persons and ourselves. Behaviorism begins with an abstraction and not a given. One must first remove precisely what are experienced as the subjective attributes belonging to the other organism. The organism, however, is initially experienced as a living totality that is transcendent to each of my perceptions, observations, and statements. Husserl (1970a) wrote about the one-sided "exaggerations of the behaviourists, who operate only with the external side of modes of behaviour, as if behaviour would not then lose its sense (*Sinn*), i.e., the sense given to it by empathy, the understanding of 'expression'" (p. 247).

The present concern, however, is not the evaluation of behaviorism as a scientific method or even as a theory of human functioning. More important are the widespread, insidious, and commonsensical behaviorist assumptions that pervade our current worldview and efforts to classify and treat mental disorders. Behavioral assumptions are not specific to the behaviorist approach but are common to nearly all contemporary scientific approaches that concern human beings and mental disorder. I am not suggesting a return to a metaphysics of the soul or other archaic worldviews. The phenomenological approach can serve, rather, as antidote to the concealed metaphysical prejudices of *scientific* approaches to abnormal *behavior*. By appealing to common sense, the acceptance of the assumptions of methodological behaviorism (as well as behaviorism as a worldview) is shielded from criticism. Phenomenology serves as a form of criticism of taken-for-granted presuppositions (Seebohm, 1962). By means of historical traditions of thought, these have entered our common sense. They are passed on as if they were given in our experience and not to be questioned in their obviousness. The distinction between *inner* and *outer*, for example, was present in medieval Christian theology and found its way into the methodological doubt of Descartes in his *Meditations* (Straus, 1949, p. 141). In contemporary thought, this distinction is connected to the oppositions *public/private, overt/covert, body/mind*, and *self/other*. These are fundamental to behaviorist assumptions about what constitute legitimate observables.

Behaviorist and materialistic approaches to the explanation of mental disorder, just as much as their counterparts, cognitive and psychodynamic approaches (the latter tending to be more idealistic by making inferences about "internal" events and *explaining* behavior in terms of these internal events) attempt to overcome Cartesian dualism by stressing one side of the interconnected oppositions: body/mind, outer/inner, materialism/idealism, and other/self. These approaches inadvertently preserve dualism and the whole host of accompanying formal oppositions by their one-sided emphasis. The oppositions have become part of our common sense and stock of knowledge. They form the basis for the manner in which we *talk* about our experience. They do not necessarily reflect the way we really experience the world.

It is generally acknowledged that the formulation of hypotheses is restricted in advance by the artifacts of our experimental methodology, the instruments used, and by the limitations of formulating everyday language into operationalized experimental procedure and formal languages (see the Margolis and Goodman chapters in this book). What is not questioned is that ordinary language is already a reformulation and translation of our everyday experience of reality. Ordinary language contains the presuppositions of common sense. Presupposed commonsensical oppositions enable us to isolate abstractively idealized objects of psychological research, for example, behaviors, cognitions, psychodynamic processes, the synaptic transmission of neurotransmitters, and family systems.

There is the additional problem of isolating these basic units for analysis and measurement. Any isolated behavior, cognition, psychodynamic process, or neurological synapse is a Gestalt isolated from a background of other possible conceptual units with wandering dimensions. These dimensions depend on the thematizing activity of the researcher (what the researcher attends to), who then tries to test hypothesized causal relationships between abstracted parts of meaningful wholes.

Language structures the units of organization in conjunction with our perceptions. Common sense presuppositions contribute, unmonitored, to the meaning distinctions that generate the abstract categorizations of our languaged experience. This occurs precisely through an unexplained obviousness in the connecting of language to experience. The putatively unproblematic connection of language to experience is considered as part of the heuristic, early phases of scientific research which need not be examined in themselves. Because the phenomenological method is burdened with cumbersome technical language, its strengths (e.g., descriptive access to the subject's paralinguistic organization of experience) are not appreciated. This organization is more basic to our everyday experience than the oppositions or paradoxes that first arise in our commonsensical ordinary language.

Subjectivity, when acknowledged, is regarded as opaque or impenetrable compared with reliable observation in the study and classification of mental disorders. Historically, this prejudice was expressed in the behaviorist critique of introspective attempts to quantify and experimentally study internal processes. Subjectivity was seen as the black box, inaccessible to scientific method. The behaviorist critique of introspection depended on the commonsensical opposition between internal and external, private and public events. The latter are assumed to be made up of isolatable units, accessible to consensual direct observation.

Behaviorism shares with its adversary, introspective structuralist psychology, the assumption that the human experience of meaning can be broken down into atomistic parts that have causal or mechanistic relationships to one another. Despite the behaviorist critique, Wundt's introspective psychology of structural elements pervaded not only traditional psychiatric classification beginning with Kraepelin (Hoff, 1992; Kraepelin, 1896) and Jaspers (Conrad, 1958; M. Spitzer, 1989), but also the later division in cognitive psychology between higher and lower processes. Cognitive psychology still assumes that internal processes can be studied atomistically without taking into account the problem of evidence these abstractions engender. Since psychiatric classification does not develop a phenomenologically clarified concept of the human subject, it depends on such unsystematic chartings of subjectivity. Many of these assumptions have not been tested since the work of the early introspectionists.

For the description of clinical behavior proposed by DSM-III-R as well as the various approaches to the explanation of mental disorder which depend on it, the isolation of observable behaviors relies on an "abstractive reduction" (Gurwitsch, 1974; Husserl, 1970a)[7] of everyday experience. The reduction is obtained only by suppressing one side of a structurally interconnected pair in assumed formal opposition. DSM-III-R explicitly emphasizes the observation of outward behavior and a restriction of inferences about the inner subjectivity of the patient. This presupposes the common sense opposition between outer and inner, as well as the interconnected oppositions other/self and body/mind. None of the above oppositions can be given as evident in everyday experience, however, without the presence of its counterpart in what Viktor von Weizsaecker (1968) called a relationship of *mutual concealment*. Each term presupposes the other and yet excludes it, depending on the momentary perspective of the subject. He called this the *revolving door principle of* the Gestalt-circle (p. 21).

COMMONSENSE OPPOSITIONS AND MUTUAL CONCEALMENT: EMPIRICAL EVIDENCE

Viktor von Weizsaecker demonstrated that the concept of *subjectivity* is indispensable in interpreting experiments he conducted in sense physiology. He then attempted to introduce the resulting concept of subjectivity to the theory and practice of clinical medicine, including neurology and psychiatry. He is generally considered the founder of German psychosomatic medicine. The Gestalt-circle principle was first derived from the relationship between the organism's perception and movement in the perception of Gestalten (meaningful forms), but it can be applied to other oppositions that appear separate in common sense. In the following, I will limit the discussion to only two of these experiments.

There is a Bavarian custom in which a prospective wedding couple must saw a log together with a double-handed lumberman's saw before the wedding ceremony. This is meant to symbolize their future belonging and working together in the common task of life. Using this custom as a model, Viktor von Weizsaecker and his assistant Paul Christian decided to test experimentally the relationship of physiological, psychological, and social processes as part of one overriding organization. This organization is found in social interaction when one is undertaking common tasks. In the laboratory they constructed a double-sided "saw," which in reality was a metal bar with handle grips attached. It could move back and fort, up and down, and was able to register all variations of movement. The device was able to measure "form, direction, magnitude and duration of the movements of the steel bar, i.e., the 'saw,' and the respective force applied by the two partners (form, magnitude, direction, duration, amount of time)" (Christian cited by Klinger, 1986).

Klinger (1986) described the results of the experiment:

> If one of the experimental subjects is instructed to reduce the amount of force which he contributes, this is usually unnoticed by the partner and compensated for in a flowing manner. The total achievement remains the same. In the act of doing the work together, no separation of the persons involved was possible. Only in the dramatic absence of contribution from one of the partners did this become notice-

able to the other——although the requirement of additional energy for the later partner was adjusted to be the same as in the previous cases. (p. 182, my translation)

There is connectedness but mutual concealment between the partners in that
each anticipates and compensates for the other's movements in on-going but
unnoticed adjustments. These are based on the prior experience and anticipa-
tions of the partner's contribution. They occur implicitly while the attention
of the experimental subjects is directed thematically toward the goal of sawing. Physiological processes of muscle tension, psychological anticipation of
the others' movements, and the mutual rhythm of social interaction come into
play with each other in one organization. This can only be abstractively analyzed into levels in retrospect. There is an ongoing system of balances and
counterbalances which enables each subject to preserve the coherence of the
mutual effort. Organized contact with the environment is maintained precisely
by overlooking the compensations that one brings to match the rhythm and
force of the other's movements. This is improvisational in that there is no
completely matching precedent for the unique fit of working together with the
idiosyncrasies of the present work partner.

In their monograph *Wesen und Formen der Bipersonalitaet* (1949),
Christian and Haas described the principles that may be derived from the
seemingly banal results of the experiment. They argued that inmost human
behavior or in human activities such as "thinking, feeling, perceiving, and
doing——there is from the beginning relationship to others" (p. 8) and otherness
as such. Following von Weizsaecker, Christian called this *dual* or *bipersonality (Bipersonalitaet)* as a fundamental organization of the subject's experiential field.[8] This is not to restrict human relationship to the dyad. Instead, it
shows that these principles of organization first reveal themselves experimentally when two or more people are present.

The relationship to self is also bipersonally structured in that one transcends
one's past self through envisioning new possibilities.[9] It is also this structure,
however, that in part makes possible, for example, depersonalization disorder;
the ability of the anorexia nervosa patient to consider her or his body image
and interoceptive stimuli primarily from an external point of view; or even the
schizophrenic hallucinating of voices commenting on the subject as if issuing
from an other. In each case, self-transcendence is compromised in the ongoing
exchange between self and other.

It is possible to formalize the various disturbances of the function of bipersonal organization in different disorders for empirical research. Bipersonal
organization is conceptualized as *simultaneously* a relationship to otherness
and to self. Such subjective organization is more fundamental than the psychoanalytic intrapsychic defenses such as splitting and even repression. Currently,
there are efforts to operationalize defenses by means of rating scales in terms
of a hierarchy of levels of adaptive maturity as a prospective axis for DSM-IV

(Perry & Cooper, 1989; Vaillant, 1985). They gauge themselves largely on be-havioral criteria, instead of raising the phenomenological question of anchor-ing such defensive operations in subjectivity. More primitive, or less adaptive defenses, for example, tend to focus on the other *or* self, with less flexibility for reversal of bipersonal organization (self-reflection), for example, projective identification, splitting, or autistic fantasy.

Cooperativeness in working together, as indeed in all forms of human communication, such as play or eroticism, involves deception (*Taeuschung*). Deception is necessarily built into the perspectival structure of subjective experience. Precisely when one feels most free, most independent as oneself in interaction with an other, one is, at that moment, unconsciously most the other and most dependent on the other. Hans-Georg Gadamer expressed his indebtedness to von Weizsaecker in his own phenomenological analysis of playing a game. He wrote that the

> game is . . . the formation of the movement as such, which in an unconscious teleology, subordinates the attitude of the individuals to itself . . . neither partner alone constitutes the real determining factor, rather, it is the unified form of move-ment as a whole that unifies the fluid activity of both. We can formulate this as an theoretical generalization by saying that the individual self, including his activity and understanding of himself, is taken up into a higher determination that is really the decisive factor. (pp 53—54)

In game playing, as in human interaction in general, there is one organization-al dynamic structure that connects the participants. It necessarily conceals its totality by revealing only partial and complementary aspects to the players. Each player anticipates the other's moves in his or her own movements, as in tennis or chess, for example. For that moment, one *is* the other but in a way hidden to oneself, according to the revolving door principle. This is an alter-nating reversal and exchange of active and passive attitudes of the embodied subjects. In a different way, this is also fascinating to a spectator who has internalized this bipersonal structure from still another vantage point.

One is simultaneously and unconsciously the other with whom one interacts in an ongoing Gestalt-circle as bipersonal structure. Paradoxically, the more one unconsciously becomes the other, the more one feels free to conduct the situation from one's own side of things. Just as self/other are *simultaneously* structured, the physiological and psychological levels of the organization of experience are by no means at first experienced as separate from one another. They coordinate effort in the subjective structuring of meaning, even if this subjective structuring is from the very first bipersonal. Similarly, the distinc-tions between *inner and outer*, and especially *overt* and *covert*, so essential to behaviorist methodology and behavioral approaches to description of mental disorder, have no relevance on this level. There is a prior unity of inextricable involvement, an intertwining (*Verschraenkung*) between abstract terms, terms held separate in common sense. These are, instead, in a prior interlocking relationship of mutual concealment according to the revolving door principle of the Gestalt-circle. This principle is found to function in everyday experience and clinical diagnosis.

Bipersonality enables the "atmospheric between" (Tellenbach, 1987b, p. 231) of the mutual structuring and anticipation of meanings in the clinical interview. Communication, in general, involves the sharing of imparted and received themes as Gestalten that are in ongoing transition. Bipersonal exchange is the structural basis for typifications in diagnostic practice.[10] As stated above, this is sometimes unnecessarily mystified as "tacit knowledge."

Viktor von Weizsaecker and his assistants conducted a series of sense-physiological experiments involving a striped cylinder drum rotating about the subject. This artificially produced vertigo presented a crisis in the relationship between the subject and his or her environment (von Weizsaecker, 1968). The amount of disturbance could be manipulated as a *quantitative* factor by increasing the speed of the drum. Corresponding *qualitative* changes in perceptual organization were then reported by the subjects. This enabled the determination of the degree of disturbance to subjective perceptual meaning in regard to new strategic efforts toward preserving a coherent Gestalt as the experiential point of contact between subject and environment. These strategies are automatic and spontaneous (what von Weizsaecker called *improvisational*) and not consciously reflected upon. They involve selectively preserving certain aspects of the perceptual Gestalt while sacrificing others disturbed by the movement. (An example is the considerable disturbance that the rotary movements of a propeller blade bring to perception. This is overcome, however, by preserving/sacrificing features in the resultant blur.) If the subject is instructed to focus on his hand or an object that he hold in front of him, the rotating cylinder, with enough velocity, will suddenly appear at rest. The subject's own body, however, appears to spin in the opposite direction. Depending on what is taken as the point of reference during the experimentally induced vertigo, the self or rotating object, the field organization may reverse what is taken as mobile and what remains stable.

We have seen similar principles at work in the experimentally demonstrated concept of bipersonality. These principles may also underlie the psychoanalytic concept of *defense*. The threshold between what was preserved and sacrificed, that is, what remained thematic and what was overlooked, was relative to the goal of the mutual work of sawing. It is not the absolute threshold that is assumed in experimental psychophysics.

Von Weizsaecker applied this concept of the situationally labile threshold to the problem of illness. Illness changes the threshold between what is subjectively experienced as voluntary and involuntary. The modern medical view of illness presupposes the metaphysical dualism between mind and body. It reduces the involuntary aspect of illness to its site of occurrence in the body as no longer at the voluntary disposal of the conscious subject. Because this involuntary aspect is not seen as a fluctuating boundary relative to the person's total situation, the distinction between voluntary and involuntary in illness loses all significance as a subjective factor. In the modern view, illness is restricted to the local site of its occurrence in the body. The range of voluntary behavioral competence of organic patients, however, such as dressing in apraxia, varies from day to day, depending on the subjective mood of the patient and the patient's experience of the total situation. Von Weizsaecker (1957) pointed out that what illness makes involuntary is not something that remains fixed.

> It sometimes happens that a hemiplegic patient is only able to innervate the muscles of the stricken side by straining the muscles on his will side, or by yawning. Clearly, we have no right to call such a "co-movement" any less voluntary; nevertheless, we know that the patient is not in a position, even on the healthy side, to directly innervate "the muscle itself" voluntarily. He finds himself rather wanting to perform certain "actions," such as clenching his fist. No one should hinder us, then, from calling the accompanying, "co-movement" of the unhealthy side any less voluntary. . . . Such an achievement by detour can quickly become a habit and, therefore, is just as voluntary as any other. (pp. 57–58; my translation)

Illness involves a transformed relationship to one's own body in which certain parts of one's body, or body-self, previously under one's disposal, now take on an alien character as resisting one's subjective will. These parts become a resistant *it*. They are no longer under the free disposal of the *I*, but are experienced as foreign or *other*. The threshold between voluntary and involuntary, between the *I* and *it* aspects of bodily experience, is variable depending on subjective factors.

How does this apply to the problem of illness or disease in mental disorder? It is possible to arrange in hierarchical typology the range and extent of disturbance to voluntary functioning in different disorders. This could range from considerable disturbance in, for example, psychosis, to less pervasively impaired voluntary functioning in, for example, substance abuse or anxiety disorders. (This does not mean that the degree of meaning disturbance is subjectively experienced as a proportional limitation of freedom. It remains an interesting research question that in many of the more severe disorders, the inverse occurs, e.g., confabulation in organic patients, lack of insight in psychotic patients, subjective feelings of unlimited capacity during manic episodes, etc.). In acute and/or chronic mental disorder, rather, what was once a part of the conscious experience of self and at one's free disposal is lost below the threshold of what is voluntary. It reappears in inverted form as involuntary in the symptom.[11] Von Weizsaecker called this the *unlived life*, which he applied to his concept of psychosomatic and functional "illnesses," but which can also throw light on mental disorders (Mishara, in press; von Weizsaecker, 1957).

A SKETCH FOR A PHENOMENOLOGICAL CLASSIFICATION OF SUBJECTIVE MEANING DISTURBANCE

The chapter by Sadler and Hulgus in this book suggests that the multiaxial system could be used for accounting for sorely neglected idiographic data of the patient. From a different point of view, Vaillant, Perry, Bond and others are attempting to develop a reliable coding system for inferring the patient's use of defenses during the clinical interview as a possible axis for DSM-IV. It was stated above, however, that the latter approach, although consonant with the DSM-III-R behavioral assumptions, does not inquire into how such defenses fit into a phenomenology of the patient's subjective organization of experiential meaning as bipersonal structure.

The avoidance of the patient's subjectivity could be impoverishing for research and possibly the diagnosis itself. Unforeseen advances could result from accounting and recording idiographic or subjective data as proposed by Sadler and Hulgus and by bringing them into statistical covariation with factors on the other axes. The resulting data and questions could redirect the clinician's or researcher's thematic concerns to new aspects of mental disorder.

The phenomenological method encourages the development of research questions with respect to the following categories of the patient's subjective experiencing; spatiality, temporality, embodiment, self-other relationship as bipersonality, and the relationship to self as an ongoing task of self-transcendence. Questions that arise in the clinical application of such categories may appear initially to be rather rudimentary and difficult to formalize: How does the subject experience and structure his or her world? Space? time relationships? Relations with others? How does the subject manifest bodily presence during the interview (i.e., through posture, expressions, voice tone, statements, etc.)? How does the subject express, move, and define space as embodied subject? Is there a tendency to take an external or internal perspective to one's body, actions, expression and self and under what situational circumstances? What is the patient's ability to transcend bodily self as the momentary and fluctuating center of experiences? What is the ability to empathize with others? Does it have a certain quality?

At first sight, such questions may appear to be empirical questions that merely take into account more aspects of the patient's subjective experiencing and organization of experience. Another objection may be that such subjective variables would present methodological problems in quantifying these for reliability studies through the usual instruments—questionnaires and rating scales, for example. Even if we were to formalize the above variables into related or intersecting dimensions, which, in fact, the phenomenology theory indicates, it appears that all statements made by the clinician are still merely inferences, admittedly of a somewhat different type, which are drawn from the patient's behavior and utterances.

The problem here is not the reality of the patient's subjectivity. This is presupposed in any diagnostic or therapeutic interaction with the patient. The interaction is anchored in everyday experience and its basic structure of bipersonality. The problem is instead methodological. How does the clinician or researcher have access to the patient's subjectivity such that formalizable statements could be made with a certain amount of reliability and then, empirically tested?

Phenomenology offers a theory of human subjectivity which is developed methodically and goes beyond the commonsensical assumptions that uncritically inform other approaches. Husserl (1970a) showed that it is possible to have theoretical access to others' subjectivity as well as one's own. This is achieved by means of the imposed shift of attitude which comes with his method of phenomenological reduction.[12]

The listing of phenomenological categories of experience and their structural changes, however, allows us at best to develop a primitive typology. The establishing of a formal typology of subjective meaning disturbance first requires some groundwork: (a) Apply Husserl's method of free fantasy variation to uncover the essential structure of what we mean when we diagnose different disorders (Sadler, 1992; Uehlein, 1992); this enables us to counter the danger of theoretical fragmentation which comes with over-splitting of diagnostic classifications. (b) Use a genetic phenomenological approach to such categories of subjective structural meaning; it is possible to formalize the universal laws of the genesis of experience for human subjects by abstracting levels of meaning (Mishara, 1992). This provides a theoretical framework for detecting the level and depth of meaning disturbance in various disorders and formalizing them into a typology.

To take one example: we might hypothesize that an antisocial personality disorder is deficient in an ability to empathize in structuring relationships with others. We would have no criterion for distinguishing how this deficiency may differ from narcissistic, borderline, and sadistic (proposed in American Psychiatric Association, 1987, p. 376) personality disorders, or for that matter, from schizophrenics who may also be deficient in such a proposed basic empathy function. If we turn to empirical research, we see, for example, that psychophysiological recordings of skin conductivity and heart beat with socio-paths have shown a "lower emotional reactivity" and an "ability to block out arousing sensory input and thus stem cortical arousal" when stressful stimuli are applied (Davidson & Neale, 1990, p. 270). It is assumed that their emotional responsiveness to others in distress would therefore also be less.

On the other hand, antisocial personalities sometimes demonstrate empathic or caring responses to others whom they perceive to be in a situation similar to their own (i.e., other antisocial personalities). It follows that the antisocial's empathic deficiency may manifest different subjective structural meaning than the empathic deficiency, for example, suggested by the DSM-III-R description of the interpersonal exploitativeness or lack of empathy of the Narcissistic Personality Disorder (American Psychiatric Association, 1987, p. 350). Empirical research has considerable difficulty in operationalizing such distinctions, which ostensibly involve situational variability. The difference, however, could lie in these disorders' structural development regarding the subjective experience of other persons. In any case, neither antisocial, narcissistic, nor even sadistic personality disorders have such a fundamental disturbance of empathy that they would have difficulty in perceiving the reality of other person's views on things, or that they would mistakenly ascribe personal agency in inanimate things or states of affairs, or be persistently unable to *perceive* certain matters beyond their own perspective. These are nevertheless disturbances in the genesis of the perception of otherness which are often found in schizophrenic delusions. It is clear that schizophrenia involves a more fundamental—that is, genetically earlier and more pervasive—and qualitatively different kind of disturbance in the genesis of empathic responses than the above stated personality disorders.

The above example can only provide a rough idea of the possibilities in formalizing such differences in the genesis of subjective structural meaning. It would then be possible eventually to undertake empirical studies that would take such variables into account. Other examples in which a phenomenological approach could sharpen diagnostic criteria in DSM-III-R can only be suggested but not discussed in detail here. Regarding the disturbance of body image in Anorexia Nervosa (American Psychiatric Association, 1987, p. 65), current research and its instruments are geared toward measuring an overestimation of self's body size. This one-sidedly emphasizes the dimension of breadth along the horizontal axis of body image. It neglects the vertical dimension of bodily experience in which the experience of gravitational pull and the striving against weight occurs. As another example, the subjective experience of temporality which accompanies the slowed (depressive) or accelerated (manic) reactions of patients with mood disorders (American Psychiatric Association, 1987, pp. 218 and 215, respectively) could be considered, along with the corresponding experience of space as narrow-oppressive or open-expansive (see the loss of depth dimension in the spatial experience of depressive patients reported by Tellenbach, 1956, p. 18). In DSM-III-R post-traumatic stress disorder is "more severe and long lasting when the stressor is of human design" (American Psychiatric Association, 1987, p. 248), an acknowledgment that the *meaning* of the stressor is critical for the course of the disorder. It is simply easier to explain, that is, to cope with, a natural disaster than one resulting from human neglect or intent. Phenomenology is able to show how the subjective need to find *meaning* in experience in general as a means of coping also applies to traumatic experience (see also Straus, 1930). DSM-III-R uses a disturbance of empathy as a criterion for the diagnosis of Autistic Disorder in that there is a "marked lack of awareness of the existence of feelings of others" and a "qualitative impairment of reciprocal interaction" (American Psychiatric Association, 1987, p. 8). The genesis of the subjective empathy response in autistic disorder needs to be clarified and compared with the level and scope of disturbance in schizophrenic as well as various personality disorders.

CONCLUSION: PHENOMENOLOGICAL METHODOLOGY ENCOURAGES A DISCIPLINED CLINICAL ATTITUDE

What Blankenburg (1981) wrote about existential analysis (*Daseinsanalyse*) is also an ideal of the application of phenomenological method to problems of psychiatric classification, diagnosis, therapy, and research: "There belongs to existential analysis a far-reaching oscillation between participating empathy and contemplative, respectively, reflective distance" p. 51; my translation). By encouraging both empathy and distance, phenomenology offers a discipline for acquiring a change in attitude which maximizes the use of subjective experience without itself becoming subjective. It enables a new realm of research to develop: how meaning structures itself in experience as at first atmospheric or physiognomic.[13] Phenomenological method enables a maximizing of the subjective sources of cognition and the clinician's thematizing of the subjective experiencing of the patient. At the same time, it provides a maximizing of distance with respect to the reality claims of these subjective cognitions of self and others by placing them into methodical suspension or brackets. Although it opens up a realm of meaning structure for descriptive analysis in phenomenological reduction, it makes no theoretical claims concerning the nature of these structures. It requires the suspension of theoretical prejudices that would too quickly bias our interpretation of meaning structure in terms of the presently existing approaches. These attempt to explain mental disorder in terms of underlying etiology: biological, cognitive, psychodynamic, behavioristic, systems theory, for example.

In his or her descriptions, the researcher or clinician abstractively isolates regions of being depending on his or her theorizing interests. The pertaining ideal objects or constructs (e.g., the classificational types and genera), are products of his or her own formalizing activity. They are arranged hierarchically and have provisional existence as the nomenclature of a discipline based on direct intuitions (observations) and/or an acquired stock of knowledge (Schutz, 1962). This abstracting process has its basis in preconceptual typifications in everyday experience. The latter occur unobtrusively in their own right and are usually not thematized or questioned unless they lead to ineffective practices as operational assumptions. Phenomenology does not claim independent existence for these regions. They dictate, rather, the necessary structure of any object in terms of basic essential properties that enable membership in a particular ideal classificational region (e.g., the region of mental disorders).

As a method of abstract thought, phenomenology cannot compete with empirical approaches in producing reliable results. It is rather a shift of internal attitude which develops incrementally through practice and is eventually acquired as habit. It provides a means by which clinicians and researchers could be trained through observation and thematization to enhance their experience of the atmospheric as the realm in which meaning first interactively structures itself in experience as physiognomic Gestalt perceptions. Schwartz and Wiggins (1987b) demonstrated the importance of this realm in the preconceptual typification processes that first lead to diagnosis. It is also the realm that is disturbed in mental disorder. Disturbances of the subjective achievement of meaning can be formalized into a typology that takes into account temporal, spatial, bodily, interactive, self-, and genetic aspects as part of one *subjective* organization. In addition, genetic phenomenology offers access to levels of the organization of experience which would otherwise remain unthematized by means of abstractively removing layers of experience.

The mere excluding, exiling, or forbidding of subjectivity from objective research considerations, or the injunction to keep subjective inference to a minimum in the objective description of behaviors (as in DSM-III-R) is no guarantee that the subjective has actually been removed from our considerations. I have argued that the common sense that is presupposed as an unquestioned basis for such approaches is actually a return of a subjective perspective in concealed form. It generates a problematic leap from the observation and description of behavior in ordinary-language diagnostic practice to an explanatory realm (whether this is biological, psychodynamic/cognitive or behavioral/social) without being able to give a step-by-step account of deriving one's formal idealizations from the evidence of everyday experience (i.e., *metabasis in allo genos*). Finally, I have sketched a direction for classifying disturbances of subjective organization and experience of meaning in the ongoing bipersonal structure of reversible relationship between self and otherness.

5   Phenomenological and Criteriological Diagnosis
Different or Complementary?

ALFRED KRAUS, M.D.

The worldwide application of operationally defined diagnostic criteria in psychiatry, as in the diagnostic manuals of ICD-9 and DSM-III-R, has provoked change in the daily practice of diagnosing. This change has as yet been insufficiently examined. In the scientific field the application of methods of multivariate statistics, such as factor and cluster analysis, has led to new diagnostic entities and a growing crisis of taxonomy. An enormous literature about diagnostic problems in psychiatry is concerned with methods of generating data, evaluating data, and revising classifications, whereas the process of diagnosing itself has rarely been investigated. This process seems especially important to us because we are convinced—this should be posed as a thesis at the beginning—that the making of a diagnosis in psychiatry, especially by the experienced psychiatrist, comprises much more than is represented in the diagnostic manuals and, therefore, that ICD-9 and DSM-III-R are far from real reconstructions of the diagnostic process.

DIAGNOSTIC PRACTICE

Interested not only in the assessment of symptoms, the course of illness, biological features, genetic factors, and so forth, psychiatrists are also concerned with the holistic impressions that they get from a patient and his or her situation. The better their training, the more they control or support their diagnoses by considering the patient in all his or her aspects and whole context. Diagnosticians themselves may not always be aware of this; however, it often seems to give them final diagnostic certainty. Thus, according to Irle (1962), in an inquiry of 1,246 psychiatrists from West Germany, 54% of them considered the praecox feeling described by Rümke (1958) to be reliable for the diagnosis of schizophrenia, and 25% of them considered it to be even more reliable than the actual symptoms of schizophrenia.

We are especially concerned here with the impact on the practice of diagnosing, as well as on the training of the physician, if in operationalized diagnosis holistic aspects of the patient are not considered. It is obvious that an orientation toward so-called *hard signs* will invariably neglect soft signs, such as symptoms of expression, as well as other holistic aspects of the patient, such as his or her way of living and life events.

BASIC CONCEPTS OF CLASSIFICATION AND DIAGNOSIS

The tendency to eliminate all nonempirical, nonoperational concepts in the classification or diagnosis of psychiatric disturbances has led to the devaluation of holistic categories of description, such as Bleuler's (1911) basic symptoms of schizophrenia (disturbance of association, ambivalence, autism). It is often historically overlooked that in the development of many of our nosological entities, such as manic-depressive illness and schizophrenia, the intuitive grasping of a psychopathological Gestalt, a naive phenomenology, has probably played a more important role than any presumed causes in the sense of natural science. Moreover, until now the nosological entities of psychiatry have mostly been founded in psychopathology instead of etiology. Psychopathological entities such as the endogenous psychoses are mostly related to causes that remain more or less hypothetical. This relationship to causes, however, should not deceive us about the way in which we conceive of these entities. Originally with cyclothymia and schizophrenia, according to Schneider (1959), we have to make do with "pure psychological facts" (p. 90) that by their very nature can be differentiated only typologically. Therefore, Schneider maintained that these are not diagnosis in a medical sense but rather the assessment of a differential typology. To say that these entities of "illness" are established in a typological way is ambiguous, as is the concept of typology itself.

Typological can mean a type of correlation which indicates a frequent correlation of symptoms or a philosophical type of essence gained in an eidetic way. Insofar as illness entities are types gained only by correlative statistics, and as long as their causes are unknown, these entities can be looked upon as merely nosological conventions. But as far as the entities of illness are eidetic types, they have an immediate evidence foundation in phenomenological experience. This is especially the case with schizophrenic and affective disturbances, the endogenous psychoses. Over against the correlative-eidetic mixed nature of these entities, DSM-III-R (and some other authors, such as Janzarik [1989]) leave out an eidetic-typological foundation of illness for disturbance entities, and take a generalized nominalistic position. Schneider (1959), to whom the authors of DSM-III-R often refer, was himself ambiguous regarding typology. On the one hand, with schizophrenia and cyclothymia he spoke merely of denominations, and, on the other hand, he conceived of the psychotic patient phenomenologically as a "unified microcosmos" (p. 96), his typological understanding being not only a correlative but also an eidetic one.

As we have shown, the classifying of psychiatric disorders is a typological concern not only historically, but today as well, in the sense of an orientation toward the entities of essence. If this is true, why should we, as DSM-III-R proposes, suddenly eliminate this approach as a principle of classification and as a method of diagnostic practice? Instead, would it not be better to make explicit and scientifically grounded what has until now been practiced imminently and prescientifically? Schwartz and Wiggins (1987b) showed the significance of typification not only for the organization of the field of our experience in general but also for the diagnostic process in psychiatry.

Here we are to take the first step toward describing the cognitive processes and toward a holistic understanding of the patient—that is, at a diagnosis consisting of more than symptoms and hard data. In a second step we want to portray phenomenological methods as the via regia in the recognition of types of essence. Although restricting ourselves to phenomenological methods, we want at least to mention the great contributions to holistic diagnosis made by psychoanalytic, Gestalt/theoretical, structural/ dynamic, interactional, and other approaches, whereby the intended whole is not always of the same kind.

DIFFERENCES AMONG PHENOMENON, SYMPTOM, AND CRITERION

Above all, phenomenological authors such as Blankenburg (1980b), Häfner (1959); Hofer (1954); Müller-Suur (1958); and Tellenbach (1987a) have referred to the difference between phenomenon and symptom. Unfortunately, there is often an undifferentiated use of the terms *phenomenon* and *symptom*. Even in the different phenomenological schools these terms do not always have the same meaning. For instance, Jaspers (1965) wanted to reduce his phenomenology merely to a vivid representation (*anschauliche Vergegenwärtigung*) of mental states. *Phenomenology*, as we understand it here, refers to the essential structure of a phenomenon. The emphasis lies on the *logos* (*eidos* or essence) of the phenomenon.

Since we want to focus upon the special features of phenomenological diagnosis, symptomatological/criteriological diagnosis, characteristic of ICD-10 and DSM-III-R, will be discussed less extensively, and then usually as a form of deprivation when compared with phenomenological diagnosis. However, this does not mean that we devalue symptomatological/criteriological diagnosis.

The special practical and scientific usefulness of this method stem precisely from the reduction of the phenomena to terminological formulas. The reliability of criteriological diagnosis is founded in this reductive simplification.

The fact that we speak of symptoms at all in psychiatry is the consequence of a model of psychic illness founded in natural sciences which relates special symptoms or syndromes to special causes. However, with most psychiatric illnesses this is only partially possible. On the one hand, it is difficult to differentiate psychiatric illnesses from one another, much less from normality. On the other hand, special causes are often unknown. Therefore, Schneider (1959) was of the opinion that the notion of symptom, as well as that of illness in psychiatry, is different from that found in somatic medicine. Speaking of characteristics instead of symptoms, he was one of the initiators of the criteriological approach. Referring to disorders rather than to illnesses, DSM-III-R also takes into account problems associated with the notion of illness in psychiatry in a manner similar to that of Schneider (1959). Characteristics become criteria when it is specified in advance which characteristics in which combination are sufficient to justify a certain diagnosis.

Regarding the differentiation of *phenomenon* and *symptom*, the difference between illness as a subjective experience and as a medical notion has often been pointed out. The difference between a phenomenon and a symptom could be better grasped if we asked ourselves, for example, whether a patient has an endogenous psychosis or neurosis in the same way that he has a fracture of a bone or hepatitis. Is schizophrenia as an illness to be differentiated from the person at all? Are we not primarily dealing with a certain kind of being, manifesting itself in phenomena that in referring to a medical model, can be taken as the symptoms of an illness?

Compared with symptomatological diagnosis, phenomenological diagnosis tries to describe the special modes of experience and behavior of a patient and his relationship to himself and to the world. Thus, phenomenological diagnosis is more person oriented, whereas symptomatological diagnosis is more morbus oriented.

Since the patient not only *has* schizophrenia, mania, or depression but is a person who *is* schizophrenic, depressed, or manic, the clinical intuition of the psychiatrist is completely different from that of the internist. With the aid of intuition and experience, the internist links certain symptoms together to form a picture of the somatic illness of the patient (Wyrsch, 1946). In contrast, the intuition of the psychiatrist grasps something that is neither to be found in the individual symptoms nor in their accumulation but rather in a certain mode of being of the patient. Not considering the whole mode of being of the patient, symptomatological diagnosis instead selects some aspects from a mass of data about mental states and behavior and gives them a special significance and weight.

THE DIAGNOSTIC PROCESS IN CONVENTIONAL AND IN CRITERIOLOGICAL DIAGNOSIS

To differentiate more clearly between phenomenological and criteriological diagnosis, it is useful to consider the diagnostic process of the experienced psychiatrist. When this psychiatrist makes a diagnosis, both kinds of diagnosis work together and complement each other. The psychiatric practitioner is not only oriented toward symptoms and objective findings but also toward the whole being-in-the-world of the patient. Not only his way of looking, walking, or shaking hands, or his style of living and communicating, but the whole of his biography is important. Very soon, often as the patient is crossing the threshold, the practitioner may gain a hypothesis about the patient's disturbance. This holistic scheme will decide all of his further diagnostic steps. On the other hand, with the aid of the data gained, the holistic scheme of the disturbance can become more defined, retroactively allowing for an ever-increasing distinction of diagnosis. Thus, diagnosis is a dialectical process, consisting of an anticipating, proleptic part and a retrospective (or retro-versive) determination.

Through this dialectic in conventional diagnosis, the single phenomenon remains connected with the whole, both part and whole giving each other clarity and distinction. However, this is the case only when the single phenomenon is integrated into an understandable whole, as in the phenomen-ological whole of the being-in-the-world of schizophrenics or manics. This is not analogously valid for mere syndromes, even when a syndrome can be re-duced to a known cause or causes.

For a trained practitioner, the whole of the experience with this single patient *and* the whole of experience with many patients determines his or her diagnosis. The more experiences influence diagnosis, the more precise the grasping of individual phenomena. If the diagnostician asks only about in-dividual symptoms and then puts them together into syndromes, as the inexperienced diagnostician often does, this dialectical process is lost. Above all, there is no prolepsis. To a certain degree this is the case in criteriological diagnosis, insofar as there is only the question of the presence of a certain criterion. Because the issue of diagnosis, in a certain sense, is always already at hand with the criteria set, there is no dialectical becoming of a diagnosis. Since these entities are not supported by a concept of wholeness (*Ganz-heitsschau*), the combination of the single criteria into a diagnostic entity can only be reached by counting and proceeding logically. Therefore, the pro-cedure of diagnosing could even be done by a computer.

In addition, the end of the diagnostic process is different in criteriological as opposed to phenomenological diagnosis. In criteriological diagnosis, by means of the fulfillment of previously fixed inclusion and exclusion criteria, the diagnostic process has come to an end. Alternatively, because of the dialectic already mentioned, the phenomenological diagnostic process remains open and cannot be closed. New experiences with the patient can always lead to a wholly new evaluation of the individual phenomena. The diagnosis can always be questioned, and it can be ever more deepened.

In criteriological diagnosis, the regulative idea of wholeness is missing, at least in the sense of the whole of an essence—that is, of an internal connection, an essential unity of the individual criteria. Also, the whole of the experience and behavior of the psychiatrist in determining the individual phenomena is excluded from the diagnostic process. Learning to make phenomenological contact with the patient is not to be mistaken for training in the application of criteria to a patient.

In actual diagnostic practice these differences do not appear as grossly as we have depicted them here because a holistic approach to diagnosis is always concomitant.

THE PROBLEM OF SPECIFICITY OF PHENOMENON AND SYMPTOM

There are usually two arguments against holistic diagnosis. One argument states that the whole of a patient is not recognizable. Our answer here is that even if the whole is not recognizable in its totality, it is always possible to be directed to the whole. Moreover, we should not forget the ideal type character of a phenomenological description of essence or structure (Binswanger, 1961; Jaspers, 1963; Kraus, 1991; Schwartz, Wiggins & Norko, 1989; and this book). A second argument against holistic diagnosis is the claim that the intuition of a specific wholeness is never more than a feeling that can never be described clearly or investigated scientifically. However, even if the practitioner cannot generally found his holistic diagnosis scientifically in the same way as his symptomatological diagnostic procedures, we have to ask ourselves whether we are only dealing with a feeling, or if a real recognition is taking place. Later on we will show that what the practitioner does in a prescientific although protophenomenological way can also be founded in phenomenological science. We have to admit, of course, that such a scientific approach is only in its beginnings.

The practical as well as the scientific significance of phenomenological diagnosis will become clear if we recognize that symptomatological/criteriological diagnosis not only makes the reality of the patient accessible in a very reduced way but also portrays the pathological phenomena in a very imprecise and broad manner. For this reason the emphasis on operationally exact definitions of criteria should not be mistaken for an exact grasping of the essence of clinical phenomena. The two methods are fundamentally different from each other.

The reduction of phenomena to symptoms and criteria has as its consequence a loss of specificity. In 1957, Weitbrecht had already demonstrated the unspecificity of symptoms, and this lack of specificity has been confirmed subsequently by several empirical investigations. For example, depressive symptoms are to be found in 50% of schizophrenics according to Helmchen and Hippius (1967) and in 80% of schizophrenics according to Möller and von Zerssen (1981). Even Schneider's first rank symptoms have been proven to be unspecific (Bland & Orn, 1980; Carpenter, Strauss & Muleh, 1973).

As against this fundamental lack of specificity of the symptom, diagnosis oriented toward the holistic experience or intuition (such as the praecox feeling) seems to provide the experienced practitioner with specificity for the phenomena. Rümke (1958) thus maintained that blunting of the emotions, decrease of mental capability, the loss of energy, and even Schneider's first-rank symptoms could only be considered as distinguishing features of schizophrenia if we could put the qualifying words "an entirely specific kind of . . ." before each of these symptoms. Rümke (1958) even went so far as to say that without this very specific schizophrenic coloring such symptoms as catatonia or delusional structures have nothing to do with real schizophrenia.

Müller-Suur (1958) pointed out that with the intuition of schizophrenia we have to do with not only a vague feeling of something "indistinctly incomprehensible" but by all means with something "distinctly incomprehensible." In other words, we have to do with "phenomenal specificity" (Müller-Suur, 1961, pp. 146, 149). This distinct apprehension of the schizophrenic quality is not already given by the first physiognomic impression of something odd (Müller-Suur, 1958, 1961). What is at this point indistinctly incomprehensible gains diagnostic profundity only in connection with the symptomatological process of differentiation. In this manner phenomenological diagnosis should always be used in connection with symptomatological/criteriological diagnosis. By means of the so-called praecox feeling, the diagnosis of schizophrenia is raised to a higher level, namely, that of phenomenal distinctness.

What is distinct about the praecox feeling? It is the very special *form* of another kind of being-in-the-world, the difference as such remaining incomprehensible. What is designated as *form* here is different from what, on the symptomatological level, Schneider (1959) called the form of a psychotic content, such as hallucination or delusion. *Form*, as we intend it, aims at a more comprehensive description of the patient-person than symptoms could express. Phenomenologically speaking, not only in schizophrenia but also in depression or mania the changed relationship of the self to itself and the world gives specificity to the individual phenomena. If this were generally accepted, then Schneider's thesis (that the decisive element of endogenous psychoses is not their content but their form) could be confirmed in a broad sense. Or, as Rümke postulated (1958), "The secret of schizophrenia is a secret of form."

However, to transform this intuition of a specific wholeness into a scientifically valid expression requires much new scientific work. Above all, for this aim we need very different descriptive categories, not reducing the patient to an object but taking human subjectivity into account. Such categories have been developed by the phenomenological/anthropological (Binswanger, 1961; Blankenburg, 1978, 1980a, 1980b; Kraus, 1977, 1978; Spiegelberg, 1972; Tellenbach, 1987a, 1987b), daseinsanalytical (Binswanger, 1955a, 1955b; Blankenburg, 1977), and interactional psychopathology (Glatzel, 1978, 1981) approaches. These categories allow us to describe the structure of the encounter with others, as well as the formation of identity, the temporalizing (*Zeitigung*), the spatializing (*Räumlichung*), and other aspects of the patient.

THE SCIENTIFIC FOUNDATIONS OF THE SYMPTOMATOLOGICAL/ CRITERIOLOGICAL AND THE PHENOMENOLOGICAL/ ANTHROPOLOGICAL APPROACHES

The symptomatological/criteriological and the phenomenological approaches have entirely different scientific foundations. Symptomatological/criteriological systems of classification and diagnosis, as exemplified by manuals such as DSM-III-R and ICD-10, mainly follow the scheme of scientific explanation of Hempel and Oppenheim (1948), founded in the logical empiricism of the circle of Vienna and the critical rationalism of Popper (1965). On the other hand, the phenomenological/anthropological approach, also used in other sciences, in the social sciences, e.g., has its roots mainly in the phenomenology of Husserl and in existential philosophy. The frequent devaluing misunderstanding of the phenomenological approach is predominantly a result of the (mis-)application of the intentions and the scientific criteria of logical empiricism to it. Consequently, from the viewpoint of logical empiricism, the phenomenological approach is not recognized as an independent scientific paradigm.

DIFFERENT UNDERSTANDINGS OF EXPERIENCE

The main difference between the two methods of diagnosing results from differing approaches to the understanding of experience. As is true with operational/empirical methods in general, with the criteriological approach the range of possibilities of expected or experiential clinical phenomena is, to a great extent, defined in advance. Therefore, the patient diagnosed with manuals such as DSM-III-R and ICD-10 either fulfills the criteria of a certain kind of disturbance or does not. That means that a certain picture of illness is provisionally applied to the patient. Whereas here, in a methodologically controlled way, certain expectations are to be confirmed, with the phenomenological approach (as in hermeneutic sciences in general) experience is something that makes us see the object in a new way, changing ourselves as well (Gadamer, 1976). Entirely different from the notion of experience in empirical sciences, which is only a derived one, every real experience in everyday life contradicts or nullifies an expectation. It is important to realize that, because of methodological rules in criteriological diagnosis, the very essence of the investigated object as well as the lifeworld experience (*Lebensvelterfahrung*) of the investigator are *excluded* as criteria of verification. Thus, the investigator sometimes has to make a particular diagnosis even if it is contradictory to his clinical experience.

The task of the phenomenological/anthropological approach is to reflect that special understanding that proceeds (*Vorverständnis*) and enables every experience. Objectifying/empirical methods, however, take their data from experience as objectively given. Nevertheless, we have to take into account that these data are loaded with theory, so that we could say that a so-called fact is given only if a corresponding theory has already allowed for it. To quote Wolfgang v. Goethe (1981): "All that is fact is already theory."

Therefore, phenomenological methods strive for a description of the object as free as possible from theoretical prejudices and presuppositions. We should keep in mind the warning of Husserl (1968) that descriptive notions enter into the final results of pretended scientific judgments of experience. In the same manner, in the biological model of illness, certain concepts of causality even determine our language of description.

For example, if we speak of an inhibition of motion and thought in a depressive state, we infer a disturbance of drive. Phenomenologically, we can observe a global transformation of the lived space and time of the patient. Not only have the distances between things and people become larger but also those between the single ideas of this patient. Things are no longer at hand (*zuhanden*), and the social boundaries between the patient and other people become insurmountable. The patient experiences not only a loss of the perspective of the future and a dominating relationship to the past but also a slowing down, or even standstill, of subjective time. There is a loss not only of prospection but also of protention (Janzarik, 1965) of the directedness to the future. With phenomenological description, which keeps very near to the phenomena themselves (Husserl pleaded: *zu den Sachen selbst*, to the things themselves), we get another view. We see how many possibilities of our experience get lost when symptomatologically we speak of an inhibition of drive as if it were a disturbance of some function. This is actually a reductionistic abstraction of the holistic change of the relationship of the depressed patient to the world and the self.

Therefore, the first step of the phenomenological method, as given to us by Husserl, is to turn back from a theoretical to a natural attitude. This means to turn toward the lifeworld (*Lebenswelt*) of the patient and to allow things to be seen as they show themselves. Or, to quote Heidegger (1963): "*Um das, was sich zeigt, so wie es sich von ihm selbst her zeigt, von ihm selbst her sehen zu lassen*" (to let that which shows itself be seen precisely in the way in which it shows itself) (p. 34).

THE PROBLEM OF DESCRIPTION

One of the main problems of the symptomatological/criteriological diagnosis is the achievement of an adequate description of psychotic phenomena. In our view, every classification stands and falls with such description. If we establish new diagnostic classes and the phenomena are not clear because they are insufficiently described in their essence, it is, as Hoche joked, like pouring a dirty fluid from one glass into another, the fluid remaining unchanged.

On the one hand, our language does not provide a sufficient richness for this task. Therefore, we tend to describe psychotic phenomena univocally, equivocally, or analogically to phenomena of nonpsychotic mental states. On the other hand, operationalized definitions of symptomatological criteria which are oriented toward a possible quantification (e.g., of the degree of severity of an illness or symptom) can lead to reductionistic descriptions of the originally given phenomena.

For example, we designate very different mental states as depressive. But depression in mourning, neurosis, epilepsia, schizophrenia, dementia, and melancholia (endogenous depression) have very different qualities. Indeed, even if DSM-III speaks of the special quality of depressive mood in the melancholic type of major depression, nowhere is there a further, clearer definition to be found. DSM-III-R only points to the loss of interest, of pleasure, and of reactivity, all of which are qualitatively nonspecific. In contrast, from the viewpoint of phenomenological diagnosis, in melancholia, compared with other kinds of depressed mood, there is a changed relationship to oneself, a not-being oneself in the melancholic "mood." Freud (1967) spoke of an emptiness of the I [*Ich*]). Therefore, this kind of mood is experienced as strange and forced upon one. Characterized in this way, the core of melancholia would not be an alteration of mood but, as we show elsewhere, a special kind of depersonalization (Kraus, unpublished manuscript). It follows that the main characteristic of the so-called affective psychoses in DSM-III—that is, mood disturbances as merely a presumed elevation or lowering of mood—would be entirely questionable, at least for the melancholic type of major depression. We see that insufficiency in description may have incalculable consequences not only for classification but also for many kinds of empirical research and therapy.

RELIABILITY AND VALIDITY

The operational/symptomatological methods of diagnosis have greatly improved the reliability of diagnoses, nationally and internationally, and have given a fresh impetus to empirical research. However, this agreement, reducing mutual understanding to the smallest common denominator, offers no possibility of an interchange of deeper experiences and is perhaps even an obstacle to this. Reliability seems to have been purchased by renouncing essential aspects of psychiatric experience. The pronounced weak point of the prevailing operational/symptomatological diagnosis is, as the German publishers of DSM-III (Köhler & Sass) admit, that most diagnostic categories have only partial or no sufficient validity. This, in our view, is mainly a result of poorly differentiated qualification of the phenomena. Because of the lack of specificity of individual symptoms (or characteristics), diagnostic significance arises only through correlations with other symptoms. Formed in this way, diagnostic classes are nothing more than serial summing-up formulas, stating the smallest number of symptoms necessary for the probability of a certain diagnosis.

To characterize this "necessary and sufficient model" Klerman (1980) spoke of a "Chinese-restaurant-menu-approach to diagnosis" (p. 1310). Through the isolation of each symptom from a whole way of being, individual symptoms lose their coherence with each other. In such aggregates of symptoms and characteristics there are only "and"-connections. In contrast, the phenomenological approach assumes a "psychological whole" (Jaspers, 1963, p. 510) as the basis of schizophrenia as well as of manic-depressive illness. Even Jaspers, a most ardent critic of all striving for wholeness, maintained that the psychopathologist has "an intuition of a whole which is called schizophrenic, but we cannot grasp it, but enumerate a quantity of singularities" (p. 478). Wyrsch (1946) spoke of a specific schizophrenic kind of being which is more than the individual symptoms. The phenomenological approach strives to discover the essence revealing itself in these individual phenomena. Thus, the hermeneutic circle, making understandable the individual elements out of the whole context as well as the whole context out of the individual elements, is of central importance.

RELATIONSHIP OF THE INVESTIGATOR AND THE OBJECT OF INVESTIGATION

In the two kinds of diagnosis there is also a different relationship between the investigator and the person being investigated. In the morbus-oriented symptomatological/criteriological diagnosis, the investigated person, as a supplier of data, tends to be viewed as an object. In the person-oriented phenomenological diagnosis the investigated person is, as Schütz (1962) formulated for qualitative social investigation, "on principle a person capable of orienting, theorizing, and interpreting" (p. 118). Instead of being made into an object, a bearer of symptoms and qualities, he reveals himself from the side of his freedom and his relation to the future. As understanding requires a common basis for the investigator and for the person investigated, the investigator is to a large extent dependent upon the cooperation of the patient. The investigator has to show himself to the patient in a way that is different from that of the first method. Moreover, instead of keeping the influence of himself as a person as small as possible, in the phenomenological method, there must be for mutual understanding a certain closeness between the investigator and the investigated person. Because the investigator is more interested in detecting than verifying, a "disciplined spontaneity" (Giorgi, 1985, p. 14) and creativity are allowed for him to get the hermeneutic process going.

THERAPEUTIC ASPECTS

The close reference of phenomenological diagnosis to the lifeworld of the patient makes it obvious that guidelines and norms for rehabilitative and therapeutic interventions issue out of the diagnostic process itself, without having to be added after the diagnostic encounter. Exclusively symptomatological/criteriological diagnoses are mostly unable to determine norms for judgments about the pathological status of quantitative or qualitative deviances. In the introduction to DSM-III-R, it is admitted that there is no satisfying definition of the concept *psychic disturbances*. In this case there are also no exact norms to judge indications for treatment. Such norms often are not derived from the symptoms themselves but from their consequences for the patient and his surroundings. In other words, these norms are gained from the relationship of the patient to his lifeworld and from a holistic understanding of the patient. What is done intuitively in daily practice should be explicated by phenomenological investigation.

CONCLUSION

Our criticism of symptomatological/criteriological diagnosis should in no way diminish its necessity or success. This criticism should actually be complemented by a criticism of phenomenological diagnosis to show the limits of this method also. However, in this chapter we have been concerned primarily with presenting phenomenological diagnosis as a methodologically independent approach that, as a scientific paradigm, deserves further development. We want to call attention to the fact that this method, presently neglected, has great complementary significance not only for the practice of diagnosing but also for research in classification and diagnosing and, last but not least, for therapy.

This chapter appeared in German in 1991, *Fundamenta Psychiatrica*, *5*, 102–109. Reprinted, slightly revised, with permission.

II PSYCHOPATHOLOGY

6 The Basis of Psychiatric Diagnosis

MANFRED SPITZER, M.D., Ph.D.

DESCRIPTION

Perspectives

Psychiatric diagnoses are based on the interaction of two people. One of them, whom we usually call the patient, suffers from some mental disturbance and seeks help or is brought by others to receive help; the other, the psychiatrist or other mental health professional, is trained in providing such help. However, to make appropriate decisions, the interaction must result in a proper description of what is wrong with the patient, that is, the patient's symptoms. Any further clustering of such symptoms into disorders as well as any hypothesis about the etiology of the symptoms rest on an accurate description of what is wrong with the patient.

To describe something, whatever it is, we have to use concepts. These concepts select some category of what is to be described and specify features. "This is cylindrical, red, 6 inches long, a third of an inch thick, and used for writing" describes my pen. We see that the description selects the categories of shape, color, size, and function to do descriptive work. How do we describe another person? What categories should we pick? Actual clinical practice provides an answer to these questions, reflected by the format of the mental status examination. Here we find categories used in describing a patient, such as motor behavior, speech, affect, form of thought, content of thought, perception, intelligence, orientation, memory, and so on.[1] However, we may ask, Where do these categories (or dimensions) come from? What is their scientific status? How are they, or how can they be, justified, and do they make sense?

First of all, it is striking that questions like these are rarely asked. Psychiatrists worry about clustering symptoms into syndromes or about the biological basis of syndromes, but the fundamental processes are neglected.

Second, when we look at the way the mental status examination is done, we easily recognize the elements of 19th-century "faculty psychology." However, whereas psychology has developed in the meantime, it seems that psychiatrists are stuck with old categories or dimensions that were fashionable during psychiatry's beginnings as a medical specialty. Moreover, it is often argued that psychiatrists should be more "holistic" in their approach toward patients; that is, the patient's unity of experience should not be divided into arbitrary categories, such as perception, affect, and thought, for example. In other words, the mental status examination is sometimes said to represent the "splitter's approach" which is, in principle, inappropriate when it comes to the description of mental events.

Let us take an example of description: the pen I use for writing can be described as cylindrical, red, and as used for writing. It is easy to see that the holism argument does not work with the pen: I must choose the categories of form, color, and purpose to describe what I hold in my hand. Holistically, I could only say "there is something." In other words, every description has to select categories and place the object or event to be described in them. In the example of the pen, we choose the category of length, among others, and then place the object—quite literally—on that category at the mark of 5 inches. To use the terminology of phenomenology, we have to take *perspectives*, the perspective of color, the perspective of shape, for example. Yet the same is true for the mental state of another person; it requires certain perspectives.

Note that although the placement of events or things or categories—the way the perspectives are used in a given case—may be *right* or *wrong*, the application of a peculiar perspective itself is *appropriate* or *inappropriate*, *useful* or *useless*. The perspective (category) of loudness, for example, is inappropriate and useless to describe the pen, whereas it makes sense to be used for describing sounds.

Are the perspectives that we take in psychiatry to describe patients appropriate and useful? The answer to this question is partly yes and partly no. First of all, these perspectives have been used now for at least 100 years and have therefore stood the test of time. However, as a look at several psychiatric textbooks plainly reveals, there seems to be no general agreement as to how many appropriate perspectives (descriptive categories) there are or what they should be called. Furthermore, the perspectives are often presented as if they were orthogonal or independent of each other, but they are not. Kaplan and Sadock (1988, pp. 158–159), to take just one textbook as an example, listed *speech activity* and *form of thought, perception* and *sensorium, thought process* and *cognition, consciousness* and *judgment* as different headings[2] in the section on the mental status examination, although it is clear that these categories overlap. Lastly, the relationship of descriptive categories to diagnostic criteria is sometimes vague. There is a striking difference between the way the perspectives of *appearance* or *attitude* toward the examiner enter a diagnostic decision tree (if they do at all) as compared with perspectives such as *formal thought* or *perception.* Psychiatric research seems to be invested in how to combine criteria properly but not in how such criteria come into existence.

Concepts

To describe an entity by placing it on a dimension or category implies the use of concepts. We use the concept of *redness*, for example, to describe something as red. Although the use of such concepts can be correct or incorrect (i.e., the thing may be red or not), the concepts themselves, like perspectives, are not subject to the question of correctness,[3] but rather of appropriateness and usefulness. In ordinary language, concepts are in constant development, changing according to what we (as individuals, as a community, and even a species) know. To handle these developments as well as the problem of the general meaning of concepts, it is helpful to distinguish between the *intension* and the *extension* of a given concept. What we usually call the *meaning* of a concept is its intension. The extension of a concept is the set of all its instantiations. To give an example, the extension of the concept *table* is the set of all tables, the intension is the meaning of the word *table*, that is, something like "object that one can sit at, eat from, work at . . . usually has four legs and a flat surface."

With regard to psychopathological concepts such as *hallucinations* and *delusions*, the extension poses a problem of reliability, that is, the problem of determining whether a given case reliably belongs as a member to a given set. The problem of intension bears a close relationship to the problem of validity——the question of the factual basis of a given concept. By regarding conceptual problems as merely statistical problems of reliability and validity, though, one may miss important issues. Hence, in this chapter we will use extension and intension, instead of reliability and validity, as our conceptual framework to deal with concepts.

HALLUCINATIONS

Hallucinations,[4] like other symptoms of mental disorder, cannot be observed directly; hallucinations cannot be seen or heard as can, for example, an inflammation of the skin or a wheeze in the lungs. The investigator always has to rely on the patient's statements and/or behavior and thus can only indirectly infer the presence of hallucinations. If hallucinations are identified by certain signs or utterances, one might expect a definition and characterization of hallucinations to refer to such signs and utterances. Thus we would expect a definition of hallucinations to read as follows: "A patient hallucinates if he says this and that and/or behaves such and such." Although people who want to *explain* hallucinations (e.g., from the physiologist to the psychoanalyst) would be expected to refer to the phenomenon in terms of overt theoretical constructs, we would expect purely descriptive *psychopathologies* to define hallucinations with reference to specific communications and behaviors of the hallucinating individual, that is, with reference to the situation of two interacting people.[5]

Although many of our concerns apply to many nosologies, let us take a particular example. In the *Diagnostic and Statistical Manual of Mental Disorders, Third Edition, Revised* (DSM-III-R, p. 398) we find the following definition:

> Hallucination. A sensory perception without external stimulation of the relevant sensory organ. A hallucination has the immediate sense of reality of a true perception, although in some instances the source of the hallucination may be perceived as within the body (e.g., an auditory hallucination may be experienced as coming from within the head rather than through the ears). . . . There may or may not be a delusional interpretation of the hallucinatory experience. For example, one person with auditory hallucinations may recognize that he or she is having a false sensory experience whereas another may be convinced that the source of the sensory experience has an independent physical reality. . . . Hallucinations should be distinguished from illusions, in which an external stimulus is misperceived or misinterpreted, and from normal thought processes that are exceptionally vivid.

It is striking that these sentences do not have the form we expect them to have. The fact that hallucinations are identified indirectly is not taken into consideration at all. Moreover, almost any feature that is given in this definition can be questioned.

Feature: Hallucinations are like perceptions.

Problem: Clinical experience shows that most patients can distinguish between their perceptual and their hallucinatory experiences, even though they are often unable to name any differences. About 60 years ago, the psychiatrist Zucker (1928) demonstrated experimentally that even those patients who claimed that their hallucinations were exactly like their perceptions could in fact distinguish their hallucinations from perceptions that were made to resemble the hallucinations as closely as possible. Zucker simulated voices, put electrical wires into the beds of the patients to simulate electrical sensations, sprayed patients with ethylenechloride to simulate tactile sensations and alleged these to be hallucinations. Despite his efforts, in no case was he able to fool his schizophrenic patients.[6] Merleau-Ponty (1966) later emphasized that patients as well as doctors cannot help but use perceptual language to refer to the experiences of the patients but that this does not mean that these experiences are exactly like perceptions. Perception is instead used as a model or analogy by patients and psychiatrists to refer to such strange experiences that could otherwise not be communicated at all. Note furthermore, that the notion of *hearing voices* is a strange one which under normal circumstances is not used to refer to normal auditory perceptions by normal people. In fact, as Wernicke (1906) pointed out, the notion of hearing voices was not invented by psychiatrists but rather was a brainchild of patients, who used it to indicate that their experience was somehow like hearing other people talking but somehow different from this as well.

Feature: ". . . without external stimulation of the relevant sensory organ . . ."

Problem: How can one determine that such stimulation, in fact, is not present? Wundt already noted that according to this definition, strictly speaking, only blind people can have visual hallucinations. Do all the others have illusions? If not, how shall we distinguish these two phenomena, as we are told that we should? It seems not only that the relevant organ is without stimulation but also that the relevant stimuli must be missing from the phenomenal field. But this is just to displace the problem, because how do we determine the meaning of relevant here?

Feature: "external" stimulation.

Problem: What is the boundary between internal and external? Are floaters (i.e., black moving spots that sometimes are interpreted as flies[7] and are caused by small benign deposits of some degenerated proteins in the vitreous body of the eye) hallucinations, because the stimulation takes place "inside?" Are afterimages hallucinations because the stimulation takes place "inside?"

Feature: ". . . the immediate sense of reality of a true perception . . ."

Problem: What is an "immediate sense of reality"——do normals always have it? How often? When? What is a "true perception?"——If I see a stick that is bent in the water, is this a true perception of a stick that is bent by refraction in water, a false perception of a bent stick, because the refraction of the water is disregarded, or is it simply a perception, whatever the conclusions about the things seen?

Moreover, from a clinical point of view, it is false that all patients who are said to have hallucinations experience this immediate sense of reality. First of all, there are patients who know that their hallucinations are unreal but suffer from them nonetheless. Second, the careful investigations of Aggernaes (1972) have shown that there is no such thing as a simple concept of reality. If hallucinating patients are asked questions about various aspects of reality, they give different answers that do not represent a single, uniform, coherent underlying concept or structure of reality, but rather a complex net of reality features or qualities, as Aggernaes (1972) called them. The vividness of the perceptual experience, the relevance to overt behavior, the conviction that others perceive the same thing, independence from voluntary control, the possibility

of perceiving with several modalities, the conviction of its independent existence—these features do not correlate as we might expect them to. Hence,
there is no empirical basis for the concept of *one* reality.

Feature: "relevant" sense organ.

Problem: Are there irrelevant sense organs? Which ones? What is the relevant
organ when a patient says that he feels electrifying rays in his stomach?

Feature: ". . . false sensory experience . . ."

Problem: Although the notion of false sensory experience is common, it is
problematic. Can an experience of a patient really be called false? Of course,
claims of its validity may be false, but this does not necessarily apply to the
experience itself. Furthermore, the notion of *false* is often meant to denote the
deceptive nature of hallucinations. However, the clinician uses the term *hallucinations* to denote experiences that by definition exclude the possibility of
deception. Bleuler (1911), for example, noted that pain can be hallucinated.
For logical reasons, however, sensations of pain cannot be the subject of deception; that is, I cannot be deceived if I feel pain.[8] Therefore, if there are
reasons to use the concept of hallucinations with respect to pain, and there are
such reasons,[9] hallucinations cannot be deceptions.

Feature: ". . . physical reality"

Problem: The very notion of *physical*. Although we all seem to share a vague
idea of what might be meant here, a careful investigation reveals that more detailed explications of *physical* create problems. We do not know whether
physics really matters; and in clinical settings, physics certainly does not matter. In physics, the notions of red, bitter, or loud do not occur. Moreover, what
are we to make of the notion of an *independent* physical reality—does this
imply that there could be a dependent physical reality?

A look at how some special forms of hallucinations are defined in DSM-III-
R reveals further difficulties:

> Hallucination, somatic. A hallucination involving the perception of a physical exper-
> ience localized within the body. . . . Somatic hallucinations are to be distinguished
> from unexplained physical sensations; a somatic hallucination can be identified with
> certainty only when a delusional interpretation of a physical illness is present. A
> somatic hallucination is to be distinguished also from . . . a tactile hallucination, in
> which the sensation is usually related to the skin.
> Hallucination, tactile. A hallucination involving the sense of touch, often of
> something on or under the skin. Almost invariably the symptom is associated with
> a delusional interpretation of the sensation. Examples: . . . [A man] complained of
> experiencing pains, which he attributed to the Devil, throughout his body, although
> there was no evidence of any physical illness. . . . Tactile hallucinations of pain are

to be distinguished from Somatoform Pain Disorder, in which there is no delusional interpretation. (DSM-III-R, p. 399)

Feature: ". . . physical illness is present."

Problem: This may be a matter of wording, but if a physical illness really is present, then what is experienced within the body should not be called a hallucination although it might be interpreted by the patient in a delusional way. A second problem is that in the general definition quoted above, it is explicitly stated that hallucinations may be interpreted in a delusional way. This contradicts the statement that a delusional interpretation is a necessary condition for something to be a hallucination.

Feature: ". . . unexplained physical sensations."

Problem: It is not clear how somatic hallucinations are to be distinguished from "unexplained physical sensations" as the obscurity of bodily sensations may be the only criterion for determining that the experience is hallucinatory.

Feature: "A somatic hallucination is to be distinguished . . . from a tactile hallucination" by means of the criterion of relatedness to the skin.

Problem: When tactile hallucinations are explained, we find given as an example, "pains . . . throughout his body." Therefore, the distinction is not clear-cut.

From the historical point of view, the concept of hallucinations as proposed by DSM-III-R can easily be traced back to Karl Jaspers, who explicitly defined hallucinations as being like true perceptions (Jaspers, 1963, p. 64). However, the Jaspersian clear-cut notion of hallucinations has been criticized by other investigators from the time of its first publication in 1913. Schröder, as early as in 1915, maintained that the Jaspersian concept was too narrow to account for most clinical cases, that it left one with the impression that clinically there are only few "real" hallucinations (which are, by definition, like "real" perceptions and deceptive). Beringer (1927), who was the first to experiment with mescaline in the early 1920s, explicitly criticized Jaspersian terminology in the realm of perception because it could not account for many aspects of the drug's hallucinogenic effects. Later, researchers in the field of sensory deprivation found themselves in the same position as Beringer. They did not find the concept of hallucinations as defined in psychiatric textbooks to be useful and instead made up terms such as *non-object-bound phenomena* to refer to the experiences of subjects in the dark (Spitzer, in press). At about the same time, Penfield conducted his famous experiments on direct electrical brain stimulation and explicitly turned away from the concept of hallucinations because it did not properly represent the subjective reports of his patients regarding their experiences (Penfield & Perot, 1963; Vernon, 1963).

To summarize: From a clinical as well as from an experimental point of view, a concept is required to describe the experiences of patients and subjects which are to some extent, or in some respects, like perception. The term *hallucinations* would have been ideal if it had not been defined in terms of its identity with perception. The fact that hallucinations have been defined this way led to constant dissatisfaction, and this, in turn, often led to dispensing with the concept. The second defining feature of the concept of hallucinations, deception, suffers from a similar inadequacy. Many patients hallucinate and at the same time distinguish this hallucinating. Hence these patients are not deceived by their experiences, which we nonetheless want to call hallucinations.

The arguments stated above suggest a revision of the definition of hallucinations, a revision that might reflect a more "open" spirit that could be more receptive to clinical phenomena. It may run about as follows:

Hallucinations are mental dysfunctions that are in various ways similar, or analogous, to perception, and which are described by patients as well as by physicians in the language of perception. They may occur in all sense modalities and are in most cases of a productive kind ("negative hallucinations," i.e., not perceiving something that is there, are not ruled out by this definition). The experiences are not necessarily like perceptual experiences in all respects but rather often lack several perceptual features, such as clarity, vividness, or the conviction of some aspects of the reality of what is perceived.

One might add:

As we do not know which features of the hallucinatory experiences are important for specific clinical tasks such as differential diagnosis or therapy response, the notion should rather serve as a "blank" category to be filled with descriptive material—such as modality, complexity, length, frequency, constancy over time, precipitating situation, degree of perceptual similarity such as brightness of color, clarity of sound, and so on; concomitant affect; and modes of appreciation of reality, such as delusional interpretation in general; the relevance to overt behavior; the conviction that others perceive the same thing; the independence of voluntary control; the possibility of perceiving with several modalities, and the conviction of independent existence.

Only by careful observation of features like the ones mentioned above will the physician be able to judge the clinical relevance of the experience, and only by taking into account as many of these features as possible will scientific studies progress beyond the notion that hallucinations are unspecific with respect to diagnosis. Hence, a more descriptive and less inferential and theory-laden approach to hallucinations is desirable.

DELUSIONS

Our second example of a basic psychiatric concept is that of delusions. In DSM-III-R we find the following definition:

Delusion. A false personal belief based on incorrect inference about external reality and firmly sustained in spite of what almost everyone else believes and in spite of what constitutes incontrovertible and obvious proof or evidence to the contrary. The belief is not one ordinarily accepted by other members of the person's culture or subculture (i.e., it is not an article of religious faith). When a false belief involves an extreme value judgment, it is regarded as a delusion only when the judgment is so extreme as to defy credibility. (DSM-III-R, 1987, p. 395)

Like the definition of hallucinations, this definition of delusions poses several problems, which we shall examine step by step.

Feature: ". . . false . . ."

Problem: Although falsity in fact characterizes delusions in many cases, there are also cases of delusions in which, nevertheless, the question of truth and falsity is either (a) not applicable (as in religious delusions) or (b) applicable but hardly likely to be relevant to the acute making of the diagnosis (empirical falsification is often not carried out, as for example, in delusions of being persecuted by a satellite, being punished by rays etc.) or even (c) applicable but solved in the sense that the content of the delusion is in fact true. Karl Jaspers (1963, p. 106) gave the following example: "A delusion of jealousy, for instance, may be recognized by its typical characteristics without our needing to know whether the person has genuine ground for his jealousy or not. The delusion does not cease to be a delusion although the spouse of the patient is in fact unfaithful——sometimes only as a result of the delusion."

Feature: ". . . personal . . ."

Problem: It is not clear in what respect the adjective *personal* is meant to contribute to the definition of delusions. We may suggest that it implies that the belief in question is not shared by others or is peculiar in content. Kräupl-Taylor's (1983) reference to this aspect of delusions as "idiosyncrasy" may be a better account of the feature in question. In particular, in the case of shared delusions, the belief is not held by just one person and thus, strictly speaking, is not "personal"; the content in question, however, is likely to be rather idiosyncratic.

Feature: ". . . based on incorrect inference about external reality . . ."

Problem: Instances of "incorrect inference" should be described as formal thought disorder rather than as thought disorder with respect to content——delusion. Moreover, empirical research has not clarified yet whether incorrect inferences in fact play a major role (if any) in the formation of delusions. Although it is true, for instance, that schizophrenics do make more mistakes in tests that involve certain types of logical reasoning, it is not true that patients with delusions make more mistakes with regard to inference than patients without delusions (the opposite finding is even more likely); in addition, there is no specific impairment of inference which can be attributed to schizophrenics, especially delusional schizophrenics (Spitzer, 1989). Furthermore, the very fact that a theory about the etiology of delusions is part of the definition is problematic. We know almost nothing about the psychological genesis of delusions——whether they result from abnormalities in inference, drive, motivation, or some other defect, to name just a few mechanisms that have been proposed. Such an etiological proposal also runs counter to the atheoretical stance of the DSM. Lastly, it can be argued that making incorrect inferences about external reality presupposes the correct apprehension of such a reality (i.e., only the inferences are wrong) and that this presupposition is not necessarily true from a clinical point of view.

Feature: ". . . external reality . . ."

Problem: The statement that delusions are about "external reality" is inconsistent with what is said about delusions in other parts of DSM-III-R, especially about the symptomatology of schizophrenia. Here we find the following statements:

> Certain delusions are observed far more frequently in schizophrenia than in other psychotic disorders. These include, for instance, the belief or experience . . . that thoughts that are not one's own are inserted into one's mind (thought insertion); that thoughts have been removed from one's head (thought withdrawal); or that one's feelings, impulses, thoughts, or actions are not one's own, but are imposed by some external force (delusions of being controlled) (DSM-III-R, 1987, p. 188).

As we can see, the concept of *delusion* is meant to describe phenomena that do not refer to things in the external world but instead to subjective experiences such as thought insertion and thought withdrawal. Although we can leave it open for now whether it is possible to refer to somebody else's subjective experiences as false beliefs, we want to stress the inconsistency brought about by these statements: Thought insertion and thought withdrawal are either concepts by the use of which the clinician describes the actually experienced changes of the experience of the patient (in this case the clinician neither describes the patient's beliefs about the *external* world nor anything *false*, but instead what the patient's actual experience is like), or thought insertion and thought withdrawal refer to false beliefs uttered by the patient (in which case they are not about external reality). Therefore, the statements in the glossary and the statements in the description of the symptomatology of schizophrenia are inconsistent.

Feature: ". . . firmly sustained . . ."

Problem: Although it certainly is a feature of delusions that they are firmly sustained by the patient, it is not clear how delusions "in remission" can be called delusions. As every experienced clinician knows (although rarely sees written about) delusions do not disappear in an instant; they are not an all-or-none phenomenon. If delusions are successfully treated with neuroleptic drugs, for example, the patient may first find them less and less relevant to his life and may act according to this diminishing relevance (he might, for example, start worrying more about his unemployment than about the persecutory acts of the CIA). On questioning, however, at this stage, the patient will continue to make all of the delusional claims which he made prior to treatment. Only later in the course of the remitting disorder will he admit that he may have been wrong in his suspicions. However, if "firmly sustained" is a necessary condition of mental phenomena to be called delusions, "delusions in some stage of remission" cannot be diagnosed. Therefore, we propose that delusions also refer to statement(s) that once were firmly sustained by the patient but actually are no longer firmly sustained. In these cases, the degree of distance should be noted, for example with terms such as *not acting upon, not actively engaging in dialogues about, admitting some doubts*, and the like.

Finally, a critical point can be raised about the assumption that delusions are *beliefs*. The notion *belief* does not add anything to the definition of delusions and is misleading. For example, patients rarely say that they "believe such and such," but rather state that they "*know* such and such." That is to say, patients with delusions express *conviction and certainty* about certain statements instead of suggesting that these statements are subject to discussion and inquiry. Of course, from an objective standpoint these knowledge claims are merely subjective. However, this argument can only be made after having classified a certain statement as delusional. It follows that we give a wrong account of the clinical process of diagnosing delusions if we claim to do so by, first, asking the patient about his beliefs and, second, finding that some of them are delusional. What actually happens, rather, is that some of the patient's knowledge claims are evaluated by the clinician as being "merely" beliefs. In short, from the subjective point of view delusions are not beliefs, and from the objective point of view the notion that delusions are some form of beliefs is true by definition but has no practical meaning.

We have argued elsewhere[10] (Spitzer, 1990) that *delusions may be defined as statements about external reality which are uttered like statements about a mental state; that is, with subjective certainty and incorrigible by others. A statement that once was, but no longer is, uttered with subjective certainty and incorrigible by others may still be called a delusion. The degree of "conviction" may range from, and/or may be inferred from, "not acting upon," "not actively engaging in dialogues about," "admitting some doubts about his or her conviction," to "being able to reasonably discuss the issue."*

CONTEXT OF DISCOVERY AND CONTEXT OF JUSTIFICATION

We have gone a long way from description and concepts to clinical phenomena to understand basic aspects of psychiatric diagnoses and to give examples of how such an understanding changes the way we conceive certain phenomena. To shed further light upon the diagnostic process, we will now introduce a basic distinction from philosophy of science. The distinction between the context of discovery and the context of justification of a scientific hypothesis is commonplace in the philosophy of science (Popper, 1976). Medawar (1974) illustrated this distinction as follows:

> First, there is a clear distinction between the acts of mind involved in discovery and in proof. The generative or elementary act in discovery is "having ideas" or proposing a hypothesis. Although one can put oneself in the right frame of mind for having ideas and can abet the process, the process itself is outside logic and cannot be made the subject of logical rules. (p. 284)

However, what is of interest in science is not the peculiar way in which a scientist arrived at a hypothesis but rather, very simply, whether this hypothesis is true. In other words, what is of interest is the justification of the hypothesis, not its discovery. In the case of Einstein's theory of special relativity, for example, we ordinarily would not be interested whether Einstein had coffee or tea at the insightful moment when he realized that the speed of light, rather than time, is constant. We simply want to know: Is this true? We know from Einstein himself that the basic ideas were the easy part of his work and that he had a hard time sitting at his desk doing the necessary calculations to prove them to be true. Generally speaking, in science we are concerned whether statements are true——whether and how they can be justified.

The emphasis on justification is crucial to all sciences and also for medicine as a science. However, medicine is more than a science: It is often stated to be an *applied science* or even an *art.* From a clinician's point of view, the reason for this is clear: He is usually concerned with making a diagnosis rather than with justifying one. In fact, in most cases it is easy to justify a diagnosis once it is made; but in many cases it may be hard to have the right idea at the right time. *Clinical judgment, clinical experience and wisdom, countertransference, praecox feeling*——the heterogeneity of the terms that have been used to indicate the history of a statement (i.e., the way in which it came into being) indicates that there is no general theory about this historical aspect. It may well be that there cannot be any comprehensive theory of clinical insights, but nonetheless it is possible to say a little bit more about it.

At the beginning, the process of making a diagnosis has all of the features which are required to be appropriately called *hermeneutic*. When the clinician *starts* to make a diagnosis, he does *not* yet possess the guiding principle of sorting out relevant from irrelevant data and of organizing the data in a meaningful way. He somehow does that, and the more experienced he is the better he will be at these selection tasks. He will take into account the verbal and nonverbal cues provided by the patient and may start with his own initial reactions to the patient (what else does he have at the start?), assign weights to the data, try out tentative hypotheses, reorganize the data, and so on. The whole process may take the experienced clinician no longer than a few minutes or even a few moments (students may need hours), but nonetheless it is important that such processes always take place in the process of making a diagnosis.

It might be argued that the existence of diagnostic computer programs and algorithms provides evidence that this proposed view is wrong. However, on the level of symptoms, that is, on the level of the raw data to be entered into the computer, the process takes place again. Hence, these models rely on a functioning hermeneutic process already in place; they merely provide a structured way to make the somewhat final decision about the proper diagnostic entity. Moreover, to be able to replace that last bit of hermeneutics in the process, these algorithms have to be detailed and hence, cumbersome, so as not to miss anything. Finally, the more sophisticated the computer-based algorithms become, the more they resemble a clinician engaged in hermeneutic processes.[11]

Diagnostic manuals are important when it comes to the question of why patient X suffers from disorder Y, that is to say, when it comes to the *justification* of a diagnosis. Sets of necessary and sufficient criteria provide a basis for answers to such questions and are indispensable as long as medicine is also a science. Hence, a useful answer to the question of why patient Z suffers, from, for example, schizophrenia, is not that the psychiatrist had that peculiar praecox feeling, but instead consists of a list of criteria met by the patient. It is equally as ridiculous to answer the question, "How did we get at the correct diagnosis of schizophrenia in this patient?" by stating, "We checked all criteria we found in the entire DSM-III-R, and ended up with the ones for schizophrenia being met."[12]

Why is this important? It might be argued that we do not have to worry about the historic aspect of psychiatric diagnosis because the experienced clinician (in any event) will *do* the right things, that is, apply the relevant criteria for practical reasons. However, if we disregard this aspect of psychiatric diagnosis we run the risk of being blind to essential features of the diagnostic process and also of diagnostic criteria. As these criteria are meant to aid the clinician by providing basic concepts for descriptive purposes, they have to reflect the patient-doctor interaction accurately. As we have already seen with respect to hallucinations and delusions, the definitions of basic criteria may contain unjustified and distorting presuppositions, and hence their clinical applicability may be less than optimal.

The issue of mood congruence may serve as a last example to illustrate this point.

UNDERSTANDING MOOD CONGRUENCE

Mood-congruent psychotic features are defined in DSM-III-R as follows:

> Delusions or hallucinations whose contents are entirely consistent with either a depressed or a manic mood. If the mood is depressed, the content of the delusions or hallucinations would involve themes of either personal inadequacy, death, nihilism, or deserved punishment. If the mood is manic, the content of the delusions or hallucinations would involve themes of inflated worth, power, knowledge, or identity or special relationship to a deity or famous person. (DSM-III-R, pp. 401–402)

The concept of mood congruence was formed by Karl Jaspers, a psychiatrist who had worked for 7 years at the Heidelberg Psychiatric University Hospital and later became a philosopher. Jaspers emphasized that *understanding* is an essential part of the psychiatrist's function in seeing a patient (Jaspers, 1965). He stressed the hermeneutic nature of understanding—that is, as we already have pointed out, the fact that the clinician is engaged in a dialogue with the patient. This process has circular features, going back and forth between the two. In this course of this process of understanding, the subject matter of the dialogue could be described as *incomplete pictures* instead of as *stringent arguments*. Progress is made by a progressively comprehensive view of what the patient is saying, a view in which the details are arranged to fit best.

With respect to affective and psychotic symptoms, such fit can be difficult to assess: Whereas in some cases the relation between the predominant mood and a particular hallucination or delusion is easily understood, in other cases such understanding is difficult. Nonetheless, understanding may reach a point at which it becomes clear that there is such a relationship. In a manic patient, for example, delusions of grandeur are readily interpreted as understandable in terms of the prevailing mood. In yet another manic patient whose mood is more restless, agitated, and hostile, and hardly elevated, the delusion of being persecuted by a specific person may also be understood in terms of the prevailing mood, although delusions of persecution are not listed under the standard set of mood-congruent delusions in mania. By the same token, delusions of grandeur may occur in a patient who does exhibit a slight elevation of his mood sometimes. In this case the clinician may try to understand these relationships, may decide which features are the most prevailing ones, and may make a differential diagnosis between mania and schizophrenia. The point here is that the metaphor of a simple fit—as in the case of congruent triangles—does not reflect what actually goes on in the diagnostic process, which goes back and forth, tries out interpretations and discards them, until the most coherent story is found. The notion of understanding captures this clinical process and therefore seems to be more appropriate.

CONCLUSIONS

The basis of psychiatric diagnosis is the series of events that occurs during the interaction of the patient and the psychiatrist, in particular, events regarding the mental life of the patient as perceived and understood by the psychiatrist. The description of the patient's mental life necessarily has the character of perspectival viewpoints; that is, it happens within dimensions and categories. It further has to use descriptive concepts, such as *hallucinations*, *delusions*, and *mood congruence*.

   With respect to any psychiatric diagnosis, the process of getting at it (discovery) and the task of explaining why it is valid (justification) have to be distinguished. Contrary to other scientific disciplines, in which the historic aspect of discoveries is of little systematic interest, in medicine, and especially in psychiatry, the process of getting at a diagnosis deserves special attention. Therefore, descriptive concepts should not only reflect the task of justifying, but also the task of discovering the diagnosis. In other words, basic psychiatric concepts should take into account the hermeneutic nature of the diagnostic process.

   To be as descriptive as possible—that is, as little theory driven and as little inferential as possible—the definition of psychiatric symptoms and the wording of diagnostic criteria should be based upon a clear appreciation of this basic dialogic interaction. As we have tried to show by using *hallucinations*, *delusions*, and *mood congruence* as examples, DSM-III-R falls short of its own standards of being etiologically atheoretical and minimizing inference. We have proposed some suggestions to improve this unsatisfying situation, which hopefully will enhance respect for actual clinical work.

7 Voices and Selves

G. LYNN STEPHENS, Ph.D.
and GEORGE GRAHAM, Ph.D.

Nowadays, an increasing number of philosophers hold that the psychological phenomenon of self-consciousness or self-awareness is best understood as the sense of being actively involved in our own mental lives (Dennett, 1984; Flanagan, 1991; Frankfurt, 1988; Taylor, 1976). We do not feel that we are merely spectators of our occurrent mental episodes (thoughts, sensations, passions) but agents in charge of our own mental conduct. We castigate ourselves for our stupidity and ignorance, congratulate ourselves on our own cleverness and intelligence, and remonstrate ourselves for faulty reasoning and sloppy thinking. Active involvement in one's own mental life is not easy and is often upsetting. Daniel Dennett wrote, "It is hard to be . . . optimistic in the cold hours of the morning when one reflects back on one's own appalling weakness and stupidity, at the width of the chasm between one's public self-presentation and the unpresentable private thinking that apparently determined one's action" (1984, pp. 165–166).

According to Dennett, we all know the dreadful feeling at times, "the terrible existential funk in which we recognize that we have slid self-defeatingly into the passive spectator attitude, fecklessly wondering what we are going to do, or think next" (p. 167).

Luckily, however, for most of us, these slumps into mere passivity pass. "We break out of our slump, like the golfer who finally sees the wisdom in the curious advice of the pro: keep your head down and follow through" (p. 168).

Keep your head down and follow through: remain active and involved in your own mental life. Monitor, shape, and if necessary realign and recast your psychological conduct.

Now having promoted the conception of people as self-conscious agents who are active in their own mental lives, philosophers are immediately faced with the chore of trying to make that conception intellectually tractable and understandable. Elsewhere (Stephens & Graham, in press) we have argued that active self-consciousness involves taking the *intentional stance* toward ourselves and constructing a representation (picture, theory) of ourselves which enhances the prediction, explanation, and control over our own mental lives. We find this conception of active self-consciousness immensely plausible, and we think it goes a long way toward capturing the idea of persons as self-conscious participants or agents in their own mental lives. Nor are we alone in finding it plausible and useful. Flanagan (1991, pp. 133—158), for instance, deployed a similar conception in his analysis of the determinants of self-esteem. Dennett (1991) appealed to such an idea in his treatment of the biographical emergence of a person's sense of self.

The concept of *intentional stance* originated with Dennett (1981, 1987; Strawson, 1962). The main idea goes roughly like this: We take the intentional stance toward something (ourselves, another, a computer, whatever) when we view it as a dynamic system of past and present beliefs, desires, wants, aspirations, and commitments, whose behavior (and mental life) can be predicted, explained, and controlled by viewing it as such a system. In the language of contemporary philosophy of mind, an intentional system is anything that is viewed as a *folk psychological subject*——a bearer of beliefs, desires, and other attitudes. Dennett himself sometimes explicitly introduced other notions into the concept of intentional system, such as that it is *very* rational and that nothing *really* is a true believer. Here we shall not be employing a concept of intentional system in Dennett's more special (instrumentalist?) sense. For us, an intentional system need not consist of even remotely ideal rational agency. In particular, it can exemplify marked failures of consistency and cohesion in its attitudes, including reflexive (self-referential) attitudes. Further, we wish to allow that the representations that people possess and the constructs of themselves may be dim and inchoate, fluid and indeterminate. Whether taking the intentional stance toward ourselves provides an accurate picture of ourselves——whether ascribing beliefs and desires to ourselves represents us as we really are——is a more complicated matter (Horgan & Graham, 1991). But regardless of how ultimately that question is answered, one thing will be assumed in this chapter. The self represented in self-consciousness is standardly or ordinarily viewed as an *actual* bearer of beliefs, desires, and other attitudes. To ourselves, in our own minds, we are accurately depicted by the intentional stance.

We have one primary and two secondary objectives in this chapter. The primary objective is to make the concept of active self-consciousness available to psychiatrists and psychopathologists involved in the development of DSM-IV. We shall argue that the concept is a valuable theoretical tool for classification in psychiatry. The demonstration of the utility of the concept motivates two secondary objectives. First, we would like to focus upon and criticize the account of verbal hallucinations (or "voices") as auditory hallucinations presupposed by DSM-III-R (American Psychiatric Association, 1987). We shall argue in favor of reclassifying voices as disturbances of a subject's sense of self rather than as auditory hallucinations. Second, we shall advance an argument in favor of describing disturbances of the sense of self as disorders of active involvement in one's own mental conduct, that is, as disturbances of self-representation.

BACKGROUND

It sometimes happens that in the absence of any appropriate environmental stimulus, a person has a strong impression of being addressed by another or of overhearing another speak. Such experiences, called *voices*, are prominently associated with schizophrenia, although, as noted in DSM-III-R, they occur in connection with other sorts of mental disorders——for example, Alcohol Hallucinosis (1987, p. 131) and Bipolar Disorder, Manic Episode (p. 216)——and are not rare even in individuals without known mental disorder (p. 398; see also Posey & Losch, 1983).

DSM-III-R discusses voices at several points (pp. 110, 131, 135, 144, 216, 398), most extensively as part of the symptomatology of schizophrenia.

> The major disturbances in perception are various forms of hallucinations. Although these occur in all modalities, the most common are auditory hallucinations, which frequently involve many voices the person perceives as coming from outside his or her head. The voices may be familiar, and often make insulting remarks. . . . Voices speaking directly to the person or commenting on his or her ongoing behavior are particularly characteristic. . . . Occasionally the auditory hallucinations are of sounds rather than voices. (p. 188)

This passage reveals several presuppositions about voices. Generally, they are disturbances of perception. As such they are grouped together with, for example, hallucinations in various sensory modalities, hypersensitivities to sound, smell, and other sensory stimuli, and synesthesias; and, they are contrasted with, for instance, disturbances of thought content (e.g., delusions of thought insertion and of being controlled by outside agents) and disturbances of volition. More specifically, they are hallucinations, which DSM-III-R defines as "A sensory perception without external stimulation of the relevant sensory organ" (p. 398) and which it describes as having "the immediate sense of reality of a true perception" (p. 398). Still more specifically, voices are a subspecies of auditory hallucination, "a hallucination of sound," distinguished from other auditory hallucinations because they involve speech sounds rather than "clicks, rushing noises, music, etc." (p. 398).

The passage also mentions various more or less typical features of voices. They are "frequently" perceived by the subject as "coming from outside his or her head" (though the glossary entry on hallucinations notes that "an auditory hallucination may be perceived as coming from within the head rather than through the ears") (Junginger, 1986, p. 398). The voices are characteristically perceived as "speaking directly to the person" or as speaking about the person, and they are perceived as speech acts, for example, commands, insults, comments. It is implied, though not explicitly stated, that the voice is perceived as that of another person or agent rather than as the subject's own voice and that the relevant speech acts are attributed to the other person instead of the subject.

Taken together the various references to voices in DSM-III-R emphasize the apparently auditory character of the experience; the subject has the impression of *hearing* someone speak. They are described as *disturbances* because the subject has such an impression in the absence of appropriate stimulation of the organs of auditory perception—because they are not "true" perceptions.

Just above we have expounded the brief and apparently obvious remarks on voices in DSM-III-R at perhaps inordinate length because we want to take issue with them in detail. We shall argue that the best current research on voices indicates that they are not, in general, auditory hallucinations. Indeed, they need not involve apparent sensory experiences of any sort; they need not have for their subjects the immediate sense of the reality of true perception. Although we shall not deny that voices sometimes do involve auditory hallucinations, we shall argue that what is essential to voices is the impression that the voice is of nonself origin: that it is a communication from another person and is not produced by the subject. Such an impression we shall refer to as their *alien quality*. We shall argue that the alien quality of voices can be neither identified with nor explained by any perceptual or auditory quality of the experience. This is important for the diagnostic classification of voices because our view is that they should be classified as disturbances in the person's self-consciousness instead of as perceptual disturbances (as matters of nonveridical perception). The voices that the subject "hears" are the subject's voice—his or her own thoughts or inner speech—and the speech acts expressed in those voices are his or her own mental acts. The problem is that the subject has the impression that the voice and the speech acts it expresses are those of another. Seen in this light, voices are more akin to delusions of thought insertion and other delusions of control by outside agencies rather than to auditory or other sorts of hallucinations. In particular, we shall propose that the basis of the alien quality of voices is best sought in the intentional or volitional aspects of the subject's cognitive activities. We shall attempt to develop this proposal by appealing to the conception of active self-awareness discussed above.

The first step in our argument is to examine the experimental and clinical work on voices and the theories or explanations that have been used to integrate this work to date.

DATA AND THEORY

Those who suffer from voices have the strong sense or impression that they are aware of another person's speech, in the absence of any appropriate stimulus—no other person is talking. It is possible that this impression has no basis in their experience: that it is directly produced by neurological processes of which the subject has no awareness. Most investigators suppose, however, that there is some basis for this impression in the subject's experience. There are two general sorts of proposals concerning the experiential basis of voices. Some investigators suppose that the experience of voices arises from the subject's awareness of his or her own inner or subvocal speech (Flor-Henry, 1986; Hoffman, 1986); that is, they suppose that the subject produces the message expressed by the voice but that for some reason the subject has the impression that the message is produced by another and that he or she is merely receiving or apprehending the other's speech production. The subject is talking (silently) to himself or herself but feels that someone else is doing the talking. Thus, voices involve genuine speech production and awareness of speech production, but the subject misattributes the relevant speech acts. Call this the *misattributed act theory* (MAT) of voices.

Another proposal is that voices involve a mishearing or misinterpretation of a genuine auditory stimulus. Frith (1979), for example, hypothesized that the subject is in fact hearing some nonspeech sound, the sound of running water or the droning of an air-conditioner, for example, which is misinterpreted as the sound of someone speaking. Hallucinations that are elaborations of genuine perceptual experiences have been called *functional hallucinations* (Fish, 1962). Let us call this proposal, then, the *functional theory* (FT).[1]

On the surface, each sort of account has its own explanatory advantages, which we may notice by distinguishing two aspects of voices. The first aspect is that they have a verbal or linguistic quality. They consist in words, phrases, and sometimes sentences. The subject regards them as semantically significant. They frequently appear as speech acts: criticisms, insults, warnings, commands, and so on. Second, voices have what we call an alien quality. The subject perceives them as originating outside himself or herself, as communications from another person.

MAT readily accounts for the verbal quality of voices. The experience seems verbal because it *is* verbal. It arises from the subject's awareness of a genuinely linguistic episode, an instance of his or her own inner or subvocal speech. The difficulty for MAT is to explain why the subject's own inner speech appears; why it seems to have been produced by another person.

In contrast, FT offers a plausible explanation of the alien quality of voices. The voice seems to come from outside the subject because the subject is actually hearing a sound produced by an object that is external to the subject. The corresponding difficulty for FT is to explain the verbal quality of voices ——to explain why the subject hears nonspeech sounds as another's speech.

How do MAT and FT fare when tested against the clinical and experimental data on voices? FT receives support from a recent study by Bentall and Slade (1985) which found that subjects who experience voices are more likely to interpret nonspeech sounds as verbal than subjects who do not. But FT encounters the problem that subjects readily report experiencing voices in the absence of external auditory stimuli (Hoffman, 1986, p. 512). One proponent of FT, Frith (1979), suggested that in such cases the subject is mishearing the sounds of his or her own heart beats and respiration. This suggestion, however, sounds like an ad hoc rescue operation constructed merely to save the account, since it allows that voices can be experienced as external or coming from without even when the sounds on which they are based originate in the subject's own body. Gone is the main explanatory strength of FT——the idea that the apparent externality of the voice can be explained by reference to the external origin of the relevant auditory stimuli.

MAT garners support from studies of the activation of the vocal system, neurological and muscular, during inner speech and concurrent with voices. A variety of studies have established that normal inner speech (e.g., during silent thinking and reading) is associated with physiological activity in the vocal system (Flor-Henry, 1986). Early work in this area has been criticized, and it is questionable whether speech is invariably accompanied by detectable muscle movements (Woodworth & Schlosburg, 1955). However, more careful recent studies bear out the correlation between inner speech and myogenic activation of the vocal system (Faaborg-Anderson, 1957; Faaborg-Anderson & Edfelt, 1958; Luria, 1960, 1961). Several studies, beginning with the work of Gould (1948, 1949, 1950), establish that such activation likewise accompanies the occurrence of voices (Cerny, 1964, 1965; McGuigan, 1966; Inouye & Shimizu, 1970). This work suggests that subvocal speech co-occurs with voices and supports the hypothesis that the experience of voices is based on the subject's awareness of his or her inner speech.

INNER SPEECH AND THE ALIEN QUALITY OF VOICES

The empirical data suggest that MAT is superior to FT, and we urge adopting MAT. However, as noted previously, the explanatory problem for MAT is to say how the subject's inner speech could appear as a perception of someone else's speech——in other words, to account for the alien quality of voices. A natural suggestion here is that the voice seems alien because it "sounds" like someone else's speech to the subject. To flesh out this suggestion briefly: It is plausible to suppose that the subject's typical experience of his or her own inner speech is phenomenologically quite different from his or her typical experience of hearing someone speak. Think of the qualitative difference between, for example, reciting Coleridge's *Kubla Khan* silently to yourself and hearing it read aloud. Although it is notoriously difficult to provide precise descriptions of the phenomenal qualities of experience, it seems reasonable to characterize the latter experience as more vivid or forceful than the former. It is likewise plausible to suppose that these phenomenological differences provide part of the explanation of how the subject normally distinguishes his or her awareness of inner speech from the auditory perception of speech. But suppose that, on occasion, a subject's experience of his or her own inner speech exhibits the phenomenal properties typically associated with hearing someone speak, that it has the vivid, forceful quality of a typical auditory perception of speech. Then it would seem to the subject as if the voice was someone else speaking. However, since the subject is aware that he or she is not speaking audibly, the relevant inner speech episodes might appear as a perception of someone else's speech. Hence, the alien quality of the voice.

Several investigators, notably Mintz and Alpert (1972) and Slade (1976), argued for this sort of explanation of the alien quality of voices. Mintz and Alpert asserted that the "imagery" associated with voices is "more like external auditory stimuli on the dimension of vividness and therefore more readily confused [with it]" (p. 314). Slade proposed a mechanism that might account for the relative enhancement (greater clarity or vividness) of verbal imagery in voices vis-à-vis normal inner speech. However, such enhancement might be explained; the idea is that voices have the subjective feel of normal auditory experiences (i.e., they are auditory hallucinations), and this provides the key to understanding why they seem to the subject to be of alien or nonself origin.

Although the phenomenological explanation of the alien quality of voices has considerable intuitive appeal, it is challenged by a wide variety of clinical observations and experimental work. The phenomenological explanation supposes that voices are phenomenologically very similar to auditory perceptions and quite distinct from the normal experience of inner speech. However, some of the earliest clinical descriptions of voices, dating back to the mid 19th-century, note that patients often deny that their voices appear as auditory events heard through the ears (Baillarger, 1846; Maudsley, 1886). Bleuler (1934) noted that for many patients, "the voices are unlike spoken voices but are as of thoughts." In his classic study of schizophrenia (1950) he remarked that patients often characterize the voices as "soundless" and as like "vivid thoughts." He quoted one patient's report, "It was as if someone pointed his finger at me and said, 'Go drown yourself.' It is as if we were speaking to each other. I don't hear it in my ears, I have a feeling in my breast" (p. 111).

Sedman (1966) offered several quotations from patient self-reports to the same effect. One patient said of her voice, "I felt it within me: It doesn't sound as though it's outside" (p. 487). Another described the voice as "like a loud, strong thought" (p. 487).

Most important, a recent study by Junginger and Frame (1985) bore out these observations. They asked their subjects to rate the "sensory" qualities of their voices on a scale from 1 to 10, with 1 indicating an experience very similar to their ordinary experiences of their inner speech and 10 representing an experience very like hearing another person speak. More than 40% of Junginger's and Frame's subjects rated their voices below 5. In a later study (reported in Junginger, 1986) they found that patients reliably reported that a headphone voice presented at a level approximating normal speech appeared "louder, clearer, and more outside the head than their most recent [verbal hallucination]." Junginger concluded, "that hearing a hallucinated voice is not that different a sensory experience from normal verbal imagery, but it does differ from normal auditory perception" (p. 528).

The data discussed above provide conceptual room to support the phenomenological explanation of the alien quality of voices. For instance, the above data might result from the cognitive penetrability of phenomenological description of mental processes. Even among psychotics, many people who experience voices do not believe that anyone is actually speaking to them. They realize or suspect that the voices are "only in their heads." Perhaps, when asked to describe the sensory qualities of their voices they modify their reports so as to accord with their views of the reality behind the experience. Thus, they would describe their voices as unlike normal auditory perception and more like thoughts because they believe that the voices really are thoughts, even if the voices sound similar to auditory perceptions.

This proposal for saving the phenomenological explanation of the alien quality of voices is ruled out by more careful examination of the clinical cases. Bleuler (1950) noted that "many patients do differentiate between what they really hear from what is 'imposed' on them." But he continued, "Nevertheless, even they are frequently inclined to attribute reality to . . . these hallucinations" (p. 110); that is, the patient may recognize that he or she is not hearing the voice, but nonetheless regards the voice as a genuine communication from another person. Allen, Halperin, and Friend (1985) reported a case that makes this point quite clearly. "The voices are not received as auditory events coming from without through the ears. . . . They feel distant and diffuse, like thoughts, she adds ironically. Ironically because she cannot accept them as her own thoughts, but as messages sent to her by beings external to herself" (p. 602).

Junginger and Frame (1985) also noted that their subjects' estimates of the similarity between voices and auditory perception varied independently from their convictions concerning the external origin of the voice. Subjects who recognized the self-produced character of their voices were as likely to rate them as highly similar to auditory perceptions as those who regarded the voices as genuinely alien. Conversely, subjects who were firmly convinced of the external origin of the voices were no less likely to describe the voices as thoughtlike than those who recognized that the voices were all in their heads.

The work cited above has two main implications. First, it shows that the phenomenological explanation of the alien character of voices cannot be generally adequate. People are quite capable of experiencing the voice as alien, as that of another person, even when the voice does not seem to them like an auditory perception. Therefore, phenomenological similarities between the experience of voices and the normal experience of auditory perception cannot be an essential part of the explanation of the alien quality of the voice. Further, clinical and experimental studies of voices suggest that voices cannot be regarded, in general, as auditory hallucinations, or experiences that exhibit the sensory or phenomenal properties of auditory perceptions while lacking the latters' causal connections to external stimuli. For some patients, at least, the experience of the voice is qualitatively quite distinct from their ordinary experience of external auditory stimuli and rather similar to their typical experience of their own inner speech. Of course, subjects talk about "hearing" voices and ascribe various acoustical properties to them—being loud or soft, clear or indistinct, for example. But people also talk this way when reporting their awareness of inner speech. We speak of hearing or being unable to hear ourselves think; we can talk "loudly" or "softly" to ourselves without making any noise, and so on. Although we do not deny that many subjects experience their voices as vivid, auditionlike episodes, this apparent auditory quality is not something common to all voices and, hence, does not provide the explanation of their alien character.

So what does? Within the theoretical embrace of MAT, we need some other sort of explanation of the alien quality of voices. Before turning to the discussion of what sort of explanation we favor, we should comment on the significance—for the development of future DSMs—of the finding that voices are not, in general, auditory hallucinations.

APPLICABILITY OF CRITICISM OF VOICE CLASSIFICATION TO DEVELOPMENT OF FUTURE DSMs

The problem of categorizing voices as auditory hallucinations highlights the issues involved in developing an appropriate classification for the symptoms of mental disorder. Many traditional psychiatric categories of symptoms are classified, either alone or in concert with others, as either disturbances of perception or disturbances in the subject's sense of self. This second category includes delusions of thought alienation, delusions of being controlled, depersonalization, and other disturbances in one's sense of being involved in one's own mental and bodily activities.

Conceptualizing the voices phenomenon has direct and profound research implications. Classifying voices in the manner of DSM-III-R, as hallucinations, as disturbances of perception, suggests that the problem faced by people who experience voices is primarily a matter of "hearing" things that are not there, just as the problem with visual hallucinations is a matter of "seeing" things that are not there. This approach suggests that the understanding of voices depends not on examining a subject's sense of self, but on considering the normal operations of our auditory perceptual system and searching for defects or anomalies within the hallucinator's auditory perceptual system. This approach also suggests that the sorts of comparisons with other psychological phenomena which are most likely to shed light on the experience of voices are comparisons with other sorts of perceptual disturbances such as auditory hallucinations of nonspeech sounds and visual and other modalities of hallucinations and illusions. However, if voices need not involve auditory hallucinations—that is, if those who hear voices need not be suffering from any disturbance of sensory perception—then we should look elsewhere for an account of what is going on in people who hear voices.

VOICES AND SELVES

What explains the apparently alien character of voices? Why do subjects misattribute their own inner speech? Our answer here must be tentative and somewhat sketchy. We shall suggest a general sort of explanatory approach, without attempting a detailed account of the full range of problems presented by the clinical data.

In our view the key to understanding how the subjects come to attribute certain episodes of their own inner speech to others lies in understanding how they come to attribute most such episodes to themselves. To get a handle on this latter question we need to consider the larger question of how people come to regard various of the events in their life histories (speech or otherwise) as their *actions*—as things they *do*—as opposed to things done to them by others or things that just happen to them; that is, we need to consider our sense of ourselves as *agents* rather than as spectators or patients. Following a line suggested by Dennett (1991), among others, we propose that whether subjects regard an event *e* as one of their actions—as something they do or did—depends upon whether they believe that *e*'s occurrence is best explained by reference to their own intentional states (Eagle, 1988; Flanagan, 1991; Stephens & Graham, in press). A person operates with a theory or picture (perhaps not a very accurate or adequate theory or picture) of his or her own psychology. Among other things this theory ascribes to him or her various relatively persistent or enduring dispositional states, notably beliefs, desires, and aversions. The aim of such theorizing is to make sense of and anticipate his or her own behavior, both overt and covert. Thus, for instance, the person is walking in a certain direction carrying a purse because she wants to buy some cigarettes, believes she can easily obtain cigarettes from the corner drug store, and believes the store lies in the direction in which she is walking. She anticipates that, on arriving at the drug store, she will open her purse because she believes that cigarettes cost money, that her money is in her purse, and that she intends to purchase cigarettes with the money in her purse. It is because she regards her walking or her opening of her purse as a direct upshot or expression of her beliefs and desires that she regards it as her action and pictures or sees herself as its agent.

Suppose, by contrast, that the person is unable to account for her ambulatory behavior given her theory of her own intentional states. She does not take herself to have any beliefs or desires that would explain or "rationalize" her behavior or which the behavior would appropriately express. To her the behavior seems not something that *she* does. In this case, she must either revise her theory of her own psychology, decide that she does indeed have the relevant sorts of intentional states and that the behavior *is* an action of hers, or she must regard the movements as something that is merely happening to her.[2] As mere happenings, they are episodes in which she is involved only as patient and not as agent.

It is worth noting that although the person might refuse to acknowledge that the relevant episode is *her* action, she might nevertheless conclude that it is *someone's* action. In delusions of possession and in some experiences associated with multiple personality disorder, subjects have the sense that their behavior is under the control of another agent, that their bodily movements are expressions of another person's beliefs and desires rather than the subject's own intentional states.[3] We shall return later to the question of why a subject might regard her movements as another's actions rather than merely as automatisms or involuntary movements.

We would argue that the sorts of factors which determine self-ascription of overt behavior also operate in the case of inner speech. As Harry Frankfurt has emphasized, we often, perhaps generally, experience inner speech as something in which we are actively involved as agent or speaker (Akins & Dennett, 1986; Frankfurt, 1988). We talk to ourselves offering advice, encouragement, self-criticism; we silently recite poetry, rehearse arguments, perform calculations. Although we sometimes experience inner speech as mere verbal imagery, running willy-nilly through our heads without exciting in us any sense of active involvement on our part, we may also experience it as voluntary, purposive, and even fully deliberate activity. As with their overt behavior, whether the subjects regard an episode of their inner speech as something they do—as their own speech act—depends upon whether they find its occurrence explicable in terms of their theory of their own intentional states. Do they take themselves to have beliefs and desires of the sort that would account for the occurrence of the relevant episode of inner speech?[4] If so, then they will regard the episode as their own speech act; if not, then they must either revise their picture of themselves so as to include intentional states of the appropriate sorts or refuse to acknowledge the episode as an action.

A question can of course be raised about why, given that the episodes of inner speech which constitute voices are produced by the subjects themselves, they should seem to the subjects to be independent of or discordant with their own intentions? Why should they appear to the subjects as out of kilter with their own attitudes? Although we have no account or answer of our own to offer here, there are some interesting suggestions in the clinical literature. Hoffman (1986) proposed that speech production (inner and overt) is controlled by structured cognitive states that he called *discourse plans*. Although these states are not themselves consciously accessible to the subjects, they do result in them having tacit expectations regarding the form and content of their speech output. If an inner speech performance fails to accord with such expectations, the subjects recognize that the resultant inner speech is not what they "meant" to say. Then, their performance will have the quality of *felt unintendedness*, to use Hoffman's terminology. Hoffman offered evidence that breakdowns or disruptions of discourse planning, and hence production of unintended inner speech, occur frequently in schizophrenia. He suggested that disturbances of discourse planning, and the resultant proclivity to produce unintended inner speech, play a critical role in the etiology of schizophrenic verbal hallucinations. Similar, perhaps more transient or less severe, disruptions of discourse planning may account for the apparently unintended character of voices generally.

Hoffman's way of viewing people as subject to potential breakdowns in speech production contrasts with a second and alternative suggestion from Frith and Donne (1988). They located the problem not in the production of inner speech, but in the subjects' ability to monitor their inner speech production. They supposed that in the normal case, subjects are able to somehow keep track of whether an inner speech episode is produced by their "willed intentions." They suggested that under certain conditions, this monitoring—not the production—breaks down. Although the subjects intentionally produce an episode of inner speech, they are unaware of its intentional etiology; so, it seems to them that the episode occurs independent of their intentions.

As just mentioned, it is not our purpose here to endorse either of the above accounts. We mention them only to suggest how it might be possible for the subjects' own inner speech to seem unintended by them, despite the fact that they do produce the speech in question.

Of course, those who suffer from voices do not merely have the impression that the relevant inner speech episodes fail to count as their own actions—that they constitute examples of involuntary verbal imagery or cognitive automatisms—they feel as though the voice is that of *another* person; that is, they do not feel that they are involuntarily producing inner speech. Instead, they feel as if they are receiving a message or a communication from some external agent. Why then do the hallucinators experience the voices as *alien* rather than merely as nonvoluntary or unintended? Why do they take them to express another's beliefs and intentions?

An episode of inner speech which the subjects refuse or fail to acknowledge as an expression of their own attitudes and intentions may nevertheless seem quite intentional to them. It may be topically relevant, for example, speaking to concerns that are very much present in their thoughts. Unlike involuntary verbal imagery such as snatches of doggerel running unbidden through our heads, which are notable for their lack of connection with and tendency to distract us from our current concerns, the content of voices tends to be personally salient to the subjects (Bleuler, 1950, p. 97; Mott, Small & Anderson, 1965). Likewise, voices typically exhibit the sorts of grammatical forms typical of conversational or communicative speech. They are frequently in the second person, for example (Linn, 1977). A young mother, concerned about her child's welfare and her own maternal responsibilities, may find the utterances "Bad mother" or "You're hurting your child" occurring in her consciousness. She does not acknowledge in herself the sorts of beliefs and desires which would naturally find expression in such utterances. As she represents herself to herself, she is a person with no doubts about her maternal competence or devotion to child. These are not comments she would say or wish to say to herself. Nonetheless, it is hard for her to dismiss this verbal episode as random verbal imagery. It seems to betray an agency, an intelligence that accounts for its coherence, its salience, and its directedness. Thus, she may have the strong impression that she is hearing another speak: that God, her mother, or her divorced husband is addressing her.[5]

A nonvoice example may be helpful here to understand the overall phenomenon. Suppose I discover that my hand is writing a love letter to a young woman named Virginia. I do not represent that behavior as mere bodily movement. Because the letter is a letter, I interpret it as intelligent action. But suppose I do not seem to myself to be monitoring the letter; and, I do not recall anyone named Virginia. Indeed, suppose I do not seem to myself to have any beliefs or desires that the letter would appropriately express.

I have two options. One is to make "attribution to self" and to revise my self-conception so that writing to Virginia is interpreted as something that I perform. I provide ex post facto intentional explanation of the writing behavior. The other is to make "attribution to other." If the action impresses me as so grossly out of kilter with my intentions and attitudes (including memories), the author may strike me as being alien. Another performs the letter writing through me. Similarly, consider the case of voices. One option is to revise my self-conception and to represent the inner speech as my speech. If, however, the evidence available to me is that I am not speaking, the speaker may strike me as alien. Another performs speech acts in me. My speech issues forth as the speech of another.

APPLICABILITY OF PROPOSAL TO DEVELOPMENT OF DSM-IV

As noted in a recent report by several members of the DSM-IV Task Force of the American Psychiatric Association, the recommendations for making revisions in DSM-III-R to be reflected in DSM-IV, "must be substantiated by explicit statements of the rationale and by systematic review of the relevant empirical data" (Widiger, Frances, Pincus, Davis & First, 1991, p. 7).

The proposal introduced above was supported by extensive criticism of the DSM-III-R classification and by the suggestion that it accommodates the alien quality of voices better than does the DSM-III-R classification. It also fits nicely with suggestions of Hoffman and of Frith and Donne about why inner speech produced by the subject should appear out of kilter with his or her own attitudes, but without requiring that either of those two suggestions be endorsed. And by retaining voices and their linguistic properties, it avoids the objection to FT that FT strips voices of their linguistic character.

We now wish to comment on two features of our proposal of interest in the development of future DSMs.

First, if our proposal is correct, the way to understand those who hear voices is not to consider the normal operations of our auditory system and to ferret out defects, but instead to consider the normal operations of human self-consciousness and to search out defects or anomalies within the hallucinator's self-representation which would account for such disturbances. For instance, in the last 2 decades a great deal of empirical work has examined the role of motivational factors in the creation of self-representation. Much of this work has been conducted within one of two rather distinct theoretical orientations. One paradigm stems from the segment of social psychology known as attribution theory (e.g., Taylor & Fiske, 1975), whereas the other stems from cognitive approaches to behavior modification and psychotherapy (e.g., Turk, Meichenbaum & Genest, 1983). According to attribution theory, the self-representor possesses motivated inclinations to ascribe some traits to himself or herself rather than to others—for example, to make self-serving attributions. Cognitive psychotherapists argue that self-representations can be influenced by hedonic qualities of associated mental imagery. Of two mental images of oneself the more pleasant will be preferred.

One message of our proposal is to make the literature on motivated self-representation germane to the study of voices. Perhaps whether the subjects other-attribute a speech intention or judge the intention their own depends on motivational biases they have as well as on the hedonic quality of the image of themselves as bearers of the intention. In the earlier example, the subject did not like the image of herself as a self-critical mother; she was biased to see herself as self-appreciative. So when the speech act "bad mother" occurred she experienced this as another's assessment rather than her own.

Second, we recognize that our proposal leaves a number of unanswered questions. This chapter is not an attempt to give a full account of the voice phenomenon. That must involve a great deal more articulation of the concept of active self-consciousness. We, however, see no need to apologize for the fact that there are gaps in our proposal and that the proposal is not fully developed. We predict that having such a proposal and developing it will help to focus discussion away from the phenomenology of voices and toward their self-represented personally unintended and alien character. That would be all to the good. Indeed, we suspect that the concepts and principles involved in our proposal will be useful in understanding and classifying a wide variety of symptoms of mental disorder other than voices.

Perhaps a continuum of disturbances in active self-consciousness and thus symptoms of mental disorder is involved here. On one extreme of this continuum are subjects who experience episodes in their own psychological life as not being part of the self (as voices, thought alienation, thought insertion, etc.). In the middle range lie those who experience such episodes as their own but uncontrollable (e.g., as obsessive thoughts or compulsions). Finally, on the other and perhaps potentially mentally healthy extreme are those who experience episodes as discordant with their sense of self, but which force or promote revision or modification in their self-representation (e.g., as characterological anomalies or novel reactions) so as to self-attribute them.[6]

Let us sum up. DSM-III-R says that voices are perceptual disturbances; we say that they are disturbances of active self-consciousness. DSM-III-R proposes that voices are best understood by comparison with the normal, accurate operation of the perceptual system. We propose that voices are best understood by picturing persons as self-conscious intentional systems, actively involved in interpreting their own mental life. If we are right, the voices of DSM-IV should not echo the voices of DSM-III-R. They need to speak in the language of new and improved classification.

8 Subjectivity, Self-Identity, and Self-Description

Conceptual and Diagnostic Problems in Autism, Schizophrenia, Borderline Personality Disorder, and the Dissociative Disorders

PETER J. CAWS, Ph.D.

The following essay is conjectural. This is not an apology: as Karl Popper (1963) held, the advance of science proceeds by conjectures and refutations, rather than by the mere accumulation of an empirical base for inductions. Working scientists cannot always allow themselves the luxury of a really sweeping conjecture; they may feel obliged to keep for the most part to the paths of what Thomas Kuhn (1970) called "normal science." Philosophers are professionally freer in this respect, which is one reason why it makes sense to have philosophers comment on scientific questions.

Freedom of conjecture does not mean license to forget the refutation side of the ledger. There are two main strategies of refutation: empirical, in which what comes under attack is the *evidence*; and logical, in which what comes under attack is the *argument*. Philosophers can generally be trusted to take care of the logical refutations themselves and not to offer conjectures that do not hang together. But empirical refutation is the business of science: when conjectures have empirical contents or consequences, they should be brought under scientific scrutiny. The latter is a part of the agenda here. I am sure I can count on my medical colleagues to challenge anything that is clearly inconsistent with their clinical experience.

My topic is individual human subjects: how they are to be understood, how they come into being, what can go wrong with them, and whether these considerations might have anything to contribute to the problem of diagnosis in psychiatry. By the *subject* I mean the self-identical individual, however eventually to be defined, who in a given particular episode of experience (and experience only comes in particular episodes) feels, knows, acts, fears, remembers, and so on. This subject may perhaps seek help from psychiatry. Ambiguities abound from the start; "subjects" have been the subject matter of philosophical argument for centuries (*subject matter* itself is one of the ambiguities), and most of these ambiguities will have to be passed over, but a couple of obvious ones can be dealt with briefly.

A trivial case: *subject* sometimes means a subject of an experiment or trial, one of the units that add up to the *N*; that is not what is meant here. More seriously: sometimes *subject* is taken to refer to the domain of the *subjective*, and *that* is taken as something necessarily unscientific. To cite the first example that comes to hand: the authors of a recent book on object relations theory remarked that they "feel the current emphasis by self psychologists on 'subjective reality' or 'subjective validity' in determining the selfobject experience constitutes a tacit, but potentially fruitful, acknowledgment of the contribution of phantasy to that experience" (Bacal & Newman, 1990).[1] *Subjective* here is implicitly contrasted to *objective*, where the terms have roughly the connotations, respectively, of private, fantastic, unrealistic, and affect laden on the one hand; and public, realistic, and free of fantasy and affect on the other.

This is a distinction worth making, but it will not get rid of the subject or subjectivity. The project of eliminating "the subjective" from objective scientific discourse has been common to positivism, behaviorism, and some versions of structuralism. But it would leave science without scientists, who, while properly doing their best to control for the self-interested aspects of subjectivity, can hardly be expected to become decentered or disembodied. (This is a point that goes back to Kierkegaard's criticism of Hegel, whose followers, said Kierkegaard, did their best to be "speculative philosophy in the abstract" [1941].) The very notion of *object* is *relative to* a subject, as can be seen from the derivation of the terms: Latin *sub* "under" and *ob* "in front of" combine with *iacio* "throw" to give *subiectio* "a laying under" and *obiectus* "a placing over against, putting opposite." The fact that one of the roots is "throw" underlines the contingency of the situation: each of us, in our awareness, finds ourself occupying a *point of view*, which rests on its own subjectivity *here* and confronts the world's objectivity *there*. There can be no "opposite" or "over against" except from such a point of view. Subject and object thus complement and supplement one another, are necessary correlatives of one another: there can be no object except for a subject.

Still, the ordinary intuitive distinction has some point to it: we do want science to be objective rather than subjective. Indeed, the distinction between subjective judgment and objective judgment can be made objectively—but only by a subject. I can try at least to factor out contingent influences (whether momentary or systematic), emotions, preferences, biases, and the like that may compromise my objectivity, but it is still I who must do this, from my own point of view. Psychiatric patients may not be very good at it— indeed, their not being very good at it may be one of the reasons they are psychiatric patients. Thus, the conditions of their subjectivity are of great diagnostic interest. To understand those conditions better it is necessary to elaborate further on the concept of subjectivity itself.

THE THEORY OF SUBJECTIVITY

It may be asked why the other concepts that have become familiar in this domain will not do the job: individual, self, ego, person. The difficulty with all such concepts is that they bring with them theoretical baggage from elsewhere. Theories are ways of looking at things (the Athenian *theoros* was an official observer), but things can be looked at only from a point of view: taken as objects, the self, the person, the ego, the individual are, again, objects *for a subject*. The subject is always here and now (i.e., *here* and *now* are defined as where and when the subject is). Also, the subject is by definition conscious; although the idea of an unconscious ego function makes sense, the idea of unconscious subjectivity does not. In (philosophical) phenomenology consciousness and subjectivity are sometimes used interchangeably. *Consciousness*, however, is an unsatisfactory substitute because it is a general function, and our concern must be with the particular and the individual. Further, *consciousness* does not have a robust non-functionalist referent——if we say *the conscious* the natural question is "whose 'conscious'?" and the answer will be: that of the (conscious) subject.

The object is whatever occupies the subject's attention here and now. This attention can be thought of as a *directedness toward* the object, along a line of sight or *sagittally*, that is, with the directedness of an arrow——indeed the subject-object relation is sometimes diagramed with an arrow.

$$S \text{ ------} > O$$

I call this arrow the *vector of intentionality*, following the usage established in philosophical phenomenology. Why *in*tentionality when the directedness in question was introduced in connection with *at*tention? If the subject simply attends to the object (as, e.g., in the case of normal perception), its directedness is (relatively) passive; attention is the selection of a focus, but once directed to that focus its content is whatever happens to present itself. But active directedness is also possible. For example if I *want* something that is within perceptual range I will not just pay attention to it, look at it passively, but will most likely begin a movement toward it. If I want something that is not within perceptual range, I may look *for* it, or initiate action to bring it within range, or think about ways in which to secure it.

These activities will reveal *intentions* in the ordinary sense of that word, but it has a more general sense: if I think about something, bring it to mind, imagine it perhaps, my relation to it will be *intentional* even if it is not (and perhaps cannot be) perceptually available for attention. Objects that were once perceptual may become intentional in this sense when remembered; objects that have never been perceptual for me may be intentional for me if I am told about them, or anticipate them, or even think about their impossibility. (In phenomenology some objects are recognized as purely intentional objects—the golden mountain, for example, or the round square, one of which is physically improbable and the other geometrically impossible; note that to be an intentional object it is not necessary for the object in question to be *imaginable* or able to be *visualized*.)

The subject, then, is intentionally related to a domain of objects. This indeed may be taken to be its defining property: whatever it is that bears this relation to objects, which constitutes them as objects in relation to itself, is the subject. Thus in the history of philosophy the subject has been defined in seemingly odd ways: as a transcendental unity (in Husserl, 1970b; and Kant, 1965) or as an empty center of consciousness constituted by the negation of facticity (in Sartre, 1966).[2] (A later Sartrian formulation sees the subject as temporarily objectified by the Look of another subject [1966]; since the Other for Sartre is initially encountered as an object we may find here an anticipation of object relations theory.)[3] We might say that the subject lives in, or animates, an intentional domain, a life-world, much of which, however, is taken over, preempted, or commandeered by perception when the subject system is exposed to the external physical world through the senses.[4] This way of looking at the matter preserves a unity in the subject-object relation: the life of perception is continuous with the life of thought. Thought does not have to be treated as anomalous or as belonging to a different domain from perception. At the same time the object domain is complex and will have a feedback effect on the subject. A general working principle then might be this: the subject is defined at any moment in the first instance as the correlate of what it attends to or intends—what it is directed toward.

We can distinguish several possible kinds of object of this directedness, each of which will generate an aspect of subjectivity:

- one's own body (generating what we might call *embodied subjectivity*)
- other people (generating *interpersonal subjectivity*; object relations)
- things, places, ideas, and so on (generating *positional subjectivity*)
- oneself and one's own thought contents, memories, and so on (generating *reflexive subjectivity*).

The basic idea is that the subject is *situated* in relation to classes of objects; specific members of these classes react upon it and in so doing help to constitute it as what it is. Indeed, a good name for the position being developed here would be the *situated subjectivity model*. It is fully compatible with the biopsychosocial model (Engel, 1977, 1980) but goes beyond it—or one might say beneath it, in that its engagement with the subject is on a more fundamental level.

The biopsychosocial model, it should be remembered, was intended as a model for the conceptualization of medicine in general, not just of psychiatry, even though psychiatry is assigned a special role to play in activating it and is charged with a special responsibility not to allow itself to be reduced to the biomedical model. The biopsychosocial model offers a systemic view of the patient as a person in his or her interconnectedness with the rest of the world, inner and outer. But the subject is not identical with the person and is not necessarily a person to itself, *person* representing primarily what one is to other people. (One might say that the subject is related to the person as body to clothing, *persona* being originally a mask; we may of course come to think of ourselves *as* outward appearance, as we would wish to present ourselves to others, but this would not count as the immediate self-knowledge of a subject.) The subject is situated at the *place* of the person in Engel's scheme of things (it looks outward toward the biosphere, inward toward molecules, and reflexively back on itself) but occupies this position in a different way from any of the entries in the systems hierarchy, the person included. It is as it were in a different dimension, orthogonal to the plane of the page on which the relation of the person to the rest of the hierarchy is represented. The subject is not biological or psychological or social, it is the one for whom the distinctions among these categories make sense. The clinician is a subject as much as the patient is: the challenge is to find a way of dealing with the patient as subject. The biopsychosocial model is not of much help with this, even though it is no doubt the best working model we have at the moment and is entirely adequate to specialties outside psychiatry as well as for a good many disorders within it.

The subject is not even *mental*—again, it is the point of view from which a distinction between *mental* and *physical* makes sense. This suggests a comment on a recent candidate to replace the biopsychosocial model: *organic unity theory* (Goodman, 1991b). To propose an interpretation of the mind-body problem as an answer to the deficiencies of the older model is to miss the point that the essential duality in the situation of the patient is not mind versus body but subject versus object; from this perspective both mind and body count as objects. I can exhibit psychophysical identity from the point of view of some other subject, but as subject I cannot be identical with the objects I intend. The organic unity model rests on a mental-physical identity theory according to which "there exist 'pure psychophysical events' that the subject and the observer experience differently" (*subject* being understood here as a subject of experiment or inquiry) (Goodman, 1991b, p. 557). But it simply is not the case that we experience, say, the release and uptake of neurotransmitters in a different way from an observing neurological researcher; we do not experience *them* at all, we experience depression or cognitive closure or whatever. The fact that the central postulate of the mental-physical identity theory is that for every mental concept there exists a physical concept with the same referent gives the game away: if there are *concepts* on either side of the identity there has to be a conceiving subject to see and assert the identity, whose status will be ontologically prior to them both.

To return to the exposition from this argumentative digression: each of the aspects of subjectivity listed above may, again, operate in either of several pairs of modalities:

- relating to its objects actively or passively
- relating to its objects cognitively or affectively
- relating to its objects atemporally or temporally (i.e., in the present moment, or directed to past or future; the contrast is between *momentary* and *enduring*——the latter of which may be construed as *lasting* or *progressing* or both——and is sometimes expressed by the terms *synchronic* and *diachronic*).

The force of these oppositions is fairly obvious, and in combination they lead to a large number of possible states or conditions of the subject. A further modal opposition, whose cogency in this context, however, would depend on as yet unresolved questions about the function of lateralization in the normal brain, might be:

- originating in the left or right hemisphere; this would be the subjective counterpart of what Suzanne Langer (1948), long before the evidence from commissurotomy, postulated as the opposition between *discursive* and *presentational* forms of thought.

In addition to the various aspects and modes of subjectivity generated by the analysis of the subject-object relation, a question arises about the development of subjectivity. It is tempting to assume a primitive subjectivity or proto-subjectivity, atemporal, objectless, undifferentiated, a locus of nondirected feeling, as the starting point of the life of the self. Some such state, determined presumably as a function of some underlying neurophysiological substrate, seems necessary to bridge the developmental gap between biology and psychiatry. Such a protosubjectivity also seems to correspond intuitively to the threshold of consciousness (frequently experienced, e.g., in slow awakening from sleep) at which the subject becomes aware of itself as self-identical, but as floating, and nondirectional, compared with usual experience. Such a primitive subjectivity might constitute the theoretical limit of regression short of complete unconsciousness and might be postulated as underlying catatonic states. However, for obvious reasons it would be difficult to operationalize and can therefore be introduced only as a conjectural inference from other aspects of subjectivity.

SUBJECTIVITY IN PSYCHIATRIC DIAGNOSIS

We are now in a position to begin to ask what all of this means for psychiatric diagnosis. In spite of the complexity of the picture that has been painted so far, there seems little difficulty in the idea that in the "normal" case

- all aspects of subjectivity would develop
- under all modalities, and
- would become integrated
- into a single self-identical subject.

Each of us, as a rule, in our waking (or dreaming) moments, is such a subject, unproblematically; we encounter no trouble in transitions from cognitive to affective relations, from dealing with people to dealing with things, from concentrating on the present moment to remembering the past or anticipating the future. We remain our self-identical selves through all of this (the *self* being just what the subject calls itself). But this normal picture can go wrong in many ways. In particular, pathologies could be expected if

- some aspect of subjectivity failed to develop, or
- some modality was lacking, or
- these various subjectivities failed to integrate, or
- they "integrated" into multiple subjects.

The question is, do any of these pathologies correspond to recognized psychiatric disorders? In particular, are any of them found among the categories of the *Diagnostic and Statistical Manual, Third Edition, Revised* of the American Psychiatric Association, the DSM-III-R (1987)?

On purely intuitive grounds, given the meanings of their names and their primary symptomatologies, a few well-known disorders virtually select themselves as candidates for this sort of analysis:

- autism (or Autistic Disorder), because of the failure of the autistic patient to establish the connections with the world which constitute subjectivity according to the foregoing account;
- Schizophrenia, because of the failure of schizophrenic patients to hold together the early integration of cognitive with affective modes of subjectivity;
- Borderline Personality Disorder, for a reason very similar to that given for Schizophrenia but with a different emphasis, the cognitive remaining in place but the affective being in some crucial respects split off from it;
- the dissociative disorders, especially Multiple Personality Disorder, in which the integration of the aspects and modes may take place but at more than one focus, so that the subject is confused as to the point of view it occupies. In more dramatic cases, the subject may actually share

its occupancy of a central point of view sequentially with one or several distinct alters, sometimes a fairly large number of them, each a subject in its own right.

Given these formulations, it is a reassuring confirmation of the approach taken here to find that precisely these disorders have some slight acknowledgement in DSM-III-R of the patient-as-subject. (One other is also mentioned there: Identity Disorder, which might be construed as a special kind of dissociative disorder.) DSM-III-R is not, of course, intended as a theoretical work but as an eminently practical one, so that to remark on its scanty theoretical content does not count as criticism of its original project. On the other hand, part of my point is to suggest that what seem like purely theoretical considerations may be of great practical utility in a diagnostic context. The point is general—practical people in many domains tend to dismiss "theorizing" as irrelevant, when in fact theory is a rich source of thoroughly practical insights—and it has rarely been put more forcefully than by Kant (1974), who concluded his small but powerful essay "On the Old Saw: That May Be Right in Theory, but It Won't Work in Practice" with the remark that "what is valid in theory, on rational grounds, is valid also in practice."

In all events what DSM-III-R does say, even indirectly, about subjectivity, and subjective self-understanding and self-expression, amounts to no more than can conveniently be cited *in extenso*.

Autistic Disorder

Autistic Disorder is described as "marked abnormalities in the form or content of speech . . . use of 'you' when 'I' is meant (e.g., using 'You want cookie?' to mean 'I want a cookie')" (American Psychiatric Association, 1987, p. 39).

Autism might seem to be an excess of subjectivity rather than any kind of deficiency. R.J. Campbell, for example, in his *Psychiatric Dictionary* (1981), defined it as "a form of thinking more or less genuinely of a subjective character," and explained this as meaning that the autistic patient's thinking consists of "material derived from the subject himself," that "the content of thought is largely endogenous." On reflection, however, it appears that *subject* and *subjective* here are being used informally, in the ordinary language sense discussed earlier: *subjective* in the first citation could be replaced by *private*, and *subject* in the second could be replaced by *patient*, without changing the sense. An established and formed subject would naturally use the pronoun *I*. However, the accepted view of autism, echoed by DSM-III-R, is that *I* is what the autistic patient means when he or she says *you*. But what supports this view? To assume that the autistic speaker in fact means what a healthy speaker *would* mean is surely to waste precious diagnostic evidence: namely that the autistic speaker does not say what the healthy speaker says, but something else.

What if autism were, as I suspect it is, a generalized failure of subjectivity above the primitive protosubjective level, a failure to establish intentionality, more specifically a failure of active interpersonal subjectivity? Then there might not *be* an *I* for the autistic speaker to refer to in interpersonal communication. Further, bearing in mind the difference between what words mean and what speakers mean (which may be very great), it may be that although the autistic speaker's *words* mean something anomalous ("*you* want cookie?") the *speaker* is not in a position to mean *anything*, *meaning* being an intentional function of a subject. There seems no reason why a language processing capacity might not develop without its being activated by a subject——indeed there is plenty of suggestive evidence, in aphasia, parapraxes, and other speech disorders, of relatively autonomous linguistic functions, and if language can function independently of a conscious subject in such relatively benign cases it may well do so in autism.

Identity Disorder

DSM-III-R describes Identity Disorder as "severe subjective distress regarding inability to integrate aspects of the self into a relatively coherent and acceptable sense of self. . . . The person experiences . . . conflicts as irreconcilable aspects of his or her personality and . . . fails to perceive himself or herself as having a coherent identity. Frequently the disturbance is epitomized by the person's asking, 'Who am I?'" (American Psychiatric Association, 1987, p. 89).

"Inability to integrate" suggests dissociation, but it assumes that integrating is something worth trying to do. If there really is an attempt to integrate irreconcilable aspects of the self, and subjective distress at the failure to do so, then it would seem (in the light of the theory of subjectivity) that there already exists a unitary subjective agent, namely the one who makes this attempt and suffers this distress. It may be, then, that the question "Who am I?" is not only a healthy question on the part of someone who has perhaps learned from the culture to expect the wrong *sort* of answer, but also a question that has a relatively simple right answer. The inquiry to pursue here may be what the patient takes to be an "acceptable" sense of self, and why. If the question "acceptable to whom?" makes any sense at all it will have a good chance of evoking a robust subject, since it is not clear what it would mean for *my* sense of self to be unacceptable to someone *else*. If it does not evoke a robust subject that may be because a genuine dissociative disorder is present.

Another possibility here is that Identity Disorder might reflect a failure to integrate the subject from one moment to the next, or over time, which, in the terms of the theory, could be seen as a failure of the diachronic or temporal modality in interpersonal or positional subjectivity; not having a coherent identity would mean not recognizing oneself as the same person as at some other time. Here again, however, the question may be of how strict the conditions are for self-identity. Let us say that the subject is defined as an element in the system subject-object. If this *system* is stable over time, the subject aspect can be expected to change every time the object part does. Normally the mature subject in my sense will consider itself the owner and animator of the structure of such a stable, though internally dynamic, subject-object system, and will occupy in relation to it a position analogous to that of the transcendental ego in phenomenology. However, the phenomenologists (Husserl at least [1970b]) recognize also a "naively interested ego," more liable to be buffeted by changes in its world, and if the subject assumes this position its continuity may be more problematic. Even so, in any Identity Disorder short of full dissociation it would seem that the transcendental position should be accessible (a remark that may have more therapeutic than diagnostic relevance).

Schizophrenia

Of Schizophrenia, DSM-III-R says, "the sense of self that gives the normal person a feeling of individuality, uniqueness, and self-direction is frequently disturbed. This is sometimes referred to as a loss of ego boundaries, and frequently is evidenced by extreme perplexity about one's own identity and the meaning of existence" (American Psychiatric Association, 1987, p. 189).

Schizophrenia is too complex and multifarious a disorder to make this descriptive excerpt the basis for a penetrating comment about it—indeed the suggestion has been made that it may turn out to be a cluster of several distinct disorders. Individuality, uniqueness, self-direction, and identity are all attributes of the normal subject, which experiences the sense of self. Just how are these attributes distorted in schizophrenia? Certainly the active/passive modality is commonly distorted, in cases in which the patient reports being instructed or controlled by voices or forces from elsewhere. Certainly the cognitive/affective modality is distorted in flat affect and in the sometimes quite placid attribution to others of bizarre and fantastic intentions and powers. In terms of the present theory, schizophrenia may perhaps be viewed as a failure of integration of interpersonal and positional subjectivity. On the one hand, this may be manifest in social withdrawal, and on the other, in the population of the world with weird and sinister agencies. In addition to the modal distortions already specified, some temporal distortion might be expected as well. A tempting question in the light of the usual age of onset of schizophrenia— but again perhaps not one of immediate diagnostic relevance—is whether the full integration of the interpersonal and the positional is *normally* delayed until adolescence, so that its failure would not be noticeable before that stage: whether things in the world may be more personalized, and persons considered more thing-like (in line with the "selfobject" concept of the object-relations theorists), in childhood and adolescence than in maturity.

Dissociative Disorders

DSM-III-R says of Dissociative Disorder that it is "a disturbance or alteration in the normally integrative functions. . . . If it occurs primarily in identity, the person's customary identity is temporarily forgotten, and a new identity may be assumed or imposed (as in Multiple Personality Disorder), or the customary feeling of one's own reality is lost and is replaced by a feeling of unreality (as in Depersonalization Disorder)" (American Psychiatric Association, 1987, p. 269).

"If it occurs primarily in identity": the other possibility cited is occurrence primarily in memory, as in psychogenic amnesia or fugue, cases that I leave aside here. Depersonalization Disorder seems to have something in common with Identity Disorder, as discussed earlier: *someone* feels unreal, since any feeling properly so called requires a subject, and a reasonable diagnostic (and possibly also therapeutic) line of questioning might seek to establish who the patient thinks that is. This might be called the Cartesian strategy, Descartes (1960) having had the insight that though I may be deluded or deceived it is still *I* who am deluded or deceived. If a depersonalized patient responded to the Cartesian inquiry, "I am the one who doesn't feel real, but I don't feel like a person," the strategy would be to point out that he or she is, all the same, capable of saying "I," which is a criterion for subjectivity (though not necessarily, as we have seen, for personhood).

Multiple Personality Disorder may have a claim to be recognized as belonging to an entirely different category from Identity or Depersonalization Disorder. The DSM-III-R language refers to "the person's customary identity," which recalls the comment above that the subject is not a person to himself or herself, only to other people: it is the *persona*, the outer mask, that identifies the person. The implausible thing about Multiple Personality Disorder——so implausible that many otherwise reasonable clinicians refuse to recognize its existence——is that it is apparently the *same person* who suddenly speaks in a different voice or exhibits a different pattern of behavior. The association of *personality* with *person* serves to confuse the issue, so that the disorder might better be called Multiple Subjectivity Disorder. For any one of the subjects affected by the disorder all may be perfectly normal in his or her subjective life (*his* or *her* in this case having no necessary connection to the gender of the *person* in question): agency and passivity, cognition and affect, even temporality and memory, may be fully exemplified in all of the aspects of subjectivity, embodied, interpersonal, positional, and reflexive.

The one "abnormality" is likely to be in the continuity of the subjective life; there will be periods, perhaps long periods, in which a particular subject is not active, and these periods may be experienced as "lost time." However I put "abnormality" between quotation marks precisely because these lapses might seem as normal to one of a set of multiple subjects as the lapses we all experience in sleep, daydreaming, or inattention do to us. We lose time every night and do not feel called upon to offer an explanation for this—we call it *sleep*, but that is a name, not an explanation. The difference is that we do not find things in pockets or closets or on desks, for example, which some other subject has put there with what we think of as "our" hands. (There is a hint of this in sleepwalking disorder, when the patient may wake in a place other than where he or she went to sleep, but there is no evidence of the activity of another subject in that case.) It is presumably the fact that other people do not have these experiences which convinces the multiple of his or her abnormality.

Multiple Personality Disorder seems to be the most straightforward case for the theory: it is simply integration into more than one subject. The double subjectivity of commissurotomized patients is a special and factitious case in which the functional separation of the subjects results from a surgical intervention; in Multiple Personality Disorder proper the neuroanatomical and neurophysiological substrates are by no means so clearly abnormal. But the recognition of separate subjectivities in the split-brain case does make it easier to acknowledge such a possibility as arising developmentally in other cases. The astonishing thing about normal development, it seems to me, is that it does so regularly lead to a single fully integrated subjectivity. The organism's behavior, especially in response to situations of extreme stress, can become so complex that on reflection it seems not at all implausible that special subjectivities might emerge to play special roles. These special roles may display a pattern of mutual accommodation and protection, a kind of symbiosis, not consciously devised or monitored by any one of the subjectivities in question. The diagnostic lesson here is that a lot of time may be wasted if the clinician insists on looking for the integrated subject or "personality" in the face of flagrant evidence of multiplicity. Indeed, this may be one reason for the difficulties in classifying personality disorders.

Borderline Personality Disorder

DSM-III-R describes this as "a marked and persistent identity disturbance . . . . [that] is often pervasive, and is manifested by uncertainty about several life issues, such as self-image, sexual orientation. . . . The person often experiences this instability of self-image as chronic feelings of emptiness or boredom" (American Psychiatric Association, 1987, p. 346).

Here again, the description of the subjective state is only part of a longer characterization of the disorder, which includes affective instability, mood shifts, impulsive behavior, and so on, as well as the apparently entitled and manipulative pattern of interpersonal relations which has come to be the trademark of the borderline personality. What is interesting in the citation is the stress on the patient's self-image and the suggestion that instability in that respect may be experienced as chronic feelings of emptiness or boredom. Emptiness and boredom, as well as mood shifts and impulsivity, suggest an imperfect engagement with objects on the part of the subject, at least in the mode of affect. Not that there is nothing in the subject position or that it is confused regarding its identity *as* a subject (clearly the notion of *identity disturbance* needs further clarification), rather whatever is there is labile, does not have staying power, lacks substance. What it might mean for subjectivity to have substance has puzzled philosophers, and one suggestion has been that there may be a kind of longitudinal intentionality in which what the subject is intentionally directed toward is its own past and future states——in other words, one facet of what I have called *reflexive subjectivity*. The fact that the problem with the borderline is said to be one of self-*image* suggests that the failure may be one of reflexive subjectivity in this sense. Along with Identity Disorder (which is cited in DSM-III-R under the differential diagnosis of Borderline Personality Disorder) there may be a temporal problem here, one of stability and continuity. That does not however account for the other features——looking at borderlines as, for example, Kernberg does (1987) and applying the theory developed here, the obvious conclusion would be that the disorder is a splitting between the cognitive and the affective in interpersonal subjectivity. Still, it might be that this disorder arises from an inability to maintain a constant interpersonal subjectivity over time.

A NEW ROLE FOR THE SUBJECT IN PSYCHIATRY?

So much for the somewhat slim overlap of my topic and the content of DSM-III-R. Once again, my purpose is not to fault DSM-III-R for not concentrating on subjectivity. The conceptual traditions of psychiatry and philosophy have different origins (psychology was once part of philosophy, but the relations between psychology and psychiatry have their own complexities). It is not surprising that empirically minded clinicians have not had the phenomenological literature high on their reading lists. There have of course been plenty of psychiatrists——especially psychoanalysts——who have dealt at length and in detail with phenomenological issues (see especially Atwood & Stolorow, 1984) and with questions of self-identity (see especially Erikson, 1968), but they have not been centrally placed in the profession, and their work has not much influenced the mainstream diagnostic categories represented by DSM-III-R. The serious question is whether in the preparation of DSM-IV (or DSM-V or VI . . .) there might be something to be gained by focusing on the concept, and the manifestations or indicators, of subjectivity.

Diagnosis or *knowing-through* suggests a process of inference: from symptoms to underlying conditions or, even better, to recognized and classified disease entities of which the symptoms in question are pathognomonic. One difficulty with psychiatric diagnoses is that disorders (there are not many robust diseases in this area) almost never have unambiguously pathognomonic symptoms. There may be a family resemblance, in Wittgenstein's sense, between clusters of symptoms, but any of them singly might be present transiently or factitiously in normal individuals. This accounts for the statistical or Chinese menu aspect of diagnostics in psychiatry and the need for criteria of persistence or duration.

Viewed from the perspective of other medical specialties this seems like an unsatisfactory situation. The old ideal, still within reach in many branches, construed disease whenever possible as caused by a lesion or pathology of a specific organ or system. Expertise about the system in question gave the specialty a name suggestive of knowledge: cardiology, hematology, neurology. Although it is inadvisable to lay too great weight on details of terminology which may be partly accidental, it is worth noting that psychiatry shares with a couple of other major specialties (pediatrics, geriatrics) an explicit reference in its very name to the healing process, as if its object were a sick whole rather than some malfunctioning part. Pediatrics deals with the health of the child as a whole, geriatrics with the health of the elderly person as a whole, psychiatry with the health of the . . . psyche as a whole?

That line of thought would take us beyond the limits of this chapter, but it is suggestive all the same. The psyche, whatever it is—just *mind* according to the APA's *Psychiatric Glossary* (whatever mind is)—is certainly not a localizable organ or system like the heart or the gastrointestinal tract. But it would be a mistake to conclude that it is not to be treated seriously, either conceptually or therapeutically—that it somehow does not really exist and has to be eliminated after the manner of the behaviorists. No doubt the reason for the approximate character of a lot of psychiatric diagnosis lies in the fact that the underlying physiology is a system, a neurological system having on the order of 10^{11} elements, each multiply connected, any one or any subset of which can malfunction in indefinitely many ways, of which we know only a few of the most general—regional excesses or deficiencies of one or another neurotransmitter, gross anomalies of projection, and the like.

But psychiatry is not neurology. That the neurological substrate is what makes the life of the mind possible cannot be in doubt; mental activity can reasonably be regarded as a normal and natural function of neurological complexity. It is that activity as experienced by the individual subject, however, which commands the attention of psychiatry. If it can be shown—as is becoming the case with more and more disorders—that intervention at the level of neurophysiology or its underlying neurochemistry will relieve the distress reported by the subject, then that is obviously one of the ways treatment can go, but what is being treated remains the subject in his or her distress, and only instrumentally the neurological carrier. *The object of psychiatry is the subject in its relation to its objects.* It is perhaps the only medical specialty that has a relational object rather than a physical or a systemic one.

If that is the case—if it were agreed to be the case—then the situation in the profession would I think be greatly simplified if it were openly acknowledged to be the case and made the basis of the inquiries upon which diagnosis rests. How might this work out in practice? Here I can only give some hints, since things work out in practice only as tested in practice. It would certainly involve a good deal of education of the patient, although this would not be the drawback it might seem because I suspect that that education would itself be therapeutic. The form the education would take would be the explicit encouragement of the patient to think of himself or herself as a relational being, not simply in the family or social context but in the more fundamental sense developed earlier in this chapter. This would include attending in detail to the different kinds of object which occupy the distal pole of the relation and then becoming aware of, and focusing attention reflexively on, the specific state of the subject that occupies its proximal pole. An important part of the difficulty that patients encounter—as the DSM-III-R account testifies—is in self-conceptualization. As long as the attempt is made to think of the self as fixed and substantial, as something to be "found" ("finding oneself" being a popular ambition on the part of many people who wind up under psychiatric care), failure is almost certain.

The kinds of question which might form the basis of a diagnosis using this approach are suggested by the categories of subjectivity, its aspects and modes, outlined in the theoretical treatment at the beginning of this chapter. Is the patient's subjectivity now—in relation to the therapist—the same as or different from what it was when alone, or in the street, in a family setting, with things, with animals? Is there a sense of continuity over time, or are there breaks? If so, when, and under what circumstances? Is the patient's subjectivity effective as an agent in its world, is it at the mercy of that world, or is it sometimes one and sometimes the other? Again, under what circumstances? What provokes the change? In shifting attention from his or her own body to things, from things to people, does the patient experience a corresponding subjective shift, or is the transition smooth and accompanied by feelings of stability? Do the knowing and the feeling subject seem to be the same or different? Is there slippage between the positional and/or interpersonal on the one hand, and the reflexive on the other, in the sense that the patient's subjective state is taken to be determined by things and people when it is in fact determined by his or her own thought contents? In other words, is there a confusion of the perceptual with the intentional? If so, is this systemic, or can it be corrected by reality testing?

My conjecture is, as must be clear by now, that pursuing this line of inquiry in the light of a theory of subjectivity such as the one expounded in this chapter would lead to diagnostically and therapeutically useful developments. But I return to my opening remarks: the conjecture is open for clinical refutation. This is a challenge to empirical investigation. If it were to remain unrefuted, that would be as much as any conjecture could hope for. (Even the most robust of scientific theories is never finally confirmed, only provisionally unre-futed.) Surviving the test of attempted refutation might, in turn, qualify the practical criteria based on the theory for inclusion along with other diagnostic criteria in some future edition of the DSM.

I am grateful to Nancy Breslin, John Sadler, and Stephen Shanfield for invaluable criticisms of earlier drafts of this chapter.

III VALUES

9 Closet Logics

Hidden Conceptual Elements in the DSM and ICD Classifications of Mental Disorders

K. W. M. FULFORD, D.Phil., M.R.C.P., M.R.C.Psych.

DSM-III (American Psychiatric Association, 1980) and its successor DSM-III-R (American Psychiatric Association, 1987) represent major advances in the classification of psychiatric disorders. Building on the descriptive principles established in ICD-8 (World Health Organization, 1967) and ICD-9 (World Health Organization, 1978a), the introduction of detailed criteria for each category of disorder, together with a multiaxial format, have encouraged clearer thinking and greater consistency in the diagnosis of mental illness, both in clinical work in psychiatry and in research.

Yet considerable difficulties remain. Many of the criteria adopted are subject to continuing revision; the very inclusion of certain categories is hotly debated (Pincus, Frances, Davis, First & Widiger, 1992); and the ICD, although in its latest edition following the DSM in overall format (World Health Organization, 1991), reflects unresolved international differences. Moreover, classifications of this general kind, notwithstanding their relative success in mainstream hospital psychiatry, are proving less readily applicable in other clinical contexts: in primary care (Jenkins, Smeeton, Marinker & Shepherd, 1985), for example, in psychodynamic and family therapies (Frances et al., 1991), and in liaison psychiatry (Mayou & Hawton, 1968). Indeed, in relation even to some of the more contentious areas of psychiatric practice—such as involuntary treatment and forensic assessments of responsibility—the relevance of these classifications is uncertain. DSM-III was subject to a caution about its use in medicolegal contexts, and in DSM-III-R this has been elevated to a full-page disclaimer (American Psychiatric Association, 1987, p. xxix).

The authors of DSM are among the first to acknowledge that modern psychiatric classifications, although more successful than their predecessors, remain provisional (Frances et al., 1991). However, the changes that they envisage in future editions would be primarily scientific in nature. There is a recognition that if a classification is to be acceptable across a wide range of clinical opinion, scientific purity has sometimes to be diluted by pragmatic considerations; but as far as possible the development of our classifications should be based solely on the accumulation, as they put it, of new "data" (American Psychiatric Association, 1987, p. xxvii).

The theme of this chapter, on the other hand, will be that this approach is only partly right. It depends on the belief that ICD and DSM are not just scientific but *exclusively* scientific in nature. Whereas, as we will find, these classifications, although predominantly descriptive in their overall structure, also contain an evaluative element of meaning. The philosophical method of linguistic analysis will be used to make this element explicit. This will in turn suggest a framework for future research, philosophical as well as scientific, directed toward the development of a classification in which evaluative and descriptive elements are equally represented. Such a classification, although more complex than existing systems, will be closer to the contingencies of everyday clinical practice.

CURRENT CLASSIFICATIONS: OVERT DESCRIPTIONS AND COVERT EVALUATIONS

There is no mystery about the firmly scientific self-image of ICD and DSM. The success of these classifications is a direct result of the adoption of a descriptive approach to the definition of mental disorders, more or less consciously emulating the scientific basis of disease classification in physical medicine. The history of this is well known (see Wallace's chapter in this book): the emergence of Kraepelin's classification—based on the symptoms and course of mental disorders—from the relative nosological chaos of the nineteenth century; the proliferation of classifications based on premature etiological theories; the report by Stengel to the World Health Organization recommending a return to a symptomatic basis for psychiatric classification (1959); the subsequent publication of ICD-8 (World Health Organization, 1967) and ICD-9 (World Health Organization, 1978) with a glossary of discursive definitions; and the development of specific "operational" criteria in DSM-III (American Psychiatric Association, 1980) and DSM-III-R (American Psychiatric Association, 1987).

Why, then, it will be asked, should this process not continue seamlessly into the future? We need more clarity about the symptoms of mental disorders, certainly. But this is ongoing in psychiatric phenomenology. Moreover, just as in physical medicine a symptomatic stage of disease classification was a necessary preliminary to the development of well-founded etiological theories, so also in psychiatry. With progress in the brain sciences, we should thus look forward to the emergence of disease categories that are as uncontentious, as universally applicable, and as forensically unambiguous as their counterparts in physical medicine.

Given all this scientific momentum, then, it is surely the more remarkable that we should find value terms, terms expressing judgments of good and bad (see below), liberally distributed throughout both ICD and DSM. Both classifications, at the risk of stating the obvious, are classifications of mental *disorders*. Similarly, in the bodies of both classifications, frequent use is made of a range of terms with *prima facie* evaluative connotations. For example, in the DSM-III-R section on Developmental Disorders (American Psychiatric Association, 1987, pp. 28–32), there are no less than seven value terms (*disorders* used three times; *disturbance*, twice; and *failure* and *distortions*) in the first six lines describing the disorder, and even in the statement of specific diagnostic criteria there are three (*subaverage*, *deficit*, and *impairments*). Moreover, notwithstanding its greater descriptive rigor, value terms are, if anything, more prominent in DSM than in ICD. Indeed, certain of the definitions in DSM appear to rely explicitly on evaluative criteria. This is especially true of conditions on the margins of our classifications: the essential feature of Conduct Disorder, for example, is "a persistent pattern of conduct in which the basic rights of others and major age-appropriate societal norms or rules are violated" (American Psychiatric Association, 1987, p. 53); and patients with paraphilic disorders are described as tending to come to medical attention only "when their behavior has brought them into conflict with sexual partners or society" (American Psychiatric Association, 1987, p. 280).

These are merely observations, of course. Nothing has been said thus far about how the presence of value terms in our classifications should be interpreted. But notice, first, that the value terms in question are indeed terms expressing judgments of good and bad. We need to be clear about this. The expressions *evaluative* and *descriptive* can be used with a variety of different meanings. In DSM, for example, *descriptive* is used in the classification itself to mean that it is based on symptoms rather than etiology, on what is directly observable rather than theoretically postulated. Similarly, *evaluative* can mean a judgment that, although descriptive in the sense of being concerned with some matter of fact, is subjective, vague, or intuitive. DSM, despite its emphasis on operational criteria, sometimes falls back on judgments of this kind: the distinction between *bizarre* and *non-bizarre* delusions, for example (American Psychiatric Association, 1987, p. 202); and judgments of the *symbolic* significance of the symptoms of Conversion Disorder (American Psychiatric Association, 1987, p. 257). We should not be surprised to find judgments of this kind even in a purely scientific classification. We should expect, moreover, that with progress in the science concerned, they would be replaced by more objective measures——rather as the wavelength of light is now used in optics in place of subjective color impressions. Yet these aside, ICD and DSM, it seems, contain evaluations that are not descriptions at all, but, genuinely, as in morals or esthetics, judgments of good and bad.

From a scientific point of view, value judgments of the former (subjective/descriptive) kind are readily recognizable for what they are. Genuine value judgments, on the other hand, often are not. This is one sense in which they are in the closet: they are hidden, camouflaged. They are also in the closet in the sense of being a touch disreputable, something to be hidden away, a skeleton in the scientific/psychiatric cupboard. Hence, even where they are correctly identified, there is a strong tendency to minimize their significance. They are considered a residuum of prescientific terminology (Boorse, 1975), largely definable away if sufficient care is taken with our definitions (Campbell, Scadding & Roberts, 1979), or, at worst, provisional on future advances in scientific understanding (Roth & Kroll, 1968).

From a philosophical point of view, on the other hand, and specifically from the point of view of linguistic analysis, the presence of value judgments in our classifications can be shown to be highly significant.

LINGUISTIC ANALYSIS; MAKING COVERT EVALUATIONS OVERT

The essence of the linguistic analytical approach to philosophy is to explore the meanings of our concepts, not passively by reflective definition, but actively, by examining the ways in which they are actually used (Wittgenstein, 1958). This is developmentally sound. We learn the meanings of our concepts largely by shared use within a social context rather than by explicit definition. Moreover, many concepts that are indispensable in everyday usage are for different reasons highly resistant to explicit definition—the concepts of *baroque*, for example, and *time*. At all events, as Austin (1968) pointed out, our powers of direct reflection on the meanings of our concepts are severely limited. We tend to latch on to one or another aspect of a concept or family of concepts, to see only part of the full picture. Hence, to the extent that use reflects meaning, exploring the ways in which our concepts are employed could lead to a more complete picture, a less biased or slanted view, of the concepts with which we are concerned.

Austin's approach helps us to understand the general features of ICD and DSM outlined in the preceding section. As we saw there, the conventional understanding of these classifications is that their predominantly descriptive structure is the result of a progressive approximation to a purely scientific nosology. An Austin-led approach, on the contrary, suggests that the descriptive focus in these classifications may be no more than a particular instance of a general tendency to focus too narrowly when reflecting on the meanings of our concepts. Moreover, in this instance, this tendency has been given a particular (descriptive) direction by the success of medical science.

Similarly, and correspondingly, if use is a surer guide to meaning than reflective definition, then the persistence of value terms in these classifications, far from being a mark of their scientific incompleteness, could point directly to the presence of an evaluative element of meaning alongside the descriptive. The relative distribution of these value terms between ICD and DSM suggests, moreover, that this is a conceptually important element. If it were merely a prescientific contaminant, we should expect to find value terms, if anything, *less* prominent in the more rigorous DSM. But they are *more* prominent. The likelihood, therefore, is that this element is woven into the very criteria for inclusion in these classifications, into the very meaning, that is to say, of mental disorder.

The Concept of Mental Disorder

An Austin-led interpretation of our classifications thus leads beyond them to the concept of mental disorder. This in itself is a useful result. There is, of course, a large literature on the concept of mental illness and, indeed, on the general concepts of illness and disease (Clare, 1979). Yet there has been remarkably little contact between this area and psychiatric classification. Authors concerned with concepts of disorder tend either to write in general terms or to concentrate on one or other limited areas of pathology. There is little attempt to tie general theory, as the linguistic analytical method requires, to the full range and detail of the rich phenomenology of illness, physical as well as mental. Equally, the authors of our classifications, focusing more directly on the range of psychopathology, have tended to neglect the general concepts by which the very scope of their classifications are defined.

DSM is, again, ahead of ICD in this regard in offering a definition of *mental disorder*. This definition, consistently with the descriptive orientation of DSM, reflects many of the various science-based definitions developed in the literature, for example by Boorse (1975). By analogy with physical disease, it emphasizes the syndromal nature of mental disorders, defined by such ostensibly descriptive criteria as pain, risk of death, and disturbed functioning. Thus, a mental disorder is taken to be a "clinically significant behavioral or psychological syndrome or pattern that occurs in a person and that is associated with present distress (a painful symptom) or disability (impairment in one or more important areas of functioning) or with a significantly increased risk of suffering death, pain, disability, or an important loss of freedom." There then follow two important qualifications, excluding, on the one hand, an "expectable response to a particular event" and, on the other, "deviant behavior" and "conflicts that are primarily between the individual and society" except where these "are a symptom of a dysfunction in the person" (American Psychiatric Association, 1987, p. xxii).

There is not space here to analyze this definition in detail. Nor would this be appropriate, given that the reasoning behind it is not spelled out. I have argued elsewhere, however, on Austin-led linguistic analytical lines, that definitions of this science-based kind, like the science-based classifications of ICD and DSM, reflect a one-sided view of the conceptual structure of medicine (Fulford, 1991a). They do indeed contain elements that are genuinely descriptive (e.g., "behavioral or psychological syndrome or pattern" and "pain"). However, leaving aside merely tautological elements (e.g., "clinically significant," "symptom") these are not in themselves sufficient to define a disease, and when we look at what more has to be added, we find a whole series of value terms (e.g., *distress, disability, impairment*).

The natural response to this, from scientifically minded philosophers as well as physicians, is that it should be possible to establish value-free criteria for the use of terms such as these. Boorse (1975), for example, defined disease, ultimately, by reference to the purely descriptive notions of reduced life and/or reproductive expectations. But the essential Austin-led point is that, however carefully a value-free definition of disease is developed, as soon as the concept is actually used, value judgments slip back in. In Boorse's paper, for example, the descriptive "environmental causes" slips to become the evaluative "hostile environment" (1975, p. 59). Moreover, there is something of this even within the wording of the DSM definition. The onus of the second qualification to the definition is that it is not merely *deviant* behavior from which disease has to be differentiated, but negatively *evaluated* deviant behavior. In DSM-III, indeed, this is made explicit, it being said of such behavior that it may or may not be "commendable" (p. 6).

The implication, therefore, is that, stipulate as we may a purely descriptive definition of disease, the concept is simply unable to do the work that is required of it in actual use without the reintroduction of an evaluative element into its meaning. The alternative, therefore, is to accept that disease is indeed a value term and to explore the consequences of this. A number of authors have adopted one or another variant of this approach (e.g., Agich, 1983; Sedgwick, 1973). In my own work I have used it as a basis for examining the ways in which philosophical work on the logic of value terms can help to illuminate the meanings of the medical concepts, focusing on illness and disease in particular (Fulford, 1989). It should be emphasized straightaway that this is not an antiscientific approach. On the contrary, the strategy is to clarify the ways in which evaluative and descriptive elements of meaning are woven to-gether into the conceptual structure of medicine. The resulting "model" of the medical concepts can be considered at two levels. At the first level, illness and disease are treated as value terms *simpliciter*. Illness and disease, however, are not just value terms *simpliciter*. They express a particular kind of value, medical as distinct from, say, moral and esthetic values. This leads to the second level of analysis, in which illness and disease are interpreted as terms expressing specifically medical value. As we will see, the second level is more complicated than the first, leading as it does into the relatively uncharted philosophical waters of the philosophy of action. Both levels, however, yield useful results for our understanding of the structures of ICD and DSM.

Level 1: Illness and Disease as Value Terms

A value-based analysis of the medical concepts completely repolarizes our picture of current classifications of mental disorders. A science-based analysis, as we have seen, leads to a picture of these classifications as predominantly descriptive, with, at most, evaluative fringes. A value-based analysis inverts this picture. It turns it upside down because it shows the descriptive parts of these classifications to be no more than criteria—extended criteria, to be sure—for the value judgments expressed by the medical concepts. This is a consequence, simply, of the way that value judgments in general are related to the (descriptive) criteria for their application. To judge something to be good or bad of its kind is to imply certain descriptive criteria for the value judgments in question. A good apple, to take a nonmedical example, is (in most contexts and for most people) an apple that is sweet, clean-skinned, and so forth. To the extent, therefore, that bodily and mental conditions are like apples, to judge a condition to be a disease is to imply that the (descriptive) features by which that condition is defined are criteria for the (negative) value judgment expressed by disease.

This repolarization of view has many consequences. In the first place, it is consistent with the predominantly descriptive (surface) structure of our classifications. A science-based view is also consistent in this respect, but for different reasons. According to a science-based view, our classifications appear to be predominantly descriptive simply because they are, indeed, largely scientific in nature. In a value-based view, on the other hand, this appearance is a consequence of a property that illness and disease, if value terms, would be expected to share with value terms in general. This property arises from the fact that all value terms, even *good* and *bad,* carry descriptive as well as evaluative connotations. And as Hare (1972) and others pointed out, value terms may have *predominantly* descriptive connotations in those contexts in which the descriptive criteria for the value judgments they express are largely settled or agreed upon. Thus, *good apple,* to return to our nonmedical example of a moment ago, has the descriptive connotations "sweet, clean-skinned, etc.," because most people in most contexts take sweet, clean-skinned apples to be good. Compare this, on the other hand with, say, *good picture.* This has largely evaluative connotations because the descriptive criteria by which people judge pictures to be good or bad are highly variable. There is no consistent descriptive meaning to latch onto, as it were, whereas with *good apple* we come to notice the descriptive meaning because it is relatively stable from one occasion to the next. In some circumstances, moreover, we may by (more or less tacit) convention come to settle once and for all the descriptive criteria for a value judgment. This is possible where there is already a good degree of agreement, within a given "evaluating community," as it were, on the criteria for the value judgment in question. With respect to apples, again, Urmson (1950) argued that Ministry of Agriculture criteria for grading them as "fine," "superfine," and so forth, amount to conventional definitions of value terms. Disease definitions can be understood in certain respects similarly. Our classifications can be understood in part as extended and comprehensive statements of the conventional definitions of the disease concepts adopted within our own "clinical community."

With respect to the predominantly descriptive structures of our classifications, then, a science-based view and a value-based view converge. With respect to the persistence of value terms in our classifications, however, they diverge. For in a value-based view, the persistence of value terms, far from being a residue of prescientific thinking, emerges as a second consequence of the logical property of value terms just noted. As we have seen, where the descriptive criteria for a value judgment are generally settled, the value term in question will have largely descriptive connotations. Correspondingly, therefore, where the criteria are not settled, the value term in question will have evaluative connotations. We have already noted *good picture* as an example of this. Hence, if the medical concepts are, through and through, evaluative concepts, we should anticipate, as turns out to be the case, that their evaluative connotations should be most apparent in relation to those conditions described earlier as being on the margins of our classifications. If the attribution of disease involves a value judgment, if this is an essential part of the meaning of disease, then one source of difficulty about the status of a condition *as* a disease will be disagreements about whether the condition in question is or is not a bad condition to be in. In the cases at least of conduct disorder and the paraphilias, the DSM definitions—with their references to the values of society *as opposed to* those of the individual concerned—reflect just such disagreements. (In Russell's chapter in this book, this latter dispute is raised also.)

This explanation for the more overtly evaluative connotations of certain conditions in our classifications can be extended to explain the more overtly evaluative connotations of mental illness as a whole compared with physical. The evaluative connotations of mental illness are an important source of debate in the literature. They are a central concern of Boorse's argument, for example (1975). Along with other supporters of the concept of mental illness (e.g., Kendell, 1975), his objective is to define them away, to show that "mental disease" [*sic*] is really as value free, as scientific, as the concept of physical disease. Similarly, Szasz (1960) and other opponents of mental illness have taken its evaluative connotations to be an indication that it is not really illness at all. The criteria of (so-called) mental illnesses are indeed, Szasz argued, social/evaluative, rather than, like those of genuine illnesses, biological/ scientific.

However, from a value-based perspective the more overtly evaluative connotations of mental illness are seen to be a consequence, simply, of the fact that the descriptive criteria by which we evaluate typical symptoms of mental illness are, overall, less settled or agreed upon than the corresponding criteria by which we evaluate typical symptoms of physical illness. Physical pain, for example, is (for most people in most contexts) at best a necessary evil; it is true that even here we can make good come of evil, but we have to work at it. Whereas anxiety, as a typical symptom of mental illness, although avoided by some people, may, without perversity, be sought out by others— we speak of the thrill of fear, for example. Hence, mental illness constituted by anxiety will for this reason alone be more value laden than physical illness constituted by pain.

A similar analysis can be applied to other psychiatric symptoms, although some are more complicated than others (Fulford, 1989, chaps. 5, 8–10). The overall approach, however, shows the relatively value-laden nature of disease classifications in psychiatry in a quite different light from the prejudicial slant of the science-based view. Instead of this being a mark of deficiency, the evaluative connotations of mental illness are shown to reflect the properties (the logical properties) of its constituent symptoms (such as anxiety) and to reflect these properties as faithfully as the more descriptive connotations of physical illness reflect the corresponding (logical) properties of its constituent symptoms (such as pain). In this respect, mental illness and physical illness are thus on a par. Indeed, to the extent that there is an evaluative element in the meanings of the medical concepts generally, mental illness has the edge on physical illness in being the more transparent. We will return later to the significance of this for our classifications. But in general terms, we can see already that if this is true, there is not the same pressure to exclude value judgments from our classifications. If they are there, and genuinely contentious, the conventional science-based objective of defining them away could be fundamentally misdirected, increasing as it does the vulnerability of psychiatry to abuse (Fulford, Smirnov & Snow, 1993).

The misdirectedness of this approach can be seen in a different way by applying the same point about the logic of value terms to the relationship between illness and disease. These terms are, of course, often used as synonyms. However, as a number of authors have pointed out (e.g., Barondess, 1979), insofar as they are distinct in meaning, illness tends to refer to the patient's experience, whereas disease refers to the doctor's specialized scientific

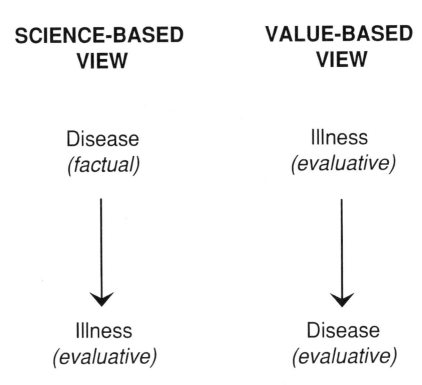

SCIENCE-BASED VIEW	VALUE-BASED VIEW
Disease (factual)	Illness (evaluative)
↓	↓
Illness (evaluative)	Disease (evaluative)

Figure 9.1 Two Views of the Primacy of the Meanings of Illness and Disease

In the conventional science-based view of medicine, the meaning of the ostensibly value-laden notion of illness is derived from that of disease, which in turn is defined in terms of descriptive criteria of disturbed functioning. In a value-based view, this relationship is reversed. Descriptively defined conditions, whether of body or of mind, are marked out as diseses by the negative value judgment expressed by illness. This repolarization of view has a number of important consequences for our understanding of the logical structures of ICD and DSM (see text).

knowledge. It has been natural, therefore, given a science-based perspective, to seek to define illness in terms of disease rather than vice versa—Boorse (1975) defined illness as a serious disease. The corresponding tendency in our classifications has been to seek to model mental disorders on concepts of physical disease (see the foreword to this book).

From a value-based perspective, on the other hand, the logical relationship, the relationship of meaning, can be shown to be the other way. This is illustrated in Figure 9.1. According to this approach, illness is the primary concept, our concepts of disease owing their logical properties, ultimately, to the patient's experience of illness. Again, there is a good deal of detail to be gone into here (Fulford, 1989, chap. 4). But the key step is to see that symptomatically defined diseases are a subcategory of illnesses. Illness has the more overtly evaluative connotations (partly) because it can be used for any condition that may be negatively evaluated as an illness; disease has more descriptive connotations because it refers to the subcategory of illnesses that are uniformly evaluated in its way (i.e., by most people in most contexts). From this latter subcategory, other disease concepts can evolve—by association, by causal links, and so forth. These further subcategories, moreover, once evolved, can achieve a degree of logical autonomy (covering, e.g., the use of disease in respect of asymptomatic conditions). However, the essential point is that the flow of meaning throughout is from the patient's experience through to derived disease concepts, not vice versa. Disease concepts, in this view, thus presuppose the meaning of illness. Hence if it is the logical structure of our classifications with which we are concerned, we should be focusing not, with the science-based view, on disease, but, directly, on the concept of illness. This brings us to the second level at which our analysis of illness and disease as value terms can be pursued.

Level 2: Illness as Failure of Action

Many important practical difficulties in psychiatry concern the particular kind of value expressed by illness. In depression, for example, decisions about compulsory treatment turn not so much on whether the patient's condition is a bad condition to be in as on whether it is a bad condition of the particular kind we call illness. The issue is whether the patient is merely sad or, medically speaking, mad. Similarly, issues of responsibility in law turn on whether the patient is bad or, again medically speaking, mad. Issues such as these have, of course, been widely debated (Flew, 1973). Yet surprisingly little of this debate has focused on the definition of medical value. The science-based view, in particular, subsumes the attribution of illness to the identification of disease, this in turn being subsumed to the definition of disturbance of functioning. However, as no less a supporter of the science-based view than Boorse emphasized (1975), this approach gives results that are, in important respects, counterintuitive—psychotic disorders, for instance, turn out to be peripheral rather than central cases of mental illness as an excuse in law. The difficulties with this approach, moreover, are reflected in the uncertain relevance of ICD and DSM to questions of this kind. If attributions of illness involved nothing more than the identification of diseases, there would surely not be the need, expressed as we have seen even more strongly in DSM-III-R than in DSM-III, for a warning notice between the diagnostic categories defined so carefully in these classifications and medicolegal questions.

From a value-based perspective, however, the natural approach to these issues is not in terms of failure of function but failure of action. As with value *simpliciter*, a full account of this is beyond the scope of this essay (Fulford, 1989, chap. 7 and 8). Again, though, the basic idea is straightforward enough:

if we consider the actual experience of illness, not as defined by disease but in its own right, then it is most directly analyzable in terms of failure of intentional action rather than failure of function.

Thus, actions are the things that people (and higher animals) characteristically do: functioning is what bodies and minds, and the parts of bodies and minds, characteristically do. The concepts of action and function are related, of course. Writing this sentence——an action of mine——is possible only if my hand and arm (muscles, nerves, memory, etc.) are functioning properly and it is by way of this relationship that the experience of illness and knowledge of disease are also related. Medical knowledge of disease is (appropriately) constructed in terms of impairments of functioning. But the patient's experience of illness is to be understood rather in terms of incapacity or failure of action——an inability to do things one can ordinarily do. The requisite failure of action, however, is internal rather than imposed. For the experience of illness involves a two-way distinction: on the one hand, from things that we do; on the other, from things that are done to us. Paralysis, for example, is different both from not moving and from being restrained; pain (as a symptom of illness) is different from hurting oneself and from being hurt (by something external). Behind this two-way distinction, furthermore, lies all the complexity of what Austin (1968) called the "machinery of action"——perception, volition, foresight, control, and so forth. This complexity is no barrier to the analysis, however. On the contrary, it allows a variety of illnesses, mental and physical, to be analyzed as failures at different points in this machinery (Fulford, 1989, chap. 3). Illness, then, according to this view, is, roughly, failure of action, whereas different kinds of illnesses are analyzable as different kinds of failure of action.

Although less familiar than the analysis of disease as failure of function, the analysis of illness as failure of action has considerable face validity. First, as Toulmin (1980) pointed out, the very word *patient* implies a loss of agency. Second, it provides the required logical link between illness and negative value. To intend something is to value it positively. Hence, a *failure* of intentional action is an inherently negatively evaluated experience. Third, and returning now to psychiatric classification, it is consistent with, and thus explains, the presence in ICD and DSM of a whole range of concepts which, if not exclusively the concern of philosophers, certainly sit as comfortably with the philosophy of action as with experimental science. The definition of mental disorder in DSM reflects this: it is said to be a "dysfunction," but, oddly for a scientific definition, a dysfunction "in the *person*"; and the criteria for a mental disorder include, in addition to pain, disability, and so forth, loss of "an important *freedom*."

In the bodies of both ICD and DSM, furthermore, we find elements both of the two-way distinction by which the experience of illness is defined (the "done by——wrong with——done to" distinction just described) and of the concept of action. Anxiety State (300.1, p. 38) and Neurotic Depression (300.4, p. 39) in ICD-9 (World Health Organization, 1978), for instance, are said, respectively, to be "not attributable to real danger" and "disproportionate"; both disorders, therefore, in the terms of the two-way distinction, are to be distinguished from things that are *done to* us. Then again, coming to the concept of action in ICD-9, the alcoholic is distinguished from the drunk by his drinking not being on his "own *initiative*" (305.0, p. 43); the hysteric, although acting on his own motives, is not acting *intentionally* because he is unaware of these motives (300.1, p. 35). In DSM, although the hysteric's symptoms are allowed to serve conscious as well as unconscious *motives*, they are nonetheless said to be not "under *voluntary* control" (American Psychiatric Association, 1980, p. 244); Factitious Disorder, on the other hand, although produced by *acts* that are *purposeful*, *intentional*, and *voluntary*, is not simple malingering; it retains an element of pathology in that it has a *compulsive* quality (American Psychiatric Association, 1980, p. 285). Similar action terms are to be found in the corresponding definitions in DSM-III-R. They are also to be found in all three classifications in relation to a wide range of other disorders.

The appearance of action terms in our classifications, like the appearance of value terms, could be a residue of prescientific thinking. Such terms could be provisional on the development of "hard," objective, scientific criteria. This is how they would be interpreted in the science-based view. Equally, though, their presence, again like the presence of value terms, could point to important, if denied or neglected, elements in the structure of our classifications. This is the linguistic/analytical interpretation of them. On this interpretation they have, in addition to face validity, construct validity; that is to say, they imply a definite construct or model in terms of which it is possible not only to interpret our classifications but also to develop them further. We will turn to this next. Inevitably, much of this will be speculative, anticipating as it must future developments in psychiatry, philosophical and, indeed, scientific. A value-based view, nonetheless, leads to a number of specific predictions about the future of our classifications.

FUTURE CLASSIFICATIONS: OVERT EVALUATIONS AND OVERT DESCRIPTIONS

There are important respects in which, at least for the present, a fact+value classification (as we may now call it) will appear identical to a purely factual classification. There are two reasons for this. First, simply, a fact+value classification is just that, a fact *plus* value classification. There is no question of replacing fact with value, of turning a fact classification, as it were, into a value classification. The approach described here, as indicated in the preceding section, seeks rather to add evaluation to description and, correspondingly, the experience of illness to knowledge of disease, and the analysis of illness as failure of action to the analysis of disease as failure of function. Thus, any genuinely descriptive elements that are properly included in our present classifications remain unchanged.

The second reason is more fundamental. It has to do with the relationship between description and evaluation outlined earlier. In a fact+value classification, descriptive criteria are understood as defining disease categories, not in their own right but by virtue of their status as criteria for the value judgments expressed by the medical concepts. Where the criteria for a value judgment are widely agreed, however, these, rather than the value judgment itself, will be most prominent in the use of the value term in question (as with *good apple*). Hence, to the extent that the criteria for the value judgment expressed by disease *are* widely agreed, so the definitions in our classifications will continue predominantly descriptive in form. Only where the value judgment is problematic will it become visible. Similar considerations apply, *mutatis mutandis*, to the range of moral philosophical concepts——arising from the experience of illness as action failure——which reflect the particular kind of value expressed by the medical concepts. These, too, to the extent that they are unproblematic, will remain implicit rather than explicit in our classifications.

All in all, then, there is much that will look no different. Large areas of the classification of mental disorders will appear exclusively descriptive and, hence, similar to the even larger areas of the classification of physical disorders which, for similar reasons, also appear exclusively descriptive. As against this, however, the evaluative element in a fact+value classification, instead of being ignored or trivialized, would be taken seriously. Facing up to the evaluative element, facing it full square, is not all there is to handling it better. But it is a start. Thus it could help to avoid confusions, as between different senses of *evaluative*, for example——of the two cases of evaluative delusions instanced in DSM-III-R (American Psychiatric Association, 1987, p. 395), one (that the patient is the "worst sinner in the world") is indeed a genuine good/bad evaluation, but the other (that the patient "is fat") is an evaluation only in the subjective/descriptive sense of the term noted earlier. Similarly, it could help to avoid contradictions, as between the definition of mental disorder and particular disease categories——the DSM definition, notably, excludes merely social value judgments as criteria of disease (explicitly in DSM-III, implicitly in DSM-III-R); but the definitions of both conduct disorder and the paraphilias, as noted earlier, rely directly on criteria of just this kind. It could be, of course, that such confusions and contradictions in our classifications reflect the actual state of our thinking about the concepts in question. However, this makes it all the more important that we should recognize them for what they are. Otherwise, how are they ever to be resolved?

So much for the present. What about the future? Here we might anticipate changes of a more radical nature. These all flow from the reversal of the (logical) relationship between illness and disease in a value-based view, disease being derived from illness rather than illness from disease. This role reversal of illness and disease could lead to changes in (a) the use that is made of other pathological concepts, such as trauma and disability; (b) the ways in which disease concepts themselves develop; and (c) the extent to which the elements of the experience of illness are made explicit in our classifications.

The first change follows directly from the reduced emphasis on disease in a value-based view. So long as disease is regarded, as in a science-based view, as the primary concept, it is natural that we should seek to mold our concepts of psychiatric disorder to the disease concepts deployed so successfully in physical medicine. One effect of this has been that other pathological concepts have tended to be underutilized. As we noted earlier, once illness is recognized to be the primary concept, the pressure to focus on disease is much reduced. There is thus more room, more conceptual space, for the employment of other pathological concepts. To the extent that this results in greater use being made of the concepts of trauma and disability, psychiatric classification, in a value-based view, would follow classification in physical medicine more closely even than it does now. This is well illustrated by ICD. Physical disorders are organized in ICD into a series of chapters covering diseases of different bodily systems together with separate chapters for traumas and disabilities. On the other hand, mental disorders are lumped together in a single chapter, in which, despite its being called Mental *Disorders*, the diagnostic concepts are treated as though they were all diseases——diseases of the "mental system," as it were, alongside diseases of the cardiovascular system, the respiratory system, and so forth.

The result of this conflation has been awkward stresses and strains within our classifications of mental disorders. In ICD, for instance, Adjustment Disorders are included, but with an apology from the authors of the classification for what they see as a departure from their self-imposed descriptive (as opposed to etiological) definitions of disease (World Health Organization, 1978, p. 11). But adjustment disorders, surely, are more like wounds or traumas than diseases. The framework of illness theory, moreover, suggests a basis for the distinction between disease and trauma, not, as such, in etiology, but in one side of the two-way distinction by which the primary experience of illness is defined——trauma being, quite literally, a *done to* experience. Then again, Personality Disorder has an equivocal place in our classifications. In respect of this concept, it is true, DSM has already shifted somewhat to a more open structure by placing it in a separate axis. However, by including it in the same axis as Developmental Disorders, it implies a definite etiological theory. Whereas Personality Disorder——as a very long-term condition with little expectation of change——is conceptually closer to disability than to disease. The long-term nature of disability, moreover, being outside the scope of the experience of failure of action, suggests an analysis of it in terms of the other side of the two-way distinction by which illness is defined, the distinction between illness and things that we do (Fulford, 1989, chap. 7).

Illness theory thus opens up our thinking in classification. It gives us more elbow room. Through this effect, too, it could have its most significant influence on the development of disease theory in psychiatry. If disease is logically primary, it is natural to expect that as psychiatry develops scientifically, so the disease concepts it employs will become ever closer to those of physical medicine. In a discussion paper the authors of DSM-IV (Frances, Pincus, Widiger, Davis & First, 1990) made this explicit, arguing that the end result of the Human Genome Project could be the abolition of mental disorders altogether! But if illness is the primary concept, if disease is derived *from* illness, then there is scope for disease concepts in psychiatry to develop independently, along different branches albeit of the same tree.

There is no *requirement* that they should do so. Nor is there any suggestion that disease concepts derived from physical medicine cannot be helpful in psychiatry. On the contrary, they are already of proven value. The point is rather that if disease is the derivative concept, psychiatry is free to develop its own disease concepts, drawing where expedient on physical medicine but not yoked to it. Even in physical medicine, after all, our choice of disease concepts is governed as much by clinical opportunism as by science. There is a form of natural selection at work here, and the selective pressures could well be different in some respects in psychiatry. Indeed, given the diversity of perspectives in psychiatry (McHugh & Slavney, 1983), they surely *are* different. Hence one virtue of a value-based model is that it provides the conceptual degrees of freedom for psychiatric disease concepts to evolve, where appropriate, independently.

It is, however, through its emphasis on the importance of the experience of illness that a value-based view could have its most profound long-term influence on classification. In a science-based view, the patient's experience of illness is important diagnostically only to the extent that it is a preliminary to the application of scientifically derived concepts of disease. In a value-based view, as we have seen, it is important in its own right. This is no mere gesture to patient autonomy, significant as this may be (McKee, 1991). It makes available to psychiatric classification a wide range of new diagnostic concepts derived from the elements of the experience of illness analyzed as failure of action.

These new diagnostic concepts have potential applications both in relation to individual symptoms and conditions and to groups of conditions within the structure of our classifications as a whole. As to the former, we have already noted the wide range of conditions the definitions of which, even in our present science-based classifications, draw on components of the experience of illness. In a fact+value classification, all of these elements would be recognized squarely for what they are, this being, as with the element of value itself, a step toward avoiding, or at any rate acknowledging, confusions and contradictions—the conflation of *loss of control* and *failure to resist*, for example, in the definitions of Impulse Control Disorders (American Psychiatric Association, 1987, pp. 321–328). Illness theory, indeed, goes one step further in this respect than the logic of value terms *simpliciter*. It not only makes plain the nature of difficulties of this kind but also supplies a rich conceptual framework within which to explore them. I have shown elsewhere, for example, that some of the problems associated with the diagnosis of alcoholism can be analyzed as difficulties that arise in the attribution of intentions in respect, specifically, to desires (Fulford, 1989, chap. 8).

The framework of illness theory, however, takes us beyond conditions such as these, in which the elements of action are more or less transparent, to other conditions less self-evidently defined in action failure terms. It suggests, in particular, a novel approach to the ever-contentious concept of psychosis, an approach that helps to display the phenomenological properties of individual psychotic symptoms while at the same time clarifying the general place of psychotic disorders within our classifications.

Again, I have discussed this in detail elsewhere (Fulford, 1989, chap. 10). The line of argument broadly recapitulates much of the argument of this chapter. Thus, the concept of psychotic disorder is, on the face of it, something of a nosological paradox. The key phenomenon of psychotic loss of insight has proved so resistant to scientific definition that, from Aubrey Lewis onward (1934), ever more heroic attempts have been made to exclude it from our classifications (American Psychiatric Association, 1980; World Health Organization, 1978). Yet it persists. In everyday medical discourse it persists linguistically in the use of phrases such as *antipsychotic drug* and *puerperal psychosis*, and it persists substantively in relation to compulsory treatment (Fulford, 1991a), assessments of responsibility in law (Flew, 1973), and other medicolegal and ethical issues. It also persists in ICD and DSM themselves— in ICD-9 as a main subdivision of mental disorders, in DSM as a subcategory of a wide variety of disorders, and in both classifications in catch-all categories such as Psychotic Disorder Not Elsewhere Classified. As with so many other features of our classifications, this could be regarded merely as a persisting symptom of prescientific thinking. But from a linguistic/analytical point of view—in which the use of a concept is a surer guide to meaning than received definitions—it suggests rather the need for a new approach to understanding the meaning of psychotic loss of insight.

Illness theory—at both levels of abstraction—helps to provide this. At the level of value terms *simpliciter*, it explains the connection just noted between the concept of psychotic disorder and areas of clinical decision making which are as much moral as scientific in nature. In any value-based theory, this connection is integral (Fulford, 1989, chap. 10). Then, at the second level, the notion of (specifically) psychotic loss of insight (so elusive to definition in

Table 9.1. A Differential Diagnosis of Thought Insertion, Illustrating the Interpretation of Psychotic Loss of Insight in Terms of the Experience of Illness

	CONSTRUAL					
PHENOMENON	BY PATIENT			BY OTHERS		
Thoughts in patient's mind	Done by	Wrong with	Done to	Done by	Wrong with	Done to
Normal thoughts	+			+		
Forced thoughts (epileptic)		E			E	
Obsessional thoughts	O			O		
Thought insertion			+	I		

Note: The notion of psychosis remains important clinically but has an equivocal place in ICD and DSM. A value-based view of the medical concepts suggests that psychotic loss of insight should be understood as a misconstrual by the patient across the two-way distinction by which the experience of illness is characterized. This generates differential diagnostic tables, illustrated here for thought insertion. Normal thinking is experienced as something that we do: obsessional thoughts, although often alien in content, are experienced as one's own thoughts; forced thoughts, as in temporal lobe epilepsy, are acknowledged for what they are once their nature is explained to the patient. Only thought insertion is experienced fully as something that is "done to" the patient. As described in the text, a deeper understanding of the concept of psychotic disorder can be achieved by extending the analysis from the primary experience of illness to the interpretation of this experience in illness-theory terms as failure of action. Different kinds of action failure are represented here schematically by the letters O, E, and I.

conventional scientific terms) is straightforwardly analyzable in illness theory terms as a misconstrual across the two-way distinction (described earlier) by which the experience of illness itself is defined.

This simple idea can be used to generate differential diagnostic tables, differential illness diagnostic tables, for a variety of individual psychotic symptoms. This is illustrated for Thought Insertion in Table 9.1. Genuine thought insertion appears as a mismatch between the way the experience is construed by the patient (as something that is being done to him) and the way it is construed by everyone else (as something wrong with him). Similar though more complicated tables can be produced for hallucinations. Delusions, however, although interpretable in part in these terms, require a deeper analysis. This leads directly to an interpretation of the form of delusional thinking in action failure terms as, or as implying, defective reasons for action (Fulford, 1989, chap. 10).

Despite its unfamiliar appearance, this way of understanding delusions, like the general analysis of illness in action failure terms, has considerable face validity. The conventional understanding of delusions in terms of impaired cognitive functioning has proved difficult to substantiate (Hemsley & Garety, 1986). In illness theory terms, the irrationality involved in delusional thinking is not, as such, cognitive rationality. It is the rationality of rational action. This can be shown to be consistent with the full range of delusional phenomenology——evaluative as well as factual delusions, true as well as false factual be-liefs, and the paradoxical delusion of mental illness (Fulford, 1989, chap. 10). It is consistent, too, with the particular clinical significance of psychotic disor-ders, providing as it does a direct conceptual link between the irrationality of delusions and the loss of responsibility for our actions which is the basis both of compulsory treatment and of the status of mental illness as an excuse in law. At the present stage of its development, this interpretation is not complete in itself. However, taken within the overall framework of illness theory, it provides a basis for research which could bring together, where ICD and DSM seek to separate, medicolegal and clinical approaches.

CONCLUSIONS: IMPLICATIONS FOR CLINICAL RESEARCH AND PRACTICE

At their most general, the claims of this chapter could have been dressed up to appear more palatable to scientifically minded physicians. Call what we have been concerned with theories, models, concepts even, and it is accept-able. Call it philosophy, and it is not. Yet even in science an interplay is need-ed between data and the constructions we place on the data. This is true, indeed, especially at the cutting edge of science, as in quantum mechanics and artificial intelligence at the present time. Historically it has been true of phe-nomenology: Jaspers, for instance, combined philosophical insight with close attention to clinical case material. It has been true more recently of psychiatric classification: Stengel's report to the World Health Organization (1959), on which our current descriptive classifications are based, was crucially influ-enced by a paper on classification by the philosopher Hempel (1961; see Appendix, this book).

So why have philosophers not been involved in the development of either DSM or, I understand (N. Sartorius, personal communication, 1988), ICD-10? It may be that future classifications will develop solely by the accumulation of data within existing conceptual structures. Yet this seems unlikely, given the nature and extent of the difficulties that remain. The general claim of this chapter, therefore, is that we should keep both sides going, the conceptual with the empirical, the philosophical with the scientific.

Specific claims have also been made, however, methodological and substan-tive. The methodological claim is for the particular relevance in this area of linguistic analysis. This is not an exclusive claim, of course. Phenomenolog-ical and existential methods are clearly relevant as well. Philosophical work, in general, moreover, does not exclude anthropology, ethnography, sociology, psychology, let alone the more biological sciences of medical psychiatry. Indeed, one of the particular virtues of linguistic analysis is that, with its em-phasis on use rather than definition, it is uniquely well suited to employment in partnership with empirical disciplines (Fulford, 1990a). This partnership, as I have argued elsewhere (Fulford, 1991b), is potentially two way: medicine (and psychiatry, in particular) having as much to offer philosophy as philosophy has to offer medicine. The partnership between medicine and philosophy could thus be as fruitful as the two-way partnership that exists between medicine and science.

The substantive claim made in this chapter is more contentious. Dress it up as we may, the idea that there is an essential (logically essential) element of evaluation in our classifications, and hence that diagnosis itself entails value judgments, cuts right across the scientific ethos of medicine. However, this too is not an exclusive claim. Other philosophical disciplines, in addition to the logic of value terms and the philosophy of action, are relevant to psychiatric classification—issues in the philosophy of science are raised by Margolis, Goodman, and Spitzer (all in this book); and the authors of DSM-IV found themselves at one point embroiled in the mind-body problem (Frances et al., 1990).

Similarly—and this bears repetition—to recognize an evaluative element in medicine is not to exclude the descriptive. It is, rather, to acknowledge both elements for what they are and thus to clarify their respective contributions to the conceptual framework of the subject. This tactic, moreover, is already yielding results in areas as diverse as medical education and questionnaire design (Fulford, 1990b). In respect to classification, in particular, both levels of the model of mental illness outlined here are represented elsewhere in this book: the evaluative element *simpliciter* in Agich's study of personality disorder, and the analysis of illness as action failure in the comments by Stephens and Graham on the intendedness of hallucinations. As already emphasized, the model as described is not complete. Nor should we expect it to be. The attention to actual usage required by linguistic analysis means that research into the evaluative element in psychiatric classification will involve the same long-term assiduous application as research into the descriptive element. That such research could prove worthwhile, however, is suggested by the fact that the topics touched on here are all among those recognized to be problematic in ICD and DSM. These problems are summarized in Table 9.2. They include the medicolegal significance of psychotic and other mental disorders; the nosological place of adjustment disorders; the equivocal disease status of conditions such as the paraphilias; and, crucially, the meaning of mental disorder itself. Making the hidden logical elements in our classifications explicit, therefore, while not in any way undermining their scientific integrity, could help to bring them closer to the requirements of everyday clinical practice.

We must recognize, however, that the results of philosophical research will be different from the results of scientific research. Science aims at convergence. Philosophy is often at its most effective as a foil to (premature) convergence. The outcome of linguistic analysis, specifically, should be not neat

Table 9.2. Redistribution of issues identified by the authors of DSM-IV in a fact+value framework

Problem issues identified by authors of DSM-IV	Location of these issues in a fact+value classification			
	Descriptive	Evaluative		
	Value simpliciter		Medical value	
			Primary experience of illness	Analysis of illness as action failure
Frances et al. *Guide to DSM-IV Conundrums* (1991)				
Status of personality disorder	+		+	
Relevance of test results	+			
Categories versus dimension	+			
Sensitivity versus specificity	+			
Overly rigid use of DSM	+			
Research versus clinical	+			
Broad base for categories	+	±		
Hierarchical relationships	+			
Definition of mental disorder	+	+	+	+
Use of clinical judgment	+	±		
Universal versus culture-specific	+	±	±	+
Aggregation versus differentiation	+			
Outmoded mental-physical dualism		±	±	±
New diagostic entities	+	±		
Data versus expert opinion	+	+		
Categories as prototypes	+			
Avoiding inconsistencies		+		+
Subclinical categories	+	±	±	±
DSM in primary care, etc.	+		+	
DSM in family/dynamic therapy	+			+
DSM in forensic/reimbursement cases	+	+		+
Validation issues	+	+		
Timing/format of publication				
Compatibility with ICD-10				
Future form of classification	+	+	+	+
Controversial categories	+	+	+	+
Frances et al. *Work in Progress* (1990)				
Anxiety disorders	+		+	+
Child/adolescent psychiatry	+			
Eating disorders	+			
Late luteal phase dysphoric syndrome	+	+	±	
Mood disorders	+		+	
Choice of axes	+			
Terminology for organic disorders		±	±	±
Personality disorders	+		+	±
Psychotic system interface disorder	+		+	+
Definition/subdivision of schizophrenia	+			
Subdivisions of sexual disorders	+			±
Definition of sleep disorders	+			
Criteria of dependence	+		±	+

NOTE: An exclusively science-based view of mental disorders leads to a preoccupation with empirical aspects of classification to the exclusion of other considerations. A value-based view, on the other formulas (see the foreword to this book) but a recognition of the full complexity of the concepts we so lightly deploy in everyday discourse.

This is not an argument against progress, however. It is true that in showing the significance specifically of the evaluative element in the language of medicine, linguistic analysis also shows that there is a limit to consensus formation in psychiatry (Fulford, in press). But the recognition of this limit, reflecting as it does our individuality as human beings, is important clinically. It is important in psychiatry as a basis for reconciling Jaspers' causal and "meaningful" connections (Jaspers, 1974) and, hence, psychodynamic and biological (Frances et al., 1990), Meyerian and Kraepelinian (Double, 1990) approaches to the classification and diagnosis of mental disorders.

It is perhaps still more important in medicine generally. Doctors may be satisfied with a purely scientific view of their subject, but their patients certainly are not. Indeed, as medical science has become ever more powerful, so patient satisfaction has actually declined! This is an area, then, as noted earlier, in which the difficulties presented by psychiatric classification, far from being a mark of deficiency, could point to important lessons for medicine as a whole. Not just in psychiatry is a humanistic rather than merely mechanistic basis for clinical practice urgently needed. In responding to this need, linguistic analysis could contribute a rigorous methodology. This in turn could generate a model of medicine in which the evaluative element in the meanings of illness and disease, instead of being considered a skeleton in the cupboard of scientific psychiatry, would be recognized as the living bones that give shape to the empirical flesh provided by medical science.

---

hand, provides a framework within which descriptive and evaluative elements can be distinguished and studied in their own right. In this table the problem issues identified by the authors of DSM-IV (and *only* so identified) are factored out across the principle components of a (hypothetical) fact+value classification generated by a value-based analysis of the medical concepts. The continuing importance of science in such a classification is emphasized by the large number of issues shown to be either exclusively or in part descriptive in nature. But evaluative considerations, both in their own right (value *simpliciter*) and as reflected in the phenomenology of illness (medical value), are now seen to be important as well. Some of the issues to which evaluative considerations are relevant are discussed in more detail in the text.

10 Evaluative Judgment and Personality Disorder

GEORGE J. AGICH, Ph.D.

In this chapter I examine the extent to which value judgment is involved in diagnosing personality disorders, taking as my primary example the DSM-III-R Antisocial Personality Disorder (APD). As background for my analysis of APD, I first review the general debate regarding the value neutrality of disease concepts and the particular debate over psychiatric disease and diagnosis. Second, I summarize criticisms of the DSM-III-R claimed atheoretical approach which are central to the dominant critical treatment of APD, and I consider what an atheoretical psychiatric nosology might involve. Third, I argue that APD does reveal several significant deficiencies, but that these point more toward the role of evaluative judgment in the construction and application of the diagnostic category than toward any particular theoretical bias. APD reveals a range of value commitments that need to be distinguished for both practical and theoretical reasons. Making these points, however, does not necessarily commit me to a critique of either this diagnostic category or the atheoretical stance of DSM-III-R, but does suggest a need to analyze the pragmatic assumptions and implications of any psychiatric nosology, including DSM-III-R.

DISEASE AS DESCRIPTIVE AND EVALUATIVE

The debate over the status of disease language involves two fundamentally opposed views. The first is so-called *functionalism*, which defines health and disease descriptively in terms of those functions that are typically found within members of a species (Boorse, 1975, 1982). The claim is that judgments of health and disease are descriptive and so entirely avoid being evaluative. Such a theory involves two unsustainable theses: a methodological thesis that divorces the analysis of disease language from the actual context of medical practice, and the thesis that disease language is evaluatively neutral and simply a matter of empirical description (Agich, 1983). For present purposes, it is reasonable to assert that functionalism or a value-neutral theory of health and disease has been persuasively—even if not conclusively—rejected. The second view might be termed *normativism*; it views judgments regarding health and disease as involving both descriptive and evaluative (or normative) elements. Normativism in this sense, it should be stressed, is a *weak* normativism insofar as it includes *both* descriptive as well as evaluative components. Such a view has to be distinguished from *strong* normativism, which holds that health and disease judgments are *purely* evaluative and without descriptive meaning or content at all. Strong normativism claims that disease language is purely ethical or political, lacking an anchor in empirical reality.

Critics of the medical model in psychiatry and the political use/misuse of psychiatric diagnosis during the 1960s and 1970s, such as David Cooper, R. D. Laing, and Thomas Szasz, argued that the language of mental illness and mental disease is a myth or mere label used to stigmatize nonconformist individuals (Cooper, 1971; Laing, 1967; Szasz, 1961, 1970a, 1970b). These critics are committed to a strong normativism with respect to concepts of psychiatric disease. They view psychiatric diagnosis as always and only an exercise of political power. Some, notably Szasz, also hold a biologically reductionistic version of the functionalist view with respect to nonpsychiatric or medical disease. Real disease is seen as physical; the medical model of disease is accepted uncritically for all of medicine except psychiatry, which is limited to treating problems in living.

Central to this approach is a binary opposition of a medical model of disease and a strong normativistic model of psychiatric disease as myth. These critics do not see, or do not accept, that all disease language involves both descriptive and evaluative elements. Because they do not acknowledge, much less accept, a weak normativism, they conclude that the value-laden character of psychiatric diagnosis is ethically paradoxical or problematic by definition. The political purpose of these critiques of psychiatry should be judged on its own terms; but, however one views that purpose, the political goal is distinguishable from its interpretive framework. Once this point is appreciated, it is reasonable to contend that the value-laden character of disease language is a philosophical thesis that does not necessarily commit one to an ethical or political critique of psychiatric diagnosis. Weak normativism, however, commits the psychiatric nosologist to the project of understanding the interplay of descriptive and evaluative elements in psychiatric diagnosis and nosology.

These general points are relevant to APD because critics of that diagnostic category frequently criticize the claimed atheoretical stance of DSM-III-R by arguing that this stance implies an epistemologically naive view of diagnosis and disease language. To be sure, psychiatric diagnostic categories are not only evaluative but also usually theory laden. The theory involvement of these concepts, however, is less fundamental than is commonly assumed. Evaluative commitments are far more basic and important than theory commitments as such, because theoretical commitments themselves reflect preferences regarding principles of causation, explanation, or relation.

Since theories are not constructed by some transhuman reason, they inevitably involve and reflect cultural, historical, and social preferences and values outside those that are defined or expressed within specific theories of disease. Psychiatric disease categories are thus inevitably bound up with evaluative judgment. Critics of the DSM-III-R atheoretical stance, however, fail to see that the issue of the theory ladenness of diagnostic categories is really an aspect of the larger issue of the relation of descriptive and evaluative elements. Whether the claimed atheoretical stance of DSM-III-R represents a naive epistemology or points to an important and unexamined feature or function of contemporary psychiatric nosologies is a question that warrants further discussion.

A PRAGMATIC VIEW OF DSM-III-R

DSM-III-R, to be sure, presents a veritable universe of contrary (if not contradictory) tendencies of which the claim to being atheoretical is but one. For example, DSM says of mental disorder, "whatever its original cause, it must currently be considered a manifestation of a behavioral, psychological or biological dysfunction in the person" (American Psychiatric Association, 1987, p. xii). At the same time, it is maintained that "there is no assumption that each mental disorder is a discrete entity with sharp boundaries (discontinuity) between it and other mental disorders, or between it and no mental disorder" (American Psychiatric Association, 1987, p. xxii). DSM-III-R also claims that its approach is descriptive and atheoretical with regard to etiology or pathophysiological process and that its multiaxial structure provides a biopsychosocial approach to assessment (American Psychiatric Association, 1987). Hence, it is not committed to a biological or organic definition of valid or real disease.

Critics point out nonetheless that the DSM-III-R hierarchical principles cast doubt on this claim. For example, diagnostic categories are structured hierarchically according to two principles: first, when an organic mental disorder can account for the symptoms, it preempts the diagnosis of any other disorder that can produce the same symptoms; and second, when a more pervasive disorder has associated symptoms that are the defining symptoms of a less pervasive disorder, only the pervasive disorder is diagnosed if both its defining symptoms and associated symptoms are present. Only schizophrenia, not schizophrenia and dysthymia, should be diagnosed when the defining symptoms of schizophrenia are present along with chronic mild depression, which is a commonly associated symptom of schizophrenia (American Psychiatric Association, 1987).

Critics contend that commitment to this hierarchical structure involves undefended etiological and theoretical preferences. This criticism is made even though the principles are asserted to be taxonomic rather than explanatory. Critics are quick to point out that facts do not create a theory, but are defined only within the context of a theory (Bursten, 1989). The view that disease concepts are inevitably bound up with theoretical assumptions is a corollary of the widely embraced contemporary view of science: namely that observations are inevitably based on theory; observations are always connected to an implicit or explicit theoretical framework that makes them possible (Kuhn, 1970). As a result, there are no theory-neutral concepts of disease. On this view, we invent categories and classifications and do not discover or simply find them in nature. There are thus no descriptive or atheoretical concepts upon which to build a nosology. DSM-III-R claims to be atheoretical only to smuggle theoretical claims and commitments into the nosology by way of hierarchical principles.

These—and other—points of tension are cited by critics as evidence of the problematic nature of the DSM-III-R classificatory framework, but there is another line of interpretation. The alleged presence of contradictions, paradoxes, or tensions in the DSM-III-R classificatory scheme can be regarded as an expected outcome of its *pragmatic* approach to nosology. A pragmatic approach is atheoretical in that it is not committed to any particular theory of psychiatric disease, but nonetheless need not be completely neutral regarding etiological explanation. It can eschew general etiological theory while accepting particular etiological explanations as the best available or most useful for its classificatory purposes. The basic point, after all, is not to explain, but to classify. Such an approach is congenial to the whole classificatory procedure of DSM-III and DSM-III-R. This procedure is a collective enterprise governed by consensus and compromise; rigorous commitment to specific theories of psychiatric disease is nowhere to be found. In this view, the atheoretical commitment represents not an abnegation of theory, but rather the acceptance of a specifically pragmatic approach to nosology.

Such an approach to psychiatric nosology is admittedly inchoate and not at all defended in DSM-III-R, but it is at least a plausible, and possibly the only sensible, way to read DSM-III-R as an effort to provide a single classification system that meets the various requirements of contemporary psychiatric practice. These requirements include record keeping for clinical and research purposes, quality assurance, reimbursement, and forensic purposes (Mirowski & Ross, 1989). Even psychiatrists who are critical of diagnostic reification and sensitive to the perils of classification and diagnosis in psychiatry accept the necessity of contemporary psychiatric nosology for political and pragmatic purposes (Kendell, 1988; Vaillant & Schnurr, 1988). The problem is that this approach is just that, an approach, a way of doing things, not an account explaining or justifying how the nosology was constructed.

A pragmatic approach is unified not by an articulated pragmatic *theory*, but by commitment to an overriding set of practical goals and purposes. In the case of DSM-III-R these goals seem to involve general purposes of record keeping, diagnostic consistency and efficiency, and coherence with current knowledge and research programs on the diagnosis and treatment of mental disorders. Allen Frances and colleagues (1991) noted in this regard, "we have resolved fully, and indeed expect to resolve fully, none of these issues. Instead we are attempting to find balanced, if imperfect, solutions to reflect our best available knowledge and further the research that will hopefully allow for more incisive solutions in DSM-V" (p. 407). There is a studied agnosticism regarding explanatory and theoretical commitments at the level of the enterprise as a whole.

When empirical or practical reasons persuade the DSM-III-R authors of the *validity*, namely, the practical compellingness or utility, of a diagnostic category and its defining criteria, they embrace it; its theoretical appropriateness is beside the point so long as it meets the test of consensus and practical utility. In this way, DSM-III-R seems committed to a pragmatic concept of validity. It is beyond the scope of this chapter to explore further the pragmatic nature of the DSM nosologies; rather, I want to show that the view has important and useful implications in the case of APD insofar as the pragmatic approach helps highlight the evaluative commitments associated with this diagnosis.

Critics of DSM-III-R, even those who accept that all observational and descriptive judgments are theory laden, usually fail to note that the concept of validity retains meaning in the context of a specific research program. Although validity certainly cannot be absolute, rejecting an absolute validity does not entail that validity cannot be understood contextually. In this sense, one can argue that the concept of validity in DSM-III-R has a pragmatic cast. The concept boils down to something like *workable, generally agreed to*, or *the best we can do all things considered*. This concept of validity will certainly sound odd to many. It sounds more like a set of rules of thumb than an epistemologically or logically justified concept. That, however, is precisely what one would expect a pragmatic approach to entail. The meaning of validity is functionally related to specific diagnostic categories. Validity thus depends on the variety of variable kinds of empirical data available to support the category and its defining criteria; these, in turn, reflect various conceptual and value commitments that themselves are products of the multiple, and possibly inconsistent, overall purposes driving the classification effort.

Many critics who complain that DSM-III-R is committed to an epistemologically naive view of scientific explanation and that its atheoretical rhetoric really masks an ontological commitment to a medical model of disease—that "real" disease is discrete and organic—seem to adopt this strategy to argue or press for additions or emendations to the nosology (Birley, 1990; Bursten, 1989). In the pragmatic view I have suggested, disputes over specific categories or their defining criteria are best interpreted in terms of the practical advantages or utility of proposed additions or emendations to the nosology, not simply asserted as alternative to the DSM-III-R broadly claimed atheoretical posture. Being atheoretical is neither an advantage nor a disadvantage for a pragmatic approach; it is simply a corollary of the view that what is acceptable, and so valid, must be workable as measured by scientific consensus and utility for the main purposes of the nosology. It is not surprising that disagreements regarding the formulation of specific categories and their criteria have arisen. As a matter of fact, we should expect just such disagreement to materialize because of the complexity and possible incommensurability of the inadequately stated, and certainly undefended, goals of the nosological enterprise as a whole. What recommends the pragmatic approach is precisely the vague or indeterminate "consensus" about the classification effort which forces compromise on specific diagnostic and classificatory issues that nonetheless remain open for future examination and debate.

I do not think that all classificatory schemes need involve theoretical or explanatory commitments, though many clearly do. The claim of DSM-III-R is that it does not; critics contend that it does. Rather than attempt to resolve this particular issue, I prefer to concentrate on the way a hierarchical classificatory scheme involves value commitments regarding the ordering, relation, and meaning of the various categories. Some of these value commitments may entail commitments to theory, although it appears that this is purely an empirical rather than a logical matter. In any event, the claim of DSM-III-R that its classification scheme is taxonomic rather than explanatory seems to represent an important statement of its purpose or intended use rather than a justification of its structure, because etiological and theoretical preferences are clearly included. I think it plausible to suggest that the oft-criticized "atheoretical" claims of DSM-III-R are better understood as a statement—inadequate, to be sure—of a pragmatic approach to psychiatric nosology. The issues then shift from the general to the specific diagnostic categories and their defining criteria.

EVALUATIVE JUDGMENT AND ANTISOCIAL PERSONALITY DISORDER

Unlike earlier classificatory systems, DSM-III-R provides specific diagnostic criteria to enhance reliability, even though it is admitted that most diagnostic criteria are based on clinical judgment and have not been fully validated by empirical research (American Psychiatric Association, 1987). DSM-III-R is far more concerned with reliability and objectivity than with categorial discreteness (Bursten, 1989). Since the categories of mental disorder have been shaped by consensus and compromise, they need not have sharp boundaries (i.e., discreteness). To the extent that they do compromise discreteness, they inevitably build in relationships. At the same time, the ideal for the diagnostic criteria is to provide identifiable behavioral signs and symptoms that require a minimal amount of inference on the part of the observer; this reveals a preference for a reliability that presses toward discreteness even though this may come at the expense of clinical utility (Frances & Cooper, 1981).

To assume that a classification scheme as such can significantly establish reliable and valid diagnosis involves a rather essentialist conception of the nature of psychiatric disease. It does not seem to me that DSM-III-R is committed to such a view, although critics contend that it is. Some commentators, for example, have insisted that DSM-III-R is in fact committed to an essentialist ontology of disease. Birley (1990) argued that "DSM-III is an essentialist wolf dressed up as a nominalist sheep" (p. 117). One thing is clear: the classification scheme does involve important evaluative commitments regarding the nature and function of diagnostic categories which may or may not be tied to specific theories. For DSM-III-R, reliability means agreement in clinical use; such agreement is itself a normative ideal even if the entire project can be plausibly interpreted and defended on pragmatic grounds. The practical price of such agreement, however, appears to have resulted in the creation of some diagnostic categories that are clinically problematic. APD seems to be one such category.

All classifications reveal similarities and differences; these are products of how the data are arranged and interpreted. If they are arranged differently, then different relationships emerge. Which relationships are better, more valid, or more useful depends both on what *better, more valid,* or *more useful* means as well as on the interests of clinicians and researchers. Even if complete agreement regarding the classification system were attained, it would still be necessary for individual clinicians to apply the criteria in a variety of clinical settings and circumstances. Variations of judgment and problems in application thus will arise. If one is primarily concerned with consistently applying a diagnosis without regard to the context or circumstances of application—in other words, without regard for the validity of the diagnosis—categorial choices can be constrained by designing the classification to minimize inconsistency and, hence, to enhance reliability. This goal, however, has important valuational implications that can be explored in summary fashion in the case of APD.

In the case of APD a *lumping* as opposed to a *splitting* approach to classification seems evident. Combining and reducing diagnostic options seem to be a high value. This is evident in the polythetic nature of the diagnostic criteria comprising APD. The focus is on behaviors, so reference to psychological traits is eliminated, and with them, an important source of complication and differentiation (Millon, 1981). Diagnostic criteria under a polythetic format provide more *alternative* ways of making the same diagnosis than does a monothetic format; hence, reliability is increased. Some critics of APD complain that the criteria are too coarse; the criteria do not include personality features such as narcissism, interpersonal manipulativeness, or other nonaggressive behaviors believed by these critics to be essential elements of antisocial personality (Bursten, 1982, 1989; Kernberg, 1989). At the same time, the behavioral criteria of APD permit inclusion of a potentially motley range of cases. Since APD as defined focuses on aggressive antisocial behavior, one must examine the purposes that the diagnosis serves in specific circumstances and contexts. The diagnostic net will by definition work reliably (despite its failure to discriminate certain types of personality) when it is employed in circumstances in which aggressive behaviors are prominent. That may or may not be a virtue, depending on the chosen context of use. The difficulties associated with choosing a context of use, however, should not be underestimated. A parallel problem arises for cases of nonaggressive antisocial behavior because the diagnosis does not discriminate what some critics contend are therapeutically and prognostically relevant features, such as the presence or absence of narcissistic personality features (Blackburn, 1988; Bursten, 1989; Kernberg, 1989).

The polythetic format assumes a "fuzzy" view of categories as organized around a set of properties or clusters of related attributes which are only *characteristic* or *typical* of category membership. There are no essential or defining features of membership in a category; instead, diagnostic criteria are probabilistically based on a list of characteristic features that describe the category. The categories are thus organized according to a family resemblance principle (Blashfield, Sprock, Haymaker & Hodgin, 1989). However, as Douglas L. Medin (1989) pointed out, this probabilistic view of categories can embrace either of two rather different epistemological interpretations.

First, categories that are summarily represented by prototypes can be probabilistically organized according to a family resemblance principle. The general idea is that people abstract out the central tendency or prototype that becomes the summary mental representation for the category based on experience with examples of a category (Medin, 1989). A second and more radical principle of representation is the exemplar view (Smith & Medin, 1981). This view holds that categories are represented by means of a series of examples and denies that there is a single summary representation adequate for a category. Empirical research contrasting exemplar and prototype representations tends to suggest that prototypes serve untrained diagnosticians well, but that exemplars prove to be more helpful to experienced clinicians (Genero & Cantor, 1987; Medin, 1989). Prototypes, after all, help organize seemingly disparate phenomena and so simplify complex phenomena, whereas exemplars readmit complexity and variation into a conceptually unified pattern.

One aspect of the prototype view of categories which is especially important for APD is that prototype theories necessarily regard concepts as independent of context (Medin, 1989). The simplifying process eliminates the very frame within which the categorial judgment is made. However, empirical research has shown that judgments of what is typical vary as a function of context (Roth & Shoben, 1983). Context is thus a crucial, indeed, an essential, feature of the meaningful use of actual categorial judgment. For example, tea is a more typical beverage than milk in the context of secretaries taking a break, but the order reverses in the context of truck drivers taking a break. Context thus plays a significant role in the *actual* employment of prototypes, although prototype theory tends to abstract from context.

One common way around this problem involves having multiple prototypes. In effect, APD permits multiple prototypes; by employing a polythetic format, members of this category need to share only the features of being at least 18 years of age, having evidence of a Conduct Disorder with onset before age 15, and the antisocial behavior did not occur exclusively during the course of Schizophrenia or Manic Episodes. The crucial determination of a pattern of irresponsible and specifically antisocial behavior since the age of 15 is determined on the basis of the presence of only 4 of 10 additional criteria (American Psychiatric Association, 1987). The authors of DSM-III-R are clearly aware of this feature. They note that all people described as having the same mental disorder are not alike in all important ways. All they need share are the defining features of the disorder; in other respects they might differ significantly (American Psychiatric Association, 1987). There are thus at least two aspects of the disorder which need to be considered: the adequacy or inadequacy of the defining features of the order, a concern that has been the focus of much of criticism and discussion of APD; and the context or frame in which the prototypical diagnostic criteria are employed.

Critics contend that the prototype of APD uniformly involves aggressive and criminal behaviors and excludes relevant psychological or personality characteristics. A general aspect of prototype classifications mentioned earlier is this tendency to discard information as it simplifies classification. A problem occurs when too much information that can be shown to be relevant is discarded. In the case of APD information about the individual's personality is presently ignored. Medin (1989) pointed out that prototype theories generally assume conditions or constraints that are simply not observed in studies of human categorization; these conditions and constraints presume an insensitivity to information that people regularly and readily use in their practice. Practitioners tend to simply ignore the context dependence that is an evident feature of any process of categorization.

Sensitivity to this context-dependent nature of categorization partly underlies the objections to APD which are made on the grounds that such a category is a fiction (Karpman, 1948; Vaillant, 1975). For example, J.P. Wulach

(1983) suggested that the notion of a specifically APD exaggerates the difference between the deviant individual and the conforming individual while, at the same time, minimizing variations and differences among the antisocial. Cleckley's and others' work on the concept of Psychopathic Personality, however, seems to establish that the concept is clinically important and useful, although this work has not quieted concern about the concept in all quarters (Cleckley, 1976; Hare, 1986).

In a general way, of course, all diagnoses are fictions; they are interpretations of findings which have an empirical basis in the clinical and experiential reality of the patient. So, complaining that the diagnosis of APD is a construction or fiction can only be the starting point for discussion, not a very insightful or helpful conclusion. With regard to the point that the diagnosis is a fiction because it simply fails to include psychological features, it should be pointed out that the architects of DSM-IV appear to be aware of the need for inclusion of psychological criteria to allow further differentiation of the disorder. Even if the majority of critics of APD would be satisfied if this disorder were to be modified in this way in DSM-IV, a more basic concern would remain unaddressed, namely that judgments of antisocial personality——no matter what their defining criteria——should not be treated as context-independent (and by extension value-neutral) prototype judgments. Simply adding psychological criteria to the present behavioral ones would not sufficiently address this latter concern.

Several authors have pointed out that the history of the concept of antisocial personality involves two rather different universes of discourse: the universes of personal and social deviance (Blackburn, 1988; Millon, 1981; Pichot, 1978). In DSM-III-R APD focuses on specific acts or behaviors and so does not describe personality traits as such; traits are inferred tendencies and are distinct from specific acts or occurrences. For this reason APD does not define a concept of personality at all, but rather defines a concept of social deviance. Importantly, a judgment about deviance is not simply a description or observation of behavior; it is an interpretive judgment regarding behavioral appropriateness. Hence, these judgments are clearly dependent on an evaluative frame of reference and cannot be justified without due regard for the specific circumstances and context of the behaviors. The very meaning of the criteria involves basic value judgments that require interpretation.

Lee Robins (1989), in discussing the general problem of translating diagnostic criteria into interview questions, noted that difficulties occur when the criteria are either incomplete or nonspecific. For example, some criteria seem to omit distinctions between normal and pathological behavior. Robins' examples include the DSM-III-R criteria for childhood antisocial personality:

If one followed their language literally and asked "Have you been physically cruel to animals?" and "Have you deliberately set fires?", responses might include "I stepped on a roach in my house," "I went hunting," and "I'm a Boy Scout and had to pass my fire-starting test." To avoid such answers, I wrote questions adding in restrictions that I thought the criteria implied. For example, our question about fire setting asks whether the respondent ever started a fire in a situation where someone else's property was likely to be damaged. The problem with this solution is that my judgment as to what a criterion "really" means may not match a clinician's interpretation of the same item. It is easy to imagine that not everyone would agree that our questions have "face validity." (p. 66)

Kernberg (1989) pointed out similar problems with the behavioral criteria for APD. For example: "ran away from home overnight at least twice while living in a parental surrogate home or once without returning" omits considering whether the child is running away from an impossible home with physically abusive parents or from a well-constituted home. Similarly, the criterion: "has never sustained a totally monogamous relationship for more than one year" includes a spectrum of behaviors which involves socially determined patterns and values in addition to personality traits. The identification of such behaviors as diagnostic of APD is dependent upon a frame of reference which necessarily requires interpretation by the clinician and involves reference to behavioral norms of acceptability. In effect, the diagnostic criteria belong to the domain of social deviance and presuppose value commitments. That fact alone should not surprise or form the basis of a critical rejection of APD because all disease concepts inevitably involve both descriptive and evaluative components. The problem is that the prototypical category of APD seems to suppress the context of judgment and so the evaluative component. A central problem is that social deviance may be found with various forms of personality deviance or with none. It is neither necessary nor sufficient to identify a personality disorder as such, although it may reliably identify certain behavior patterns in particular contexts (Guze, 1964a, 1964b).

These points are especially compelling in light of the DSM-III-R claim that deviant behavior or conflicts that are primarily between the individual and society are not to be regarded as mental disorders "unless the deviance or conflict is symptom of dysfunction in the person" (American Psychiatric Association, 1987, p. xxii). This statement would seem to suggest that social deviance as such cannot be the basis for diagnostic considerations, despite the fact that "dysfunction" is a broad umbrella indeed. Many commentators have called attention to the behavioral and indeed criminal focus of APD criteria as opposed to psychological or personality traits (Guze, 1964a, 1964b; O'Neal, Robins, King & Schaefer, 1962; Robins, 1989; Shaw, 1986, 1989). The DSM-III-R criteria exclude the nonaggressive variety as well as the inadequate or passive type of APD which manifests itself in chronic parasitic and/or exploitative behaviors rather than directly aggressive ones (Fuloer, 1986; Kernberg, 1989). By restricting social personality disorders to predominantly aggressive interactional patterns and criminal behavior, individuals with very different personality makeups are included, and the distinction between socio-cultural and economic determinations of delinquency on the one hand, and psychopathology on the other is blurred (Kernberg, 1989). As a result, sensitivity for this diagnosis is probably high, whereas specificity is probably low. The goal of reliability is thus achieved, but validity is sacrificed. The validity sacrificed may well be the pragmatic utility of the diagnosis outside certain restricted contexts. The use of concrete and broad behavioral criteria instead of personality traits thus probably permits including all patients with predominantly aggressive interactional patterns. However, these criteria override the philosophical problem of defining *antisocial* and whether such a concept can be defended, much less defined, in abstraction from value commitments.

SUMMARY

Some very tentative conclusions can be drawn from these points. First, the criteria of APD involve, no matter how inchoately, evaluative judgments regarding appropriate behavior and the inappropriateness of aggressive antisocial behavior. Exploitative or manipulative behavior that is related psychologically to aggressive antisocial behavior, however, is omitted. Inclusion of psychological criteria, despite the recommendations of many commentators, will not itself answer the basic conceptual problem that APD displays—namely, its apparent insensitivity to context and the evaluative commitments that underlie its very meaning.

Second, even if this significant issue were adequately addressed, the problem of evaluative judgment associated with APD will not disappear; it will remain at the level of application. The criteria not only permit, but *require* an interpretive latitude that is fraught with value assumptions and implications.

Third, although I have steered away from specific issues such as sex bias in the diagnosis of APD (Ford & Widiger, 1989; Heilbrun & Gottfried, 1988) or the use of psychiatric diagnosis in the courts (Shuman, 1989), these are important problems that remain to be addressed.

Finally, to reiterate a point made in my introductory remarks: my analysis does not commit me either to a rejection of psychiatric diagnosis as myth or a political critique of the clinical use of the diagnosis of APD. However, I do share with critics of psychiatric diagnosis and APD a belief that psychiatric diagnosis is essentially a matter of practical ethics; unlike them I accept the descriptive aspect of diagnosis and believe that nosology is an eminently practical and pragmatic exercise. My hypothesized pragmatic view of contemporary classification of psychiatric diseases reinforces this point.

The political and practical issues forcing the shaping and justifying of DSM-III and DSM-III-R need further exploration and analysis. Such analysis, I have suggested in the course of discussing APD, is a rather different kind of enterprise than that practiced in the 1960s and 1970s by various critics of psychiatric diagnosis. Such an analysis focuses attention on the evaluative dimensions of the language of diagnosis and its employment in practice without assuming the posture of the privileged observer so common in the earlier work. In my view, the philosophical analysis of psychiatric nosology is itself an exercise of practice ethics; its first task is one of interpretation and understanding and only secondly a matter of criticism.

11 Psychiatric Diagnosis and the Interests of Women

DENISE RUSSELL, Ph.D.

Psychiatric diagnosis should be a tool in the understanding and treatment of psychiatric disorders. Conceptual distinctions embodied in the diagnoses may further the understanding of the disorders, and it is hoped that the diagnostic categorization will provide a basis for different treatment directions. In sum, psychiatric diagnosis is a crucial starting point for psychiatric theorization and practice.

In this chapter I focus on the basic concept of psychiatric diagnosis in DSM-III-R (American Psychiatric Association, 1987) and on some of the conceptual distinctions in the particular categorizations. I want to show that there may be some problems that will be of particular concern to women.[1] I highlight the way in which a particular behavior or experience is viewed rather than how it is caused. This is an important distinction for particular categories, as there may be disagreement about the domain of psychiatric concern, which means that a debate about causes cannot even get off the ground.

Keeping the aims of diagnoses in mind, when we look at DSM-III-R three key philosophical/feminist problems emerge. The first relates to the conceptual foundations, the second to certain subjective features, and the third to the narrowness of focus.

DSM-III-R emerges from the American Psychiatric Association and, as such, is firmly embedded in the medical psychiatric tradition. It is therefore very interesting to note that the use of the terminology of *mental illness* has declined with successive schemes. Gradually, in the descriptions of specific categories, the notion of *mental illness* is replaced by the notion of *mental disorder*.

It is the notion of *mental disorder* which forms the crucial underpinning of the structure of psychiatric diagnosis in DSM-III-R. It is explained as follows:

[a mental disorder] is conceptualized as a clinically significant behavioral or psychologic syndrome or pattern that occurs in a person and that is associated with present distress (a painful symptom) or disability (impairment in one or more important areas of functioning) or with a significantly increased risk of suffering death, pain, disability, or an important loss of freedom. (American Psychiatric Association, 1987, p. xxii)

The definition appears so clear-cut and medical, how could it possibly disadvantage women? The trouble is that beneath its crystal clear appearance lies a nest of value judgments. If one does not happen to share the same values, different decisions will be reached about whether a mental disorder exists or not. Two aspects of the definition illustrate this point: distress and disability.

Distress is defined as a painful symptom. A *symptom* is defined in DSM-III-R as a manifestation of a pathological condition (American Psychiatric Association, 1987). Yet for most of the DSM-III-R disorders it is acknowledged that the etiology is unknown. If the etiology is unknown, then the pathological condition has not been isolated and is, as yet, a mere conjecture. If there is uncertainty about the pathological conditions that are supposed to give rise to symptoms, then there will be consequent uncertainty about the symptoms. The judgment that something is a symptom must remain tentative until some underlying pathological condition is substantiated. Because in most cases no underlying pathological condition is substantiated, the declaration that aspects of thinking or behaving referred to, can be regarded as *symptoms*, must be treated with caution. The authors want to avoid the vexing problem of etiology, but they run the risk of conceptual incoherence in their talk of symptoms. It does not make sense to talk of symptoms in the absence of even conjectures about what the symptoms are symptoms *of*. The authors claim that when a mental disorder exists, there is an inference that there is a behavioral, psychological, or biological dysfunction (American Psychiatric Association, 1987), but no justification is offered for this inference; rather, it is undercut by the claim that "for most of the DSM-III-R disorders . . . the etiology is unknown" (p. xxiii).

It could be countered that for at least some physical disorders, such as AIDS and multiple sclerosis, the etiology is unknown, and yet the symptoms are real or present. For mental disorders too, the symptoms may be real and debilitating even though there is no clear-cut agreement on etiology.

This argument does not get over the conceptual problem. The person may be experiencing something abnormal and debilitating without it being appropriate to describe their experiences as symptoms. For that description to hold, there must be agreement about the appropriate way to look at the individual and about the terms of some underlying pathology in the individual. This is not, of course, the same as saying that the pathology has been located. There is substantial agreement to this approach in physical medicine, and hence talk of the "symptoms" of AIDS is usually regarded as unproblematic. But there is dissent in the psychiatric area. Some theorists reject the individual pathology model (Basaglia, 1987; Laing & Esterson, 1970) and hence the appropriateness of talk of "symptoms." Laing and Esterson provided a long argument for this position in reference to Schizophrenia. I agree with the argument, but there is not space to present it here. A less controversial example might be the Adjustment Disorder with Disturbance of Conduct, in which "the predominant manifestation is conduct in which there is violation of the rights of others or of major age-appropriate societal norms and rules. Examples: truancy, vandalism, reckless driving, fighting, defaulting on legal responsibilities" (American Psychiatric Association, 1987, p. 331). These manifestations are breaches in morality. There is no need to take the further step and say that immorality is symptomatic of mental disorder.[2]

In DSM-III-R the vague inference to underlying pathological conditions in the discussion of distress is particularly relevant to women. Numerous psychological studies have pointed out that what in the West is generally regarded as the woman's role happens to coincide with what is regarded as mentally unhealthy. This relationship appears to hold for people unconnected with mental work and for professional mental health workers. In a 1970 paper, Broverman and others reported on a study done with a group of 79 clinicians: psychologists, psychiatrists, and social workers. They found that the clinicians strongly agreed on the behaviors and attributes that characterized a mentally healthy man, a mentally healthy woman, or a mentally healthy adult independent of sex (Broverman, Broverman, Clarkson, Rosenkrantz & Vogel, 1970). The description of a healthy adult independent of sex closely matched the description of a healthy man but not that of a healthy woman. This confirmed the notion that a double standard of health is applied. Healthy women are perceived as significantly less healthy by adult standards. Clinicians are significantly less likely to attribute healthy adult traits to a woman than they are likely to attribute these traits to a man (Broverman et al., 1970). These differences parallel the sex role stereotypes in the West and also relate to what is socially valued.

According to the Broverman study, healthy women differ from healthy men by being more submissive, less independent, less adventurous, and more easily influenced, less aggressive, less competitive, more excitable in minor crises, having their feelings more easily hurt, being more emotional, more conceited about their appearance, less objective, and disliking math and science. In general, these are traits that are devalued, and hence, the authors argued, the judgments involve a powerful, negative assessment of women (Broverman et al., 1970).

These results were confirmed in a study reported in 1972 involving 982 subjects, both men and women, married and single, from different age groups and educational and religious backgrounds (Broverman, Vogel, Broverman, Clarkson & Rosenkrantz, 1972). Such studies reveal that women are caught in an impossible situation. If a woman breaks out of the female role she may be regarded as mentally unhealthy as she is not fulfilling her role, but if she stays within the role she may be regarded as mentally unhealthy on an adult standard. Vague talk about psychological and behavioral dysfunction conceals this underlying problem that *dysfunction* embodies a moral evaluation, and that works strongly against women.

The Broverman studies have been criticized. Stricker (1977) pointed out that there is some arbitrariness in the categorization of certain responses as *logical* or *illogical* when the actual scores are not radically apart on a scale. The categorization suggests bipolar opposites, but it is more a matter of degree.

This is a worry about how the study has been reported, but it does not amount to a challenge to the findings. The general direction and tenor of the Broverman studies have been supported in later research (Abramowitz, Abramowitz, Jackson & Gomes, 1973; Brodsky & Holroyd, 1975; Brown & Hellinger, 1975; Fabrikant, 1974; Maslin & Davis, 1975; Penfold & Walker, 1983; Sherman, 1980). Some authors make particular mention of the "Catch 22" situation that exists for women: "The very state of being a woman, it has been argued, contains so many contradictions and so much suffering that what appears as deviant behavior is, in fact, an unwillingness or an inability to fit the oppressive stereotype of health" (Jordanova, 1981, p. 102). Furthermore, as Marcie Kaplan suggested (1983), the double bind that exists here could itself drive a woman crazy (1983). Other research indicated that biases relating to class (Briar, 1961), skin color (Chesler, 1973), or sexuality (Reiss, 1974) may interact with a sex role bias.

A variety of explanations have been proposed for the different attitudes toward the mental health of women and the mental health of men. Such explanations try to answer why sex roles are the way they are. There is not space to do justice to these issues here. One interesting approach appeals to the early oral dyadic relationship between mother and child with the need for males to reverse their early helplessness and dependence on a powerful female object (Lerner, 1981). This may be tied in with fantasies about women's destructive power (Bayes, 1981; Chodoff, 1982).

In this section I began with what appeared to be an uncontroversial notion: *distress*, which is in this context equated with *a painful symptom*. This notion suffers from conceptual problems and, at least in the present state of psychiatry, is inextricably bound up with particular value judgments. As these value judgments circumscribe the role of women in an unjustifiable manner, they can be seen to work against the interests of women; any diagnosis that relies upon these values should be regarded with a high level of suspicion.

Let us turn now to *disability*, another key notion in the DSM-III-R definition of mental disorder, and another source of trouble. According to the definition cited above, for a syndrome to be a mental disorder it must be associated with a painful symptom or *impairment in one or more important areas of functioning (disability)* [emphasis mine]. Looking into the details of the various classifications, it becomes clear that important areas of functioning concern social, occupational, academic, and legal activities. Many references are made to impairment in occupational functioning. Examples are absence from work, loss of job, deterioration in work relations, interference with work efficiency, work inhibition, and occupational difficulties relating to authority figures or co-workers.

Impairments in academic functioning cover the difficulties that some children experience in the classroom, with school work, or difficulties that students and/or academics have in writing papers. Impairment of functioning in the legal sphere is mentioned in the descriptions of the categories entitled Alcohol Dependence and Cannabis Abuse. The phrase "[impairment] due to the legal consequences of being apprehended" forms part of the description of the diagnostic categories of Kleptomania and Pyromania (American Psychiatric Association, 1987, p. 323).

"Impairment in social functioning" is the description that occurs most frequently in the DSM-III-R classification. It is supposed to incorporate attributes such as the incapacity to develop socialization skills, deterioration in friendships and family relationships, loss of friends, strained social relations, stormy and ungratifying interpersonal relations, and so on. This is another point at which the sex role stereotyping and different attitudes to the mental health of men and women may play a role. Some studies prior to DSM-III-R showed that women who follow the feminine role closely by revealing emotional responsivity, naiveté, dependence, and childishness may be subject to the diagnosis of Hysteria or Hysterical Personality (Chodoff, 1974; Hollender, 1971; Lerner, 1974; Wolowitz, 1972). On an adult "scale," there is impairment in social functioning. Marcie Kaplan compared the impairment in social functioning occurring in the DSM-III description of Histrionic Personality Disorder (previously called Hysterical Personality) (American Psychiatric Association, 1980, p. 315) with the Broverman findings mentioned above. This disorder is far more frequently diagnosed in women than in men. Although the description of this disorder has changed slightly in DSM-III-R, the analogy still holds. Note in Table 11.1 the comparison of the DSM-III descriptions of personality traits with the findings of Broverman and colleagues.

Kaplan (1983) concluded, "via assumptions about sex roles made by clinicians, a healthy woman automatically earns the diagnosis of histrionic personality disorder" (p. 789).

A sex bias in judgments about social functioning has been unearthed in another area: left-of-center political deviance was regarded as more indicative of maladjustment when the purported patient was female than male (Brodsky & Holroyd, 1975). Feminists, beware!

Table 11.1   Descriptions of Personality Traits Associated with Histrionic Personality Disorder in DSM and Descriptions of Healthy Women from the Broverman Study

DSM-III	Broverman et al. (1970)
Self-dramatization; (e.g., exaggerated expression of emotions); overreaction to minor events	Being more emotional; more excitable in minor crises
Irrational angry outbursts or tantrums	More excitable; more emotional; and less objective
Vain and demanding	More conceited about appearance
Dependent, helpless, constantly seeking reassurance	More submissive; less independent; less adventurous; more easily influenced

Thus, when one looks into the details of what is meant by *disability* or *impairment of functioning* it amounts to a breach in a particular way of behaving or experiencing. This "standard" way of behaving or experiencing is not one that emerges from medical theory; rather it is based upon certain judgments, which perhaps enjoy the agreement of many, but by no means all, folk in Western societies. The basic values embodied in this notion of disability center around the desirability of having stable and peaceful relationships with one's family, friends, employer, and the law. There is little room to express dissatisfaction with one's lot, without being regarded as impaired. This suggests that there may be values that override those that simply support the status quo; but this type of conceptual debate concerning key notions in DSM-III-R cannot even get off the ground if the dominant values are disguised as medical phenomena. Yet if these medical phenomena do amount to values, and if it is the case, as I believe it to be, that there is no uniformity in these values across all sections of Western society, then any discrepancies in the values underlying decisions about disability or impairment will lead to corresponding discrepancies in the diagnosis. It is quite possible for a psychiatrist to diagnose mental disorder when there is simply a clash of values between the patient and the psychiatrist, who may be conforming to the values of society. A collection of summaries of case histories from the practice of the family psychiatrist Susan Penfold illustrates this point. The relevant descriptions concern encounters between male psychiatrists and female patients. In particular, they reveal that lesbian relationships may be viewed by psychiatrists as a mark of mental disorder, and by the patient, as a preferred lifestyle (Penfold & Walker, 1983).

The diagnosis of mental disorder may considerably decrease the self-esteem of the diagnosed person, who may also be encouraged to embark on a treatment program that at best may be irrelevant and at worst may be deadly. The toxicity of some of the psychiatric drugs such as lithium and the phenothiazines may be death. If it is desirable for the "patient" to change her values, there are more relevant and humane ways of promoting this other than by medical psychiatric treatment.

There may be some instances of agreement on the values that underpin decisions about impairment, but this does not necessarily mean that such values should remain unquestioned. The values bearing on the acceptability of certain sorts of behavior for women and the acceptability of other behavior for men, relating to sex role stereotypes, seem to be widespread. These stereotypes are commonly incorporated into the self-concepts of both men and women (Broverman et al., 1972). This might reveal the difficulty of change but in no sense invalidates feminist initiatives toward change.

The problems in the conceptualization of "distress" and "disability" are compounded in the new clause: that the syndrome is associated "with a significantly increased risk of suffering death, pain, disability, or an important loss of freedom." This introduces a new looseness into the definition. What is "a significantly increased risk of suffering disability" for instance, when the disability is in the social or occupational realm? It could amount to a risk that the person will experience difficulties in the relationships with family and friends or employer, not that she actually does now. If there are biases in the determination of distress or disability as argued above then these biases could certainly also affect the assessment of the risk of such suffering, and again, this could relate to the interests of women.

An exclusion clause is added to the basic conceptual framework in DSM-III-R: "Neither deviant behavior; e.g., political, religious, or sexual, nor conflicts that are primarily between the individual and society are mental disorders unless the deviance or conflict is a symptom of a dysfunction in the person" (American Psychiatric Association, 1987, p. xxii). This clause is an attempt to disassociate the concept of mental disorder from the realm of politics, but it does not work. A political difference could easily fall under the label of *dysfunction*. Suppose, for example, that one's political deviance amounts to rejection of authority figures and the desire to create egalitarian structures. It could be said that according to the DSM definition this deviance amounts to an occupational dysfunction——rejection of authority figures——and hence it satisfies the definition for mental disorder.

Conflict between an individual and society could always be seen as dysfunctional, given that normal functioning is defined in such a narrow way. The category of Adjustment Disorder with Disturbance of Conduct illustrates this point. This aspect of the definition is also of relevance to women. If it is the case that most Western societies are dominated by patriarchal norms (as the above discussion indicates), then women rejecting such norms may find it very difficult to be viewed simply as experiencing a conflict between an individual and society and not simultaneously dysfunctional.

The failure of the DSM to be clear about (and to examine) the values that are operative in the discussions about distress and disability is a serious weakness. In uncovering ways in which values do enter the apparently neutral diagnostic scheme, I hope to have shown how it may be used as a weapon to keep women "in their place." One positive move in DSM-IV would be to drop the facade of value neutrality. At least if it is admitted that values enter into the conceptual foundations, then this could form the basis for a debate about their appropriateness—a debate that should extend beyond the domain of medicine because the values concern the right way to live, and medicine has no particular authority on that question.

PROBLEMS OF SUBJECTIVITY

Many of the descriptions of the categories in DSM-III-R leave room for variable interpretations. There is also a strong element of subjectivity embedded in the application of various criteria within some diagnoses. This is of particular significance to women. It is women who are more likely to be persuaded, cajoled, or forced to submit themselves for assessment by psychologists or psychiatrists. As mentioned before, the label of mental disorder can be devastating to one's self-image. It may also affect how one comes to be regarded by others. The label almost invariably sets one up as a candidate for drug therapy, and the drugs currently in use often have significant irritating and/or damaging side effects. Hence, it does matter if someone is classified as mentally disordered or as sane. If that classification depends to a large extent on subjective factors, then it is a problem.

Two diagnoses that are supposed to be much more commonly attributed to women than men are Borderline Personality Disorder and Dependent Personality Disorder. In DSM-III field trials, this difference in attribution with these two disorders was confirmed as extremely significant for the diagnosis of Dependent Personality Disorder (Kass, Spitzer & Williams, 1983).

The Borderline Personality Disorder is characterized by "instability of mood, interpersonal relationships, and self-image" (American Psychiatric Association, 1987, p. 347). One problem here is that what counts as instability is very much an open question. It will be up to the assessor to decide, and there will be great variability in these decisions. Moreover, the assumption that instability is a mark of mental disorder is not free of subjective elements. A further problem is the covert inclusion of bisexuality in the defining criteria. Increasingly, homosexuality is regarded as a normal variant of human sexual experience, and this is acknowledged in DSM-III-R in the abandonment of the category of Ego-Dystonic Homosexuality. If homosexuality and heterosexuality are both considered to be normal variations, why then should bisexuality be regarded as a mark of a disorder? Placing bisexuality in the defining criteria of Borderline Personality Disorder leaves open the possibility that some psychiatrists will apply the criteria in a different way than others because they hold varying judgments about normal sexuality. This is of particular concern to women, as women more often receive the diagnosis of Borderline Personality Disorder. The problem is that a disorder diagnosis could be given to someone who has simply chosen a life-style different from the norm.

The Dependent Personality Disorder also contains subjective elements. The disorder is marked by "a pervasive pattern of dependent and submissive behavior, beginning by early childhood and present in a variety of contexts" (American Psychiatric Association, 1987, p. 354). This has a familiar ring. It is very close to what we are expected to be as women. If we succeed in our role as women then we may be diagnosed as having Dependent Personality Disorder. If we do not succeed in our role as women, we will be punished in other ways.

Marcie Kaplan (1983) elaborated on the subjectivity of the description *Dependent Personality Disorder*, pointing out three major assumptions: (a) that dependence is unhealthy; (b) that extreme dependence in women marks an individual dysfunction rather than merely reflecting women's subordinate social position; and (c) that whereas a woman's expression of dependence merits clinicians' labeling and concern, a man's expression of dependence [relying on others to maintain his house and take care of his children] does not. Kaplan challenged the three assumptions. Williams and Spitzer (1983) responded by pointing out that the description is open enough to cover dependence in males as well as females. This argument concerned the challenge to the third assumption, but it did not counter Kaplan's point that specific male behaviors are often not acknowledged to involve dependence when they are just as good candidates for this description as certain female behaviors. Kaplan's challenge to the first two assumptions was simply ignored.

Kass, Spitzer, and Williams (1983) made another attempt to undermine Kaplan's position by citing empirical findings that there is no overall tendency for women to receive a Personality Disorder diagnosis more often than men, and hence sex bias does not exist in the DSM-III criteria for Personality Disorder. This misses the point: if a woman conforms to the female role, she runs the risk of being labeled under one of the categories, Dependent Personality Disorder, Histrionic Personality Disorder, or Borderline Personality Disorder. Even if fewer women than men received Personality Disorder diagnoses, this would not show that the bias did not intrude.

Two of the proposed diagnostic categories for DSM-IV which apply mainly to women are Late Luteal Phase Dysphoric Disorder and Self-Defeating

Personality Disorder. The former has a tight definition in terms of onset "symptoms in [criterion] B occurred during the last week of the luteal phase and remitted within a few days after onset of the follicular phase" (American Psychiatric Association, 1987, p. 369), but a very loose definition in terms of symptoms. No change is necessary for the diagnosis, but a range of changes covering many different mental and physical factors is sufficient. This is an improvement on the results in a 1985 survey of the literature and clinical experience relating to premenstrual syndrome in which the authors stated that at least 200 symptoms and complaints had been reported to occur premenstrually (Halbreich, Endicott & Lester, 1985). However, the DSM-III-R definition still has a "catch-all" nature. Judith Bardwick (1974) commented on three of the listed symptoms—depression, irritability, and hostility—saying that they were predictable and normal emotional states in women. This is another variant of the theme emerging from the Broverman studies: that it is normal for women to be disordered. Bardwick and others promoting this diagnostic category are implicitly adopting a male norm. Men are viewed as less changeable than women, and men are used as the standard to evaluate acceptable levels of changeability. There may be positive aspects to fluctuations in mood and in energy levels, so it may not be appropriate to call such changes symptoms of a disorder.

Another aspect of the diagnostic description is that "the disturbance seriously interferes with work or with usual social activities or relationships with others" (American Psychiatric Association, 1987, p. 369). This aspect does not adequately keep in check the problems of subjectivity in the symptoms list. Suppose an irritable, angry, tense woman were to rebel against an oppressive work situation on two occasions just before the onset of menstruation. She might be labeled as suffering from the Late Luteal Phase Dysphoric Disorder. Another way of looking at what is going on may be to regard her anger as giving her the strength to rebel against an oppressive occupational arrangement. The diagnostic category directs us to see what may be merely *changes* of emotional or bodily state as *symptoms* of a disorder. It also assumes that serious interference with past social or occupational arrangements is necessarily negative. An alternative view is that the changes that the woman experiences in the premenstrual phase may give her the motivation and energy to make positive changes in her life.

Although it cannot be denied that some women experience undesirable cyclical changes, the diagnosis of Late Luteal Phase Dysphoric Disorder should not be introduced into DSM-IV. The subjective nature of the proposed criteria could have very dangerous implications for women. The diagnosis could be used to defuse rebellious moves by women which may have a sound basis. There are indications in the work of Katharina Dalton, a leading British researcher/practitioner in the field, that this diagnosis could be used to justify women's unequal position in the workforce.

Dalton asserted (1977) that the "cost to industry of menstruation is high" (p. 146); she then detailed the harmful effects in various industries in Sweden, the United Kingdom, and the United States: "in the retail and distributive trades there may be a variety of effects ranging from errors in stocktaking and billing to bad tempered service to customers and breakages from clumsiness. In the office the irritability may result in a sudden argument with the boss, the cleaner spilling the bucket of water across the room, the secretary hurling spoilt letters into the basket" (p. 146). Dalton (1978) recommended that employers handle these problems by giving women time off or assigning them to less skilled jobs: "packing and stacking . . . rather than remaining on tasks which are harder to remedy later, such as soldering or filing" (pp. 119–120). This suggestion could easily be taken as encouragement to employers not to employ women at all. Dalton's approach very easily leads to the view that women's unequal position in the workforce is, in fact, fair.

The diagnostic category of Self-Defeating Personality Disorder also contains dangers for women. The DSM-III-R criteria are an improvement on the 1985 draft for Masochistic Personality Disorder, but some of the problems raised by the APA Committee on Women (mentioned in Ritchie, 1989, pp. 696–698) remain: (a) it is implicitly sex biased and will be misapplied primarily to women; (b) it ignores the fact that our culture fosters behaviors in women which could be misinterpreted as self-defeating (there is a striking parallel between this proposed disorder and Pope John Paul II's 1988 pronouncement on the role of women (Ritchie, 1989); and (c) it pathologizes normal responses to the experience of victimization.

The new definition attempts to handle point (c) by the clause "the behaviors do not occur exclusively in response to, or in anticipation of, being sexually, or psychologically abused" (American Psychiatric Association, 1987, p. 374). This clause does not go far enough, as the determination of actual abuse may sometimes be difficult to make. There could well be variable judgments about whether abuse has occurred——especially psychological abuse. Many women complain, perhaps rightly so, that most men are blind to their perpetration of psychological abuse. Will a male psychiatrist, within a patriarchal culture, see the situation from a woman's point of view? Also, as noted by Franklin (1987), "it often takes a long time and an unusual amount of trust between a client and a therapist before the patient will admit to being a victim of abuse" (p. 53).

Whether or not a woman anticipates abuse will also be very difficult to determine. If the diagnosing psychiatrist has no evidence of actual abuse, he may find it difficult to accept that there is anticipation of abuse. Moreover, it is rare for women not to anticipate abuse, whether it is through exercising the physical freedom that men experience, for example, by walking the streets of Sydney at night, or through their desire to enter traditional male domains in the social and occupational arena.

Another reason why this clause is an inadequate response to point (c) is that victimization may fall short of actual "abuse" and still exercise a constraining effect on one's thinking and behaving.

The main danger in introducing this diagnosis is that it will act to obscure the extent of the oppression of women within modern culture. Many of the problems that women suffer seem to be attributable to their unequal social position (Brown & Harris, 1978; Miles, 1988). So if the aim of psychiatry is to improve mental health it should not be introducing categories that could perpetrate that inequality.

NARROWNESS OF FOCUS

Not surprisingly, the focus of DSM-III-R is on problems within particular individuals rather than problematic features of a particular social context. This focus on individuals may sometimes be appropriate. However, the consistent lack of a broader perspective is likely to encourage diagnoses of mental disorder when there is far more disturbance in the social environment than in the mind of the diagnosed person, and when the "treatment program" should be directed toward fixing that environment instead of continually trying to make the disturbed individual conform to it. Marcie Kaplan (1983) also mentioned this problem when she stated that in some instances "it is difficult to say when society should be labelled crazy" (p. 789). She obscured this issue though and left herself open for attack when she claimed that "it is difficult if not impossible, to say when a disturbance is only brought about by a conflict between an individual and society" (p. 789). As Williams and Spitzer (1983) correctly pointed out, this can be read simply as asserting that societal pressures may contribute to mental disturbance—a claim that is not very controversial and is much weaker than the assertion that the disturbance is wrongly attributed to the individual.

A study that could be used to throw light on this distinction was reported by Stone (1987). He looked into certain features of the diagnosis of Borderline Personality Disorder, including homosexuality, displays of temper, and suicidal threats. He found that parents' lack of acceptance of their offspring's homosexuality as manifested in mockery and abusiveness appeared to have led their children into suicidal gestures and inordinate anger.

One point that is relevant when reflecting on this study is that, as mentioned above, many people now regard homosexuality as a normal variant of human sexuality. The problem here may be more with parents' intolerance. The suicidal gestures and anger could, at least in some instances, be seen as normal reactions to what is viewed as oppressive and unfair criticism.

The narrowness of focus in DSM-III-R is a problematic feature of other diagnostic categories too. The descriptions of the categories Cyclothymic Disorder and Dysthymia, for instance, pay too little attention to the social context of people fitting the descriptions. The Cyclothymic Disorder is characterized by fairly mild changes in mood from depression to elevated states, perhaps with intervening periods of normal moods. The Dysthymic Disorder is characterized by periods of mild depression separated by periods of normal mood (possibly of a few months' duration). Both are diagnosed more in women than in men. By directing our attention away from the social context, these descriptions prevent us from viewing the relevant mental states as normal responses to a disappointing or frustrating social context. Yet, it might be more appropriate to view them in this way, to deny that there is disorder in the individual, and to impute a problem to the social context, if indeed there is a problem at all. It could be that the normal variability in the context is reflected in the variability of peoples' moods. This emerges only as a problem in the social or personal domain if it is assumed that stability and nonvariability have a higher value. This is quite debatable, especially if one seeks a rich and complex life.

Two studies pointed out a sex bias in the diagnosis of Histrionic Personality Disorder, with clinicians tending to diagnose female case histories rather than males as Histrionic Personality Disorder even though the diagnostic information is the same (Ford & Widiger, 1989; Warner, 1978). This bias seems to relate to the diagnostic label rather than the specifics of the criteria, leading Ford and Widiger to conclude, "removing sex-typed features from the criteria sets may neither eliminate nor substantially inhibit sex bias" (Ford & Widiger, 1989).

These are just a sample of the problems stemming from a narrowness of focus, which affect a wide range of diagnoses in DSM-III-R. The scheme brings in broader considerations in some of the diagnostic criteria and under Axis IV. The former is very limited, and Axis IV concentrates on psychological stresses. This does not go far enough; it will not alert the diagnostician to the fact that cultural biases—those relating to sex or sexuality or the desirability of narrowly defined emotional stability—might affect diagnoses inappropriately. Improvement is not going to come simply by increasing the list of psychological stresses under Axis IV, although an expansion of this axis or even adding to the specific diagnostic criteria for some categories may be the way to go. This takes us back to the point mentioned above: that values are very important in the diagnostic process, a fact obscured by the use of medical terminology. It is possible that the problems of the narrowness of focus will only be addressed adequately when the facade of value neutrality is dropped.

IV FUTURE PROSPECTS AND ALTERNATIVES

12 Enriching the Psychosocial Content of a Multiaxial Nosology

JOHN Z. SADLER, M.D.
and YOSAF F. HULGUS, Ph.D.

The *Diagnostic and Statistical Manual of Mental Disorders, Third Edition* (DSM-III) (American Psychiatric Association, 1980) and the *Third Edition, Revised* (DSM-III-R) (American Psychiatric Association, 1987) marked significant advances for scientific psychiatry in the United States. These manuals re-established the importance of accurate diagnosis in psychiatry; improved diagnostic reliability; facilitated basic, clinical, and epidemiological research in psychiatry; and stimulated renewed interest in descriptive psychiatry (Tischler, 1987). The influence of DSM-III and III-R has been worldwide; hundreds of thousands of copies have been sold, and they have been translated into more than a dozen languages. The successes of DSM-III and DSM-III-R need little additional comment. Nevertheless, these diagnostic systems were, and are, controversial (Chodoff, 1986; Jampala, Sierles & Taylor, 1986; Kendler, 1990; Klerman, Vaillant, Spitzer & Michels, 1984; McKegney, 1982; Mezzich and von Cranach, 1988; Tischler, 1987; Williams, Spitzer & Skodol, 1985). Criticism has come from a large variety of perspectives and interest groups, with some focusing on specific diagnostic entities, others focusing on broader conceptual issues. Without reviewing all of these criticisms, we would like to highlight a few nosological dilemmas reflected in DSM-III-R. It will become apparent that some of these dilemmas plague other major nosological systems in psychiatry and hence have significance beyond DSM-III-R.

One of the criticisms relevant to our current discussion is the DSM-III-R focus on the individual person or patient as the basic unit of psychiatric nosological concern (Wynne, 1987). In DSM-III-R, only individuals have disorders of mental function; only individuals have psychopathology. DSM-III-R asserts, in effect, that social systems or communities, families, and couples *as units* do not have psychopathology or disturbed mental functions, only individ-

261

ual persons do. The notion of context-dependent psychopathology, communicative or interactive pathology of social groups is foreign to this nosology. Indeed, the whole notion of *mental function* under the DSM-III-R rubric betrays an individualistic metaphysics: minds reside in brains, which in turn reside in individual persons. Minds, and subsequently mental disorders, do not reside in the social world (Bateson, 1972). (In her chapter, Denise Russell discusses the implications of this for women.) This choice favoring the nosological primacy of the individual makes practical sense in that the traditional and most common clinical encounter involves only the clinician and the individual patient. The problem is that all psychiatric disorders are embedded in a social, community, family, or similar network——networks that have profound practical importance for the clinician. The vast literature in preventive psychiatry, social psychiatry, and family and marital psychiatry attests to the etiological and practical relevance of these social systems to psychiatric disorders. The primacy of the individual in DSM-III-R relegates the diagnosis and treatment of social system "pathologies" to a nosological Siberia. The predictive advantages and treatment implications of these areas of psychiatric knowledge are lessened because of this nosological "disinterest." Indeed, this problem is not limited to DSM-III-R; the focus on the individual holds true for most medical nosologies——certainly the *International Classification of Diseases, Ninth Revision* (ICD-9; World Health Organization, 1978a).

A second area of criticism relevant to our task has been most strongly voiced from psychoanalysts and other psychodynamically oriented clinicians (Chodoff, 1986; Klerman et al., 1984). This critique focuses on, among other issues, the problem of historical emptiness in DSM-III-R. What we mean by this is that DSM-III-R provides no means for placing the psychiatric patient into a personal life history context——what McHugh and Slavney (1983) succinctly called the "life story" perspective of psychiatry. A related concern for those working on DSM-IV is *reification*——seeing the DSM nosological entities as concrete diseases rather than useful abstractions. The reification of nosology results in the false sense that if one knows the diagnosis, one knows the patient (Frances et al., 1991). Although historical life events may be a part of the diagnostic criteria for a DSM-III-R disorder, these are usually life events of *symptoms*. Historical life events such as divorce; job loss; catastrophe; parental death, abuse, or abandonment; and other stressful life events may be incorporated into Axis IV as a global rating, but even then only if they were recent. The etiological, clinical, and practical significance of these and other life events in the patient's past are pushed into the nosological background. Furthermore, the perspective of human development and its relevance to psychiatric disorder are also defined out of DSM-III-R. Again, a vast literature detailing the relevance of recent and remote historical life events to psychiatric illness, as well as a vast literature on human development is also nosologically marginal. If a recent review is representative, this is true to a large extent in other nations' nosologies as well (Mezzich and von Cranach, 1988).

A third criticism has to do with the alleged atheoretical stance of DSM-III-R. This is discussed elsewhere in this book (see the chapters by George Agich, Denise Russell, Joseph Margolis, K. W. M. Fulford, Aviel Goodman, and Schwartz & Wiggins). Although DSM-III-R does not overtly declare allegiance to a particular etiological theory or theories, it describes or gives structure to the diagnostic reality so that some etiological theories are more applicable or relevant than others (Faust & Miner, 1986). DSM-III-R declares, as any nosology must, some clinical data relevant to diagnosis and other data not relevant. The DSM-III-R diagnostic approach selects operationalized, individualistic signs and symptoms as relevant clinical data, whereas other kinds of clinical data are ignored as *nosologically* irrelevant. This descriptive, syndrome-bound approach to diagnosis fits the needs of a biological psychiatry much better than other etiological models, as, for instance, a family interactional model (as in family systems models) (Beavers & Hampson, 1990) or a developmental, life story approach (as in psychoanalytic and related therapies) (McHugh & Slavney, 1983). Presuming that the primary functions of diagnosis are treatment selection and the prediction of patient course, it follows that diagnosis would prefer those etiological theories whose terms most closely match those used by the particular diagnostic nosology (Sadler & Hulgus, 1991). For example, the operationalized, descriptive, symptom-based diagnostic approach of DSM-III-R records the sort of clinical data or evidence which matches biological psychiatry's terms better than (for instance) a family systems psychiatry; the interactional data utilized by the latter would be unaccounted for by the individualistic, symptom-oriented DSM-III-R. Because DSM-III-R categories fit biological psychiatry's theory base better than other psychosocially oriented therapies, the DSM-III-R diagnosis tends to make biological conceptualizations of the patient primary and the psychosocial secondary. In summary, DSM-III-R may not state a theory, but the metaphysical structure of its classification prefers the theoretical bases of descriptive/ biological psychiatry.

The theory ladenness of DSM-III-R appears in other, less subtle ways. For a DSM-III-R disorder to have an identified etiology, the scientific evidence must be deemed adequate. In fact, only biological etiologies are considered to have adequate enough evidence, as in the Organic Mental Disorders (such as Cannabis Delusional Disorder). However, the so-called functional disorders are not considered to have adequate enough evidence for any etiology to be defined——this despite the fact that the necessary condition for the development of Post-traumatic Stress Disorder (PTSD) is a catastrophic life event: "an event that is outside the range of usual human experience and that would be markedly distressing to almost anyone" (American Psychiatric Association, 1987, p. 250). Surely the condition of this catastrophic life event would be as etiologically relevant as cannabis abuse would be for Cannabis Delusional Disorder, and we would bet the actual quantity of published evidence for the life event cause of PTSD to be a huge order greater! It is true that cannabis use is a necessary condition for the development of Cannabis Delusional Disorder, and cannabis use is recognized as the "cause" of Cannabis Delusional Disorder. However, the catastrophic stressor is *not* (at least formally) identified as the cause of PTSD; instead, it is built into the *description* of the PTSD entity. There appears to be a double standard in DSM-III-R regarding what things are considered causally neutral descriptive criteria and what things are considered etiologically significant. In one case, cannabis use is considered causal, and the other, catastrophic stressors, are not. This double standard affirms the theoretical bias we have already described.

Do these criticisms have anything in common? We think so. The DSM-III-R nosological approach loses clinical data that mental health clinicians often find essential in their everyday work with patients. The lost clinical data include, for example, their understanding of traumatic life events, their patient's practically difficult life circumstances (e.g., homelessness), the maladaptive communicational patterns manifest in the patients' family, the warped set of reinforcement contingencies present in the workplace, and so on. These factors may have dramatic effects on etiology, treatment, and prognosis, yet they evaporate when the DSM-III-R classification is enacted.

One could counter, however, that diagnosis is not intended to solve all treatment problems. Could not a DSM-III-R diagnosis and treatment formulation suffice? We would say no. Having an acontextual diagnostic system perpetuates the hegemony of biological psychiatry——a hegemony that is so pervasive that some practitioners actually believe there is no diagnostic alternative. Please do not get us wrong. We are not "anti-" biological psychiatry. We would like to minimize hegemonies in diagnosis. Having a contextual diagnostic system would give the power of the DSM-III-R operationalized approach to a multiplicity of theoretical approaches to treatment and would possibly make the classification usefully multitheoretical. How can we deal with these relevant historical and environmental factors in a psychiatric nosology? How can we do it and continue to have a manageable and tidy diagnostic system? How can we do it without saying that *everything* is important in treating the patient? The focus of this chapter is to illustrate how a critique of the nomothetic/idiographic distinction can bear fruit for the above nosological problems.

NOMOTHETIC AND IDIOGRAPHIC SCIENCE

The German philosopher Wilhelm Windelband (1848—1915) sought to polish the then-tarnished status of history as a scientific discipline. His response to positivist criticisms of history (as well as other social sciences) was to distinguish two kinds of science: nomothetic and idiographic. We will show how the distinction that Windelband made almost a century ago can frame the nosological problems posed above.

Windelband described the complementary relationship between the natural sciences (such as physics, chemistry, and astronomy) and the social sciences (such as history and sociology). This complementarity is reflected in his concepts of nomothetic and idiographic. *Nomothetic* science seeks to describe the particular scientific problem as an example of general laws, such as Boyle's law. *Idiographic* science seeks to describe the structural form of the singular, unique event (Oakes, 1988; von Wright, 1971; Windelband, 1980). To use Windelband's own (translated) words, nomothetic science is "concerned with what is invariably the case," and idiographic science is "concerned with what was once the case" (Windelband, 1980, p. 175). Nomothetic science reasons from particular to general laws, and idiographic science reasons within the particulars themselves. Although some intellectual domains lend themselves to nomothetic science (such as physics) and other intellectual domains lend themselves to idiographic science (such as history), this dichotomy is not axiomatic. Indeed, Windelband provided a brief example of nomothetic and idiographic science investigating the same subject matter. The example given is evolutionary biology. As a taxonomy or nosology, it has a nomothetic character, as it develops laws to explain and predict organismic development over time. When evolutionary biology is considered as a historical development of the biosphere, however, this viewpoint is idiographic (the viewpoint that studies this particular evolution as a whole). However, nowhere is the complementary nature of nomothetic and idiographic more profound than in the discipline of psychology, in which the nomothetic character is reflected in such sciences as behaviorism (where the emphasis is on the laws that determine human behavior), and the idiographic is reflected in psychoanalytic psychology (where the emphasis is on understanding the person in his or her uniqueness).

Let us proceed with our critique of the distinction. The nomothetic/idiographic distinction is a useful means to divide up scientific reality, but the blurring of the distinction occurs in psychiatry as well. This blurring of the distinction will be important to understanding our later nosological proposal. Windelband's distinction depends on what is considered the unit of study, or level of observation. Using Windelband's evolutionary biology example, the unit of study is "the historical development of the biosphere" for the idiographic aspect, and the units of study for the nomothetic aspects are individual lines of phylogeny. In clinical psychiatry we often evaluate a patient's life history as a whole (idiographic aspect), but within that history there will be recurrent behavior patterns (such as obsessional checking of locked doors or cycles of marital violence) that can be reliably predicted (nomothetic aspect). Indeed, much of contemporary psychological single case study research (idiographic aspect) relies on repeated measures of thought/behavior patterns (Barlow & Herson, 1984) which, when evaluated with techniques such as nonparametric statistics (Siegel, 1956), can provide lawlike predictions and thus give a nomothetic aspect to a single case study. Thus, the psychiatrist can focus on the life history and develop an overall understanding of the idiographic structural form of the unique patient. Alternatively, when the focus is on particular thought or behavior patterns, an impressive predictive ability can be developed as well—as in nomothetic science. So, the psychiatrist uses tentative idiographic knowledge of the individual person to aid in recognizing recurrent patterns of thought and behavior, and conversely, those thought/behavior patterns from nomothetic understanding contribute to understanding the individual as idiographic whole (Ricoeur, 1981). In other words, these recurrent patterns can in part determine the structural form of the individual, and the ability to identify the thoughts or behaviors separately is necessary to recognize the general patterns of thought or behavior.

Considered in this way, the nomothetic and idiographic are complementary and mutually dependent. The strict dichotomy suggested by Windelband's nomothetic/idiographic distinction provides a *perspective-dependent* complementarity. Perspective dependence refers to the primacy of the descriptive level or focus. The nomothetic and idiographic are complementary because the development of one fosters the development of the other, and both broaden the comprehension of the phenomenon.

To summarize, although structural forms promote an understanding of the whole (as in idiographic science), they may also have predictive value (a characteristic of nomothetic science). Whereas the development of laws of prediction enhance explanation (as in nomothetic science), the recognition of predictive laws or lawlike behavior may also enhance empathic understanding of the individual (a characteristic of idiographic science). In these ways the sharp distinction between nomothetic and idiographic blurs. Windelband's fuzziness in this area will provide a bridge for developing a more contextually rich psychiatric nosology.

It is precisely this ambiguity of nomothetic and idiographic perspectives which suggests a possible resolution to the psychosocial impoverishment of DSM-III-R. To preserve the complementarity of nomothetic and idiographic science in a field as complex as psychiatric diagnosis, a diagnostic nosology must embrace more than one unit or level of observation: clinical data used in diagnosis must address holistic, historical data, as well as components of these historical wholes. How does DSM-III-R currently measure up to this challenge, and how could it be improved?

IS DSM-III-R NOMOTHETIC OR IDIOGRAPHIC SCIENCE?

DSM-III-R is a complex nosology that attempts idiographic and nomothetic aspects. Because of this complexity, the question "Is DSM-III-R nomothetic or idiographic?" suggests that the individual axes be evaluated separately.

Axis I is characterized by clinical syndromes that rely on operationalized diagnostic criteria. This is intended to standardize psychiatric diagnosis among examiners so that investigations of etiology are facilitated while the course of illness and response to treatment can be reliably predicted. Axis III, that of the conventional medical disorders, is based on the same concept, without the criteria specified, as they represent nonpsychiatric disorders. Axis II disorders (primarily personality disorders) were also intended to reflect the categorical criterion (Axis I) approach, but for various reasons the Axis II classification has been subject to criticism from both researchers and practitioners (Frances et al., 1991; Grayson, 1987; Schwartz & Wiggins, 1989, 1991; see also the chapter by Agich in this book). In summary, the Axis I, II, and III systems attempt, with varying degrees of success, to classify the patient as an example of a group with similar characteristics, to put the patient into a syndrome. This approach enables systematic studies to be made of large numbers of the diagnostic group, subsequently allowing statistical generalizations to be made. These statistical generalizations can then be used in predicting the behavior of new members of the diagnostic group. This represents an obvious, if not classic example of nomothetic science (see the Appendix for Carl Hempel's historical nomological conception of psychiatric classification).

Axes IV and V are nosologies of a different sort (if they are nosologies at all). Axis IV is a global scale of the severity of psychosocial stressors——environmental or historical events that have occurred in the past year which are presumed to have contributed to (a) development of a new mental disorder; (b) recurrence of a prior mental disorder; or (c) exacerbation of an already existing mental disorder (American Psychiatric Association, 1987, p. 18). This clearly suggests that psychosocial stressors have causal relevance for mental disorders, although these factors are treated as if they were nosologically relevant only in a *global* sense. The assumption was made that these psychosocial stressors have little *specific* effect on the patient's clinical status, such that a global rating will suffice. For example, there is no relevant *nosological* difference among a patient's divorce, a serious illness in a patient's child, and a patient being fired from a job if the "severity" of the stressor is the same. On the contrary, it is the nonspecific, global nature of Axis IV which has generated concern about limited clinical utility (Williams, 1985a, 1985b; Mezzich, Fabrega & Mezzich, 1987).

Axis V is a rating of *global assessment of functioning* (GAF) in the psychological, social, and occupational spheres. As Axis V is of limited relevance to our concerns here, our discussion is limited to the acknowledgment that the authors of DSM-III-R wished to assist the clinician in tailoring patient assessment to include some prognostic and treatment planning concerns that are relatively unique to the particular patient. This compromise is also subject to the same criticisms as Axis IV: that the rating is too vague and unfocused to be clinically useful.

What Axes IV and V attempt to do is to provide some information about this particular patient's circumstances which may be relevant to treatment planning and outcome. This concern for understanding the *particular* circumstances of the patient, considering the past history and current environmental/ historical circumstances, represents an attempt toward an *idiographic* dimension in DSM-III-R. At the same time, Axes IV and V can also have nomothetic properties, in that they enhance the predictive ability of the clinician—that is, assist in prognosis. Axes IV and V bring the patient's personal *context* to clinical attention, albeit in a very broad way.

Thus, DSM-III-R is an interesting and original development in psychiatric nosologies (see the chapter by Wallace in this book). Two of the ways one could characterize postmodern science would be (a) a renewed interest in incorporating context into scientific observation and generalization (Bernstein, 1983), and (b) an interest in understanding scientific knowledge (theories, laws, etc.) in the light of their social and philosophical assumptions (Heelan, 1983; Longino, 1990). To use Windelband's language, post-modern science attempts to integrate scientific laws (nomothetic science) with the environmental, conceptual, and social contexts in which they arise (idiographic science). The nomothetic and idiographic are complementary in the postmodern pursuit of knowledge. Particularly in this latter sense, DSM-III and DSM-III-R are pioneering attempts at a postmodern scientific nosology for psychiatry.

However, we agree with the critics; Axes IV and V are too nonspecific to provide a truly rich and clinically useful psychosocial psychiatric science. Moreover, the DSM-III-R reach for idiographic detail is limited by the need for nomothetic reductive generalizations.

ENRICHING THE PSYCHOSOCIAL CONTENT OF DSM-III-R

After only a brief consideration it is apparent that not only are the DSM-III-R Axes I, II, and III primarily nomothetic, but general medical syndrome/disease classifications are as well. Indeed, the approach of reducing medical syndromes to clinical diseases with known pathophysiologies, courses, outcomes, and anatomical findings has been an enormously fruitful approach to medicine (Seldin, 1977). This model for medicine continues to predominate today. If psychiatric illness can be reduced to pathophysiologies of the brain, it is logical to follow the lead of our non-psychiatric colleagues and develop precise diagnostic entities with statistical predictions regarding their etiology, course, and outcome. Although this approach can and does provide a powerful approach to psychiatry, few psychiatrists will need to be convinced of the problems with this reductionistic approach. Even though a great degree of certainty is brought to clinical treatment, too many nonreducible things go wrong. The patient does not adhere to the recommended effective treatment. There are many patients whose illnesses have not been "reduced" (are curable) yet. There are innumerable practical impediments to treatment. The nomothetic laws of disease are of limited help to the clinician in dealing with the unique problems posed by the unique patient. For this reason, psychiatrists have long used a combined nomothetic *and* idiographic approach in helping their patients (even though they would not use these terms!). The wise modern clinician does not simply diagnose and administer a drug. He or she discusses the treatment plan with the patient, negotiates the treatment plan according to the peculiar needs of the patient, and deals with the practical impediments to wellness, whatever they are.

Why not nosologically support psychiatrists' actual activities with patients? Why should psychosocial dimensions, practiced every day, not be incorporated into nosology? Is there a way to embrace nosologically the idiographic-like, contextual elements of psychosocial psychiatry?

We think so. The assumption of modern medicine is that illness is "in" the individual (Foucault, 1975). Why not complement this fruitful assumption with an additional one? Why not also assume that illnesses are imbedded "in" an environmental/historical context? With this complementary assumption the same syndromatic approach could be used; but to differentiate context from person, we will call the relevant context a *syndrome of context*. The characteristics of clinically relevant events could be collected——that is, kinds of environmental and historical events could be classified through their common association with psychiatric illnesses. The clinical features of the context then would be environmental and historical instead of personal symptoms and signs, as in a classic syndrome. We will call this complementary nosology of the patient's environmental/historical world a *nosology of context*.

What Is a Nosology of Context?

A nosology of context would be an assembling of psychiatrically relevant environmental and historical factors into syndromes of context——a contextual parallel with the classic concept of *syndrome*. Conceiving a syndrome of context requires a shift of perspective which may seem odd to users of an individually centered nosology. Thought and behavior patterns of the individual patient are specifically excluded; only environmental or historical phenomena surrounding the patient are considered for syndrome inclusion. A syndrome of context can have many uses: as an etiological factor, a prognostic factor, or as a target for treatment (or perhaps more accurately, therapeutic manipulation), depending on the purpose of the nosology and the interest of the user. These collections of environmental/historical factors would need to have the coherence of the personal psychiatric syndromes. Isolated, single environmental/historical factors that may be relevant to psychiatric disorders could be included; but the inclusion of every historical fact that is relevant would be overwhelming, just as including every possible clinical feature of a schizophrenic into the schizophrenic syndrome would be overwhelming. A syndrome of context provides a shorthand for the patient's environmental/historical context, just as a DSM-III-R disorder provides a shorthand for the patient's psycho-behavioral disorder.

A Nosology of Context for Axis IV

A nosology of context should answer the problems of the current nomothetic nosologies which have been discussed above. Although we believe a nosology of contextual syndromes is a unique idea, there are precedents for this, the most obvious being the idea to specify particular psychosocial stressors in a multiaxial system (Mezzich et al., 1987; van Goor-Lambo, Orley, Poustka & Rutter, 1990). These efforts, however, tend to focus on particular stressors rather than lumping groups of related stressors into nosological categories. The proposal here is intended to provide an example of a *possible* nosology of context (others are, of course, possible, if not preferable) which is compatible, even user friendly, with the current DSM-III-R system. Our proposal involves a significant change in Axis IV to be described below.

A classification of context should (a) provide a structural form for the patient's unique environmental and historical context; (b) supply a means for tailoring etiological and treatment concerns to the individual patient; (3) expand the notion of psychopathology to include environmental and historical contexts; (4) ensure that clinically important life events are incorporated into diagnosis-based treatment planning; (5) shape the nosological reality so that psychosocial etiologies can bear equal weight with biological etiologies (i.e., have a multitheoretical nosological system).

At this point, the reader might recall our critique of Windelband's nomothetic/idiographic distinction. Our syndromes of context are a means of nomothetically classifying the traditional concern of idiographic science: the environmental/historical particularities. Indeed, the traditional psychosocial aspects of psychiatry could be conceived as idiographic concerns.

Actual examples of our proposed nosology of context may be most illustrative. We conceive psychiatrically relevant context to be divisible into three broad classes, each consisting of its respective syndromes of context. This taxonomy is illustrated in Figure 12.1: syndromes of personal history; of the interpersonal environment; and of the extrapersonal environment. These major classes are, of course, provisional, and they simply demonstrate a single example of a possible nosology of context. Nevertheless, how did we come up with these classes?

To be brief, we wanted the major classes of context to be relatively few, for the sake of simplicity. At the same time, we wanted the nosology to embrace environmental/historical data of a sufficiently broad nature to be, in theory, useful for a broad number of etiological theories. This would mean that such a nosology would make a future DSM more multitheoretical than

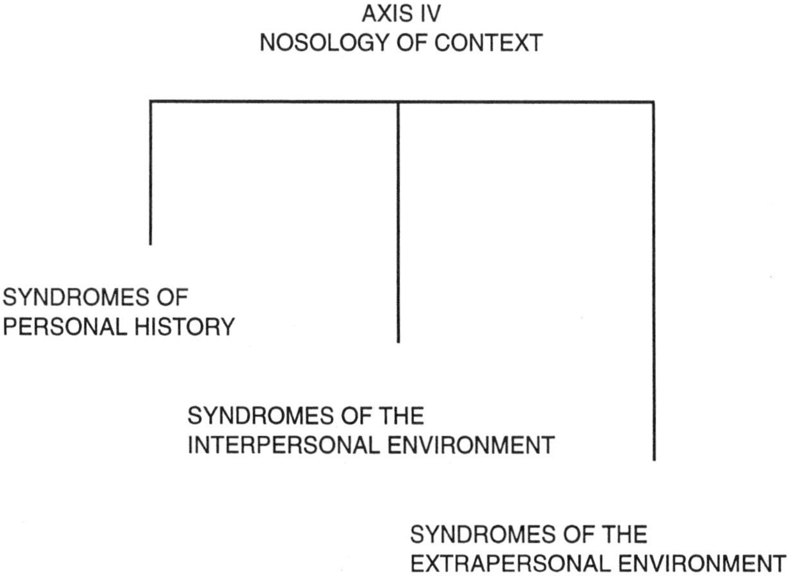

AXIS IV
NOSOLOGY OF CONTEXT

SYNDROMES OF
PERSONAL HISTORY

SYNDROMES OF THE
INTERPERSONAL ENVIRONMENT

SYNDROMES OF THE
EXTRAPERSONAL ENVIRONMENT

Figure 12.1 A nosology of context for Axis IV of the American Psychiatric Association's DSM system

atheoretical. (For a discussion of the value of multitheoretical classification, see Goodman's chapter in this book.) To describe rigorously the means of deriving our nosology of context would unrealistically prolong this chapter. However, to summarize: we considered the sort of environmental/historical data which is needed to employ a particular theory fruitfully. For example, psychoanalytic treatments are largely dependent on data of both current stressors and meaningful past events in childhood. In our scheme, to ignore either would amount to marginalizing psychoanalytic theory. Related theories, such as Jungian analysis, existential analysis, and so forth, share many of the assumptions and evidential requirements of a dynamic psychiatry. Behavioral theory (social learning theory) is dependent on both past and present environmental events as well. In contrast, cognitive therapy, largely based on here-and-now thinking patterns, would not be as dependent on past life events and so, would not need (nor be troubled by) a nosology of past historical syndromes. Alternatively, family therapy, although often based on here-and-now behaviors, largely depends on conceiving the couple or family as a dynamically interacting unit, with its own set of interactional behaviors and pathologies. Thus a nosology that only classified impersonal environmental stressors and past historical events would marginalize family therapy by excluding their primary data source: interaction/communication patterns among family members. We combined theories (and their derivatives) together according to their metaphysical assumptions and then tried to find a few broad

Table 12.1. Sample Diagnoses from Each Category of a Nosology of Context

Syndromes of Personal History	Syndromes of the Interpersonal Environment	Syndromes of the Extrapersonal Environment
Early parental death	Violent victimization	Catastrophe
Incest	Interpersonal overinvolvement	Homelessness
Childhood physical abuse	Interpersonal underinvolvement	Loss of employment
Parental neglect in childhood	Divorce process	Sociocultural transplantation
Serial — extrafamilial placement of childhood and adolescence	Family scapegoating	Cult influence
	Death of spouse	Media influence
[Others]	[Others]	[Others]

categories that could classify contextual syndromes that were relevant to those metaphysical assumptions. We were pleased to find only three categories that fit these demands: the syndromes illustrated in Figure 12.1.

Syndromes of personal history form the class of clinically important personal historical events: events from the patient's past which psychiatric research and/or clinical experience have demonstrated to be important to course, outcome, or treatment of psychiatric problems. For example, early parental loss or childhood physical abuse could qualify as clinically relevant syndromes of the historical context. *Syndromes of the interpersonal environment* consist of clinically relevant interpersonal contexts in the patient's present and immediate past. Examples here could include a violent victimization syndrome based on recent rape, mugging, or other physical assault, or a syndrome of interpersonal overinvolvement, reflecting enmeshed (Minuchin, 1974) communication patterns in the patient's family. *Syndromes of the extrapersonal environment* are those of clinically relevant extrapersonal (environmental) contexts. This class would be composed of syndromes in which the relevant context would include people with limited relationships with the patient or contexts in which the clinical relevance has *little* to do with the patient's intimate relationships: friends and family. Examples here could include a syndrome of environmental catastrophe (such as patient involvement in an airplane crash or torture) and other clinically relevant environmental situations (such as homelessness or living in a foreign sociocultural environment, as with refugees). Other sample syndromes for each of the three classes of context appear in Table 12.1. Tables 12.2, 12.3, and 12.4 provide sample operationalized diagnostic criteria

Table 12.2 Sample Diagnostic Criteria of a Syndrome from the Class "Syndromes of Personal History"

Diagnostic Criteria for Early Parental Death
The syndrome refers to adults age 18 and over
At age 15 or before, the patient lost by death one or more parent figure with whom there was a primary parent-child relationship
The syndrome does not apply to biological parent(s) with whom the patient had little or no contact
Subtype for patient age
Parental death occurred between birth and age 3 years
Parental death occurred between age 3 years and age 15 years
Subtype for
One parent
Both parents

for a particular syndrome from each major category. These are to illustrate the principles of contextual nosology and are not intended to declare an imperative for some future nosology. Note that the operational approach to diagnosis can be preserved, hopefully as successfully as in Axes I and II of DSM-III-R.

DISCUSSION

Psychiatrists have long faced an important dilemma: we wish to tailor treatments to the individual, yet treatments of demonstrated efficacy are based on generalizations about groups of individuals. Indeed, the clinician's approach to the patient moves back and forth between these dual needs: to fit the patient into a class of like individuals reliably, and to meet the unique needs of *this* person. This tension between the general and the particular is reflected in science by the dichotomy of nomothetic and idiographic science. The proposed revision to the DSM-III-R system could be useful in resolving this tension, at least in part.

How does the addition of the nosology of context to the DSM multiaxial system fit into our critique of Windelband's nomothetic/idiographic distinction? How does the contextual Axis IV complement, interact, and inform the other axes? To answer, we need to refer back to our prior discussion on the relevance of the unit of study. The unit of study of DSM-III-R Axes I, II, and III is the individual person. To have a truly idiographic science of the person, a consideration of his or her environmental and historical context is required: to understand an individual in his or her particularity, one cannot divorce the person from context. An Axis IV nosology of context provides this in a set of structural forms to apply to the unique patient, enriching the understanding of that patient. Axis IV provides historical details of the patient, details of environmental circumstances or stressors and of patterns of communication

Table 12.3 Sample Diagnostic Criteria for a Syndrome from the Class "Syndromes of the Interpersonal Environment"

Diagnostic Criteria for the Syndrome of Interpersonal Overinvolvement
The syndrome applies only to the functioning of two or more individuals cohabiting as partners-in-living or family
Persistent demonstration of at least three or more of the following patterns of communication in the (family) group
Personal pronoun use by group members is primarily limited to *we* and *us* (i.e., group members rarely make statements as unique individuals)
Interview questions directed at one capable member of the group are consistently answered by one or more other members of the group
The group frequently emphasizes the harmonious and loving (ideal) qualities of their relationship functioning
One or more group members commonly attribute thoughts or feelings to other group members without discussion with the involved other
Overt disagreement between group members is rarely demonstrated
The patterns of communication in the group represent ongoing group functioning and are not limited to crisis situations such as critical illness of a group member, death of a group member, loss of income for the group, and so on

with others. These are different units of study or observation which flesh out a more holistic or complete understanding of the unique patient. So considering Axes I, II, and III together with the contextual Axis IV embraces more idiographic *concerns* than the current DSM-III-R system while still preserving the nomothetic *practice* of the current DSM. As the repetitive behavior patterns within an individual case study provide nomothetic predictive power for an idiographic concern, so do syndromes of context provide nomothetic predictive power for idiographic concerns.

The contextual Axis IV is based on syndrome logic: cohesive groups of events within the environmental/historical context. The value of diagnosis-as-shorthand requires a nomothetic approach. To do a lengthy idiographic description of a patient's environmental and historical context would require huge amounts of time which would defeat the pragmatic purposes of a nosology: to be a conceptual shorthand.

However, it is important to note that Axis IV syndromes of context are pragmatically meaningless and useless without being considered alongside the other axes. Without the other axes the contextual Axis IV is a context without a person. It is only in considering the contextual Axis IV with Axes I, II, and III that the idiographic advantages of Axis IV are gained. *It is not that this Axis IV is more idiographic than the other Axes, but rather that the added information of the nomothetic syndromes of context brings a greater idiographic richness.* The nomothetic versus idiographic qualities of the multiaxial system proposed here depend on the level of observation—in this case, whether the level of observation is an individual Axis (nomothetic) or the multiaxial system as a whole (idiographic). Thus, the proposal here would provide for a DSM that has an enriched psychosocial, environmental/historical, or idiographic content, without the time-consuming detail of a pure idiographic

Table 12.4 Sample Diagnostic Criteria of a Syndrome from the Class "Syndromes of the Extrapersonal Environment"

Diagnostic Criteria for the Syndrome of Catastrophe

The syndrome refers to a profoundly adverse environmental event in the patient's life
At least one of the following characterizes the event
    The patient was directly involved with, or witnessed, an unexpected event that included assault, injury, and/or death of a number of people (i.e., human disasters such as an airplane crash, riot, mass execution, battle, or natural disasters such as a hurricane, flood, famine)
    The patient was subject to continuous and prolonged mental and/or physical torment by other person(s) (i.e., torture)
The adverse environment event occurred within the year preceding the time of evaluation

approach. Thus, the proposal here is emphatically a compromise between the twin goals of holistic understanding of the patient and having a user-friendly nosology.

There are several practical advantages in adding a nosology of context to the current nosology of the individual. These can be grouped loosely under the headings *research*, *practice*, and *third-party reimbursement*.

Research

The addition of a nosology of context could facilitate etiological research. For example, Axis I and II disorders could be correlated with Axis IV syndromes of context, to confirm existing views of psychosocial etiologies as well as to discover new correlative data that suggest (or refute) new psychosocial causes (Katschnig & Simhandl, 1986). Moreover, cross-correlations of Axis IV syndromes with biological/genetic factors may shed new light on somatic-environmental interactions. The cross-correlations of the four axes could also be used to predict outcomes of various treatments. For example, the Axis IV contextual syndromes of *victimization* and *catastrophe* could be compared for their predictive valence in the course and treatment outcome of Post-traumatic Stress Disorder. Epidemiological studies with comprehensive diagnosis (including the contextual Axis IV) could also have a correlative if not an etiological component.

The addition of a nosology of context facilitates the biopsychosocial ideal as well. The search for biological etiologies in Axis I disorders could continue while the research field is widened by Axis IV contextual syndromes; the psychosocial would no longer be nosologically marginalized as with the current DSM-III-R system. At the same time, the addition of a contextual Axis IV would invalidate or complicate few existing research programs that use Axis I and II diagnosis only. The operationalized categorical approach to diagnosis is preserved, so little ground is lost with the older system, and the new addition offers fresh potential.

Blashfield and colleagues (Blashfield, Sprock & Fuller, 1990) recommended several guidelines for the inclusion of new categories in DSM-IV: sufficient literature, proposed diagnostic criteria, established reliability of diagnosis, established co-occurrence of separate criteria within a category, and sufficient evidence that the category can be differentiated from other categories. These strict guidelines admittedly would eliminate some existing DSM-III-R categories. Nevertheless, in principle, categories within our proposed Axis IV nosology of context could meet these strict criteria, although they do not at present.

Practice

Recent literature has questioned the bedside utility of the biopsychosocial model for psychiatry (Fink, 1988; Sadler & Hulgus, 1990; Schwartz & Wiggins, 1985). The reasons for this are many, but we speculate that the difficulty in implementing a biopsychosocial perspective in psychiatry has to do with DSM-III-R being ill suited to a biopsychosocial approach, for the reasons mentioned in the beginning of this chapter. The proposed revision here would not solve all of the problems of implementing a truly biopsychosocial psychiatry, but it could make diagnosis a more overtly biopsychosocial statement; utilizing all five axes would be an exercise in thorough biopsychosocial assessment. The diagnostic identification of relevant environmental and historical factors would enhance the development of multimodal therapies, both in everyday practice and in the research arena. By having an Axis IV nosology of context, the pluralistic and complex treatment modalities that truly characterize our field (Karasu, 1989) could be diagnostically accounted for, validating an ideal of practice promoted by the psychiatric community.

Third-Party Reimbursement

There has been much concern about the validity and fairness of third-party payment in psychiatry, whether with diagnosis-related groups, preferred provider organizations, or fee-for-service medicine (Mezzich & Sharfstein, 1985; Taube, Lee & Forthover, 1984; Jencks, Goldman & McGuire, 1985). Part of the particular difficulty within psychiatry is the wide variability of treatment modality and treatment duration within a single diagnostic group. The insurer demands accountability for services given, and the clinician demands fair payment for tailored, good treatment. We speculate that a good nosology of context could add some correlative predictive power to Axes I and II disorders to assuage the needs of both groups. The clinician could be reimbursed appropriately for important psychosocial variables in outcome, enabling more flexibility in treatment for a particular disorder. The insurance company would receive more complete diagnostic and prognostic information, providing another check against unnecessary or inappropriately prolonged treatment.

Disadvantages of the Proposed Nosology of Context

Any substantial new addition to the existing American nosology will pose a new set of problems (Pincus, Frances, Davis, First & Widiger, 1992). Most obvious is the colossal amount of work in developing and circumscribing a nosology of context. Although there is substantial literature that discusses the clinical issues reflected in the sample contextual syndromes, even with this considerable knowledge and interest there will be little research that addresses directly the viability of these clinical issues as distinct nosological entities. The above-mentioned Blashfield criteria for including new diagnostic entities may be loosened in the same way that they would have been in the pre-DSM-III days; many accepted categories today might not have met the criteria then. It seems that some sort of commitment to a nosology of context would need to be made before studies are adequate, because without such a commitment there might not be sufficient interest or time to develop the empirical reliability and validity of such syndromes of context.

A second disadvantage is that a nosology of context could increase substantially the bulk of the diagnostic manual by adding an (unforeseen) number of new diagnostic categories. This is a critical problem as far as user friendliness goes (Pincus et al., 1992), but the complexity of nosology is probably an inevitability of growing psychiatric knowledge. The addition of a new set of contextual syndromes could decrease the utility of the classification, particularly by nonclinicians. We think this may be somewhat less of a problem than it appears. First of all, the basic premise underlying a nosology of context is one familiar to all clinicians: that environmental, interactional, and historical circumstances may influence the course and outcome of mental disorders. The nosology of context does not really add much complexity to actual practice because the complexity is one that clinicians are already routinely confronting. What the nosology of context *would* do is formalize the relevant environmental, interpersonal, and historical considerations. Adding to the actual bulk of the diagnostic manual may actually be less than expected. Indeed, DSM-III-R already devotes significant space to contextual factors under the guise of general description of disorders, associated features, predisposing factors, and complications. Various special interest groups have suggested new axes for their areas of interest; family therapists, for example, have suggested a nosology of *relational disorders* for a new axis (Frances, Clarkin & Perry, 1984; Wynne, 1987). Our own suggestions here for Axis IV may obviate such new axes while preserving the advantages of a family context in nosology.

The new use for Axis IV proposed here would also inherit similar problems shared by the current DSM-III-R and DSM-IV system (for details, see the rest of this book). For example, it will be as tempting for Axis IV to be as politicized as other axes regarding which categories are to be included or excluded. The new Axis IV would be equally as subject to the lobbying of special interest groups within and outside psychiatry as are the other axes. Practitioners of particular therapies would like to see included contextual data relevant to their skills and interests. Consensus would need to be made over nomenclature and criteria of accepted syndromes. We think there would be a role for philosophical conceptual analysis in resolving some of the debate over which contextual syndromes to include, as this analysis could help build syndromes based on shared metaphysical assumptions rather than theory-specific concepts. Philosophical analysis could also be useful in planning prospectively the set of values associated with the nosological categories. We speculate that the resultant generalized syndromes of context could reduce special interest debate by providing categories that could be used multi-theoretically rather than monotheoretically (or atheoretically) and by embracing a set of overt values which could be defended primarily rather than as an afterthought.

Some of the problems of politicization of psychiatric nosology are based on the mistaken assumption that truly scientific nosologies are value neutral (Kendler, 1990) (see also the chapters by Agich, Fulford, and Russell in this book). If a nosology is thought to be value neutral, the implied values reflected in the nosology will be unintended, yet the practical and political repercussions may be profound. Special interest groups who do not share the implied values of the nosology may then contest the nosology. An intended result of a multitheoretical Axis IV would be to reflect a greater pluralism of values in psychiatric diagnosis, rather than an accidental set of values arising out of a commitment to an atheoretical nosology.

Problems with diagnostic overlap from contextual syndrome to syndrome would emerge as well, as they have for DSM-III-R (Frances et al., 1991). A host of other, more standard nosological problems would also occur, such as lumping-versus-splitting issues, enhancing user friendliness, deciding which consumer group (e.g., psychiatrist, psychologist, psychotherapist, administrator, insurance executive), the manual should reach, and so on.

13 Psychiatry and Molecular Biology
Reductionistic Approaches to Schizophrenia
KENNETH F. SCHAFFNER, M.D., Ph.D.

A major feature of many psychiatric disorders found in DSM-III and DSM-III-R is their lack of any organic basis and etiology. DSM-III-R notes that "for most of the DSM-III-R disorders . . . the etiology is unknown" (American Psychiatric Association, 1987, p. xxiii). Further, reflecting the *a*theoretical stance of the volume with respect to etiology, schizophrenia is to be *ruled-out* if "an organic factor initiated and maintained the disturbance" (p. 195). This is a reasonable position if its intent is to exclude similar appearing but quite distinct disorders such as amphetamine intoxication. In the past few years, however, a number of researchers have begun important investigations into molecular aspects of the functional psychoses, including schizophrenia and bipolar affective disorder. These inquiries, in the case of schizophrenia, include both the elaboration of complex reductionistic models of the disorder(s) as well as attempts to determine genetic markers. Neurobiological models of schizophrenia developed by Swerdlow and Koob (1987) and by Grace (1991) can be construed as complex developments of the popular but often criticized dopamine hypothesis of schizophrenia. These neurobiological models can supplement molecular genetic studies that attempt to identify the gene (or more likely genes) that are partially causative of the disorder (Bassett, Jones, McGillvaray & Pantzar, 1988; Owen & Mullan, 1990; Sherrington et al., 1988; see also Harris & Schaffner, 1992). Both neurobiological models and genetic linkage analyses can also synergistically intercalate with an emerging ontogenetic approach to schizophrenia (Roberts, 1990; Weinberger, 1987) and potentially provide cellular and biochemical markers for the disorder, leading to improvements in diagnosis. In the light of such developments, more attention needs to be given to the possibility of important organic etiological features in disorders such as schizophrenia. However, molecular approaches to mental disorders such as schizophrenia are quite complex and partial——complications that I believe will require a careful philosophical analysis to provide an understanding of ongoing scientific advances in this area.

I will begin by defending a view of a *mental disorder* as a family of overlapping prototypical multilevel models. This defense is based on some of my previous work on the role of theory in biology and medicine (Schaffner, 1986). This prototype approach is consistent with Bleuler's classic description of schizophrenia, as well as with emerging indications of an underlying genetic heterogeneity of schizophrenia(s). In addition, the prototype approach to mental disorders has recently been argued for and undergone a test implementation in the work of Mezzich and has been commented on approvingly by Frances, Pincus, Widiger, Davis, and First (1990). Second, I will investigate this view of a psychiatric disorder for its implications for reductionistic (and molecular biological) methodology. This part of the chapter requires the development of an account of what it means for a disorder to be reduced (or to be in the *process* of reduction) to a molecularly associated/definable entity or entities (Schaffner, 1993). Finally, I will consider briefly the ramifications that this analysis has for more precise disorder definition(s), etiology, diagnosis, and therapy, as well as some implications for DSM-IV (and for later DSMs).

DISORDERS AS OVERLAPPING MODELS

Mental disorders are what are classified in DSM-III and DSM-III-R, yet the introduction to DSM-III-R admits that "no definition adequately specifies precise boundaries for the concept 'mental disorder'" (American Psychiatric Association, 1987, p. xxii). Although it is also noted that this imprecision is true of physical disorders as well, DSM-III-R does indicate that there is a working definition of sorts for the notion. Briefly,

> each of the mental disorders is conceptualized as a clinically significant behavioral or psychological syndrome or pattern that occurs in a person and that is associated with present distress (a painful symptom) or disability (impairment in one or more important areas of functioning) or with a significantly increased risk of suffering death, pain, disability, or an important loss of freedom. In addition, this syndrome or pattern must not be merely an expectable response to a particular event, e.g., the death of a loved one. Whatever its original cause, it must currently be considered a manifestation of a behavioral, psychological, or biological dysfunction in the person. (American Psychiatric Association, 1987, p. xxii)

This characterization is unfortunately all too general, and Allen Frances and colleagues (1990) wrote,

> A definition establishing precisely what a mental disorder is would have important impact on clinical practice, forensic proceedings, and decisions about which of the

conditions on the border between normality and pathology should be included in DSM-IV. Unfortunately, no previous definition of illness, disease or disorder has ever been particularly successful, and we have no illusions that we can provide a better solution. It seems unlikely that any explicit set of criteria for defining mental disorder will cover all cases or settle boundary questions. (Frances et al., 1990, p. 1442)

Frances and colleagues added later in this paper, in connection with the issue of class homogeneity of a disorder, one that is closely related to the boundary question, that a "prototypic categorization," might be useful. A prototypic approach to mental disorders, in contrast to a classic categorical approach, is more tolerant of heterogeneity and might lead to the use of DSM-IV which would be "less likely to reify categories and more likely to respect boundary cases rather than trying to force them into one or another category" (1990, p. 16). They called for further work on this approach, citing some recent work by Mezzich (1989) on prototypes in psychiatric diagnosis and research. Mezzich (1989) proposed that a prototypical approach to the definition of psychiatric illness had important advantages over alternative approaches, and he implemented such a prototypical analysis using the symptomological and functioning profiles of some 5,573 patients in the University of Pittsburgh Psychiatric Institute clinical data base. Mezzich also outlined the steps that should be taken to develop in more detail a prototypical approach to psychiatric illness.

These suggestions about the difficulties of providing any classically sharp definitions of mental disorders as well as the proposal for conceiving of mental disorders as prototypes are important. They fit some of my attempts to develop an alternative concept of scientific theory more suitable for the biological and medical sciences (Schaffner, 1980, 1986). This alternative approach to the notion of a scientific theory has, I will argue, important implications for molecular biological explanations of psychiatric disorders and will be the main theme of this chapter. To develop this theme adequately, however, I must first say a few words about the nature of scientific theories at a fairly general level.

In my view, most but not all theories in the biomedical sciences are best construed as a *series of overlapping interlevel causal models*. In a moment I will define those terms and give several examples to clarify my claim. I distinguish this approach from the more traditional construal of theory structure that is largely patterned on theory structure in the physical sciences. Theory structure in the physical sciences illustrates what might be termed the *Euclidean Ideal*—a deductive systematization of a broad class of generalizations under a small number of axioms. The physical sciences such as Newtonian mechanics and Maxwell's theory of electromagnetism lend themselves to this characterization of their structure. Some biologists and philosophers of biology have maintained that the laws and theories of biology have exactly the same logical structure as do those of the physical sciences, but this view is supportable only if one restricts one's attention to those few——but very important——theories in biology which have a very broad scope and are characterizable in their more simplified forms as a set of "laws" subject to axiomatization and deductive elaboration. Certain forms of Mendelian genetics and of simplified population genetics satisfy this characterization, but deeper analysis of even these theories will disclose difficulties with a strong methodological parallelism with the physical sciences. (The issue of parallel methodologies in the biomedical and the physical sciences is a large and complex topic that cannot be pursued in the present essay; for an introduction see Kitcher, 1984, and Schaffner, 1980; for a more systematic discussion see Schaffner, 1992.) A close examination of a wide variety of other biological theories in immunology, physiology, embryology, and the neurosciences will suggest a structure of overlapping interlevel causal models.

The models of such a structure bear family or similarity resemblances to each other, and characteristically each has a (relatively) narrow scope of straightforward application to a (few) pure types. Examples from the molecular biology of gene regulation and from the molecular neurosciences illustrate this. For example, beginning students in biology learn how genes are turned on and turned off by being taught about what is called the *lac* operon found in the simple intestinal bacterium *Escherichia coli*. Similarly, beginning neuroscience students are presented with the neural network and biochemical mechanisms found in the sea snail *Aplysia californica*, which explain simple learning, including habituation, sensitization, and classical conditioning (see Kandel & Schwartz, 1985, chap. 62). Biologists have discovered that there is a large number of different types of operon mechanisms, each bearing analogies to one another: some use positive control, some use what is termed attenuation, and some have both negative and positive controls. The picture that results led the author of one major biology textbook to speak of "a panoply of operons" (Lewin, 1990). In the neurosciences, the simple account given by Kandel and his associates concerning sensitization in *Aplysia* has in the past few years grown in complexity to reflect varying interacting mechanisms (see Frost, Clark & Kandel, 1988). Alkon (1989) found similar but not identical mechanisms in *Hermissenda*. It is these features of panoply and analogy in biological theories which represent the *overlapping* aspect I mentioned above: *the models share some assumptions but differ on others*. Philosophers may recall Wittgenstein's (1958) discussion of the concept of a game in connection with this issue.

I have already discussed that these models display subtle variations that, in the context of articulating high level comprehensive generalizations, frequently lose substantive empirical content. In addition, biological and medical models are typically *inter*level in the sense of levels of aggregation. This latter refers to these models containing component parts that intermingle behavioral, organ, cellular, and biochemical/molecular terms. Again to refer to recent work in neuroscience on *Aplysia* by Jung and Schellar (1991), a typical diagram that describes a neuroscience mechanism shows several different levels of aggregation. As an instance of this, compare Figure 5 in Jung and Schellar (1991, p. 1334), which intermingles, in the same figure, organs (the abdominal ganglion), cells (the bag cells), and molecules (the egg laying hormone).

It must be stressed that considerably more variation is actually encountered in *real* organisms because of mutations and genetic variability; thus what I have been discussing are really *highly selected idealizations or, more accurately, prototypes*. I have argued at length elsewhere (Schaffner, 1980) that this type of theory involving interlevel prototypes and causal sequences, which I termed a *theory of the middle range* (with apologies to Robert K. Merton, who first used that term in a somewhat different context), both is found and should predominate in the biomedical sciences. Because the type of theory is wide-spread in the biomedical sciences (for evidence see Schaffner, 1980), one is then likely to require *more* of the type of reasoning found in exemplar modeling than is necessary in the (simple forms of) the physical sciences.

The thesis advanced above, that exemplar or prototype thinking is more significant in the biomedical sciences than in the physical sciences, receives further confirmation in the more *clinical* sciences, including psychiatry. In the clinic, the focus is the individual patient, and generalizations such as *diseases* or *disorders* are utilized to assist in prevention, prognosis, and therapy. The individual patient is the *clinical exemplar* of an (often multiple) disease or pathological process. Clinicians bring to the examination of individual patients a repository of classificatory or nosological generalizations, as well as a grounding in the basic sciences of biochemistry, histology, physiology, and the pathological variants of the "normal" or "healthy" processes. A theory in pathology—and this will include psychopathology as well—can be construed as a family of models, each with "something wrong" with the normal or healthy process. In those cases in which the underlying *genetics* is known, such variations can be specified as families of mutants, typically producing aberrant proteins (or perhaps in the case of some deletion mutants, no proteins). Such a set of overlapping or "smeared out" models is then juxtaposed, often in a fairly loose way, with an overlapping or smeared out set of patient exemplars. This dual "smearedness"—one being in the basic biological models and the other in the patient population—typically requires that the clinician work extensively with analogical reasoning and with qualitative and at best *comparative* connecting pathophysiological principles. Thus one can find fairly frequently in textbooks of medicine as well as neuroscience, generalizations that trace causal connections through a complex system, in which a decrease in quantity A will produce an increase in quantity B, which will in turn produce a decrease in quantity C, and so on. This is a *grosser* way of articulating a generalization than, say, $f = ma$ in Newtonian physics, but it is one that is required to outflank or perhaps better to express the variation. These comparative causal generalizations are *just* the type that one finds in recent reductionistic theories of schizophrenia, as I shall illustrate in a moment.

I want to suggest that it is these loosely formulated pathophysiological principles that often constitute the *biomedical forms* of the "symbolic generalizations" described by Kuhn and other philosophers of science when they talked about the constituent parts of theories. These generalizations articulate the shared similarities or *positive analogy* in a population and sometimes across a variety of organisms. Often, however, because of variation, even the grosser comparative generalizations will have to be changed to analogous generalizations. Biological research as well as clinical problem solving, will require, if the view being developed in this chapter is correct, *close experience with specific exemplars and analogical modeling of similar exemplars with the aid of the interlevel symbolic generalizations, utilizing largely qualitative and comparative reasoning of the type discussed.* This is in contrast to the more precise mathematical models, unilevel description, and explicit quantitative reasoning widespread in the physical sciences. Such generalizations are, in spite of these differences, well suited to provide explanations in the biomedical sciences.

SCHIZOPHRENIA AS A POSSIBLE PARADIGM OF A REDUCIBLE MENTAL DISORDER

I now want to turn to some general issues associated with the molecular explanation of a specific mental disorder, schizophrenia. In this section of the chapter I shall confine myself to a brief overview of two recent accounts that provide the beginnings of such a reductionistic approach. I will then comment in more detail about the nature of such reductionistic methodologies and how they relate to the view of theory structure and the prototype approach to mental disorders discussed above.

Two Neuroscience Models of Schizophrenia

There have been a number of largely speculative attempts to propound a theory of brain activity at the chemical level which might account for the behavior and cognitive aspects of schizophrenia. One very general theory that received considerable attention in the journal *Behavioral and Brain Sciences* in 1987, and also subsequently, was proposed by Swerdlow and Koob in a target article entitled "Dopamine, Schizophrenia, Mania, and Depression: Toward a Unified Hypothesis of Cortico-Striato-Pallido-Thalamic Function." The title gives the gist of the approach, namely a variant of the dopamine hypothesis for mental illness, but now embedded in a complex series of brain circuits. In the words of one of its published critics, Wu, it used the "burgeoning advances in the delineation of neuroanatomic connection" (Wu,

Siegel, Haier & Buchsbaum, 1990, p. 169). More specifically, the Swerdlow-Koob (1987) model proposed that

> overactivity in forebrain [dopamine] systems results in the loss of lateral inhibitory interactions in the nucleus accumbens, causing disinhibition of palladothalamic efferents; this in turn causes rapid changes and a loss of focused corticothalamic activity in cortical regions controlling cognitive and emotional processes. These effects might be manifested clinically by some symptoms of psychoses . . . This model parallels existing explanations for the etiology of several movement disorders . . . , though probably [mental disorders are] several orders of magnitude of increased complexity . . . [beyond] movement disorders. (pp. 197–198)

This approach is not too dissimilar from other variants of the dopamine hypothesis. Because of certain well-confirmed findings in schizophrenics concerning the levels of dopamine as well as the numbers of dopamine receptors in these patients' brains as determined by autopsy, more complex forms of the dopamine hypothesis seem to be required. One interesting recent theory has been developed at Pittsburgh by Grace (1991), who proposed that there are two independently regulated dopamine releasing processes in the striatum:

1.   Environmental stimuli ↑ → phasic dopamine ↑ (rapidly removed by reuptake system).
2.   Prefrontal afferents ↑ → glutamate ↑ → tonic dopamine release ↑ (this yields the extracellular baseline level of dopamine).

Increases in this background amount would cause processes that would functionally oppose the first type of dopamine release response.

More specifically, Grace described his hypothesis as follows:

> In the schizophrenic, a pathological decrease in prefrontal cortical activity is proposed to cause a prolonged decrease in tonic extracellular DA [(dopamine)] levels within the ventral regions of the striatum and nucleus accumbens (hereafter referred to as the ventral striatum). The resultant decrease in baseline DA receptor stimulation would then activate homeostatic processes to up-regulate DA system responsivity. The compensatory processes activated in response to decreased tonic DA levels should be analogous to those produced by lesion-induced decreases in DA levels (i.e., decreased autoreceptor-mediated inhibition of DA synthesis and release, increased tyrosine hydroxylase activity, increased numbers of postsynaptic DA receptors, etc.). Thus, in the schizophrenic, behaviorally relevant stimuli that activate DA neuron firing would produce abnormally large phasic DA responses in the compensated ventral striatum. On this basis, the induction of DA system up-regulation leading to the increased phasic DA response in the schizophrenic thus could account for what otherwise would be a paradoxical finding: i.e., the increased levels of D_2 DA receptors in the ventral striatum of schizophrenics (which should occur with decreases in DA levels) despite pharmacological evidence for a hyper-

dopaminergic state in this disorder. Another attractive feature of this model is that the proposed DA imbalance would not be counteracted by the powerful homeostatic mechanisms that restore function in severely altered DA systems; in fact, in this model the homeostatic processes as they relate to maintaining extracellular DA levels are responsible for the induction of this hyper-responsive state. (p. 4)

Although there are additional details to be found in both the Swerdlow-Koob and the Grace models of schizophrenia, as well as extensive evidence that both papers cited in favor of their accounts, the currently formulated level of detail of proposed mechanisms is in stark contrast to that detail available in simpler organisms such as *Aplysia*. Thus, current theories of schizophrenia formulated at the molecular level are perhaps better characterized as molecular model *sketches* rather than as molecular models in any full sense of the term. The contrast with such systems as those proposed to account for simple learning or more complex behaviors such as egg laying in *Aplysia* becomes evident in a review of articles published by the research teams of Kandel and Schwartz, or the recent paper by Jung and Schellar (1991). The reader is encouraged to consult the latter article for an indication of the degree of detail which is needed to provide a molecular account of a comparatively simple form of behavior and which may someday be available, with vastly more complexity, to characterize the molecular mechanisms underlying schizophrenia. Suffice it to mention here that Jung and Schellar presented specific information concerning the genetic sequences and peptide sequences of the egg laying hormone as well as the stages of the processing of this hormone and its sorting and trafficking in the secretory pathway. In current "molecular" theories of schizophrenia, none of this wealth of detail is yet available.

REDUCTION: GENETIC AND ENVIRONMENTAL COMPONENTS

Thus far in this chapter I have been describing reductionistic accounts of schizophrenia. It is important to stress that a complete reduction of such a psychiatric disease as schizophrenia would *not* only be a reduction to molecular *genetics*. It is crucial to emphasize this point, since several authors have implied that a molecular explanation of, say, schizophrenia, would rely principally on molecular genetics. Compare, for example, Pardes, Kaufmann, Pincus, and West (1989), who wrote that "Psychiatry is being transformed by genetic research. In particular, molecular genetic strategies are expected to reveal much about the etiology and pathogenesis of mental illness" (p. 435). In a similar vein, Mullan and Murray (1989) concluded their review as follows:

It seems that we are about to move into a period when genetics will define disease entities in psychiatry. . . . It is likely that, once the gene is identified, sequenced and its protein characterized, even for a very uncommon variant, this will tell us a very great deal about the pathogenesis of the more common varieties, for it seems likely that more common causes will act through similar pathogenetic mechanisms. (p. 594)

Finally Roberts (1990), in his account of the cellular basis of schizophrenia, stated,

> The span of a decade has seen a spectacular paradigm shift from believing that schizophrenia had no organic basis to localizing the brain regions involved (medial temporal lobe) and uncovering the main aetiological factor responsible for the structural changes (aberrant brain development). The 1990s should see the final unveiling of the precise disorder in the mechanisms regulating brain development that results in schizophrenia. This knowledge will give us the *identity of the genes responsible* and thus pave the way for genetic screening, more effective therapy, and ultimately a cure. (p. 211; emphasis added)[1]

There is a consensus that strong psychiatric epidemiological evidence exists supporting a genetic *component* in the case of schizophrenia (see Pardes et al., 1989). However, as Reiss, Plomin, and Hetherington (1991) cautioned us, this genetic evidence also supports a critical *environmental* causal component for such diseases. Commenting on the articles by Pardes et al. (1989) and Mullan and Murray (1989), these authors wrote,

> Neither review recognized that the latest data in behavioral genetics support environmental causes for abnormal development and psychopathology as much as they support genetic causes. Moreover, these genetic data point clearly to a type of environmental cause with central importance: the environment that is specific or unique to each sibling in a family. (Abstract, p. 283)

Although it will not be possible to elaborate on Reiss and his co-workers' research on nonshared environmental effects in connection with psychiatric disease etiology, it should be noted that if a *completely* molecular explanation of schizophrenia is to be provided, these *environmental* causes will have to be specified in molecular terms. This point underscores again the formidable task confronting the proponents of reductionistic methodology if it be conceived of as a purely molecular (i.e., unilevel) explanation. It is difficult to identify and measure environmental variables precisely even at higher levels of aggregation, and to do so in purely molecular terms would be a very long-term project. Thus attending to the environmental as well as genetic causes of psychiatric diseases adds support to the thesis defended in the present paper: that for the foreseeable future even reductionistic approaches to psychiatric disease will of necessity be of a highly interlevel character.

I now turn to a brief discussion of reduction from a more systematic (and philosophical) point of view.

APPROACHES TO REDUCTION

Different Senses of Reduction

For biomedical scientists, the term *reduction* often suggests that biological entities are "nothing but" aggregates of physicochemical entities. This sense of reduction can be termed *ontological reductionism*. A closely related but more *methodological* position is that sound scientific generalizations are available only at the level of physics and chemistry. This methodological position can and has motivated a number of research programs in biophysics, biochemistry, and molecular biology. There are contrary antireduction positions that have been formulated on both ontological and methodological fronts.

For *philosophers*, reduction has for the past 40 or more years largely been conceived of as *intertheoretical* reduction, in which the assertions of the reduced theory are derived from the reducing theory. The *locus classicus* of philosophical analyses of theory reduction can be found in the work of Ernest Nagel (1949, 1961). Nagel envisaged reduction as a relation between *theories* in science and also assimilated it to a generalization of the classic Hempel deductive nomological model of explanation. A theory in biology, classic genetics, for example, was reducible to a theory in chemistry, such as molecular biology, if and only if (a) all of the scientific terms appearing in the biological theory were *connectable* with those in the chemical theory—that is, the gene had to be connected with DNA, and (b) with the aid of these *connectability* assumptions, the biological theory could be *derived* from the chemical theory.

It has been realized for some time now that such an approach is idealized and oversimplified, and an extensive literature has developed in the philosophy of science criticizing the Nagel model and its successors. In the present chapter I will not be able to cite any of this literature, nor even present and discuss what I think is the most viable general model for reduction. I will, however, draw on that literature as a background and offer some suggestions that I think comport with what has been said earlier about definitions of mental disorders and theories in science and discuss what the implications are likely to be for research and model building at the interface of psychiatry and the molecular neurosciences.

Unilevel versus Multilevel Reductions Involving a Prototypical Approach to Theories

The Nagel model as characterized above is a useful means of describing the relations between two branches of science, each of which involves simple unilevel theories of broad scope and in which the details of the connections have been fully worked out. Something like this occurred in physics toward the end of the 19th-century when Maxwell's theory of electromagnetism reduced phys-

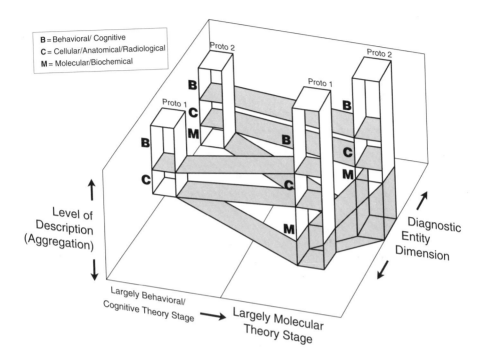

Figure 13.1 Partial Reductions of Two Prototypical Mental Disorders as Psychiatry Advances Toward a Largely Molecular Stage of Development (see text for details of the relations)

ical optics. Even here, however, there were incomplete aspects to the reduction, but that is another story. What concerns us today is what happens in science when we have two rather contrary conditions holding: (a) when the theories are better conceived of as overlapping collections of prototypical models related by similarity, and in which (b) those models are themselves largely interlevel.

In such circumstances what one will find, and will continue to find in psychiatry until well into the next century, will be only partial and very complex connections between *primarily* behavioral generalizations characterizing mental disorders and *primarily* biochemical mechanisms and their laws of working. Because of this partial character of the reduction, more traditional forms of reduction models and their successors, such as was given by Nagel (1961) and others (see Schaffner, 1997, 1993) do not fit psychiatry very easily. (See the Addendum to this chapter for a more formal account of what I term the *general reduction-replacement model* of reduction and also a discussion of its strengths and weaknesses.) The relationship that will almost certainly hold for the foreseeable future regarding psychiatric disorder reduction to "molecular" mechanisms is illustrated in Figure 13.1, but I caution the reader that it is quite schematic and considerably oversimplified.

What we see on the *left* of Figure 13.1 are two representative largely behavioral/cognitive prototypes, which have some cellular/anatomical correlates, such as increased ventricle size in schizophrenia, and possibly some fragmentary molecular features—an increased number of dopamine receptors in postmortem inspections of schizophrenic brains, for example. These "towers" represent coordinated generalizations involving intertwined levels of description (aggregation) with B representing a behavioral/cognitive level, C employing cellular/anatomical/radiological language, and M the molecular/biochemical phraseology. The C level may partially explain the B level, and the M level may partially explain the two levels above it. The two prototypes might represent two types of schizophrenia which share similar features (however, the overlap is not depicted except partially at the M level) but which are not identical, such as paranoid and catatonic types. In a reduction I assume for simplicity that each will be *largely* but not completely explained by molecular mechanisms. Behavioral (including cognitive) characteristics[2] will for the foreseeable future remain as part of the descriptions of these diseases; thus in the two prototypes depicted on the *right*, the B or behavioral/cognitive component and C or cellular/anatomical/radiological component are *retained*, but are based on and explained in a partial sense by underlying and partially common molecular mechanisms and biochemical generalizations. There is no guarantee that there will not be a reshuffling and reclassification among prototypes as a result of the molecular explanations, but I have not tried to depict such a reclassification here. In a related vein, some genetic analyses of schizophrenia suggest that if we are more inclusive, combining, for example, Schizoid Personality Disorder with classic Schizophrenia, the genetic explanation will be more adequate (at least in the sense of increased log of observed difference scores).

IMPLICATIONS FOR DSM-IV

What the above account suggests for DSM-IV is largely preliminary: a caveat that the DSM-III-R exclusion of organic etiology for schizophrenia may have to be modified to permit the use of possible anatomical, cellular, and molecular markers. I envision the influence of such organic components as being more significant in DSM-V and DSM-VI as our knowledge of the cellular basis and anatomical circuitry, as well as molecular mechanisms on both genetic and environmental fronts, grows. Such expansion of these organic elements is likely to bring increased diagnostic reliability as well as increased capacities for pharmacological interventions. Such advances will however not be easy to accomplish, and they may well not provide a simplicity and unification, except of a rather convoluted type, given the continued diversity likely to be encountered in the spectrum of prototypes which constitutes human behavior, both in its normal and pathological variants.

ADDENDUM

The literature on intertheoretical reduction is extensive and complex. Most writers working on reduction have dealt with the more syntactic requirements of Nagel connectability and derivability. The *derivability* condition (as well as the connectability requirement) were strongly attacked in influential criticisms by Popper (1957), Feyerabend (1962), and Kuhn (1962). In my 1967 essay, I elaborated a modified reduction model designed to preserve the strengths of the Nagel account but flexible enough to accommodate the criticisms of Popper, Feyerabend, and Kuhn. That model, which I termed the *general reduction paradigm*, has been extensively criticized as well as defended (for a discussion and references see Schaffner, 1993). In a form close to that of the original general reduction model, such an approach was applied in the area of neurobiology by Patricia Churchland (1986). Churchland's account is one of the most concise statements of that general model; it goes as follows:

> Within the new, reducing theory T_B, construct *an analogue* T_{R^*} of the laws, etc., of the theory that is to be reduced, T_R. The analogue T_{R^*} can then be logically deduced from the reducing theory T_B plus sentences specifying the special conditions (e.g., frictionless surfaces, perfect elasticity). Generally the analogue will be constructed with a view to mapping expressions of the old theory onto expressions of the new theory, laws of the old theory onto sentences (but not necessarily *laws*) of the new. Under these conditions the old theory reduces to the new. When reduction is successfully achieved, the new theory will explain the old theory, it will explain why the old theory worked as well as it did, and it will explain much where the old theory was buffaloed. (pp. 282–283)

Churchland proceeded to apply this notion of reduction to the sciences of psychology (and also what is termed *folk psychology*), which are the sciences *to be reduced*, and to the rapidly evolving neurosciences, which are the *reducing sciences*. In so doing she found that she needed to relax the model even further, to accommodate, for example, cases not of reduction but of replacement, and of partial reduction. She never explicitly reformulated the model to take such modifications into account, however, and it would seem useful, given the importance of such modifications, to say a bit more as to how this might be accomplished.

Some features of this type of modification can be found in what I have termed the *general reduction-replacement model* (or GRR model; Table 13.1) (see Schaffner, 1977, 1991, and 1993, chap. 9). The GRR model allows for

Table 13.1 General Reduction-Replacement (GRR) Model

T_B, reducing theory/model
T_B*, corrected reducing theory/model
T_R, original reduced theory/model
T_R*, corrected reduced theory/model

Reduction in the most general sense occurs if and only if

1a.   All primitive terms of T_R* are associated with one or more of the terms of $T_B(*)$ such that
    i. T_R* (entities) = function [$T_B(*)$ (entities)]
    ii. $T_R(*)$ (predicates) = function [$T_B(*)$ (predicates)][a]

1b.   The domain of T_R* is connectable with $T_B(*)$ via new correspondence rules (condition of generalized connectability)

2a.   Given fulfillment of condition 1a, T_R* is derivable from $T_B(*)$ supplemented with 1a.i. and 1a.ii. functions

or

2b.   Given fulfillment of condition 1b. the domain of T_R is derivable from $T_B(*)$ supplemented with the new correspondence rules (condition of generalized derivability)

3.   In case 1a. and 2a. are met, T_R* corrects T_R; that is, T_R* makes more accurate predictions. In case 1b. and 2b. are met, it may be the case that T_B* makes more accurate predictions in T_R's domain than did T_R

4a. T_R is explained by $T_B(*)$ in that T_R and T_R* are strongly analogous, and $T_B(*)$ indicates why T_R worked as well as it did historically

or

4b. T_R's domain is explained by $T_B(*)$ even when T_R is replaced

[a]The distinction between entities and predicates will in general be clear in any given theory/model, although from a strictly extensional point of view the distinction collapses.

those cases in which the T_R is not modifiable into a T_R* but rather is *re-placed*—but with preservation of the empirical domain—by T_B or a T_B* (where T_B* refers to a close analogue of the *reducing* theory). Replacement of a demonic theory of disease by a germ theory of disease, but with reten-tion, say, of the detailed observations of the natural history of the diseases and perhaps pre-existing syndrome clusters as well, is an example of reduction with replacement.

In the more complex but quite realistic case, we also want to allow for par-tial reduction; that is, the possibility of a partially adequate component of the *theory* T_R being maintained together with the entire *domain* (or even only part of the domain) of T_R. (The sense we give to *domain* here is akin to of Shapere (1974): a domain is a complex of experimental results that either are account-ed for by T_R and/or *should be* accounted for by T_R when (and if) T_R is or be-comes completely and adequately developed.) Thus, there arises the possibility of a continuum of reduction relations in which T_B (or T_B*) can participate. (In those cases where only one of T_B or T_B* is the reducing theory, we shall use the expression $T_B(*)$.) To allow for such a continuum, T_R must be construed not only as a completely integral theory but also as a theory dissociable into weaker versions of the theory and also associated with an experimental subject area(s) or domain(s). Under these assumptions the general reduction model introduced above can be modified into the GRR model characterized by the conditions given in Table 13.2. These conditions are of necessity formulated in somewhat technical language, but the concepts involved should be reasonably clear from the discussion thus far. (The italicized *or*s in the table should be taken in the weak, inclusive sense of *or*.)

The GRR model has the general reduction model as a limiting case, which in turn yields Nagel's model as a special case. The use of the weak sense of *or* in conditions 1, 2, and 4 allows the continuum ranging from reduction as subsumption to reduction as explanation of the experimental domain of the replaced theory. Although in this latter case we do not have intertheoretical reduction, we do maintain something like the branch reduction of Kemeny and Oppenheim (1956). This flexibility of the GRR model may turn out to be particularly useful in connection with discussions concerning current theories that may explain "mental" phenomena if eliminative materialism is the most plausible approach. As intricate as this GRR model is, however, when confronted with the realities of evolving sciences in which reductions are patchy and incomplete, the GRR model given in the table is in fact a simple interpretation of reduction; a more complex GRR account is also constructable and in certain cases will be more desirable. Details of the complex GRR model cannot be presented here (for this material see Schaffner, 1993, chap. 9).

I think that much of the formal complexity that appears as part of the simple and complex forms of the GRR model is bypassed in practice by scientists by their working with what Salmon (1984, 1989) termed *causal/mechanical* (or CM) explanations of a phenomenon on one level of aggregation by mechanisms formulated at a deeper level. Thus I believe that there exists a CM form of reduction which is more appropriate for patchy forms of reductions, but also which hides the true complexity of such reductions. In addition, I think that CM reduction occludes important deep structural issues, such as the scope of the explaining generalizations as well as the specific points at which *identities* need to be formulated between levels. What I have termed *CM reduction* has interesting analogies to Kitcher's (1984, 1989) idea of an explanatory extension and to Culp and Kitcher's (1989) embedding approach, although these authors would probably disagree with the strong causal character I have attributed to CM reduction and in point of fact suggest that we replace any talk of reduction with discourse about explanatory extensions and embeddings.

In Table 13.2 I list those cases in which different approaches are the most natural and why. The table is based on the fact that reductions in science frequently have two aspects: (a) ongoing advances that occur in *piecemeal* ways—that is, some features of a model are further elaborated at the molecular level or perhaps a new mechanism is added to the model—and (b) assessments of the explanatory fit between two theories (viewed here as a collection

Table 13.2 A Comparison of Intertheoretic Reduction Using the Causal/Mechanical (CM) and the General Reduction-Replacement (GRR) Models

	Approach	
State of Completion	*CM*	*GRR*
Partial/patchy/ fragmentary/interlevel	In these cases, the CM approach is usually employed; interlevel causal language is more natural than GRR connections	When reductions are patchy and interlevel, the connections are bushy and complex when presented formally, but GRR does identify points of identity as well as the generalizations operative in mechanisms
Clarified science[a]/ essentially unilevel at both levels of aggregation	Either approach could be used here, but where theories are collections of prototypes, the axiomatization/explicit generalization bias built into the GRR approach will be less simple than CM	Best match between Nagel—type reduction at and scientific practice

[a]*Clarified science* is Putnam's term and was employed by Hooker (1981) in a discussion of reduction.

of models) or even two *branches* of science. Under aspect (a), as scientists further develop reducing theories in a domain, they frequently elaborate various parts of the theories both by modifying a molecular assumption or proposing a molecular level assumption that accounts for (part of) a higher level, for example, a cellular process; and also by describing these new assumptions in *causal* terms. Thus, the results of such advances are typically complex inter-level connections with causal processes appealed to as part of the connections. (Part-whole or constituent relationships may also be appealed to in such situations.) These various theoretical developments and attendant connections—bushy and weblike though they may be—frequently have the ability to "explain" at least partially some features of a higher level domain, for example, a phenomenon such as sensitization in *Aplysia* or self-tolerance in vertebrate immunology. Such explanations are, I think, best seen as partial reductions with a strong causal character, whence my preference for terming them *CM* (recall this stands for causal/mechanical) reductions. (Additional details regarding these two general approaches can be found in Schaffner, 1993, chap. 9.)

Portions of this chapter grew out of discussions with Herbert Harris, M.D., Ph.D., during his senior elective at the University of Pittsburgh School of Medicine. That elective was arranged by the Clinical Ethics Training Program, supported in part by the Vira I. Heinz Endowment. In addition, I thank Drs. George Agich, Juan Mezzich, and John Sadler for their helpful comments on an earlier draft.

14 Pragmatic Assessment and Multitheoretical Classification

Addictive Disorder as a Case Example

AVIEL GOODMAN, M.D.

A system for classification of psychiatric diagnoses serves a number of functions, the most clinically important of which is assisting in the prediction of the natural course of patients' disorders and of their responses to available treatments. (Another important function, facilitating communication, is more directly relevant to research than to clinical practice.) DSM-III and its successor DSM-III-R were developed within a pragmatic framework that provided for an ever-improving classification system, sensitive to advances in research and clinical experience. With the objective of facilitating this process, the architects of the DSMs attempted to formulate an atheoretical classification system in descriptive terms that have no relation to theories of etiology or treatment. Their intention was to create a classificatory instrument that would accommodate and be acceptable to all of its users and which could be assessed and refined according to pragmatic criteria without contamination by advocacy for particular theoretical ideologies.

Modern developments in psychology and philosophy, however, weigh heavily against the possibility that an atheoretical classification system could be formulated. Atheoretical classification presupposes pure perception uninfluenced by thought, raw facts free of interpretation, and an atheoretical observation language—which, we realize, do not exist. There is no perceptual experience that does not involve cognitive processing directed by underlying assumptions, no fact that is not constituted by theory-guided interpretation of sensory stimuli, and no observational language that can describe experience without involving some theoretical background, whether explicit or implicit.

A broad range of psychological studies has demonstrated that cognitive sets, expectancies, frames of reference, preverbal generalizations, and implicit organizing principles significantly influence perception and conceptualization

(Gibson, 1969; Hochberg, 1964; Neisser, 1967; Piaget, 1954; Sherif & Cantril, 1947). Physiological as well as cognitive research has revealed that perception is an active process in which the perceiver interacts with stimuli to create perceptual experience. Much neural processing occurs between the stimulation of exteroceptive cells and awareness of sensation, which is correlated with activity in association areas of the cerebral cortex as well as in primary sensory areas (Barr, 1974; Thompson, 1967).

From the philosophical side, philosophers of science have presented a number of arguments against the existence in any scientific discipline of atheoretical facts or language. Consistent with the psychological studies, they conclude that observation is "theory laden" and is an active process in which theoretical background directs the observer to anticipate, interpret, and structure in advance what is to be seen (Dretske, 1969; Hanson, 1958; Lewis, 1929; Scheffler, 1967). Facts result only as interpretations of sense data, and every scientific observation presupposes a conceptual framework or set of categories which determines a number of critical scientific assumptions. These include: (a) the criteria of reality, of what qualifies as veridical experience; (b) which stimuli are abstracted from the total complexity of the stimulus field to become sense data; (c) in what factual categories these complex events will be classified; (d) which features of these events are relevant as evidence for or against the hypothesis under consideration; and (e) what conditions and measurement procedures are required for observing relevant phenomena, including instrumentation, methodology, testing situations, and control procedures (Faust, 1984; Hesse, 1974, 1980; Kuhn, 1962; Lewis, 1929; Longino, 1990; Turner, 1967).

The meaning of the language used in describing observations is also influenced by theory and associated background assumptions, and it changes when theory changes and incorporates old observational terms within a new framework of assumptions and meanings (Feyerabend, 1981a; Hanson, 1958; Harré, 1972; Kuhn, 1962; Scheffler, 1967). Some philosophers of science have claimed that observation statements are more accurately described as hypotheses than as representations of facts, since they assume (but do not guarantee) agreement with particular stimulus conditions or instrument readings (Schlick, 1959), which in turn are assumed to correlate reliably with particular situations (Feyerabend, 1981b). Furthermore, these assumptions depend on lawfulness in experience and nature, which is itself a theoretical or mind-dependent construct (Rescher, 1969/1970). A larger group agrees that there is no fixed, a priori, logical or ontological distinction between observational and theoretical languages; they belong to a unified network of linguistic/conceptual structures, and no statement is immune from correction when such correction is required to preserve the unity of the network. The distinction between observational and theoretical is continuous and diffuse, depends on theory or theoretical assumptions, varies with changing context as well as with theoretical development, and is ultimately determined by pragmatic considerations (Achinstein, 1968; Dewey, 1938; Feyerabend, 1981a; Hesse, 1974, 1980; Maxwell, 1962; Neurath, 1959; Quine, 1953, 1960; Scheffler, 1967; Shapere, 1985).

Formerly, empiricists could have dismissed the theory ladenness of observation and theory dependence of the observational/theoretical distinction on the grounds that a theory is no more than a high-order description of relationships among observable phenomena and can be rendered as a set of observation statements and logical operations. Philosophers now, however, generally recognize the underdetermination of theory by observational data— that is, that one and the same set of data is compatible with different and mutually inconsistent theories, the choice among which cannot be resolved by empirical criteria alone (Feyerabend, 1981b; Kuhn, 1962). Thus, theory and related meaning structures cannot be dispensed with by translation to determinate sets of observational statements and logical relations.

If perceptual experience inevitably involves cognitive processing, observation is theory laden, and the very distinction between observational and theoretical languages is theory dependent and context sensitive, then a classification system that is truly atheoretical cannot exist in any scientific discipline. A claim for atheoreticism in psychiatric diagnostic classification is thus unrealistic. In a similar vein, studies on statistical methods in psychiatric classification have concluded that observation combined with statistical technique alone does not lead to unequivocal classification and that interpretation of data as well as selection among statistical methods that produce differing results are necessarily involved (Grayson, 1987; Overall & Hollister, 1982; Pfohl & Andreasen, 1978).

An atheoretical diagnostic classification system is not only unrealistic as a claim but also undesirable as an ideal. Psychiatry is best served by a classification system that is not atheoretical but is multitheoretical—which encourages and embraces diverse theories, precluding none on a priori grounds while holding all equally to standards of pragmatic value. A number of philosophical arguments have been presented in support of a multitheoretical framework in any scientific discipline. John Stuart Mill (1961) recommended proliferation of views on four grounds: (a) because a view that one may now have reason to reject could still be true (since we are not infallible, and truth evolves with scientific development); (b) because a problematic view could contain a portion of truth, and since the prevailing theory is rarely the whole truth, it is only by the collision of adverse theories that the remainder of the truth can emerge; (c) even a point of view which is wholly true will, if not contested, be held in the manner of a prejudice, with little comprehension of, or feeling for, its rational grounds; and (d) the meaning of a theory is illuminated by contrast with other theories, and uncontested it will become a mere formal confession. For similar reasons, Longino (1990) stated that the greater the number of points of view in a scientific community, the more likely will its scientific practice be objective—that is, characterized by descriptions and explanations that are minimally determined by idiosyncratic subjective preferences of community members or subgroups.

Feyerabend (1981b) advanced two arguments for a multitheoretical scientific framework. The first proceeded from the underdetermination thesis (that one and the same set of data is compatible with different and mutually inconsistent theories) to the recognition that the test of a specific theory is not simply how well its predictions accord with the facts, but how it compares with a whole class of factually adequate but mutually incompatible theories. Hence, he claimed, both consistency and methodological considerations require such a class as the context for evaluating validity and interpreting meanings. The second argument focused on the value of a class of theories rather than a single theory as the most potent antidote against dogmatism. A variety of theories would encourage development of a variety of measuring instruments and of ways of interpreting results, as well as fostering conception of alternatives to the perspectives in which one believes. A multitheoretical framework also preserves the richness of scientific subject matter and encourages development of scientific theories. Since facts are not independently "out there" but depend on the conceptual interpretations of the observer (as discussed above), individuals who have more theoretical concepts at their disposal can actually see more things—that is, pattern data in more meaningful ways—than less fortunate individuals. A multitheoretical framework thus not only can more readily accommodate new scientific theories (Agassi, 1975) but also provides for a richer source of data from which new ideas may be generated.

As Sadler and Hulgus demonstrated (see their chapter in this book), DSM-III-R does not live up to its claim of being atheoretical with respect to etiology and treatment. The failing is, however, not in DSM-III-R but in the ideal of atheoreticism to which it aspired. DSM-III-R is a pragmatically oriented system and, as discussed in the preceding paragraphs, a pragmatic approach is best served by a multitheoretical framework. Future psychiatric diagnostic classification systems would thus be well advised to discard the ideal of as well as the claim for an atheoretical system and to embrace the multitheoretical framework that is more consistent both with their actual function and with current philosophy of science. What I am advocating is not a change in the pragmatic orientation of DSM-III-R, but a shift in its identity which will permit it to actualize this orientation more effectively. Fulfillment of the pragmatic objectives of a psychiatric diagnostic classification system does not necessitate that it be devoid of theoretical influence, which in any case would be impossible. A pragmatic system requires only an agnosticism regarding theoretical commitments (as noted by Agich in this book), which is sustained by receptivity to a variety of theories and openness about theoretical influences on the current composition of the system.

Adherence to an ideal of atheoreticism may moreover promote neglect or denial of theoretical and contextual (i.e., sociohistorical and personal) factors that influence the formulation and function of the classification system. To the extent that such factors operate without being subject to examination, the practical utility of the classification system may be compromised; and those who support a system but do not examine its presuppositions may unintentionally be furthering some covert ideological program (see Denise Russell's chapter in this book). Conversely, a philosophical framework that encourages open examination of theoretical and contextual factors is most likely to promote assessments and modifications that will maximize the system's pragmatic value, and to preserve individuals' freedom to choose consciously which theoretical ideologies they will support. A multitheoretical system shares with a (hypothetically) atheoretical system the objective of preventing domination by any one theoretical ideology, but it seeks to accomplish this objective through openness rather than denial. Theoretical receptivity and open examination are particularly important in light of the dialectical, mutually influencing relationship between theory and classification system (Hempel, 1965a and this book; Lewis, 1929). On the one hand, failure to consider all relevant theoretical orientations may lead to inappropriate grouping of diagnostic entities (Davis, Janicak & Andriukaitis, 1986); on the other, the characteristics of a classification system constitute the foundation for theories of psychopathology and set limits for the types of theory which can evolve from it (Blashfield & Draguns, 1976).

These philosophical issues come alive when some aspect of the current classification system is found to be serving its functions in a less than optimal manner, and options for modification of the system begin to be considered. We are then able to see how classification issues are intertwined with theoretical and contextual issues and how the pragmatic value of a classification system can be enhanced by a multitheoretical approach.

The main part of this chapter presents what amounts to a quasi-autobiographical case history of a proposal for limited modification of the psychiatric diagnostic classification system. It begins by noting observations that led me to question whether a group of several psychiatric disorders had been organized in DSM-III-R in the most clinically useful manner, proceeds to discuss the process through which I developed a proposal for modifying the organization of these disorders, and concludes by assessing the proposed modification. The case history serves two primary functions: (a) it illustrates that the relationships among classification system, theory, and context not only are significant, but moreover can have positive consequences; and (b) it demonstrates a multitheoretical framework in action by following the operation of a pragmatic method for evaluating and refining a psychiatric diagnostic classification system.

CASE HISTORY OF A PROPOSED MODIFICATION OF THE PSYCHIATRIC DIAGNOSTIC CLASSIFICATION SYSTEM

Observations

Some years ago I was working at a proprietary psychiatric hospital that included specialized units for treatment of chemical dependence, eating disorders, and what was called "sexual addiction." As I worked with alcoholics, drug addicts, bulimics, and self-described sex addicts, I observed several patterns. (a) Patients with any one of these disorders had a lifetime prevalence of the other disorders (and of pathological gambling) which was higher than their prevalence in the general population. (b) Relatives of patients with any of these disorders had a history of the other disorders (and of pathological gambling) more frequently than did the general population. (c) The disorders were characterized by similarities in many areas—patterns of symptomatic behavior, progressive development of the disorder, subjective experience of the disorder, relationships between the disorder and other aspects of the patients' lives, and ways in which patients with these disorders related to others and to themselves. (d) In a patient diagnosed with two (or more) of these disorders, as the behavior symptomatic of one disorder came under better control, behavior symptomatic of the other disorder often became less manageable. (e) In a patient diagnosed with only one of these disorders, as the behavior symptomatic of that disorder came under control, behavior symptomatic of one of the other disorders would often become problematic for the first time. These patterns suggested that the various disorders—psychoactive substance dependence, bulimia, sexual addiction, and pathological gambling—were related to each other in some significant way.

One of the purposes of a psychiatric diagnostic classification system is to provide a basis for describing important similarities and differences among psychiatric disorders (Blashfield & Draguns, 1976). This level of information is conveyed by the organizational structure of the system, through its classification of diagnostic entities into categories. A particular scheme for categorization of psychiatric disorders makes pragmatic sense when features shared by disorders in the same category are in general more clinically significant than whatever features may be shared by disorders in different categories. Although the organization of DSM-III-R meets this pragmatic criterion in most areas, it seems to fall short with respect to the disorders noted in the preceding paragraph. Each of them is listed in a separate category: psychoactive substance dependence in Psychoactive Substance Use Disorders; bulimia in

Table 14.1 Diagnostic Criteria of Addictive Disorder or Addiction

Recurrent failure to resist impulses to engage in a specified behavior
Increasing sense of tension immediately prior to initiating the behavior
Pleasure or relief at the time of engaging in the behavior
At least five of the following
   Frequent preoccupation with the behavior or with activity that is preparatory to the behavior
   Frequent engaging in the behavior to a greater extent or over a longer period than intended
   Frequent efforts to reduce, control, or stop the behavior
   A great deal of time spent in activities necessary for the behavior, engaging in the behavior, or
      recovering from its effects
   Frequent engaging in the behavior when expected to fulfill occupational, academic, domestic, or
      social obligations
   Important social, occupational, or recreational activities given up or reduced because of the
      behavior
   Continuation of the behavior despite knowledge of having a persistent or recurrent social,
      financial, psychological, or physical problem that is caused or exacerbated by the behavior
   Tolerance: need to increase the intensity or frequency of the behavior to achieve the desired
      effect; or diminished effect with continued behavior of the same intensity
   Restlessness or irritability if unable to engage in the behavior
Some symptoms of the disturbance have persisted for at least one month or have occurred
   repeatedly over a longer period of time

Disorders Usually First Evident in Infancy, Childhood, or Adolescence; sexual addiction in Sexual Disorders (as paraphilias and as example 2 of Sexual Disorder Not Otherwise Specified); and pathological gambling in Impulse Control Disorders Not Elsewhere Classified. Meanwhile, the authors of DSM-III-R seem to have recognized underlying similarities among these disorders, since the diagnostic criteria for psychoactive substance dependence, bulimia, and pathological gambling describe similar patterns of compulsivity and loss of control which differ primarily in the type of symptomatic behavior. Furthermore, bulimia is not distinguished from the other disorders by age of onset, as its category implies, since all of them usually begin in adolescence. Both the underlying similarities reflected in the diagnostic criteria and the clinically observable relationships described above appear to be neglected by the manner in which these disorders are organized in DSM-III-R, whereas the distinctions drawn by category boundaries do not seem to be the most clinically meaningful. These concerns led me to conclude that the current organization of these disorders was not adequately fulfilling its function and that reorganization could significantly enhance the clinical utility of the system.

Proposed Modifications

In an attempt to address the issues just discussed, I proposed a modification in the organization of the psychiatric diagnostic classification system (Goodman, 1990, 1991a). It entailed establishment of a new category, Addictive Disorders, which would comprise the diagnostic entities currently designated as psychoactive substance dependence, pathological gambling, bulimia (and com-pulsive overeating), kleptomania, and a number of other behavioral syndromes that meet the diagnostic criteria for Addictive Disorder but are not specifically represented in the current nomenclature (for example, sexual addiction). General diagnostic criteria for the category Addictive Disorder were formulated as a condensation, in behaviorally non-specific terms, of the DSM-III-R diagnostic criteria for psychoactive substance dependence, pathological gambling, and bulimia (see Table 14.1). Diagnostic criteria were determined by this method in part so they could be recognized as being consistent with the currently accepted system. The objective was not necessarily to devise the best possible set of diagnostic criteria for Addictive Disorder (which in any case would need to be determined empirically) but to demonstrate that such diagnostic criteria could be formulated which (a) were at least as reliable and specific as current DSM-III-R criteria, and (b) were not linked with a particular theory of etiology or treatment any more than are current diagnostic criteria.

Diagnostic criteria for specific addictive disorders were to be derived from the general, behaviorally nonspecific criteria for Addictive Disorder by substituting for the phrase "the behavior" the specific behavior that is characteristic of the disorder (e.g., ingesting alcohol or other drugs, gambling, eating, stealing, engaging in a form of sexual behavior). The diagnostic criteria were accompanied by a definition of *addiction* as a process whereby a behavior that can function both to produce pleasure and to provide relief from internal discomfort is employed in a pattern characterized by (a) recurrent failure to control the behavior and (b) continuation of the behavior despite significant harmful consequences. The terms *addiction* and *addictive disorder* were selected in preference to either *dependence*, which involves an attempt to achieve a pleasurable internal state (i.e., positive reinforcement motivation), or *compulsion*, which involves an attempt to evade or avoid an unpleasurable internal state (i.e., negative reinforcement motivation), since addiction combines both dependence and compulsion.

The proposed modification entails a significant change from DSM-III-R, yet retains much in common with it. It is at least as compatible with the rest of the diagnostic classification system as is the current disposition of addictive conditions, and it more effectively fulfills the system's pragmatic objectives. The proposed modification differs from DSM-III-R by grouping in the same category several diagnostic entities that DSM-III-R lists in disparate categories and by specifying the shared pattern of clinical features which constitutes the basis for this grouping. It retains these entities and (the essence of) their diagnostic criteria, in both content and form. It does not conflict with other areas of the diagnostic classification system and is actually more consistent with the overall organization of the system than is the DSM-III-R disposition of these diagnostic entities. How its fulfillment of pragmatic objectives compares with that of the DSM-III-R disposition will be addressed in a later section.

What I have presented so far is a reasonable account of how observations led me to perceive a pragmatic flaw in the psychiatric diagnostic classification system and to propose a modification of the system which redresses the perceived flaw without implying commitment to any particular theoretical orientation. It is, however, only a partial account. Both the content of the proposed modification and the motivation to formulate and present it were influenced by my theoretical background and personal history as well as by empirical and pragmatic considerations.

Theoretical and Contextual Factors in Development of the Proposal

My general theoretical orientation is integrative, with a background in psychoanalytic and developmental as well as biological psychiatry. In my clinical work, I was as impressed by the similar patterns in psychodynamics and object relations among people suffering from various addictive disorders as I was by the more overt observations I noted earlier; and I was also aware of similarities in the psychoanalytic theories concerning drug addiction, bulimia, paraphilias, and kleptomania. Even before I began to write my initial paper on addiction, I was already planning to follow it with a paper that would present a psychoanalytic theory of the addictive process, which I hypothesized to be the underlying pattern shared by all addictive disorders. Perhaps more saliently, I often found myself in philosophical and practical disagreement with psychiatrists and other professionals whose approach to the relationship between mind and body was either mechanistic reductionism or interactional dualism (rather than mental/physical identity [Goodman, 1991b]), who tended to neglect the distinction between behavioral syndrome and underlying pathology, and who denigrated psychoanalysis as unscientific. My sensitivity to these issues enhanced my interest in observations that supported my theoretical perspective and stimulated my motivation to write as a means of disseminating my ideas.

My personal history also contributed to the development of my proposal for modification of the psychiatric diagnostic classification system. I developed bulimia in high school, added drug addiction in college, and have used other behaviors in an addictive manner. I consequently had the opportunity to become intimately familiar with the subjective similarities among the various addictive syndromes and with their ability to substitute one for another. The hypothesis that I introduced in the initial definition paper (1990) and developed in the psychoanalytic paper (1993)——that the various patterns of behavior which meet the criteria for addictive disorder are most accurately described, not as a variety of addictions, but as a basic underlying addictive process that may be expressed in one or more of various behavioral manifestations——thus derived from my personal experience as well as from clinical observations.

Contextual Factors in "Justification"

Although the addictive process hypothesis is related to an etiological theory and to personal history, the proposed diagnostic modification that it stimulated can be assessed according to the same empirical and pragmatic criteria as any other aspect of the diagnostic classification system. Before proceeding to that component of assessment, I would like to discuss another aspect that is more often overlooked. Philosophers of science distinguish between "discovery" and "justification" of scientific theories. *Discovery* or development of theory is acknowledged to be an individual creative process that is influenced by contextual factors as well as by prior theoretical orientation. An understanding of these factors is to be sought in the domain of psychology, not philosophy. *Justification*, the assessment or validation of theory, is considered in the empiricist tradition to be the more scientifically pure process and the proper subject for the philosophy of science. It is seen as being based on logic and analytical (or noncontingent) truths that are free from influence by contextual factors. Although the theory of justification may consist primarily of logic and linguistic analysis, the practice of justification is something that people do and is thus embedded in a social network in a sense analogous to that in which observation terms are embedded in a conceptual network that includes theoretical terms. Particularly to the extent that a scientific theory has social or political implications, the justification process will be influenced by contextual as well as by scientific factors.

The initial presentation of my proposed modification of the psychiatric diagnostic classification system met with objections that derived from contextual considerations regarding the societal ramifications of diagnosis. Arguments were directed against application of the term *addiction* to syndromes other than substance addiction, particularly against the concept of sexual addiction. Although the basis of these objections was external to psychiatric theory per se, they would need to be addressed if the proposed modification were to be accepted.

One set of objections revolved around the idea that addiction is no more than a label for behavior that deviates from social norms. Some claimed that there is nothing inherently pathological in the conduct that is labeled addictive and that it is improper to label people as "sex addicts" on the basis of the number of times or appropriateness of place of their sexual behavior (Levine & Troiden, 1988). The proposed diagnostic criteria and definition have no conflict with this claim, and its criticism does not apply to them, since they neither state nor imply that any behavior is in itself an addiction. A behavior that can function both to produce gratification and to provide escape from internal discomfort has the potential to be engaged in addictively, but it constitutes an addiction only to the extent that it occurs in a pattern that meets the diagnostic criteria. It is not the type of behavior, its object, its frequency, or its social acceptability that determines whether a pattern of behavior qualifies as an addiction: it is how this behavior pattern relates to and affects the individual's life, as specified by the diagnostic criteria. Others argued that the diagnosis of sexual addiction involves judgments——for example, about degree of control and harmfulness of consequences——which are arbitrary and value laden (Coleman, 1986; Orford, 1978). This argument is less readily dismissed but is equally applicable to virtually all medical diagnoses. The distinctions in medicine between pathological and healthy are sociohistorically relative (not absolute) points on continua, and they reflect the underlying assumptions and values of the culture and the physician (Agich, 1983; King, 1954).

Another set of objections was based on a concern that the designation of a pattern of sexual behavior as an addiction undermines individuals' responsibility for their behavior. This concern was shared by groups at opposite ends of the political spectrum. Those at the conservative end feared that the concept of sexual addiction could be employed to absolve individuals of responsibility, that sex addicts would not be held accountable for the consequences of their behavior. Meanwhile, those at the liberal end feared that the concept of sexual addiction could be used to deprive individuals of personal responsibility and freedom of choice, defining sex addicts as victims who must be saved, even if they do not want to be (e.g., Szasz, 1974). These concerns reflected a failure to grasp a basic principle of medical care which is captured in the Alcoholics Anonymous aphorism, "The alcoholic is not responsible for his disease but is responsible for his recovery." People with addictive disorders are not responsible for having their addictions nor for the feelings, fantasies, and impulses they entail; but they are responsible for what they do about their addictions and for how they act in response to their feelings, fantasies, and impulses. This distinction——between responsibility for the disease and responsibility for recovery——also applies to other medical conditions, and failure to appreciate it has been a major factor in undermining the medical model.

Contextual factors of a personal nature also entered into the justification process and enhanced my motivation to defend the proposed modification. I had by now treated enough patients whose sexual behavior met the diagnostic criteria for Addictive Disorder that I had no doubt about whether the condition existed. The only question was how it should be designated. In addition to the rationale for choice of terminology which I have already mentioned, other considerations led me to prefer the term *addiction*. On the one hand, I had observed that involvement in Twelve Step groups (Sex Addicts Anonymous [SAA] and Sex and Love Addicts Anonymous [SLAA]) was an invaluable component of my sex addict patients' therapeutic program, so I believed that the addiction paradigm was of pragmatic benefit. On the other, I found this group of patients to be a particularly rewarding group to treat with mixed psychoanalytic and supportive psychotherapy, and I aspired to establish myself through a series of writings as a leader in a field that had already begun to move, unknowingly and with different jargon, in a psychoanalytic direction. The term *addiction* provided a prime opportunity to develop a theoretical and therapeutic integration of psychoanalysis and Twelve Step resources—an integration that was occurring also in my personal development.

Empirical and Pragmatic Assessment

Empirical assessment of a psychiatric diagnostic classification system is often understood in terms of reliability, coverage (or content validity), and predictive or criterion-related validity. Our discussion will focus on predictive validity, since (a) reliability is difficult to assess prior to empirical testing; (b) an inverse relationship has been demonstrated between reliability and coverage (Blashfield, 1973); and (c) the differences in reliability and coverage between the proposed modification and DSM-III-R are not likely to be very significant. Issues related to the clinical component of predictive validity, which concerns the ability to predict clinical course or response to a particular treatment on the basis of diagnostic assignment, will be considered below in the context of pragmatic assessment (which will be more speculative than empirical, since actual research studies comparing the clinical predictive validity of the proposed modification with that of the DSM-III-R formulation have not yet been conducted). The present discussion will address what could be called the nonclinical component of predictive validity, or empirical assessment as generally understood in science: that is, the extent to which observations preferentially support a modification of theory or classification by being more consistent with predictions derived from it than with those derived from its rival(s).

Kendler (1990) specified that a scientific nosology would involve the generation of hypotheses about the validity of competing diagnostic schemas and the testing of these hypotheses by examining relevant research findings to determine which hypotheses are supported by available data—for example, which hypotheses generate predictions that are confirmed by available data. My proposed nosological modification groups together in one category a set of diagnostic entities that in the current system are organized in disparate categories and thus indicates a clinically significant relationship among these disorders which is not indicated by the current system. If this relationship concerns similarities in an underlying pathological process (as I believe), then we could predict that a person afflicted with one of these disorders would be more likely to have one of the other disorders at some time in his or her life than if he or she were not so afflicted. We could also predict a familial association—that relatives of the afflicted person would be more likely than the general population to have one of the other disorders. If there is no clinically significant relationship among these disorders, we would expect risk for comorbidity with other disorders in the group and risk for familial association to be no greater than in the general population. (Of course, a third possibility exists, that the disorders are related but not through similarities in an underlying pathological process. Therefore, a lack of increased risk for comorbidity and familial association would not necessarily indicate that the proposed modification is inferior. Another test would then need to be devised which would assess more directly whatever relationship is hypothesized to obtain among these disorders.) In sum, we will be reviewing published research data to test the following predictions: (a) An individual diagnosed with one of these disorders is at significantly higher risk than the general population for (lifetime) comorbidity with any of the other disorders in the group. (b) Relatives of an individual diagnosed with one of these disorders are at significantly higher risk than is the general population for morbidity with any of the other disorders in the group.

Available studies do not assess lifetime comorbidity but only past or current comorbidity, so available data might not be as robust in confirming our first prediction as lifetime data would be. Nevertheless, the data are clearly supportive. A large number of studies have reported significant comorbidity between bulimia and psychoactive substance addiction—addiction to alcohol and/or other drugs (Beary, Lacey & Merry, 1986; Bulik, 1987; Claydon, 1987; Johnson & Connors, 1987; Jonas, Gold, Sweeney & Pottash 1987; Jones, Cheshire & Moorhouse, 1985; Mitchell & Goff, 1984; Mitchell, Hatsukami, Eckert & Pyle, 1985; Peveler & Fairburn, 1990; Pyle, Mitchell, Eckert, Halvorson, Newman & Goff, 1983; Robinson & Holden, 1986; Schneider & Agras, 1987; Stern et al., 1984; Strober, 1981; Timmerman, Wells & Chen, 1990). One of these found a significant degree of crossover between bulimia and alcoholism (Pyle et al., 1983). Several studies have reported significant comorbidity between substance addiction and pathological gambling (Haberman, 1969; Lesieur, Blume & Zoppa, 1986; Lesieur & Heineman, 1988; Miller, Hedrick & Taylor, 1983; Ramirez, McCormick, Russo & Taber, 1983), and another set has described a high prevalence of stealing and/or kleptomania in patients with bulimia (Casper, Eckert, Halmi, Goldberg & Davis, 1980; Hudson et al., 1983; Krahn, Nairn, Gosnell & Drewnoski, 1991; Pyle et al., 1983; Weiss & Ebert, 1983). Attention has been increasingly directed toward the importance of family history studies in organizing psychiatric nosology (Rainer, 1972; Robins & Guze, 1970; Stone, 1980). Such studies have revealed significant familial associations between bulimia and psychoactive substance addiction (Bulik, 1987; Hudson et al., 1987; Pottash, Jonas, Gold & Coldres, 1986; Viesselman & Roig, 1985) and between substance addiction and pathological gambling (Ramirez et al., 1983). The grouping together of the various addictive disorders is thus supported by epidemiological data, the validity of which depends neither upon my hypothesis nor on the proposed diagnostic modification.

Although empirical data provide valuable information, the important questions in nomenclature and nosology tend to be determined ultimately according to pragmatic considerations (Kendler, 1990; Panzetta, 1974). Pragmatic assessment is evaluation of the practical consequences of adopting a theoretical or classificatory modification. In clinical medicine, the bottom line "cash value" of theory or classification is the extent to which it assists in treatment and prevention of disease. Since research and further theoretical developments may also lead to improvements in treatment and prevention, pragmatic assessment of a theoretical or classificatory modification also includes its function in stimulating new research and theory. In assessing the proposed nosological modification, we will first consider its usefulness in addressing the problems that prompted its development.

The proposed diagnostic modification groups together in one category several disorders and thus indicates a clinically significant relationship among them. It consequently provides a conceptual framework with which the clinical observations noted earlier are more consistent than they are with the current classification of these disorders; and yet it is no less consistent with the remainder of the existing diagnostic classification system. It thus represents a more effective bridge between clinical observations and the body of scientific knowledge represented by the diagnostic classification system as a whole. The proposed modification additionally makes the system more elegant and internally coherent, since it focuses diagnostic questions on what actually makes a condition pathological rather than on the behavior that is only the occasion for the diagnostic questions, and thereby avoids the redundancy of having formally similar diagnostic criteria for disorders that are classified in different categories. By focusing on what makes a condition pathological, it also results in a more comprehensive system that provides better coverage of the domain of patients for which it is intended. It offers opportunity to diagnose, in a more clinically and theoretically meaningful way than "Not Otherwise Specified," addictive disorders for which current nomenclature lacks specific terms. Furthermore, it avoids the misleading implication that, of these disorders, only bulimia begins in adolescence. (Parenthetically, we might wonder to what extent age of onset is a useful basis for categorizing psychiatric disorders at all, since most emerge gradually in a continuous developmental process.) In sum, the proposed modification more effectively reflects the clinically observable relationships among these disorders and the formal similarities in their diagnostic criteria than does the current system, and it distinguishes category boundaries that are more clinically meaningful.

Our pragmatic assessment proceeds by briefly considering other potential benefits of the proposed modification. In the clinical situation, these may include: (a) assistance in asking the most effective questions to identify addictive comorbidity; (b) directing attention to the emergence of addictive use of new behavior as addictive use of the original behavior wanes, with anticipatory prevention of further addictive morbidity; (c) modification of methods for treatment of a given addictive disorder according to principles that have proven successful in treating other addictive disorders; (d) earlier identification and treatment of other addictive disorders in relatives of patients diagnosed with an addictive disorder; (e) keeping the primary focus on impaired control and harmful consequences of behavior (rather than on the behavior itself), thus weakening denial and stimulating motivation for recovery; and (f) providing patients with a conceptual framework that helps them to understand their problems. Also, the proposed modification facilitates direction of therapeutic attention to whatever underlying processes the addictive disorders may share as well as to their behavioral manifestations. A more integrated and integrating approach to treatment of the addicted person is thereby encouraged.

Full consideration of new research and theoretical developments that may be stimulated by the proposed modification is beyond the scope of this chapter. Research and theory would probably proceed together, in a dialectical or mutually influencing fashion, to explore the nature of the relationships among the addictive disorders and between them and other psychiatric conditions. It is particularly important in the context of research and theoretical development that a diagnostic classification system be explicitly multitheoretical and that classification structure and terminology be congruent with the formulation of etiology and treatment in both physical (i.e., biological and behavioral) and mental (i.e., social and psychoanalytic) concepts. Since the proposed modification is compatible with various orientations, research and theory are free to develop within the diverse frameworks of biological psychiatry, behavioral psychology, social/family psychiatry, and psychoanalysis. The hypothesis that addictive disorders share an underlying pathological process provides a useful focus and suggests a variety of approaches for investigation. A psychoanalytic theory of the addictive process has been formulated (Goodman, 1993), and a physiological investigation of stimulus barrier function in subjects diagnosed with various addictive disorders is now being designed. The latter study represents an example of how a modification that was influenced by one theoretical orientation (in this case, psychoanalytic) can stimulate research within a different orientation (in the present example, biological).

This case history ends by observing that a classification system is but one aspect of a dynamic scientific process and that information derived from further developments in theory, research, and clinical practice can be expected to lead to revision of the diagnostic criteria for Addictive Disorder, as it can with respect to criteria for other psychiatric disorders (Frances et al., 1991; Schwartz & Wiggins, 1986).

DISCUSSION

The case history of the Addictive Disorder proposal illustrates significant relationships between a proposed modification of the DSM system and the theoretical background from which the proposal emerged, the personal history of its author, and its social context. It provides an example of how contextual factors may affect both the genesis and the assessment of modifications in a diagnostic classification system and how a theory can influence the development of classificatory revisions that not only are compatible with other theories but moreover may stimulate new research within other theoretical orientations. Theoretical and contextual influences on the development of classification are inevitable but are not merely contaminants; they can have positive consequences for science which lead to progress as defined in empirical and pragmatic terms. Since these influences are ubiquitous, nothing is to be gained by denying their existence or significance. Moreover, if atheoretical empiricism is maintained as the ideal and theory and context are viewed as necessary evils, they will be less likely to be subjected to scrutiny and hence more likely to operate covertly in ways that may undermine the pragmatic value of the system. In DSM-III-R, for example, insufficient scrutiny of background assumptions—including assumptions about human nature and the nature of science as well as about etiology and treatment of psychiatric disorders—has contributed to a conceptualization that in effect excludes or devalues psychosocial data and thus undermines the system's capacity to guide the psychosocial component of formulation and treatment planning (as discussed by Sadler & Hulgus in this book).

The case history also demonstrates a multitheoretical framework in action by following the operation of a pragmatic method for evaluating and refining a psychiatric diagnostic classification system. The process, as exemplified in the case history, is similar in form to the generally recognized model of scientific method. It begins with observations that suggest that the current system is in some way not optimally fulfilling its function of assisting in the treatment and prevention of psychiatric disorders. A modification of the system which is intended to provide for more effective fulfillment of this function is then developed. In the next stage, the proposed modification is evaluated in terms of validity and practical utility. The nucleus of this method is the process of empirical and pragmatic assessment. Although this assessment stands out in a formal sense only when a modification is being considered, it is in fact an ongoing process that itself provides the initial stimulus to consider a modification. In the context of this method, empirical assessment concerns the extent to which data support a given system (or modification) of theory or classification by being more consistent with predictions derived from it than with those derived from its rivals. As noted in the case history, data concerning epidemiological variables and genetic (family) studies are particularly useful in empirical assessment. Since rival systems of theory or classification are necessary for comparisons to be made, a multitheoretical framework is required on empirical as well as pragmatic grounds. Pragmatic assessment is evaluation of the practical consequences of adopting a theoretical or classificatory system (or modification). In psychiatry, relevant practical consequences concern the extent to which the system or modification assists in the treatment and prevention of psychiatric disorders. Like empirical assessment, the pragmatic assessment of a given formulation is relative to that of alternative formulations and is of little value in isolation. Throughout the assessment process, theoretical and contextual influences are brought to light and examined. Since theoretical and contextual influences are inevitable, the purpose of this examination is not to expose them and on the grounds of their presence to disqualify a system or modification; it is rather to minimize the extent to which such influences operate covertly and, when indicated, to subject them also to empirical and/or pragmatic assessment. The import of a multitheoretical framework is thus on two levels: (a) it provides opportunity for comparison among alternatives in empirical and pragmatic assessment; and (b) it encourages open examination of theoretical and contextual influences by establishing an approach in which they are recognized to be inevitable and not necessarily detrimental.

From a metascientific perspective, the case history also represents a method of inquiry for a reflexive (or self-reflective) sociopsychology of science, which applies the naturalistic and empirical methods of science to the process of science (Bloor, 1976). On one level, this approach provides a framework within which the issues noted in the preceding paragraphs can be addressed. On another level, it suggests a direction for developing an understanding of the relationship between empirical or pragmatic science and hermeneutic science (understanding of meanings)——a relationship of deep significance for psychiatry. It represents an attempt to actualize the scientific program of Habermas, as described by Hesse (1980): "There are basically only two modes of knowledge, and the empirical and the hermeneutic both have to become self-reflective and critical to emancipate themselves from constraints that do not belong to their proper goals" (p. 210).

I would like to close with three messages. The first endorses the pragmatic orientation of our psychiatric diagnostic classification system and of the process by which it is assessed and refined, with emphasis on the importance of evaluating not only the individual diagnostic categories and criteria but also the organizational structure of the system as a whole. Adoption of the modifications entailed by the Addictive Disorder proposal is accordingly encouraged. The second message supports replacing the misguided ideal of an atheoretical classification system with a multitheoretical framework that is receptive to diverse theories and encourages open examination of both theoretical and contextual factors. The third message is an invitation to scientists of all persuasions to share their own case histories. From this information base a sociopsychology of science can develop and emerge as a valuable complement to the philosophy of science, with which it would (I envision) enjoy a mutually enriching relationship.

APPENDIX

Fundamentals of Taxonomy

CARL G. HEMPEL, Ph.D.

This paper attempts to provide a systematic background for a discussion of the taxonomy[1] of mental disorders. To this end, it analyzes the basic logical and methodological aspects of the classificatory procedures used in various branches of empirical science and indicates some implications which analysis seems to suggest for the taxonomic problems of psychiatry.

CLASSES AND CONCEPTS

A classification, as is well known, divides a given set or class of objects into subclasses. The objects are called the *elements* or *members* of the given set; the set itself will also be referred to as the *universe of discourse*, especially when it is assumed to contain as its elements all the objects with which a given investigation is concerned.

The objects of a classification may be concrete things such as stars, crystals, organisms, books, and so on; or they may be abstract entities such as numbers, kinship systems, political ideologies, religions, or philosophical doctrines.

Each of the subclasses provided for in a given classification may be thought of as defined by the specification of necessary and sufficient conditions of membership in it—that is, by stating certain characteristics which all and only the members of this class possess. Each subclass is thus defined by means of (more precisely, as the extension of) a certain *concept*, which represents the complex of characteristics essential for membership in that subclass. For ex-

Reprinted with permission from Carl G. Hempel, *Aspects of Scientific Explanation* (New York: Free Press, 1965). This appendix is the substance of a paper read at the World Conference on Field Studies in the Mental Disorders held in New York in February, 1959, under the auspices of the American Psychopathological Association. The present text incorporates some changes I made in the original version as a result of the discussion of my paper. The papers read at the conference, some of which I refer to by the names of the authors, were published in Zubin (1961), which also contains a record of the discussion.

ample, in the division of positive integers into prime and composite numbers, the condition of membership in the former of these subclasses is that the number in question be greater than 1 and be an integral multiple only of 1 and of itself. These characteristics determine the concept of prime number, and the corresponding class is the extension of this concept.

Similarly, each of the hierarchically ordered groups (cohorts, orders, families, tribes, genera, species, etc.) in a classification of mammals may be regarded as the extension of a corresponding concept, such as the concepts of marsupial, bat, primate, and so on.

Analogously, the subclasses established by a particular taxonomic system of mental disorders are determined by the different kinds of mental illness conceptually distinguished in the system; for example, in the system of the *Diagnostic and Statistical Manual* of the American Psychiatric Association, the specification of the concept of *psychotic depressive reaction* serves to determine the class of those individuals to whom the concept applies—who suffer from that type of reaction. As this example illustrates, the objects of classification in psychiatric taxonomy are not the various kinds of mental disorder, but individual cases which are assigned to various classes according to the kinds of mental disorder they exemplify. This construal accords perfectly with the conception of diagnosis as the assignment of individual cases to particular classes in a taxonomic system of diseases; and it is definitely called for by the use made of psychiatric classifications in medical statistics, which is concerned with the distribution of individual cases over the various classes provided in a classificatory system, such as that of the *International Statistical Classification of Diseases* or that of the *Diagnostic and Statistical Manual.*

An individual case of the kind here referred to is best understood to be a particular human being at a given time or during a given time span in his life history; this construal allows for the possibility that a person may belong to a class representing a certain illness at some time, but not at all times, during his life. (By contrast, the elements classified by a taxonomic system in biology are best considered to be individual organisms during their total life spans.)

Alternative ways of dividing a given universe of discourse into subclasses correspond to the use of alternative sets of concepts in singling out similarities and differences among the objects under consideration. Thus, the different typologies of physique and of temperament which have been developed from antiquity to the present employ different sets of concepts to classify or to type a given person. For example, one system of classifying individuals according to their temperaments is based on the concepts of extraversion and introversion; another on those of cerebrotonia, viscerotonia, and somatotonia; another on the concepts of cycloid and schizoid temperaments, and so on; and the resulting classificatory or typological schemes differ accordingly.

Thus, the specification of a classificatory system requires a corresponding set of classificatory concepts: Each class provided for in the system is the *extension* of one of these concepts—that is, it consists of just those objects in the universe of discourse which possess the specific characteristics which the concept represents. Hence, the establishment of a suitable system of classification in a given domain of investigation may be considered as a special kind of scientific concept formation. It seems reasonable, therefore, in a methodological study of taxonomy, first to examine the basic functions of scientific concepts in general and then to consider what demands those intended functions impose upon classificatory concepts.

In our discussion, we will distinguish, in a manner widely accepted in contemporary logic, between *concepts* and the *terms* that stand for them; for example, the term *soluble in alcohol*, which is a linguistic expression, stands for the concept of solubility in alcohol, which is a property of certain substances. Collectively, the terms used by empirical science in general or by one of its branches will be referred to as its *vocabulary*.

DESCRIPTION AND THEORETICAL SYSTEMATIZATION AS TWO BASIC FUNCTIONS OF SCIENTIFIC CONCEPTS

Broadly speaking, the vocabulary of science has two basic functions: first, to permit an adequate *description* of the things and events that are the objects of scientific investigation; second, to permit the establishment of general laws or theories by means of which particular events may be *explained* and *predicted* and thus *scientifically understood*; for to understand a phenomenon scientifically is to show that it occurs in accordance with general laws or theoretical principles.

In fact, granting some oversimplification, the development of a scientific discipline may often be said to proceed from an initial "natural history" stage[2], which primarily seeks to describe the phenomena under study and to establish simple empirical generalizations concerning them, to subsequent more and more theoretical stages, in which increasing emphasis is placed upon the attainment of comprehensive theoretical accounts of the empirical subject matter under investigation. The vocabulary required in the early stages of this development will be largely observational; it will be chosen so as to permit the description of those aspects of the subject matter which are ascertainable fairly directly by observation. The shift toward theoretical systematization is marked by the introduction of new, "theoretical" terms, which refer to various theoretically postulated entities, their characteristics, and the processes in which they are involved; all these are more or less removed from the level of directly observable things and events. For example, the electric and magnetic fields of physics and the propagation of waves in them; chemical valences; molecular and atomic structures; elementary physical particles; quantum states: all these are typical of the sorts of things and processes to which the theoretical vocabulary of physics and of chemistry refers.

In medical science, the development from a predominantly descriptive to an increasingly theoretical emphasis is reflected, for example, in the transition from a largely symptomatological to a more and more etiological point of view. Etiology should not be conceived as dealing with the causes of disease in a narrow sense of that term. In the physical sciences, the search for causes in that sense has been replaced by a search for explanatory laws and theories; and etiology has been moving in the same direction. Indeed, the various theoretical approaches to disease have brought with them a variety of theoretical concepts. For example, the *Diagnostic and Statistical Manual* (1952) characterizes the concept of conversion reaction as follows:

> Instead of being experienced consciously . . . the impulse causing the anxiety is "converted" into functional symptoms in organs or parts of the body, usually those that are mainly under voluntary control. The symptoms serve to lessen conscious (felt) anxiety and ordinarily are symbolic of the underlying mental conflict. Such reactions usually meet immediate needs of the patient and are, therefore, associated with more or less obvious "secondary gain." (pp. 32–33)

Clearly, several of the terms used in this passage refer neither to directly observable phenomena, such as overt behavior, nor to responses that can be elicited by suitable stimuli but rather to theoretically assumed psychodynamic factors. Those terms have a distinct meaning and function only in the context of corresponding theory, just as the terms *gravitational field*, *gravitational potential*, and so on have a definite meaning and function only in the context of a corresponding theory of gravitation.

Let us now survey some of the requirements which the two major objectives of description and theoretical systematization impose upon scientific concepts, and in particular upon the concepts used for classificatory purposes.

EMPIRICAL IMPORT OF SCIENTIFIC TERMS: OPERATIONAL DEFINITION

Science aims at knowledge that is *objective* in the sense of being intersubjectively certifiable, independently of individual opinion or preference, on the basis of data obtainable by suitable experiments or observations. This requires that the terms used in formulating scientific statements have clearly specified meanings and be understood in the same sense by all those who use them. One of the main objections to various types of contemporary psychodynamic theories, for example, is that their central concepts lack clear and uniform criteria of application and that, as a consequence, there are no definite and unequivocal ways of putting the theories to a test by applying them to concrete cases.

A method that has been widely recommended to avoid this kind of deficiency is the use of so-called *operational definitions* for scientific terms. The idea was first set forth very explicitly by the physicist P. W. Bridgman in his 1927 book, *The Logic of Modern Physics*. An operational definition for a given term is conceived as providing objective criteria by means of which any scientific investigator can decide, for any particular case, whether the term does or does not apply. To this end, the operational definition specifies a testing "operation" T that can be performed on any case to which the given term could conceivably apply, and a certain outcome O of the testing operation, whose occurrence is to count as the criterion for the applicability of the term to the given case. Schematically, an operational definition of a scientific term S is a stipulation to the effect that S is to apply to all and only those cases for which performance of test operation T yields the specified outcome O. To illustrate: A simple operational definition of the term *harder than* as used in mineralogy might specify that a piece of mineral x is called harder than another piece of mineral y if the operation of drawing a sharp point of x under pressure across a smooth surface of y has as its outcome a scratch on y, whereas y does not thus scratch x. Similarly, an operational definition of length has to specify rules for the measurement of length in terms of publicly performable operations such as the appropriate use of measuring rods. Again, phenylpyruvic oligophrenia might be operationally defined by reference to the "operation" of chemically testing the urine of the person concerned for the presence of phenylpyruvic acid; the outcome indicating the presence of the condition (and thus the applicability of the corresponding term) is simply a positive result of the test. Most diagnostic procedures used in medicine are based on operational criteria of application for corresponding diagnostic categories. There are exceptions, however. For example, it has been suggested that the occurrence of a characteristic "praecox-feeling" in the investigator may count as one indication of dementia praecox in the patient he is examining; but this idea does not meet the requirements of operationism because the occurrence of the specified outcome, the praecox-feeling in regard to a given patient, is *not* independent of the examiner.

Bridgman argues in effect that if the meanings of the terms used in a scientific discipline are operationally specified then the assertions made by that discipline are capable of objective test. If, on the other hand, a proposed problem or hypothesis is couched in terms some of which are not thus tied to the firm ground of operationally ascertainable data, operationism rejects it as scientifically meaningless because no empirical test can have any bearing on it, so that the proposed formulation in turn can have no possible bearing on empirical subject matter and thus lacks empirical import (see for example, Bridgman, 1927, p. 28). The operationist insistence that meaningful scientific terms should have definite public criteria of application is thusly closely akin to the empiricist insistence that meaningful scientific hypotheses and theories should be capable, in principle, of intersubjective test by observational data.

The methodological tenets of operationism and empiricism have met with especially keen, and largely favorable, interest in psychology and sociology.

Here, an operational specification of meaning is often achieved by formulating definite testing procedures that are to govern the application of terms such as *IQ* and of terms pertaining to various aptitudes and attitudes.

The concern of many psychologists and social scientists with the *reliability* of their terms reflects the importance attributed to objectivity of use. The reliability of a concept (or of the corresponding term) is usually understood as an indicator of two things: the consistency shown in its use by one observer, and the agreement in the use made of it by different observers. The former feature is often expressed in terms of the correlation between the judgments made by the same observer when he is asked to judge the same case on several occasions; the latter feature is expressed in terms of the correlations obtaining among the judgments of several observers judging the same cases, the *judgments* here referred to being made in terms of the concept whose reliability is under consideration.

The operationist emphasis on clear and precise public criteria of application for scientific terms is no doubt sound and salutary. But the customary formulations of operationism require certain qualifications, two of which will be briefly mentioned here because they are relevant to the subject matter of this paper.

First, the operational criteria of application available for a term often amount to less than a full definition. For example, criteria of application for the term *temperature* may be specified by reference to the operation of putting a mercury thermometer into the appropriate place and noting its response; or by similar use of an alcohol thermometer, or of a thermocouple, and so on. These instruments have different, though partly overlapping, ranges within which they can be used, and none covers the full range of theoretically possible temperatures. Each of them thus provides a *partial definition*, or better, *a partial criterion of application*, for the term under consideration (or for the corresponding concept). Such partial criteria of application for the terms occurring in a given hypothesis or theory will often suffice to make an empirical test possible. Indeed, there are reasons to doubt the possibility of providing *full* operational definitions for all theoretical terms in science, and the operationist program needs therefore to be liberalized, so as to call only for the specification of partial criteria of application.[3]

Second, if the insistence on an *operational* specification of meaning for scientific terms is not to be unduly restrictive, the idea of operation has to be taken in a very liberal sense which does not require manipulation of the objects under consideration: the mere observation of an object, for example, must be allowed to count as an operation, for the criteria of application for a term may well be specified by reference to certain characteristics which can be ascertained without any testing procedure more complicated than direct observation. Consider, for example, the check list of characteristics which Sheldon gives for dominant endomorphy. That list includes such directly observable features as roundness and softness of body; central concentration of mass; high, square shoulders with soft contours; short neck, short tapering limbs.[4] This is a satisfactory way of determining the concept of predominant endomorphy and thus the class of predominantly endomorphic individuals, provided that the terms used to specify the distinctive characteristics of endomorphs have a reasonably precise meaning and are used, by all investigators concerned, with high intersubjective uniformity——that is, provided that for any given subject there is a high degree of agreement among different observers as to whether or not the subject has soft body contours, a short neck, tapering limbs, and so on. And indeed, Bridgman's insistence on operational tests and their outcomes is no doubt basically aimed at making sure that the criteria of application for scientific concepts be expressed in terms which have a very high uniformity of usage.

It would be unreasonable to demand, however, that *all* of the terms used in a given scientific discipline be given an operational specification of meaning, for then the process of specifying the meanings of the defining terms, and so forth, would lead to an infinite regress. In any definitional context (quite independently of the issue of operationism), some terms must be antecedently understood; and the objectivity of science demands that the terms which thus serve as a basis for the introduction of other scientific terms should be among those used with a high degree of uniformity by different investigators in the field.

For just this reason, the operational criteria of application for psychological terms are usually formulated by reference to publicly observable aspects of the behavior a subject shows in response to a specified publicly observable stimulus situation, and this does indeed seem to be the most satisfactory way of meeting the demands of scientific objectivity. Reference to the "operations" of a highly introspective and subjective character does not meet the requirements of scientific concept formation; for example, the operational reformulation of psychoanalytic concepts proposed by Ellis (1956), which relies on such operations as thinking, remembering, emoting, and perceiving (in an enormously comprehensive sense), provides no clear criteria of application for the terms of psychoanalysis and no objective ways of testing psychoanalytic hypotheses.

To apply the preceding considerations to the taxonomy of mental disorders: if a classificatory scheme is to be used with a high degree of uniformity by different investigators, the concepts determining the various subclasses will have to possess clear criteria of application that can be stated in terms of publicly ascertainable characteristics. The importance of objective criteria of classification, or of objective diagnostic criteria, seems to me to be strikingly illustrated by observations made in some of the other papers prepared for this conference. For example, Professor Stengel[5] mentions in his contribution that among the cases admitted to mental hospitals in England and Wales during

1949, a quite improbably small fraction were assigned to the categories 315 to 317 (psychoneuroses with somatic symptoms) of the *International Statistical Classification of Diseases*; and the question arises whether lack of clearly specified criteria of application may not account in part for this apparent anomaly. Another case in point is Professor Greenberg's observation that not infrequently, technicians, assistants, and even coinvestigators engaged in a common research project differ among each other in their interpretations of the meanings of terms, disease conditions, and procedures when these are not specified in writing. In a similar vein, Professor Strömgren notes that many of the controversies between research workers in psychiatric demography can easily be traced back to inconsistencies of definition.

But while the formulation of more reliable criteria of application is certainly very desirable, it is not, I am sure, always an easy task. Professor Strömgren gives some illustrations of this point in his paper. It would therefore be unreasonable and self-defeating to insist on the highest standards of precision from the beginning; but it is important to aim at increasingly reliable criteria of application for the various categories distinguished in a classification of mental disorders.

In the interest of the objective, it may be worth considering whether, or to what extent, criteria with valuational overtones are used in the specification of psychiatric concepts. Consider, for example, the characterization of the category Inadequate Personality as given in the *Diagnostic and Statistical Manual* (1952, p. 35): "Such individuals are characterized by inadequate response to intellectual, emotional, social, and physical demands. They are neither physically nor mentally grossly deficient on examination, but they do show inadaptability, ineptness, poor judgment, lack of physical and emotional stamina, and social incompatibility." Such notions as inadequacy of response, inadaptability, ineptness, and poor judgment clearly have valuational aspects, and it is to be expected that their use in concrete cases will be influenced by the idiosyncrasies of the investigator. This will reduce the reliability of these concepts and of those for which they serve as partial criteria of application.

One interesting way of increasing uniformity in the intersubjective use of certain classificatory terms has been pointed out by Lazarsfeld and Barton (1951). Some kinds of classificatory judgment become more reliable when the *indicators*——the criteria that serve to assign individual cases to specific classes——are broken down into several components. For example, when several classifiers judge children's adjustment, reliability will be increased by simply specifying certain aspects to which the classifiers are to pay attention, such as appearance (which in turn may be further characterized by means of such subindicators as excessively untidy hair and clothing, chewed fingernails, rigid facial expression); response to interviews; attitude toward others and toward self. The authors add, significantly, that despite the increase in objectivity thus achieved, there "is still required, however, a certain body of common training and experience, such as might be found among trained child psychologists, to make a vague procedure work at all well" (pp. 166–167).

Another factor that may affect the reliability of classificatory criteria is illustrated by the Rorschach test, the thematic apperception test, and similar procedures, all of which may be regarded as providing operational criteria for diagnostic purposes. These tests differ from, say, intelligence or aptitude tests of the customary kind in that they require a good deal of interpretation and that there is no simple routine—performable, in principle, by a machine, as it were—of noting the subject's responses and combining them into an unequivocal diagnosis that assigns the subject to some particular class.

Similar observations apply to Sheldon's typology of temperaments. For diagnostic assignment of an individual subject to one of the various types distinguished in the system, the examiner has to rate the subject with respect to a specified list of traits; and while there is likely to be rather close agreement among the ratings made by different examiners, Sheldon and Stevens (1942) add this comment on the procedure: "The later (diagnostic) use of the traits, considering the traits individually, is perhaps about as objective and systematic as medical diagnosis. That is to say, we admit freely that a subjective element is present—that no machine has been built which can make a diagnosis of temperament" (p. 426).

However, the objectivity, or intersubjectivity, here under discussion is of course a matter of degree, and it should be remembered that also the results of such operations as observing an object by microscope or telescope, or a lung via fluoroscope or indirectly through an x-ray photograph, show intersubjective variation even among expert observers.[6] What matters is, I think, to be aware of the extent to which subjective factors enter into the application of a given set of concepts and to aim at a gradual reduction of their influence.

SYSTEMATIC IMPORT AND "NATURAL" CLASSIFICATION

But clear and objective criteria of application are not enough; to be scientifically useful a concept must lend itself to the formulation of general laws or theoretical principles which reflect uniformities in the subject matter under study and which thus provide a basis for explanations, prediction, and generally scientific understanding. This aspect of a set of scientific concepts will be called its *systematic import*, for it represents the contribution the concepts make to the systematization of knowledge in the given field by means of laws or theories.

The requirement of systematic import applies, in particular, also to the concepts that determine scientific classifications. Indeed, the familiar vague distinction between *natural* and *artificial* classifications may well be explicated as referring to the difference between classifications that are scientifically fruitful and those that are not: in a classification of the former kind, those characteristics of the elements which serve as criteria of membership in a given class are associated, universally or with high probability, with more or less extensive clusters of other characteristic. For example, the two sets of primary sex characteristics which determine the division of humans into male and female are each associated, by general laws or by statistical connections, with a large variety of concomitant physical, physiological, and psychological traits. It is understandable that a classification of this sort should be viewed as somehow having objective existence in nature, as "carving nature at the joints," in contradistinction to artificial classifications, in which the defining characteristics have few explanatory or predictive connections with other traits—as is the case, for example, in the division of humans into those weighing less than 100 pounds, and all others. (This is not to deny that the latter distinction, as well as other, similarly artificial ones, may be very useful for certain special practical purposes, as, for example, the classification of fingerprints for the identification of individuals, although the systematic import of the system would seem to be quite small.)

Similarly, as W. S. Jevons (1877, p. 675) pointed out (before the periodic system had been published), the elements potassium, sodium, cesium, rubidium, and lithium, which are grouped together as forming the class of alkali metals, have a great many characteristics in common: they all combine energetically with oxygen, decompose in water at various temperatures, and form strongly basic oxides that are highly soluble in water; their carbonates are soluble in water, and so forth.[7] Perhaps the most striking example of a classification reflecting general laws is the periodic system of the elements, on which Mendeleev based a set of highly specific predictions which were impressively confirmed by subsequent research. As a result of more recent advances, the system, in a somewhat revised form, has been given a deeper theoretical foundation by showing that it reflects, in the classes represented by the columns of the periodic table, certain similarities and differences in the atomic structure of the elements.

A similar development has taken place in the taxonomic methods of biology. Even in the early taxonomic systems, which are based on more or less directly observable (largely morphological) characteristics, each class represents of course a large bundle of empirically associated traits; but, as an outgrowth of the theory of evolution, the morphological basis of classification came to be replaced by one more deeply imbedded in theory, namely a phylogenetic basis. The various species, for example, are "theoretically defined, at least in principle, in phylogenetic and genetic terms" (Simpson, 1945, p. 13),[8] and the morphological characteristics now provide simply the observational criteria for the assignment of individuals to a species that is construed in phylogenetic terms.

In psychological and psychopathological research the typological systems of Kretschmer (1925) and of Sheldon and his associates, to mention two characteristic examples, illustrate the strong interest in concepts reflecting empirical uniformities and statistical associations. In Sheldon's system the three "primary components of temperament"—viscerotonia, cerebrotonia, and somatotonia—are characterized by means of three corresponding clusters of traits which were selected, on the basis of much empirical trial and error, in such a way that the traits in each group would intercorrelate positively with each other and show a negative correlation with all or nearly all of the traits in the other groups (see Sheldon & Stevens, 1942, chap. 2). In addition, one of the principal claims to scientific significance that are suggested for the system rests on the correlation between the three components of temperament on the one hand and various other psychological and somatic traits on the other: in regard to the latter, certain statistical connections are indicated between the basic components of temperament and the basic components of physique—endomorphy, ectomorphy, and mesomorphy—which are distinguished in Sheldon's theory of somatic types (Sheldon & Stevens, 1942, chap. 7; Sheldon, Stevens & Tucker, 1940, chap. 7). Kretschmer's typology of character and physique has similar objectives, and both systems attempt to exhibit some connections between somatic characteristics and a disposition to certain kinds of mental disturbance. Whatever the merits of these and similar systems may prove to be, they are mentioned here as instances of a deliberate effort to develop classificatory systems (more precisely, typologies in the sense to be discussed in the next section) whose conceptual basis has definite systematic import.

In accordance with the requirement of systematic import, the concepts used in a given field of scientific inquiry will change with the systematic advances made in that field; the formation of concepts will go hand in hand with the formulation of laws and, eventually, of theories. As was mentioned earlier, the laws may at first express simple uniform or statistical connections among observables; they will then be formulated in terms of the observational vocabulary of the discipline to which they belong. Further systematic progress, however, will call for the formulation of principles expressed in theoretical terms which refer to various kinds of unobservable entities and their characteristics. In the course of such development, classifications defined by reference to manifest, observable characteristics will tend to give way to systems based on theoretical concepts. This process is illustrated, for example, by the shift from an observational-phenomenal characterization and classification of chemical elements and compounds to theoretical modes of defining and differentiating them by reference to their atomic and molecular structures. To be unequivocally applicable to concrete cases, the theoretically specified concepts must, of course, possess clear-cut empirical, or "operational," criteria of application; but these can no longer be regarded as their defining characteristics: the specified outcome of the operational test just constitutes a readily observable *symptom* for the presence of the traits or processes represented by the theoretical concepts; the "meanings" of the latter are not fully reflected by operational-symptomatic criteria of application (diagnosis) alone but quite importantly also by the theoretical system to which they belong.

The emphasis on systematic import in concept formation has been clearly in evidence in the development of classificatory systems for mental disorders. The concepts determining the various classes or categories distinguished now are no longer defined just in terms of symptoms but rather in terms of the key concepts of *theories* which are intended to *explain* the observable behavior, including the symptoms in question, just as molecular and atomic theory accounts for the more directly observable characteristics that served as defining characteristics in an earlier stage of chemical concept formation. The trend is nicely illustrated by several of the characterizations of mental disorders given in the *Diagnostic and Statistical Manual* (1952), where an enumeration of certain symptoms is combined with an etiological or generally theoretical account: the characterizations of the various categories of psychoneurotic disorders (pp. 31–34 of the manual) are clear cases in point.

In a classificatory system with a theoretical basis, two individuals with similar symptoms may then come to be assigned to quite different classes, for some of the kinds of mental disturbance distinguished at the etiologic-theoretical level may well partially overlap in the associated syndromes, just as two different chemical compounds may have various directly observable characteristics in common. Similarly, in taxonomic systems of biology which have a phylogenetic-evolutionary basis, two phenomenally very similar specimens may be assigned to species far removed from each other in the evolutionary hierarchy, such as the species Wolf (*Canis*) and Tasmanian Wolf (*Thylacinus*).[9]

The preceding considerations have some bearing on the question of whether prognostic prospects and therapeutic possibilities may be——or perhaps even ought to be——properly included among the defining characteristics of a mental illness. It is certainly conceivable——and indeed to be hoped for as a result of further research——that concepts representing mental disorders should be used in a theoretical context which carries certain prognostic implications. In this case, the concepts in question might be defined, within the framework of the theory, by means of characteristics some of which are prognostic in character. On the other hand, it would defeat the practical purposes of diagnosis and therapy if the operational criteria of application for those concepts——the criteria forming the basis of medical diagnosis——required postponement of the diagnosis until after the illness had run its course. If they are to meet those practical needs, the criteria of application will therefore have to be couched in terms of characteristics that can be ascertained more or less immediately. To mention a parallel from physics: it would be unfortunate if the application of the term *radium* depended on the criterion that the half-life of radium is approximately 1,800 years, even though this half-life is certainly an important characteristic of radium.

We should note, however, that the distinction here assumed between prognostic and nonprognostic criteria of application is a matter of degree. Operational definitions, for example, imply conditional prognoses concerning the outcome of certain test operations: if x is a harder piece of mineral than y then the scratch test will result in a scratch mark on the surface of y; if a current of 1 ampere is flowing through that wire, the needle of a properly connected ammeter will respond accordingly; and so forth. Similarly, the Schick test, which provides an operational criterion of application for the concept of immunity to diphtheria, involves a short-range prognosis concerning a skin reaction. And in certain cases, response to particular forms of therapy might be resorted to as a diagnostic criterion. But it seems reasonable to expect that advances in theoretical understanding will increasingly provide us with etiological or structural accounts of physical and mental illness and that these in turn will imply diagnostic criteria in terms of antecedent conditions or presently ascertainable physical or mental characteristics.

It is very likely, I think, that classifications of mental disorders will increasingly reflect theoretical considerations. It is not for me to speculate on the direction that theoretical developments in this field may take and especially on whether the major theories will be couched in biophysiological or biochemical terms or rather in psychodynamic terms that lack an overall physiological or physiochemical interpretation. Theoretical systems of either kind can satisfy the basic requirements for scientific theories. In brief and schematic outline, these requirements call for (a) a clear specification of the basic concepts used to represent the theoretical entities (objects, states, processes, characteristics) in terms of which the theory proposes to interpret, and account for, the empiri-cal phenomena in its domain of investigation; (b) a set of theoretical assumptions (basic laws, fundamental hypotheses) couched in theoretical terms and asserting certain interrelations among the corresponding theoretical entities; (c) an empirical interpretation of the theory, which might take the form of operational criteria for the theoretical terms or, more generally, the form of a set of laws, statistical or strictly universal in character, connecting the theoretical traits, states, or processes with observable phenomena; (d) testability-in-principle of the theory thus specified; that is, the theory together with its interpreta-tion must imply, deductively or inductively, definite assertions about observable phenomena that should be found to occur under specifiable test conditions if the theory is correct——the occurrence or nonoccurrence of these phenomena will then provide confirming or disconfirming evidence concerning the theory. If a proposed theory has no such implications at all, it clearly has no possible bearing on empirical subject matter and thus cannot qualify as a significant theory in empirical science (not even as an unsound or false one, for these latter attributes presuppose a conflict between the theory and relevant experimental or observational evidence).[10]

This requirement of testability by reference to observable phenomena rules out, for example, the neovitalistic conception of biological processes as being determined, at least in part, by vital forces or entelechies, for the available statements of this conception yield no experimentally testable implications.

FROM CLASSIFICATORY TO COMPARATIVE AND QUANTITATIVE CONCEPTS

While it is not possible to predict the substantive changes that the concepts and theories of mental disorder will undergo as a result of further research, I think that certain changes in their logical character may well be anticipated. In this concluding section, I will attempt briefly to indicate the nature of these changes.

Classification, strictly speaking, is a yes-or-no, an either-or affair. A class is determined by some concept representing its defining characteristics, and a given object falls either into this class or outside, depending on whether it has or lacks the defining characteristics.

In scientific research, however, the objects under study are often found to resist a tidy pigeonholing of this kind. More precisely: those characteristics of the subject matter which, in the given context of investigation, suggest themselves as a fruitful basis of classification often cannot well be treated as properties which a given object *either* has *or* lacks; rather, they have the character of traits which are capable of gradations and which a given object may therefore exhibit *more or less* markedly. As a result, some of the objects under study will present the investigator with borderline cases which did not fit unequivocally into one or another of several neatly bounded compartments, but which exhibit to some degree the characteristics of *different* classes. For example, Professor Strömgren refers in his paper to the difficulties of finding a natural border separating the whole group of neuroses and psychopathies from that which does not belong to it, and he remarks that the transitions are gradual in all directions. Typologies of physique and of temperament provide another good illustration, and one in which the gradual character of the transition has received some special methodological attention. The proponents of typological systems often emphasize that "pure" instances of the basic types they distinguish are rarely, if ever, encountered in experience and that concrete individuals usually represent mixtures of several types. Sometimes, the basic types acquire the status of ideal reference points which mark, as it were, the ends of a scale along which actual cases can be arranged. Thus, Kretschmer (1925) states, "We never, even in the most definite cases, come across a pure example in the strictest sense of the word, but always the peculiar individual instances of a type, that is the type itself mixed with slight accretions out of a heterogeneous inheritance. This mixture, in the guise of which the type appears to us in any individual instance, we call the *constitutional alloy*" (p. 93).

Metaphorical statements of this kind are suggestive, but they are not sufficient for the formulation of a theory that is to take explicit and objective account of those impure cases. A conceptual apparatus is needed to describe and distinguish constitutional alloys in which the characteristics of the pure types are represented with different strengths. For example, to give a clear, objective meaning to the notion of a pure type, say *A*, which different individuals may represent in different degrees, objective criteria are required which will determine for any two individuals whether they represent type *A* with equal strength, and if not, which of them represents *A* more strongly than does the other. Suitable criteria of this kind will effect, not a division of the universe of discourse into two classes, *A* and *non-A*, but a simple (quasi-linear) ordering of the universe. In this ordering, two individuals will coincide——that is, occupy the same place——if, in the sense of the criteria they exhibit *A* with equal strength; whereas individual *x* will precede individual *y* if, in the sense of the criteria, *x* is a less pronounced case of *A* than is *y*.

A parallel from physics may serve to illustrate the point. A simple ordering of minerals according to increasing hardness can be effected by means of the scratch test criterion mentioned earlier: if a sharp point of *y* scratches a surface of *x*, but not vice versa, *y* is harder than *x* and thus follows *x* in the order of increasing hardness; if neither *y* is harder than *x* nor *x* harder than *y*, both minerals are assigned the same place in the quasi-linear order. This example illustrates two elementary but important points. (a) The "diagnostic" criteria which serve to place individual cases in the scheme are not criteria of class membership, as they would be in a strictly classificatory system; rather, they are criteria of precedence and coincidence in a quasi-linear order. (b) Such criteria can be quite objective and rather precise without presupposing quantitative measurements.[11]

We noted that recent typological systems have, in effect, replaced a strictly classificatory procedure by an ordering one (even though some of them use a classificatory terminology and supplement it by speaking metaphorically of borderline cases, mixtures, transitional forms, and the like). Such reliance on concepts and methods of an ordering character is illustrated not only by Kretschmer's system but also, to mention just a few other examples, by C.G. Jung's (1921) distinction of the extraverted and introverted types, by E.R. Jaensch's typology (1933), and by the system developed more recently by Sheldon in collaboration with Stevens and others. This latter theory, however, makes the ordering character of its basic concepts quite explicit and seeks to satisfy the requirement of objectivity (in the sense discussed earlier) for the diagnostic criteria it sets down.

Since each of the types distinguished in a typological theory will represent at least one quasi-linear ordering, typological systems usually provide for an arrangement of individuals along several axes and thus replace classificatory schemes by reference "spaces" of several "dimensions."

The advantage of ordering over classification can be considerable. In particular, ordering allows for subtler distinctions than classification; furthermore, ordering may take the special form of a quantitative procedure, in which each dimension is represented by a quantitative characteristic. And quantitative concepts not only allow for a fineness and precision of distinction unparalleled on the levels of classification and of nonquantitative ordering but also provide a basis for the use of the powerful tools of quantitative mathematics: laws and theories can be expressed in terms of functions connecting several variables, and consequences can be derived from them, for purposes of prediction or of test, by means of mathematical techniques.

The considerations presented in this section and in the preceding one suggest that the development of taxonomic concepts in the study of mental disorder will probably show two trends: first, a continuation of the shift from systems defined by reference to observable characteristics to systems based on theoretical concepts; and second, a gradual shift from classificatory concepts and methods to ordering concepts and procedures, both of the nonquantitative and of the quantitative varieties.

Notes

1. The term *taxonomy* often serves as a synonym for *classification*; but I will here use the words *taxonomy* and *taxonomic* primarily to refer to the *theory* of classificatory procedures and systems. The two concepts thus distinguished are more fully characterized in the foreword of Gregg's study (1954), where *taxonomy proper* is contrasted with *methodological taxonomy*.

2. This suggestive term is borrowed from Northrop (1947), especially chapters 3 and 4, where a distinction is drawn between "the natural history stage of inquiry" and the "stage of deductively formulated theory."

3. For a more detailed discussion of these issues, see Hempel (1958).

4. See Sheldon, Stevens, and Tucker (1940, p. 37). For detailed somatotyping, measurement of a number of diameters on the body surface, and thus the operation of applying suitable measuring devices, is required (*loc. cit.*, chap. 3).

5. This contribution and others, soon to be cited, are included in Zubin (1961).

6. See chapter 1 of Hanson (1958) for an instructive discussion of scientific seeing and observing as theory-laden undertakings.

7. See also Jevons's illuminating general discussion in chapter 30 of his book (1877).

8. See also the lucid exposition of the same subject in chapter 19, "The Principles of Classification," in Simpson, Pittendrigh, and Tiffany (1957). Concerning the systematic import of classificatory concepts in biological taxonomy, see the essays by Huxley and by Gilmour in Huxley (1940).

9. For this and other examples see chapter 19 of Simpson, Pittendrigh, and Tiffany (1957).

10. For a fuller account of these principal requirements and a critical analysis of some of their consequences, see Hempel (1952, 1958).

11. For a detailed analysis of ordering procedures, with special reference to typological theories, see Hempel and Oppenheim (1936); a short general account of the logic of classification, ordering and measurement is given in Hempel (1952, part III).

References

American Psychiatric Association. (1952). *Diagnostic and Statistical Manual of Mental Disorders*. Washington, DC: American Psychiatric Association.

Bridgman, P.W. (1927). *The Logic of Modern Physics*. New York: Macmillan Press.

Ellis, A. (1956). An operational reformulation of some of the basic principles of psychoanalysis. In H. Feigl & M. Scriven (Eds.), *Minnesota Studies in the Philosophy of Science* (Vol. 1, pp. 131–154). Minneapolis: University of Minnesota Press.

Gregg, J.R. (1954). *The Language of Taxonomy*. New York: Columbia University Press.

Hanson, N.R. (1958). *Patterns of Discovery*. Cambridge, UK: Cambridge University Press.

Hempel, C.G. (1952). *Fundamentals of Concept Formation in Empirical Science*. Chicago: University of Chicago Press.

Hempel, C.G. (1958). The theoretician's dilemma. In H. Feigl, M. Scriven & G. Maxwell (Eds.), *Minnesota Studies in the Philosophy of Science* (Vol. 2, pp. 37–98). Minneapolis: University of Minnesota Press.

Hempel, C.G. & Oppenheim, P. (1936). *Der Typusbegriff im Lichte der neuen Logik*. Leiden: Sitjhoff.

Huxley, J. (1940). *The New Systematics*. Oxford: Clarendon.

Jaensch, E.R. (1933). *Die Eidetik und die typologische Forschungsmethode*. Leipzig: Quelle & Meyer.

Jevons, W.S. (1977). *The Principles of Science* (2nd ed.). Reprinted (1958), with a new introduction by E. Nagel. New York: Dover.

Jung, C.G. (1921). *Psychologische Typen*. Zurich: Rascher.

Kretschmer, E. (1925). *Physique and Character*. (W.J.H. Sprott, Trans.). New York: Harcourt Brace.

Lazarfeld, P. & Barton, A.H. (1951). Qualitative measurement in the social sciences: Classification, typologies, and indices. In D. Turner & H. Lasswell (Eds.), *The Policy Sciences*. Stanford, CA: Stanford University Press.

Northrop, F.S.C. (1947). *The Logic of the Sciences and the Humanities*. New York: Macmillan.

Sheldon, W.H. & Stevens, S.S. (1942). *The Varieties of Temperament*. New York: Harper & Brothers.

Sheldon, W.H. & Tucker, W.B. (1940). *The Varieties of Human Physique*. New York: Harper & Brothers.

Simpson, G.G. (1945). *The Principles of Classification and a Classification of Mammals*. New York: Bulletin of the American Museum of Natural History (Vol. 45).

Simpson, G. G., Pittendrigh, C. S. & Tiffany, L. H. (1957). *Life: An Introduction to Biology*. New York: Harcourt Brace.

Zubin, J. (Ed.). *Field Studies in the Mental Disorders*. New York: Grune & Stratton.

Notes

Chapter 2. The Limits of Psychiatric Knowledge and the Problem of Classification

1. Weber was aware of the nominalistic status of his ideal types. At several points he contrasted them with naturalistic concepts. In the following passage he warns of the pitfalls involved when historians assume that their concepts are naturalistic ones:

> Nothing, however is more dangerous than the *confusion* of theory and history stemming from naturalistic presuppositions, whether in the form of a belief that one has recorded the "actual" content, the "essence" of historical reality in such conceptual images (*Begriffsbilder*); or that one uses them as a procrustean bed into which history must be forced; or even that one hypostatizes the "ideas" as a "true" reality, as real "forces" standing behind the play of appearances and working themselves out in history. (Scaff, 1989, p. 55)

2. What we have here called a *guiding idea* has been called a *perspective* by Paul R. McHugh and Phillip R. Slavney. We refer the reader to their illuminating discussion of the perspectives of psychiatry (McHugh and Slavney, 1983).

Chapter 4. A Phenomenological Critique of Commonsensical Assumptions in DSM-III-R

1. I wish to express acknowledgment to the essay by John Sadler and Yosaf Hulgus in this book for suggesting a direction that is pursued in this paper. Sadler and Hulgus suggested working with the axis system by including pertinent idiographic information. If Denise Russell states in her essay in the present collection that DSM-III-R is "subjective" in the definition of terms, I state that it is "behavioral." This is not really a contradiction because behavioral approaches are subjective in an unmonitored sense precisely because they have not thematized the problem of subjectivity. The work of Michael Schwartz and Osborne Wiggins in their various articles on typification, ideal types, and the relation of ideal types to current prototype theory on the side of diagnosis provides the impetus for examining in parallel manner disturbances of the typification process in the patient's subjective experiencing of reality. The latter may provide atmospheric (Tellenbach, 1987b, 1987c) criteria during the clinical interview for initial diagnosis which brings into motion the preconceptual typification process of

the clinician. The paper "Toward a Husserlian Phenomenology of the Initial Stages of Schizophrenia" by Wiggins, Schwartz and Northoff (1990) pointed out how a phenomenological approach to subjective meaning disturbance can be applied to beginning schizophrenia.

2. Contemporary cognitive psychology seems to acknowledge implicitly a subjective basis for experiential organization as is indicated in terms such as *cognitive map* or *cognitive representation of the world*. Cognitive representation that is "internal" to a subject nevertheless takes place within a subjective "social" field organization and can only be separated from it abstractly as an object to be studied in its own right. It is a fundamental argument of the present paper that *subjective* and *social*, the *internal* and *external*, or the *private* and *public* are not contradictory terms but belong to a more encompassing overriding, *subjective* organization of experience. *Subjective* means, therefore, from a phenomenological perspective, *intersubjective*.

3. The phenomenological approach is a method developed by the philosopher Edmund Husserl (1859–1938) for studying the origin of scientific formal classification systems in the structures of human experience. For the relevance of the phenomenological method for psychiatry as well as a concise explanation of its technical terminology see Michael Schwartz and Osborne Wiggins (1985). For the application of Husserl's method of free fantasy variation to psychiatry, see the pioneering studies by Sadler (1992) and Uehlein (1992).

4. *Natural attitude*, as opposed to the *phenomenological* or *transcendental* attitude, is the naturally occurring, unquestioned belief that objects, whether they are experienced or merely remembered or thought, "really" exist independently from the subject experiencing them.

5. I have clustered psychodynamic/cognitive and behavioral/social as belonging together, respectively, not merely for the obvious reasons that cognitive science is now being applied as a preferred model in the research of psychoanalytic process (e.g., Clippinger, 1977; Dahl, Kaechele & Thomae, 1988; Horowitz, 1979) or that behaviorism advocates a social learning theory. As will be argued in Part II, the biological, cognitive/intrapsychic, and behavioral/social realms of investigation involve abstract idealizations of their respective "objects" of research. These overlap conceptually, to a certain extent, but unfortunately more or less exclude each other methodologically, leading to a fragmented view of human subjectivity. Through providing access to the description and genesis of subjective structuring of experiential meaning which is theoretically neutral, the phenomenological method enables the integration of these various abstract levels of explanation as parts of one overriding organization of the subject.

6. Gerd Brand (1955) wrote that the "reduction" (literally a leading back, from the Latin *re + ducere*) is simultaneously a "going back towards" and an "abstaining from" (p. 30, my translation). It is a methodologically induced change of perspective in which one goes back from the natural attitude by abstaining from its unquestioned belief in the reality of the world. What is suspended is the belief in one's world as one experiences it and as it is assumed to be shared with others in one's everyday cultural environment. In abstaining from the assumptions or presuppositions one may have about this world, one shifts to a critical attitude that examines the structural conditions of these assumptions. It is a movement from the judgment about the existence of this world through suspending the "thetic positing of its being" (*Seinsthesis*) to make accessible the immanent organization of meaning as the precondition of this judgment.

The methodological moment of description which follows fixes the phenomena revealed through reduction in a technical language. Such a technical language claims transparency with respect to the phenomena it describes and a more or less immutable framework for further descriptive research to be shared with a community of practitioners.

7.   A level of phenomenological evidence is isolated by abstractive reduction. This involves beginning with a phenomenon as we experience it in everyday consciousness. Through bracketing the belief in its existence as a transcendent object or state of affairs the researcher is able to isolate genetically earlier phases of its immanent constitution. This is done by abstractively removing nonpertinent aspects until a fundamental level is reached beyond which the researcher cannot proceed.

Reduction is not meant here in the negative sense of reductionism but rather in the sense that only through actively excluding the features of a subject matter which are not relevant, a scientific analysis is able to consider other aspects that otherwise would remain concealed.

Wolfgang Blankenburg (1971) suggested that in the course of the "relatively symptom-free hebephrenic or respectively simple form of schizophrenia" there is a loss of the obviousness of what is experienced as matter of course in everyday existence. He compares this "pathological loss of natural unquestioned obviousness" with the "phenomenological method of epoché or reduction" (p. 68, my translation).

8.   Christian and Haas (1949) drew the following conclusions from the experiment: "The unity between subjects is founded in concealedness to the self. In the accomplishment of a smoothly occurring working together, the partners also disappear to a certain extent from each other. Neither is able to separate the counter-player from himself. Each is member of the total work situation. . . . Objectively, one leads, but he neither knows nor notices it; objectively, the other is being lead, but even then, one holds what the other does unconsciously to be what one does oneself" (pp. 9–12, my translation)

Such an observation has relevance for a diagnostic classification of personality disorders based on traits assessed over time by the diagnostician and/or reports by family members and significant others. Traits emerge in the polarity of interaction with others. Some persons bring out in the mutuality of interaction aspects and possibilities of an individual which others do not.

9.   The former *I* becomes an *other* to oneself in an act of self-transcendence. This is expressed in narrative accounts about oneself in a past situation: "That was the way I was. That's not me any more." For Sartre (1956), self-transcendence is an act of annihilation of the prior self.

10.   Some clinicians report that the diagnostic procedure already begins with experiencing how the patient shakes hands (as an instance of bipersonal structure). Schwartz and Wiggins (1987b) cited studies suggesting that diagnoses often take place within the first 5 minutes of the clinical interview.

11.   Keeping in mind that the threshold is always relative to subjective factors, it is possible to formalize such hypothetical relationships for eventual operationalization and empirical study. For example, a certain degree of disturbance to the subjective experience of meaning (D_1) is equal to a certain degree of voluntary action (V_1), for example, the range of envisioned life possibilities, divided by a certain degree of involuntary activity (I_1)—the symptom. It follows that the involuntary activity is equal to range of voluntary action divided by the degree of disturbance. In so far as a degree

of disturbance (D_2) is greater than D_1 $(D_2 > D_1)$, then it follows that the new range of voluntary action (V_2) is less than the previous one $(V_2 < V_1)$.

12. Husserl proposed a two-step phenomenological methodology of "reduction" and enhanced descriptive awareness for the practicing psychologist and researcher. In an incremental disciplined attitude as habitual acquisition, this methodology maximizes the subjective sources of cognition and yet, at the same time, provides maximal distance from their claims of intending reality. It enables the experiencing of the subjectivity of self and others and, at the same time, a distancing from this subjectivity. It does so by putting into parentheses or suspension—that is, by withholding judgment—any reality claims made by the immanent structuring of meaning in mental life. In this way, a certain distance is obtained with respect to the subjectively believed realities held by the self and others. At the same time it preserves them for further description. Intentional mental achievement or *intentionality* (in Brentano's and Husserl's sense, to be distinguished from *intention* in the purposeful sense), enables the subject to experience "objects" as externally "real" to himself or herself (i.e., transcendent) by means of his or her own immanent, or subjective, mental processes:

> In pursuit of a pure psychology the psychologist must never allow the validities, no matter how diverse, of the persons who make up his subject matter be valid for himself; during his research, he must have and take up no position of his own in regard to all the intentionalities of these persons which are as yet unknown, which lie in the depths of their lives and are still hidden from the psychologist, regardless, of course, of whether they are conscious or unconscious intentionalities in the special sense for the person himself. . . . If he repudiated this percept he would immediately depart from his subject. Immediately, the intentionalities through which persons (purely psychically) are what they are in themselves and for themselves, their own immanent "relating of themselves" [Sichbeziehen] and being related, would become real relations between these persons and some objects in the world which are external to them and in whose real relations they are involved. (Husserl, 1970a, p. 238)

Without such a suspending of the reality claim of the world the patient is constituting, we become "cointerested (Mitinteressiert)" and, as if in a vortex, are taken up into the reality of their world and co-constitute it along with them (Husserl, 1970a, p. 238).

13. In an essay entitled "*Martin Buber's Einfluss auf die anthropologische Wende in der Medizin*," Tellenbach (1987c) pointed to Buber's concept that the "atmospheric has priority over the world of words." He cited Buber's definition of the atmospheric: "This sphere in which humans first position themselves as humans, I call the atmosphere of the 'between.' This is an original category of human reality" (p. 268, my translation).

The term *physiognomic* was developed by Max Scheler, Maurice Merleau-Ponty, Erwin Straus, and others as indicating the initial subjective experience of "otherness" (see Straus, 1966, p. 165).

Chapter 6. The Basis of Psychiatric Diagnosis

1. Notice that we do not deal with concepts such as regression, conflict, or transference, which are sometimes referred to as descriptive concepts of a patient's mind, which they are clearly not.

2. Note that no attempt is made to give an account of the systematic nature of these headings. They are just stated without any comment on how they can be justified, how they are derived, or why they make sense.

3. We will not deal with the question of poorly defined concepts here. Such concepts—a triangle with four edges—can be said to be wrong.

4. For a detailed account of the problem of hallucinations and for further references, see Spitzer (in press).

5. Note that this does not exclude the special case in which somebody makes the diagnosis of hallucinations all by himself.

6. The only patients who turned out not to be able to distinguish between hallucinations and perceptions were patients with delirium. However, it was not clear, and by definition it still is not possible to decide, whether these patients have hallucinations that are like perceptions in every respect or whether their impaired judgment makes them incapable of proper decision making.

7. French and German psychiatrists speak of *mouches volantes* (flying flies).

8. One has to be exact here: Of course, I can be deceived with regard to my assumptions about the cause of the pain and the location of its cause. However, I cannot be deceived about the mere feeling of pain, for instance in my left foot, even if I do not have a left foot, as it happens in phantom pain.

9. One of several possible arguments runs as follows: One of my patients "saw," "talked," and "listened" to the devil as well as felt pain caused by the devil firmly shaking his hand. This holistic experience can be clinically described as a scenic hallucination in several modalities. From a clinical point of view, one wants to have and use one single concept to refer to all of the various kinds of perception-like experiences of patients rather than to split the experience into visual and auditory hallucinations as well as some other strange sensory experiences. In short, the clinician wants to have a unitary concept that is applicable to perception-like experiences.

10. For a detailed account of the problem of delusions and for further references, see Spitzer (1989, 1990).

11. Parallel distributed processing models have been proposed to mimic clinical judgment for that very reason; these models are less strict and more vague in their way of handling data and hence are able to deal with fuzzy hypotheses and incomplete data sets.

12. Note that the point here is not merely that this procedure is impractical. The procedure does also not solve the question of how we decided to apply the DSM-III-R in the first place and what it was that made us decide to use the DSM-III-R at all. Generally speaking, we cannot help but already be (some say "exist") within a context of meaning and interpretation. We always work within such contexts.

Chapter 7. Voices and Selves

1. We should note that Frith no longer endorses a functional explanation of verbal hallucinations. For his current views, which are consistent with our own account, developed below, see Frith and Donne (1988).

2. It is well known that people can and do revise their self-conception of themselves so as to self-attribute events *after* they have occurred. An interesting example of an ex post facto intentional explanation of behavior is provided by J.M.R. Delgado in *Physical Control of the Mind* (1969):

In one of our patients, electrical stimulation of the rostral part of the internal cap-
sule produced head turning and slow displacement of the body to either side with
a well-oriented and apparently normal sequence, as if the patient were looking for
something. . . . The interesting fact was that the patient considered the evoked
activity spontaneous and always offered a reasonable explanation for it. When
asked "What are you doing?" the answer [was] "I am looking for my slippers." (p.
115–116)

Here the patient, finding himself engaged in a bodily movement, explains the movement by hypothesizing that he has intentional states—a desire to locate his slippers—
of a sort that would rationalize (make reasonable) his activities. Similarly, patients a-
chieving insight via psychoanalysis may come to ascribe to themselves unconscious
states, such as, for example, Oedipal desires or fear of castration, which serve to explain their behavior intentionally. Of course, such explanations need not be incorrect.
(For a discussion of *ex post facto* rationalizations of behavior induced by posthypnotic
suggestion see also Wilkes, 1988.)

3.   "Another patient, despondent and guilty on the anniversary of her mother's
death, watched another personality put her arm in a fire. . . . The patient had no control over the movement and felt the pain as she watched her skin char" (Bliss, 1986,
p. 140).

4.   We do not mean to suggest that the subjects must take themselves to have the
beliefs and desires that would naturally be expressed by the sincere assertion of some
sentence of inner speech. If a subject says to himself or herself, "In Xanadu did Kubla
Khan a stately pleasure dome degree," the subject need not have any beliefs about the
Mongol emperor's architectural projects to regard the utterance of this sentence as one
of his or her actions. What is necessary is that the subject take himself or herself to
have beliefs and intentions of the sort that motivate or rationalize this utterance. Thus,
the subject might explain the occurrence of this sentence by supposing a desire to recite Coleridge's "Kubla Khan" to himself or herself and by believing the relevant sentence to be the poem's first line.

5.   It should be noted that the subject need not believe in the reality of the person
corresponding to the voice. Thus, for instance, it may seem to me as if God is speaking to me, although I do not believe in God; or as if my dead uncle is communicating
with me, although I would sincerely deny that the dead can truly communicate with
the living.

6.   We say *potentially* because we do not wish to leave the impression that self-
attribution necessarily marks mental health. Dissociation can be healthy. Some thoughts
come to mind unbidden, and it may be best to dissociate from them.

Chapter 8. Subjectivity, Self-Identity, and Self-Description

1.   Bacal and Newman went on to say that they adopt the *ph-* spelling for *phantasy*, following Freud's translators (as interpreted by Susan Isaacs), "in order to denote
a predominantly unconscious activity." But since the root meaning of *fantasy*, however
spelled, is "appearance," the notion of an unconscious fantasy is surely incoherent.

2.   The term *subject* appears rarely in Sartre's major works, but his doctrine of the
for-itself is in effect a doctrine of subjectivity. To establish this point in terms of the

internal history of his development would take an essay in itself. (An extended discussion may be found in Caws, 1979.)

3.   Two earlier formulations of my own are: "the subject is the animation of structure," and "the subject is the one who says 'I'." Each of these preserves the subject-object polarity and the vector of intentionality, but they do so in different modes. The first supposes a complex intentional domain instructed over a lifetime (where by *instruction* I mean "the construction of the inner" however achieved, whether genetically, epigenetically, through experience, through acculturation, etc.), the activity of the subject being the selective animation of parts of the structure of this domain. The second supposes the subject to be voiced and to address the other.

4.   A standard view in the early history of modern philosophy, and one that is still current, holds that thought is derivative form, or a degenerate form of, perception. I would maintain on the contrary that perception is an exceptionally vivid and involuntary form of thought, the contents of which are determined by sensory inputs.

Chapter 11. Psychiatric Diagnosis and the Interests of Women

1.   The oppression of women is also tied to other areas of psychiatric theory and practice, but this is not to deny that the problems in the diagnostic area are important, contrary to the view expressed by Marjorie McC. Dachowski (1984), "DSM-III: Sexism or Social Reality?" published in the *American Psychologist 39*, 702–703.

2.   For an argument against the expansion of psychiatry into criminology see my (1985) "Making Criminals Mad: Psychiatry and Criminology Enter New Domains in the 80s," published in the *Australian Left Review 92*, 20–33.

Chapter 13. Psychiatry and Molecular Biology

1.   It will not be possible in this article to review the still conflicting evidence on the genetic basis of schizophrenia and attempts to localize the disease to a specific chromosome. The interested reader should consult the articles just cited (Mullan & Murray, 1989; Pardes et al., 1989; additional comments from a more philosophical perspective on this work can be found in Harris and Schaffner (1992).

2.   I take behavioral characteristics here in a very general sense, to include environmental and even cultural factors. Cultural factors and their influence on psychiatric disease have received increasing attention in recent years in the work of Fabrega (1974, 1989) and Kleinman (1979, 1991 ms.) and would have to be incorporated in any complete explanation.

References

Abramowitz, S.I., Abramowitz, C.V., Jackson, C. & Gomes, B. (1973). The politics of clinical judgment. *Journal of Consulting and Clinical Psychology, 41*, 385–391.

Achinstein, P. (1968). *Concepts of Science: A Philosophical Analysis.* Baltimore: Johns Hopkins University Press.

Ackerknecht, E. (1966). Introduction. In T. Puschman (Ed.), *A History of Medical Education* (E.H. Hare, Trans.). New York: Hafner.

Ackerknecht, E. (1968). *A Short History of Psychiatry.* New York: Hafner.

Ackerknecht, E. (1971). *Medicine and Ethnology* (H.H. Walser & H.M. Koelbing, Trans.). Baltimore: Johns Hopkins University Press.

Ackerknecht, E. (1982). *A Short History of Medicine* (rev. ed.). Baltimore: Johns Hopkins University Press.

Agassi, J. (1975). *Science in Flux.* Dordrecht, Holland: D. Reidel.

Aggernaes, A. (1972). The experienced reality of hallucinations and other psychological phenomena. *Acta Psychiatrica Scandinavica, 48*, 220–238.

Agich, G.J. (1983). Disease and value: A rejection of the value-neutrality thesis. *Theoretical Medicine, 4*, 27–41.

Akins, K.A. & Dennett, D. (1986). Who may I say is calling? *Behavioral and Brain Sciences, 9,* 517–518.

Alexander, F. & Selesnick, S. (1966). *The History of Psychiatry: An Evaluation of Psychiatric Thought and Practice from Prehistoric Times to the Present.* New York: Harper & Row.

Alkon, D. (1989). Memory storage and neural systems. *Scientific American, 261*(1), 42–50.

Allen, J.F., Halperin, J. & Friend, R. (1985). Removal and diversion tactics and the control of auditory hallucinations. *Behavior Research and Therapy, 23*, 601–605.

American Psychiatric Association. (1952). *Diagnostic and Statistical Manual of Mental Disorders.* Washington, DC: American Psychiatric Association.

American Psychiatric Association. (1968). *Diagnostic and Statistical Manual of Mental Disorders* (2nd ed.). Washington, DC: American Psychiatric Association.

American Psychiatric Association. (1980). *Diagnostic and Statistical Manual of Mental Disorders* (3rd ed.). Washington, DC: American Psychiatric Press.

American Psychiatric Association. (1987). *Diagnostic and Statistical Manual of Mental Disorders* (3rd ed., rev.). Washington, DC: American Psychiatric Press.

American Psychiatric Association Committee on History and Library. (1979). *The History of American Psychiatry: A Teaching and Research Guide*. Washington, DC: American Psychiatric Press.

Andreasen, N.C. (1987). Schizophrenia and schizophreniform disorders. In G.L. Tischler (Ed.), *Diagnosis and Classification in Psychiatry: Unity and Diversity* (chap. 6). Cambridge, UK: Cambridge University Press.

Angst, J. (1980). Verlauf unipolar depressives, bipolar manisch-depressives, und schizo-affectives erkrangungen und psychoses. *Studie Fortschriftentes Neurologie und Psychiatrie*, *48*, 3—25.

Atkinson, R. (1978). *Knowledge and Explanation in History*. Ithaca, NY: Cornell University Press.

Atwood, G.E. & Stolorow, R.D. (1984). *Structures of Subjectivity: Explorations in Psychoanalytic Phenomenology*. Hillsdale, NJ: Analytic Press.

Auerbach, E. (1946). *Nimesis: The Representation of Reality in Western Literature* (W.R. Trask, Trans.). Princeton: Princeton University Press.

Austin, J.L. (1968). A plea for excuses. *Proceedings of the Aristotelian Society*, 57 (1956—1957). Reprinted in A.R. White (Ed.), *The Philosophy of Action* (pp. 1—30). Oxford: Oxford University Press.

Bacal, H.A. & Newman, K.M. (1990). *Theories of Object Relations: Bridges to Self Psychology*. New York: Columbia University Press.

Baillarger, J. (1846). *Des Hallucinations*. Paris: Baillière.

Baillarger, J. (1854). Note sur un genre de folie. *Bulletin of the Academy of Medicine*, *19*, 340—352.

Bardwick, J.M. (1974). The sex hormones, the central nervous system, and affect variability in humans. In V. Franks & V. Burtle (Eds.), *Women in Therapy: New Psychotherapies for a Changing Society* (pp. 27—50). New York: Brunner/Mazel.

Barlow, D.H. & Herson, M. (1984). *Single Case Experimental Designs: Strategies for Studying Behavior Change*. New York: Pergamon Press.

Barondess, J.A. (1979). Disease and illness: A crucial distinction. *American Journal of Medicine*, *66*, 375—376.

Barr, M.L. (1974). *The Human Nervous System: An Anatomical Viewpoint* (2nd ed.). Hagerstown, MD: Harper & Row.

Barrett, R.J. (1988a). Clinical writing and the documentary construction of schizophrenia. *Culture, Medicine, and Psychiatry*, *12*, 265—299.

Barrett, R.J. (1988b). Interpretations of schizophrenia. *Culture, Medicine, and Psychiatry*, *12*, 357—388.

Barzun, J. (1974). *Clio and the Doctors*. Chicago: University of Chicago Press.

Basaglia, F. (1987). *Psychiatry Inside Out: Selected Writings of Franco Basaglia*. New York: Columbia University Press.

Bassett, A., Jones, B., McGillvaray, B. & Pantzar, J. (1988). Partial trisomy chromosome 5 segregating with schizophrenia. *Lancet*, *I*(1989), 799—801.

Bateson, G. (1972). *Steps to an Ecology of Mind*. New York: Ballantine Books.

Bayer, R. (1981). *Homosexuality and American Psychiatry*. New York: Basic Books.

Bayes, M. (1981). Wife battering and the maintenance of gender roles: A sociopsychological perspective. In E. Howell & M. Bayes (Eds.), *Women and Mental Health* (pp. 440—448). New York: Basic Books.

Bayle, A.L.J. (1822). *Recherches sur l'Arachnitis Chronique*. Paris: Thèse.

Beard, C. (1934). Written history as an act of faith. In H. Meyerhoff (Ed.), *The Philosophy of History in Our Time* (pp. 140—152). New York: Anchor Books (1959).

Beard, C. (1935). The noble dream. *American History Review, 41*, 74—87.

Beard, G.M. (1869). Neurasthenia as nervous exhaustion. *Boston Medical and Surgical Journal, III*, 217—221.

Beard, G.M. (1880). *A Practical Treatise on Nervous Exhaustion (Neurasthenia), Its Symptoms, Nature, Sequence, Treatment.* New York: W. Wood.

Beard, G.M. (1881). *American Nervousness: Its Causes and Consequences.* New York: Putman's Sons.

Beard, G.M. (1884). *Sexual Neurasthenia: Its Hygiene, Causes, Symptoms, and Treatment.* New York: E. B. Trent.

Beary, M.D., Lacey, J.H. & Merry, J. (1986). Alcoholism and eating disorders in women of fertile age. *British Journal of Addiction, 81*, 685—689.

Beavers, W.R. & Hampson, R. (1990). *Successful Families.* New York: W.W. Norton.

Becker, C. (1958). *Detachment and the Writings of History.* Ithaca, NY: Cornell University Press.

Bentall, R.P. & Slade, P.D. (1985). Reliability of a scale measuring disposition towards hallucination: A brief report. *Personality and Individual Differences, 6*, 527—529.

Beringer, K. (1927). *Der Mescalinrausch.* Berlin: Springer Verlag.

Berlin, I. (1954). *Historical Inevitability.* Oxford: Oxford University Press.

Bernheimer, C. & Kahane, C. (Eds.) (1985). *In Dora's Case: Freud—Hysteria—Feminism.* New York: Columbia University Press.

Bernstein, R.J. (1983). *Beyond Objectivism and Relativism.* Philadelphia: University of Pennsylvania Press.

Berrios, G.E. (1987). Dementia during the 17th and 18th centuries: A conceptual history. *Psychological Medicine, 17*, 829—837.

Berrios, G.E. (in press). The history of psychiatric nosology. In E. Wallace & J. Gach (Eds.), *Handbook of the History of Psychiatry.* New Haven: Yale University Press.

Bichat, M.F.X. (1801—1803). Traité d'Anatomie Descriptive (5 vols.). Paris: Gabon & Cie.

Binswanger, L. (1955a). *Ausgewählte Vorträge und Aufsätze* (2 vols.). Bern: Franke Verlag.

Binswanger, L. (1955b). Daseinsanalytik und Psychiatrie. In *Ausgewählte Vorträge und Aufsätze Bd II.* Bern: Francke Verlag.

Binswanger, L. (1960). *Melancholie und Manie.* Pfulligen, Germany: Neske.

Binswanger, L. (1961). Über Phänomenologie. In *Ausgewählte Vorträge und Aufsätze BdI* (pp. 13—9). Bern: Francke Verlag.

Binswanger, L. (1963). *Being-in-the-World* (J. Needleman, Trans.). New York: Basic Books.

Birley, J.L.T. (1990). DSM-III: From left to right or from right to left? *British Journal of Psychiatry, 157*, 116—118.

Blackburn, R. (1988). On moral judgments and personality disorders: The myth of psychopathic personality revisited. *British Journal of Psychiatry, 153*, 505— 512.

Bland, R.C. & Orn, H. (1980). Schizophrenia: Schneider's first rank systems and outcome. *British Journal of Psychiatry, 137*, 63—78.

Blankenburg, W. (1969). Ansaetze zu einer psychopathologie des common sense. *Confinia Psychiatrica, 12*, 144—163.

Blankenburg, W. (1971). *Der Verlust der natuerlichen Selbstverstaendlichkeit, Ein Beitrag zur Psychopathologie symptomarmer Schizophrenien.* Stüttgart: Enke Verlag.

Blankenburg, W. (1977). Daseinsanalyse. In *Die Psychologie des 20 Jahrh.* (Vol. 3, pp. 941—964). Zürich: Kindler.

Blankenburg, W. (1978). Was heit anthropologische Psychiatrie? In A. Kraus (Ed.), *Leib, Geist, Geschichte* (pp. 13--28). Heidelberg: Hüthig.

Blankenburg, W. (1981). Wie weit reicht die dialketische Betrachtungsweise in der Psychiatrie. *Zeitschrift für Klinische Psychologie und Psychotherapie, 29*(1), 45—66.

Blashfield, R.K. (1973). An evaluation of the DSM-II classification of schizophrenia as a nomenclature. *Journal of Abnormal Psychology, 82,* 382—389.

Blashfield, R.K. (1986). Structural approaches to classification. In T. Millon & G.L. Klerman (Eds.), *Contemporary Directions in Psychopathology* (pp. 363—380). New York: Guilford Press.

Blashfield, R.K. & Draguns, J.G. (1976). Evaluative criteria for psychiatric classification. *Journal of Abnormal Psychology, 85*(2), 140—150.

Blashfield, R.K., Sprock, J. & Fuller, A.K. (1990). Suggested guidelines for including or excluding categories in the DSM-IV. *Comprehensive Psychiatry, 31*(1), 15—19.

Blashfield, R.K., Sprock, J., Haymaker, D. & Hodgin, J. (1989). The family resemblance hypothesis applied to psychiatric classification. *Journal of Nervous and Mental Disease, 177,* 492—497.

Bleuler, E. (1911). *Dementia Praecox oder Die Gruppe der Schizophrenien.* Leipzig: Franz Deuticke.

Bleuler, E. (1934). *Textbook of Psychiatry* (A.A. Brill, Trans.). New York: Macmillan.

Bleuler, E. (1950). *Dementia Praecox or the Group of Schizophrenias* (J. Zinkin, Trans.). New York: International Universities Press.

Bleuler, M. (1978). *The Schizophrenic Disorders: Long-Term Patient and Family Studies* (S.M. Clemens, Trans.). New Haven: Yale University Press.

Bliss, E. (1986). *Multiple Personality, Allied Disorders, and Hypnosis.* Oxford: Oxford University Press.

Bloch, M. (1953). *The Historian's Craft* (P. Putnam, Trans.). New York: Vintage Books.

Bloor, D. (1976). *Knowledge and Social Imagery.* London: Routledge & Kegan Paul.

Bockhoven, J.S. (1963). *Moral Treatment in American Psychiatry.* New York: Springer Verlag.

Bohannon, L. (1954). *Return to Laughter.* London: Gollanez.

Boorse, C. (1975). On the distinction between disease and illness. *Philosophy and Public Affairs, 5*(Fall), 49—68.

Boorse, C. (1982). What a theory of mental health should be. In R. B. Edwards (Ed.), *Psychiatry and Ethics* (pp. 29—49). Buffalo: Prometheus Books.

Boss, M. (1963). *Psychoanalysis and Daseinsanalysis.* New York: Basic Books.

Boyer, L.B. (1962). Remarks on the personality of shamans. *The Psychoanalytic Study of Society, 2,* 233—254.

Boyer, L.B., Klopfer, B., Brauer, F.B. & Kawai, H. (1964). Comparisons of the shamans and pseudoshamans of the Mescalero Indian reservation. *Journal of Projective Techniques and Personality Assessment, 28,* 173—180.

Boyer, P. & Nissenbaum, S. (1974). *Salem Possessed: The Social Origins of Witchcraft*. Cambridge: Harvard University Press.

Brand, G. (1955). *Welt, Ich und Zeit*. Den Haag: Martinus Nijhoff.

Breuer, J. & Freud, S. (1895). *Studien über hysterie*. Leipzig: Franz Deuticke.

Briar, S. (1961). Use of theory in studying effects of client social class on students' judgments. *Social Work, 9*, 91–90.

Bridgman, P. W. (1927). *The Logic of Modern Physics*. New York: Macmillan.

Bridgman, P.W. (1945a). Rejoinders and second thoughts. *Psychological Review, 52*(5), 281–284.

Bridgman, P.W. (1945b). Some general principles of operational analysis. *Psychological Review, 52*(5), 246–249.

Bridgman, P.W. (1950–1951). The operational aspect of meaning. *Synthese, 8*, 251–259.

Bright, T. (1586). *A Treatise on Melancholie*. London: T. Vautrolleir.

Brodsky, A. & Holroyd, J. (1975). Report of the Task Force on Sex Bias and Sex Role Stereotyping in Psychotherapeutic Practice. *American Psychologist, 30*, 1169–1175.

Brody, H. (1977). *Placebos and the Philosophy of Medicine*. Chicago: University of Chicago Press.

Bromberg, N. (1954). *Man Above Humanity*. Philadelphia: J. B. Lippincott.

Broverman, I.K., Broverman, D.M., Clarkson, P.E., Rosenkrantz, P.S. & Vogel, S.R. (1970). Sex-role stereotypes and clinical judgments of mental health. *Journal of Consulting and Clinical Psychology, 34*(1), 1–7.

Broverman, I.K., Vogel, S.R., Broverman, D.M., Clarkson, F.E. & Rosenkrantz, P.S. (1972). Sex-role stereotypes: A current appraisal. *Journal of Social Issues, 28*(2), 59–78.

Brown, C. & Hellinger, M. (1975). Therapists' attitudes toward women. *Social Work, 20*, 266–270.

Brown, G.W. & Harris, T. (1978). *Social Origins of Depression*. London: Tavistock.

Brown, J. (1795). *The Elements of Medicine* (new ed.), 2 vols. London: n.p.

Bulik, C.M. (1987). Drug and alcohol abuse by bulimic women and their families. *American Journal of Psychiatry, 144*, 1604–1606.

Burger, T. (1987). *Max Weber's Theory of Concept Formation: History, Laws, and Ideal Types*. Durham, NC: Duke University Press.

Bursten, B. (1982). Narcissistic personalities in DSM-III. *Comprehensive Psychiatry, 23*(5), 409–420.

Bursten, B. (1989). The relationship between narcissistic and antisocial personalities. *Psychiatric Clinics of North America, 12*(September), 571–584.

Burton, R. (1621). *The Anatomy of Melancholy*. Oxford: John Lichfield.

Bynum, W.F., Porter, R. & Shepherd, M. (Eds.) (1985). *The Anatomy of Madness: Essays in the History of Psychiatry* (2 vols.). London: Tavistock.

Campbell, E.J.M., Scadding, J.G. & Roberts, R.J. (1979). The concept of disease. *British Medical Journal, 2*, 757–762.

Campbell, R.J. (1981). *Psychiatric Dictionary* (5th ed.). New York: Oxford University Press.

Canguilhem, G. (1989). *The Normal and the Pathological* (C. Fawcett, Trans.). New York: Zone Books.

Cantor, N. & Genero, N. (1986). Psychiatric diagnosis and natural categorization: A close analogy. In T. Millon & G.L. Klerman (Eds.), *Contemporary Directions in Psychopathology: Towards the DSM-IV* (pp. 233–256). New York: Guilford Press.

Carlson, E.T. (1980). Charles Beard and neurasthenia. In E. Wallace & L. Pressley (Eds.), *Essays in the History of Psychiatry* (pp. 50–57). Columbia, SC: R.L. Bryan.

Carpenter, P.K. (1989). Thomas Arnold: A provincial psychiatrist in Georgian England. *Medicine and History, 33,* 199–216.

Carpenter, W.T., Strauss, J.S. & Muleh, S. (1973). Are there pathognomonic symptoms in schizophrenia? An empiric investigation of Schneider's first rank symptoms. *Archives of General Psychiatry, 28,* 847–852.

Carr, E. (1961). *What Is History?* New York: Vintage Books.

Cartwright, N. (1972). *Disease in History.* New York: Bantam Books.

Casper, R.C., Eckert, E.D., Halmi, K.A., Goldberg, S.C. & Davis, J.M. (1980). Bulimia: Its incidence and clinical importance in patients with anorexia nervosa. *Archives of General Psychiatry, 37,* 1036–1040.

Caws, P. (1979). *Sartre.* London: Routledge & Kegan Paul.

Cayleff, S.E. (1988). Prisoners of their own feebleness: Women, nerves and Western medicine—a historical overview. *Social Science and Medicine, 26,* 1199–1208.

Cerny, M. (1964). Electrophysiological study of verbal hallucinations. *Activitas Nervosa Superior, 6,* 94–95.

Cerny, M. (1965). On neurophysiological mechanisms of verbal hallucinations. *Activitas Nervosa Superior, 7,* 197–198.

Chalmers, A.F. (1982). *What Is This Thing Called Science?* (rev. ed.). St. Lucia, Australia: Queensland University Press.

Chesler, P. (1973). *Women and Madness.* New York: Avon Books.

Cheyne, G. (1733). *The English Malady: Or, A Treatise of Nervous Disease of All Kinds, as Spleen, Vapours, Lowness of Spirits, Hypochondriacal and Hysterical Distempers.* London: Straham & Leake.

Chodoff, P. (1974). The diagnosis of hysteria: An overview. *American Journal of Psychiatry, 131,* 1073–1078.

Chodoff, P. (1982). Hysteria and women. *American Journal of Psychiatry, 139,* 545–551.

Chodoff, P. (1986). DSM-III and psychotherapy [editorial]. *American Journal of Psychiatry, 143,* 201–203.

Christian, P. & Haas, R. (1949). Wesen und Formen der Bipersonalitaet. In V. Weizsaecker (Ed.), *Beitrage aus der allgemeinen Medizin, Heft 7.* Stüttgart: Enke Verlag.

Churchland, P.S. (1986). *Neurophilosophy.* Cambridge: MIT Press.

Clare, A. (1979). The disease concept in psychiatry. In P. Hill, R. Murray & A. Thorley (Eds.), *Essentials of Postgraduate Psychiatry* (pp. 55–76). New York: Academic Press.

Claydon, P. (1987). Self-reported alcohol, drug, and eating disorder problems among male and female collegiate children of alcoholics. *Journal of American College Health, 36,* 111–116.

Cleckley, H. (1941). *The Mask of Sanity.* St. Louis: C. V. Mosby.

Cleckley, H. (1976). *The Mask of Sanity* (5th ed.). St. Louis: C. V. Mosby.

Clippinger, J. (1977). *Meaning and Discourse: A Computer Model of Psychoanalytical Speech and Cognition.* Baltimore: Johns Hopkins University Press.

Cohen, I.B. (1985). *Revolution in Science*. Cambridge: Belknap Press of Harvard University.

Colby, K.M. & Spar, J. (1983). *The Fundamental Crisis in Psychiatry: Unreliability of Diagnosis*. Springfield, IL: Charles C Thomas.

Coleman, E. (1986). Sexual compulsion vs. sexual addiction: The debate continues. *SIECUS Report* (July), 7–11.

Collingwood, R. (1940). *An Essay on Metaphysics*. Oxford: Oxford University Press.

Collingwood, R. (1946). *The Idea of History*. Oxford: Oxford University Press.

Collingwood, R. (1965). *Essays in the History of Philosophy*. Austin: University of Texas Press.

Conrad, K. (1958). *Die Beginnende Schizophrenie* (3rd. ed.). Stüttgart: Thieme.

Cooper, D. (1971). *Psychiatry and Anti-Psychiatry*. New York: Ballantine Books.

Cornford, F.M. (1912). In *From Religion to Philosophy: A Study in the Origins of Western Speculation*. Princeton: Princeton University Press (1991).

Croce, B. (1921). *History: Its Theory and Practice* (S. Ainslee, Trans.). New York: Harcourt Brace.

Cullen, W. (1769). *Apparatus ad Nosologiam Methodicam, seu Synoposis Nosologiae Methodicae in Usum Studiosorum*. Edinburgh: Creech.

Culp, S. & Kitcher, P. (1989). Theory structure and theory change in contemporary molecular biology. *British Journal for the Philosophy of Science*, *40*, 459–483.

Culver, C.M. & Gert, B. (1982). *Philosophy in Medicine*. New York: Oxford University Press.

Dahl, H. (1972). *The Psychoanalytic Process: A Case Illustration*. New York: Basic Books.

Dahl, H., Kaechele, H. & Thomae, H. (1988). *Psychoanalytic Process Research Strategies*. Berlin: Springer Verlag.

Dain, N. (1964). *Concepts of Insanity in the United States, 1789–1865*. New Brunswick: Rutgers University Press.

Dalton, K. (1977). *The Premenstrual Syndrome and Progesterone Therapy*. London: William Heinmann.

Dalton, K. (1978). *Once a Month: The Menstrual Syndrome, Its Causes and Consequences*. London: Harvester.

Danto, A. (1965). *Analytical Philosophy of History*. New York: Cambridge University Press.

Davidson, D. (1980). Mental events. In D. Davidson (Ed.), *Essays on Actions and Events* (pp. 207–225). Oxford: Clarendon.

Davidson, G. & Neale, J.M. (1990). *Abnormal Psychology* (5th ed.). New York: John Wiley & Sons.

Davis, D.L. & Whitten, R.G. (1988). Medical and popular traditions of nerves. *Social Science and Medicine*, *26*, 1209–1222.

Davis, J.M., Janicak, P.G. & Andriukaitis, S.M. (1986). Scientific and pragmatic considerations for naming and classifying psychiatric disorders. In A.M. Freedman, R. Brotman, I. Silverman & D. Hutson (Eds.), *Issues in Psychiatric Classification: Science, Practice and Social Policy* (pp. 92–110). New York: Human Sciences Press.

Delgado, J.M.R. (1969). *Physical Control of the Mind*. New York: Harper & Row.

Dennett, D. (1981). *Brainstorms*. Cambridge: MIT Press.

Dennett, D. (1984). *Elbow Room*. Cambridge: MIT Press.

Dennett, D. (1987). *The Intentional Stance*. Cambridge: MIT Press.

Dennett, D. (1991). The origin of selves. In D. Kolak & R. Martin (Eds.), *Self and Identity* (pp. 355–364). New York: Macmillan.

Descartes, R. (1960). *Meditations on First Philosophy* (2nd ed., rev.) (L. J. Lafleur, Trans.). Indianapolis: Liberal Arts Press.

Deutsch, A. (1937). *The Mentally Ill in America*. New York: Doubleday.

Dewey, J. (1938). *Logic: The Theory of Inquiry*. New York: Holt, Rinehart & Winston.

Dodds, E.R. (1951). *The Greeks and the Irrational*. Berkeley: University of California Press.

Double, D.B. (1990). What would Adolph Meyer have thought of the neo-Kraepelinian approach? *Psychiatric Bulletin, 14*, 472–474.

Dretske, F.I. (1969). *Seeing and Knowing*. London: Routledge & Kegan Paul.

Drury, M. (1973). *The Danger of Words*. London: Routledge & Kegan Paul.

Duffy, J. (1979). *The Healers: A History of American Medicine*. Urbana: University of Illinois Press.

Eagle, M. (1988). Psychoanalysis and the personal. In P. Clark & C. Wright (Eds.), *Mind, Psychoanalysis, and Science* (pp. 91–111). Oxford: Blackwell.

Earle, P. (1887). *Curability of Insanity*. Philadelphia: J. B. Lippincott.

Edelson, M. (1984). *Hypothesis and Evidence in Psychoanalysis*. Chicago: University of Chicago Press.

Edelson, M. (1990). Defense in psychoanalytic theory: Computation or fantasy? In J.L. Singer (Ed.), *Repression and Dissociation: Implications for Personality Theory* (pp. 33–60). Chicago: University of Chicago Press.

Edelstein, L. (1967). *Ancient Medicine: Selected Papers of Ludwig Edelstein* (O. Temkin & C.L. Temkin (Eds.). Baltimore: Johns Hopkins Press.

Eisenberg, L. (1977). Disease and illness: Distinctions between professional and popular ideas of sickness. *Culture, Medicine, and Psychiatry, 1*, 9–23.

Ellenberger, H. (1970). *The Discovery of the Unconscious: The History and Evolution of Dynamic Psychiatry*. New York: Basic Books.

Elton, G. (1970). *The Practice of History*. New York: Thomas Y. Crowell.

Engel, G.L. (1977). The need for a new medical model: A challenge for biomedicine. *Science, 196*, 129–136.

Engel, G.L. (1980). The clinical application of the biopsychosocial model. *American Journal of Psychiatry, 137*, 535–544.

Engel, G.L. (1981). The care of the patient: Art or science? *Rhode Island Medical Journal, 64*, 95–103.

Engel, G.L. (1988). How much longer must medicine's science be bounded by a 17-Century world view? In K. White (Ed.), *The Task of Medicine* (pp. 1130–1136). Menlo Park, CA: Henry J. Kaiser Foundation.

Engelhardt, H.T., Jr. (1976). Human well-being and medicine: Some basic value judgments in the biomedical sciences. In H.T. Engelhardt, Jr. & D. Callahan (Eds.), *Science, Ethics, and Medicine* (pp. 120–139). Hastings-on-Hudson: Institute of Society, Ethics, and the Life Sciences.

Erikson, E. (1968). *Identity: Youth and Crisis*. New York: W. W. Norton.

Esquirol, E. (1845). *Mental Maladies: A Treatise on Insanity* (E.K. Hunt, Trans.). Philadelphia: Lea & Blanchard.

Ey, H. (1969). *La Conscience* (2nd ed.). Paris: Presses de Université de France.

Ey, H. (1975). La psychose et les psychotiques. *Evolution Psychiatriques, 4*, 103–116.

Faaborg-Anderson, K.C. (1957). Electromyographic investigation of intrinsic laryngeal muscles in humans. *Acta Physiologica Scandinavica, 140* (Suppl. 41), 1—148.

Faaborg-Anderson, K.C. & Edfelt, A.Q. (1958). Electromyography of intrinsic and extrinsic laryngeal muscles during silent speech correlated with reading activity. *Acta Otolaryngolia, 49,* 478—482.

Fabrega, H., Jr. (1974). *Disease and Social Behavior: An Interdisciplinary Perspective.* Cambridge: MIT Press.

Fabrega, H., Jr. (1989). Cultural relativism and psychiatric illness. *Journal of Nervous and Mental Disease, 177,* 415—425.

Fabrikant, B. (1974). The psychotherapist and the female patient: Perceptions, misperceptions, and change. In V. Franks & V. Burtle (Eds.), *Women and Therapy* (pp. 83—109). New York: Brunner/Mazel.

Falret, J.P. (1853—1854). Mémoire sur la folie circulaire. *Bulletin of the Académie Imperiale Médicin (Paris), 19,* 382—400.

Faust, D. (1984). *The Limits of Scientific Reasoning.* Minneapolis: University of Minnesota Press.

Faust, D. & Miner, R.A. (1986). The empiricist and his new clothes: DSM-III in perspective. *American Journal of Psychiatry, 143,* 962—967.

Feigl, H. (1958). The "mental" and the "physical." In H. Feigl, M. Scriven & G. Maxwell (Eds.), *Minnesota Studies in the Philosophy of Science* (Vol. 2). Minneapolis: University of Minnesota Press.

Feyerabend, P.K. (1962). Explanation, reduction, and empiricism. In H. Feigl, M. Scriven & G. Maxwell (Eds.), *Minnesota Studies in the Philosophy of Science* (Vol. 3, pp. 28—97). Minneapolis: University of Minnesota Press.

Feyerabend, P.K. (1981a). An attempt at a realistic interpretation of experience. In P.K. Feyerabend (Ed.), *Realism, Rationalism and Scientific Method: Philosophical Papers* (Vol. 1, pp. 17—36). Cambridge: Cambridge University Press.

Feyerabend, P.K. (1981b). Explanation, reduction and empiricism. In P.K. Feyerabend (Ed.), *Realism, Rationalism and Scientific Method: Philosophical Papers* (Vol. 1, pp. 44—96). Cambridge: Cambridge University Press.

Fink, P.J. (1988). Response to the presidential address: Is "biopsychosocial" the psychiatric shibboleth? *American Journal of Psychiatry, 145,* 1061—1067.

Finley, M.I. (1975). *The Use and Abuse of History.* New York: Viking.

Fischer, D. (1970). *Historians' Fallacies: Toward a Logic of Historical Thought.* New York: Harper.

Fish, F.J. (1962). *Schizophrenia.* Bristol: John Wright & Sons.

Flanagan, O. (1991). *Varieties of Moral Personality.* Cambridge: Harvard University Press.

Flew, A. (1973). *Crime or Disease?* New York: Barnes & Noble.

Flor-Henry, P. (1986). Auditory hallucinations, inner speech, and the dominant hemisphere. *Behavioral and Brain Sciences, 9,* 523—524.

Fodor, J.A. (1975). *The Language of Thought.* New York: Thomas Y. Crowell.

Ford, M.R. & Widiger, T.A. (1989). Sex bias in the diagnosis of histrionic and antisocial personality disorders. *Journal of Consulting and Clinical Psychology, 57,* 301—305.

Foucault, M. (1962). *Mental Illness and Psychology.* Berkeley: University of California Press.

Foucault, M. (1965). *Madness and Civilization* (R. Howard, Trans.). New York: Vintage Books.

Foucault, M. (1970). *The Order of Things*. New York: Harper & Row.

Foucault, M. (1975). *The Birth of the Clinic: An Archeology of Medical Perception* (A.M. Sheridan, Trans.). New York: Vintage Books.

Foucault, M. (1978a). *Discipline and Punish: The Birth of the Prison* (A. Sheridan, Trans.). New York: Pantheon Books.

Foucault, M. (1978b). *The History of Sexuality* (Vol. 1) (R. Hurley, Trans.). New York: Pantheon Books.

Foucault, M. (1980). *Power/Knowledge: Selected Writings 1972–1977*. New York: Pantheon Books.

Foucault, M. (1984). *The History of Sexuality* (Vol. 2) (R. Hurley, Trans.). New York: Pantheon Books.

Frances, A. (1982). Categorical and dimensional systems of personality diagnosis: A comparison. *Comprehensive Psychiatry, 23,* 516–527.

Frances, A. & Cooper, A.M. (1981). Descriptive and dynamic psychiatry: A perspective on DSM-III. *American Journal of Psychiatry, 138,* 1198–1202.

Frances, A., First, M.B., Widiger, T.A., Miele, G.M., Tilly, S.M., Davis, W.W. & Pincus, H.A. (1991). An A–Z guide to DSM-IV conundrums. *Journal of Abnormal Psychology, 100,* 407–412.

Frances, A., Pincus, H.A., Widiger, T.A., Davis, W.W. & First, M.B. (1990). DSM-IV: Work in progress. *American Journal of Psychiatry, 147,* 1439–1448.

Frances, A. & Widiger, T.A. (1986). Methodological issues in personality disorder diagnosis. In T. Millon & G.L. Klerman (Eds.), *Contemporary Directions in Psychopathology: Towards the DSM-IV* (pp. 380–400). New York: Guilford Press.

Frances, A., Widiger, T.A. & Pincus, H.A. (1989). The development of DSM-IV. *Archives of General Psychiatry, 46,* 373–375.

Frances, A.F., Clarkin, J.F. & Perry, S. (1984). DSM-III and family therapy. *American Journal of Psychiatry, 141,* 406–409.

Frankfurt, H. (1988). *The Importance of What We Care About*. Cambridge, UK: Cambridge University Press.

Franklin, D. (1987). The politics of masochism. *Psychology Today, 21*(1), 52–57.

Freedman, A., Brotman, R., Silverman, I. & Hutson, D. (1986). *Issues in Psychiatric Classification*. New York: Human Sciences Press.

Freud, S. (1911). *Psycho-Analytic Notes on an Autobiographical Account of a Case of Paranoia* (Vol. 12). London: Hogarth.

Freud, S. (1913). *The Interpretation of Dreams*. New York: Macmillan.

Freud, S. (1967). *Trauer und Melancholie* (pp. 427–446). Ges. Werke, Bd. 10, 4. Auflage, Frankfurt: S. Fischer.

Frith, C.D. (1979). Consciousness, information processing and schizophrenia. *British Journal of Psychiatry, 144,* 225–235.

Frith, C.D. & Donne, D.J. (1988). Towards a neuropsychology of schizophrenia. *British Journal of Psychiatry, 153,* 437–443.

Fromm-Reichman, F. (1950). *Principles of Intensive Psychotherapy*. Chicago: University of Chicago Press.

Frost, W.N., Clark, G.A. & Kandel, E.R. (1988). Parallel processing of short-term memory for sensitization in *Aplysia. Journal of Neurobiology, 19,* 297–334.

Fulford, K.W.M. (1989). *Moral Theory and Medical Practice.* Cambridge: Cambridge University Press.

Fulford, K.W.M. (1990a). Philosophy and medicine: The Oxford connection. *British Journal of Psychiatry, 157,* 111–115.

Fulford, K.W.M. (1990b). Philosophy and psychiatry: Points of contact. *Current Opinion in Psychiatry, 3,* 668–672.

Fulford, K.W.M. (1991a). The concept of disease. In S. Bloch & P. Chodoff (Eds.), *Psychiatric Ethics* (2nd ed.) (pp. 77–99). Oxford: Oxford University Press.

Fulford, K.W.M. (1991b). The potential of medicine as a resource for philosophy. *Theoretical Medicine, 12,* 81–85.

Fulford, K.W.M. (in press). Dissent and dissensus: the limits of consensus formation in psychiatry. In H.A.M.J. ten Have & H.M. Sass (Eds.), *Consensus Formation in Health Care Ethics.* Dordrecht: Kluwer Academic Publishers.

Fulford, K.W.M., Smirnov, A.Y.V. & Snow, E. (in press). *British Journal of Psychiatry.*

Fuloer, A.K. (1986). Masochistic personality disorder: A diagnosis under consideration. *Jefferson Journal of Psychiatry, 4,* 7–21.

Gadamer, H.G. (1960). *Wahrheit und Methode. Grundzüge einer philosophischen Hermeneutik.* Tübingen: J.C.B. Mohr.

Gadamer, H.G. (1976). *Philosophical Hermeneutics* (D.E. Linge, Trans.). Berkeley: University of California Press.

Gall, F.J. (1810–1819). *Anatomie et Physiologie du Systèm en Général et du Cerveau en Particulier* (4 vols. & atlas). Paris: F. Schoell.

Gardiner, A. (1961). *Egypt of the Pharoahs.* New York: Oxford University Press.

Gardiner, P. (1961). *The Nature of Historical Explanation.* Oxford: Oxford University Press.

Gay, P. (1976). *Art and Act: On Causes in History, Maret, Gropius, and Mordrian.* New York: Harper & Row.

Gay, P. (1985). *Freud by Historians.* New Haven: Yale University Press.

Genero, N. & Cantor, N. (1987). Exemplar prototypes and clinical diagnosis: Toward a cognitive economy. *Journal of Social and Clinical Psychology, 5,* 59–78.

Gershoy, L. (1963). Relativism and some problems of the working historian. In S. Hook (Ed.), *Philosophy and History* (pp. 59–75). New York: Columbia University Press.

Gibson, E.J. (1969). *Principles of Perceptual Learning and Development.* New York: Appleton-Century-Crofts.

Gilman, S. (1982). *Images of Madness.* Ithaca, NY: Cornell University Press.

Giorgi, A. (1985). Sketch of a psychological phenomenological method. In *Phenomenology and Psychological Research* (pp. 8–22). Pittsburgh: Duquesne University Press.

Glass, A.J. (Ed.). (1972). *Neuropsychiatry in World War II.* Washington, DC: US Government Printing Office.

Glatzel, J. (1978). *Allgemeine Psychopathologie.* Stüttgart: Enke Verlag.

Glatzel, J. (1981). *Spezielle Psychopathologie.* Stüttgart: Enke Verlag.

Goethe, W.v. (1981). *Werke.* Frankfurt: Insel Verlag.

Goffman, E. (1961). *Asylums.* New York: Doubleday.

Goldstein, J. (1987). *Console and Classify: The French Psychiatric Profession in the Nineteenth Century.* Cambridge: Cambridge University Press.

Goldstein, W. (1985). *An Introduction to the Borderline Conditions.* New York: Jason Aronson.

Goodman, A. (1990). Addiction: Definition and implications. *British Journal of Addiction, 85,* 1403– 1408.

Goodman, A. (1991a). Addiction concept involves theoretical and practical issues. *Psychiatric Times, 8*(6), 29– 33.

Goodman, A. (1991b). Organic unity theory: The mind-body problem revisited. *American Journal of Psychiatry, 148,* 553–563.

Goodman, A. (1993). The addictive process. A psychoanalytic understanding. *Journal of the American Academy of Psychoanalysis, 21*(1), 89–105.

Goodwin, D.F. & Guze, S.B. (1979). *Psychiatric Diagnosis* (2nd ed.). New York: Oxford University Press.

Goodwin, F. & Jamison, K. (1990). *Manic-Depressive Illness.* New York: Oxford University Press.

Goshen, C.E. (Ed.). (1967). *Documentary History of Psychiatry.* New York: Philosophical Library.

Gould, L.N. (1948). Verbal hallucinations and activity of vocal musculature: An electromyographic study. *American Journal of Psychiatry, 105,* 367–373.

Gould, L.N. (1949). Auditory hallucinations and subvocal speech: Objective study in a case of schizophrenia. *Journal of Nervous and Mental Disease, 109,* 418– 427.

Gould, L.N. (1950). Verbal hallucinations as automatic speech: The reactivation of dormant speech habit. *American Journal of Psychiatry, 107,* 110–119.

Grace, A. (1991). Phasic versus tonic dopamine release and the modulation of dopamine system responsivity: A hypothesis for the etiology of schizophrenia. *Neuroscience, 41,* 1–24.

Gray, J.A., Feldon, J., Rawlins, J.N.P., Hemsley, D.R. & Smith, A.D. (1991). The neuropsychology of schizophrenia (with peer commentary and authors' response). *Behavioral and Brain Sciences, 14,* 1–84.

Grayson, D.A. (1987). Can categorial and dimensional views of psychiatric illness be distinguished? *British Journal of Psychiatry, 151,* 355–361.

Griesinger, W. (1845). *Pathologie und Therapie der Psychischen Krankheiten.* Stüttgart: Adolph Krabbe.

Griesinger, W. (1867). *Pathologie und Therapie der Psychischen Krankheiten.* Stüttgart: Adolph Krabbe.

Grinker, R. & Spiegel, J. (1945). *War Neuroses.* Philadelphia: Blakiston.

Grob, G. (1978). *Mental Institutions in America: Social Policy to 1875.* Glencoe, IL: Free Press.

Grob, G.N. (1983). *Mental Illness and American Society, 1875–1940.* Princeton: Princeton University Press.

Grob, G.N. (1991). Origins of DSM-I: A study in appearance and reality. 43rd Annual Meeting of the American Psychiatric Association (1990, New York). *American Journal of Psychiatry, 148,* 421–431.

Grünbaum, A. (1984). *The Foundations of Psychoanalysis: A Philosophical Critique.* Berkeley: University of California Press.

Gurwitsch, A. (1974). *Phenomenology and the Theory of Science.* Evanston, IL: Northwestern University Press.

Guze, S.B. (1964a). Conversion symptoms in criminals. *American Journal of Psychiatry, 121,* 580–583.

Guze, S.B. (1964b). A study of recidivism based upon a follow-up of 217 consecutive criminals. *Journal of Nervous and Mental Disease, 138,* 575–580.

Haberman, P.W. (1969). Drinking and other self-indulgences: Complements or counter-attractions? *International Journal of the Addictions, 4,* 157–167.

Häfner, H. (1959). Symptom und diagnose. In Stolze, H. (Ed.), *Arzt im Raum des Erlebens* (pp. 29–39). München: Lehmann.

Hahn, R.A. & Gaines, A.D. (Eds.). (1985). *Physicians of Western Medicine.* Dordrecht, Holland: D. Reidel.

Halbreich, U., Endicott, J. & Lesser, J. (1985). The clinical diagnosis and classification of premenstrual changes. *Canadian Journal of Psychiatry, 30,* 489–497.

Hall, J.K., Zilboorg, G. & Bunker, H.A. (1944). *One Hundred Years of American Psychiatry.* New York: Columbia University Press for the American Psychiatric Association.

Hanson, N.R. (1958). *Patterns of Discovery.* Cambridge, UK: Cambridge University Press.

Hare, R.D. (1986). Twenty years of experience with the Cleckley psychopath. In W. H. Reid, D. Dorr, J. Walker & J.W. Bonner (Eds.), *Unmasking the Psychopath: Antisocial Personality and Related Syndromes.* New York: W.W. Norton.

Hare, R.M. (1972). Descriptivism. *Proceedings of the British Academy, 49,* 115– 134. Reprinted in Hare, R.M. *Essays on the Moral Concepts* (pp. 55–75). London: Macmillan.

Harré, R. (1972). *The Philosophies of Science.* London: Oxford University Press.

Harris, H. & Schaffner, K. (1992). Molecular genetics, reductionism, and disease concepts in psychiatry. *Journal of Medicine and Philosophy, 17,* 127–154.

Harrison, J.E. (1991). *Prolegamera to the Study of Greek Religion* (3rd. ed). Princeton: Princeton University Press.

Harvey, W. (1628). *On the Motion of the Heart and Blood in Animals* (A. Bowie, Trans.). Chicago: Hervey Regency Co. (1962).

Hecker, E. (1871). Die hebephrenie. *Archiv für Pathologische Anatomie und Physiologie und Klinishe Medizin, 52,* 394– 429.

Heelan, P. (1983). *Space-Perception and the Philosophy of Science.* Berkeley: University of California Press.

Heidegger, M. (1963). *Sein und Zeit.* Tübingen: Max Niemeyer.

Heilbrun, A.B., Jr. & Gottfried, D.M. (1988). Antisociality and dangerousness in women before and after the women's movement. *Psychological Reports, 62,* 37–38.

Helmchen, H. & Hippius, H. (1967). Depressive syndrome in verlauf neuroleptischer therapie. *Nervenarzt, 38,* 455–458.

Hempel, C.G. (1965a). A logical appraisal of operationalism. In Hempel, C.G. (Ed.), *Aspects of Scientific Explanation and Other Essays in the Philosophy of Science* (pp. 123–134). Glencoe, IL: Free Press.

Hempel, C.G. (1965b). Fundamentals of taxonomy. In Hempel, C.G. (Ed.), *Aspects of Scientific Explanation and Other Essays in the Philosophy of Science* (pp. 137– 154). Glencoe, IL: Free Press.

Hempel, C.G. (1965c). The function of general laws in history. In Hempel, C.G. (Ed.), *Aspects of Scientific Explanation and Other Essays in the Philosophy of Science* (pp. 231–243). Glencoe, IL: Free Press.

Hempel, C.G. (1965d). Studies in the logic of explanation. In Hempel, C. G. (Ed.), *Aspects of Scientific Explanation and Other Essays in the Philosophy of Science* (pp. 245–269). Glencoe, IL: Free Press.

Hempel, C.G. (1965e). The logic of functional analysis. In Hempel, C.G. (Ed.), *Aspects of Scientific Explanation and Other Essays in the Philosophy of Science* (pp. 297–330). Glencoe, IL: Free Press.

Hempel, C.G. & Oppenheim, P. (1948). Studies in the logic of explanation. *Philosophy of Science, 15*, 135–175.

Hemsley, D.R. & Garety, P.A. (1986). The formation and maintenance of delusions: A Bayesian analysis. *British Journal of Psychiatry, 149*, 51–56.

Hesse, M. (1974). *The Structure of Scientific Inference.* Berkeley: University of California Press.

Hesse, M. (1980). *Revolutions and Reconstructions in the Philosophy of Science.* Bloomington: Indiana University Press.

Himmelfarb, G. (1987). *The New History and the Old.* Cambridge: Belknap Press of Harvard University.

Hippocrates (1978). *Treatise on the Sacred Disease* (W. Switz, Trans.). In C.E.R. Lloyd (Ed.), *Hippocratic Writings.* Baltimore: Penguin Books.

Hochberg, J.E. (1964). *Perception.* Englewood Cliffs, NJ: Prentice-Hall.

Hofer, G. (1954). Phänomen und Symptom. *Nervenarzt, 25*, 342–344.

Hoff, P. (1992). Emil Kraepelin and philosophy. In M. Spitzer, F.A. Vehlin, M.A. Schwartz & C. Mundt (Eds.), *Phenomenology, Language and Schizophrenia* (pp. 115–125). New York: Springer Verlag.

Hoffman, R. (1986). Verbal hallucinations and language production processes in schizophrenia (including commentary and response). *Behavioral and Brain Sciences, 9*, 527–528.

Hollender, M. (1971). The hysterical personality. *Comments on Contemporary Psychiatry, 15*, 17–24.

Hooker, C. (1981). Towards a general theory of reduction. Part I: Historical and scientific setting. Part II: Identity in reduction. Part III: Cross-categorical reduction. *Dialogue, 20*, 38–59, 201–236, 496–529.

Horgan, T. & Graham, G. (1991). In defense of Southern fundamentalism. *Philosophical Studies, 62*, 107–134.

Horowitz, M.J. (1979). *States of Mind: Analysis of Change in Psychotherapy.* New York: Plenum.

Howells, J.G. (Ed.). (1975). *World History of Psychiatry.* New York: Brunner/Mazel.

Hudson, J.I., Pope, H.G., Jonas, J.M. & Yurgelun-Todd, D. (1983). Phenomenologic relationship of eating disorders to major affective disorder. *Psychiatry Research, 9*, 345–354.

Hudson, J.I., Pope, H.G., Jonas, J.M., Yurgelun-Todd, D. & Frankenburg, F.R. (1987). A controlled family history study of bulimia. *Psychological Medicine, 17*, 883–890.

Hughes, C. (1964). *History as Art and as Science.* New York: Harper & Row.

Hunter, R. & Macalpine, I. (1982). *Three Hundred Years of Psychiatry: 1535–1860.* Hartsdale, NY: Carlisle.

Husserl, E. (1968). *Phänomenologische Psychologie.* Den Haag: Nijhoff, p. 34.

Husserl, E. (1970a). *The Crisis of the European Sciences and Transcendental Phenomenology* (D. Carr, Trans.). Evanston, IL: Northwestern University Press.

Husserl, E. (1970b). *The Paris Lectures* (P. Koestenbaum, Trans.). The Hague: Martinus Nijhoff.

Husserl, E. (1973). *Experience and Judgment* (J. Churchill & K. Ameriks, Trans.). Evanston, IL: Northwestern University Press.

Ingleby, D. (Ed.). (1980). *Critical Psychiatry: The Politics of Mental Health.* New York: Pantheon Books.

Inouye, T. & Shimizu, A. (1970). The electromyographic study of verbal hallucinations. *Journal of Nervous and Mental Disease, 151,* 415–422.

Irle, G. (1962). Das praecoxgefühl in der diagnostik der schizophrenie: Ergebnisse einer umfrage bei westdeutschen psychiatern. *Archiv für Psychiatrie und Zeitschrift Neurologie, 203,* 385–406.

Jackson, S.W. (1986). *Melancholia and Depression from Hippocratic Times to Modern Times.* New Haven: Yale University Press.

Janzarik, W. (1965). Psychologie und psychopathologie der zukunftsbezogenheit. *Archiv Gestalten Psychologie, 117,* 33–53.

Janzarik, W. (1989). Die nosologische differenzierung der idiopathischen psychosyndrome: Ein psychiatrischer sisypusmythos. *Nervenarzt, 60,* 86–89.

Jaspers, K. (1963). *General Psychopathology* (J. Hoenig & M.W. Hamilton, Trans.). Chicago: University of Chicago Press.

Jaspers, K. (1965). *Allgemeine Psychopathologie: Achte unveranderte auflage.* Berlin: Springer Verlag.

Jaspers, K. (1974). Causal and "meaningful" connexions between life history and psychosis. In S.R. Hirsch & M. Shepherd (Eds.), *Themes and Variations in European Psychiatry.* Bristol: John Wright & Sons.

Jencks, S.F., Goldman, H.H. & McGuire, T.G. (1985). Challenges in bringing psychiatric services under a prospective payment system. *Hospital and Community Psychiatry, 36,* 764–769.

Jenkins, R. (1968). Important advances seen in new diagnostic manual. *Psychiatric News,* (Feb.), pp. 1, 24.

Jenkins, R., Smeeton, N., Marinker, M. & Shepherd, M. (1985). A study of the classification of mental ill-health in general practice. *Psychological Medicine, 15,* 403–409.

Johnson, C. & Connors, M.E. (1987). *The Etiology and Treatment of Bulimia Nervosa.* New York: Basic Books.

Jonas, J.M., Gold, M.S., Sweeney, D. & Pottash, A.L. (1987). Eating disorders and cocaine abuse: A survey of 259 cocaine abusers. *Journal of Clinical Psychiatry, 48,* 47–50.

Jones, D.A., Cheshire, N. & Moorhouse, H. (1985). Anorexia nervosa, bulimia, and alcoholism: Association of eating disorder and alcohol. *Journal of Psychiatry Research, 19,* 377–380.

Jones, K. (1972). *A History of the Mental Health Service.* London: Routledge & Kegan Paul.

Jones, K. (in press). A history of psychiatry and social work in America. In E. Wallace & J. Gach (Eds.), *Handbook of the History of Psychiatry.* New Haven: Yale University Press.

Jung, C.G. (1907). *The Psychology of Dementia Praecox.* Princeton: Ballinger Series of Princeton University Press.

Jung, L. & Schellar, R. (1991). Peptide processing and targeting in the neuronal secretory pathway. *Science*, *251*, 1330—1335.

Junginger, J. (1986). Distinctiveness, unintendedness, location, and nonself attribution of verbal hallucinations. *Behavioral and Brain Sciences*, *9*, 527—528.

Junginger, J. & Frame, C. (1985). Self-report of frequency and phenomenology of verbal hallucinations. *Journal of Nervous and Mental Disease*, *173*, 149—155.

Kandel, E. & Schwartz, J. (Eds.). (1985). *Principles of Neural Science* (2nd ed.). New York: Elsevier.

Kant, I. (1965). *Critique of Pure Reason* (N.K. Smith, Trans.). New York: St. Martin's Press.

Kant, I. (1974). *On the Old Saw: That May Be Right in Theory, but It Won't Work in Practice*. Philadelphia: University of Pennsylvania Press.

Kaplan, H.I. & Sadock, B.J. (1988). *Synopsis of Psychiatry* (5th ed.). Baltimore: Williams & Wilkins.

Kaplan, M. (1983). A woman's view of DSM-III. *American Psychologist*, *38*, 786—792.

Karasu, T. (Ed.). (1989). *Treatments of Psychiatric Disorders*. Washington, DC: American Psychiatric Press.

Karpman, B. (1948). The myth of the psychopathic personality. *American Journal of Psychiatry*, *104*, 523—534.

Kass, F., Spitzer, R.L. & Williams, J.B.W. (1983). An empirical study of the issue of sex bias in the diagnostic criteria of DSM-III axis II personality disorders. *American Psychologist*, *38*, 799—801.

Katschnig, H. & Simhandl, C. (1986). New developments in the classification and diagnosis of functional mental disorders. *Psychopathology*, *19*, 219—235.

Kaufman, M. (1971). *Homeopathy in America: The Rise and Fall of a Medical Heresy*. Baltimore: Johns Hopkins Press.

Kemeny, J. & Oppenheim, P. (1956). On reduction. *Philosophical Studies*, *7*, 6—17.

Kendell, R.E. (1975).The concept of disease and its implications for psychiatry. *British Journal of Psychiatry*, *127*, 305—315.

Kendell, R.E. (1983). DSM-III: A major advance in psychiatric nosology. In R.L. Spitzer, J.B.W. Williams & A.E. Skodol (Eds.), *International Perspectives on DSM-III*. Washington, DC: American Psychiatric Press.

Kendell, R.E. (1986). What are mental disorders? In A.M. Freedman, R. Brotman, I. Silverman & D. Hutson (Eds.), *Issues in Psychiatric Classification: Science, Practice, and Social Policy* (pp. 23— 45). New York: Human Sciences Press.

Kendell, R.E. (1988). What is a case? Food for thought for epidemiologists. *Archives of General Psychiatry*, *45*, 374—376.

Kendler, K.S. (1990). Toward a scientific psychiatric nosology: Strengths and limitations. *Archives of General Psychiatry*, *47*, 969—973.

Kernberg, O. (1975). *Borderline Conditions and Pathological Narcissism*. New York: Jason Aronson.

Kernberg, O.F. (1987). The dynamic unconscious and the self. In R. Stern (Ed.), *Theories of the Unconscious and Theories of the Self* (pp. 3—25). Hillsdale, NJ: Analytic Press.

Kernberg, O.F. (1989). The narcissistic personality disorder and the differential diagnosis of antisocial behavior. *Psychiatric Clinics of North America*, *12* (September), 553—557.

Kierkegaard, S. (1941). *Concluding Unscientific Postscript* (D.F. Swenson & W. Lowrie, Trans.). Princeton: Princeton University Press.

King, L. (1958). *The Medical World of the Eighteenth Century.* Chicago: University of Chicago Press.

King, L.S. (1954). What is disease? *Philosophy of Science, 21,* 193–203.

Kitcher, P. (1984). 1953 and all that: A tale of two sciences. *Philosophical Review, 18,* 335–373.

Kitcher, P. (1989). Explanatory unification and the causal structure of the world. In P. Kitcher & W. Salmon (Eds.), *Scientific Explanation* (pp. 410–505). Minneapolis: University of Minnesota Press.

Kleinman, A. (1979). *Patients and Healers in the Context of Culture.* Berkeley: University of California Press.

Kleinman, A. (1988). *Rethinking Psychiatry: From Cultural Category to Personal Experience.* Glencoe, IL: Free Press.

Kleinman, A. (1991). Culture and DSM-IV: Recommendations for the introduction and for the overall structure. (Privately circulated manuscript; A. Kleinman, M.D., Harvard University Dept. of Anthropology, William James Hall, 33 Kirkland St., Cambridge, MA 02138).

Kleinman, A. & Good, B. (Eds.). (1985). *Culture and Depression.* Berkeley: University of California Press.

Klerman, G.L. (1980). Affective disorders. In H.I. Kaplan, A. Freedman & B.J. Sadock (Eds.), *Comprehensive Textbook of Psychiatry* (3rd ed., Vol. 2, pp. 1305–1331). Baltimore: Williams & Wilkins.

Klerman, G.L., Vaillant, G.E., Spitzer, R.L. & Michels, R. (1984). A debate on DSM-III. *American Journal of Psychiatry, 141,* 539–553.

Kline, P. (1981). *Fact and Fantasy in Freudian Theory* (2nd. ed.). London: Methuen.

Klinger, L. (1986). *Einfuehrung in die Gestaltkreisexperimente.* Berlin: Springer Verlag.

Kohut, H. (1971). *The Analysis of the Self.* New York: International Universities Press.

Kraepelin, E. (1896). Der psychologische Versuch in der Psychiatrie. In E. Kraepelin (Ed.), *Psychologishe Arbeiten* (Vol. 1, pp. 1–91). Leipzig: Verlag von Wilhelm Engelman.

Kraepelin, E. (1912). *Lectures on Clinical Psychiatry* (T. Johnstone, Trans.). New York: W. Wood.

Kraepelin, E. (1917). *One Hundred Years of Psychiatry* (W. Baskin, Trans.). New York: Philosophical Library.

Krahn, D.D., Nairn, K., Gosnell, B.A. & Drewnoski, A. (1991). Stealing in eating disorder patients. *Journal of Clinical Psychiatry, 52,* 112–115.

Kramer, D. (1968). International collaboration: Guided "DSM." *Psychiatric News,* (Feb.), 8–9.

Kramer, H. & Sprenger, J. (1484). *Malleus Mallificarum or Witches' Hammer* (M. Sumners, Trans.) London: Pushkin Press (1925).

Kräupl-Taylor, F. (1983). Descriptive and developmental phenomena. In M. Shepherd & O.L. Zangwill (Eds.), *Handbook of Psychiatry 1, General Psychopathology* (pp. 59–94). Cambridge, UK: Cambridge University Press.

Kraus, A. (1977). *Sozialverhalten und Psychose Manisch-Depressiver,* Stüttgart: Enke Verlag.

Kraus, A. (Ed.). (1978) *Leib, Geist, Geschichte: Brennpunkte anthropologischer Psychiatrie*. Heidelberg: Hüthig.

Kraus, A. (1987). *The Significance of Phenomenology for Diagnosis in Psychiatry and Phenomenology* (A. Mishara, Trans.). Pittsburgh: Simon Silverton Phenomenology Center.

Kraus, A. (1991). Methodological problems with the classification of personality disorder: The significance of existential types. *Journal of Personality Disorders, 5* (1), 82–92.

Kretschmer, E. (1925). *Physique and Character*. (W.J.H. Sprott, Trans.). New York: Harcourt Brace.

Kroll, J. (1979). Philosophical foundations of French and US nosology. *American Journal of Psychiatry, 136*, 1135–1138.

Kuhn, T.S. (1962). *The Structure of Scientific Revolutions*. Chicago: University of Chicago Press.

Kuhn, T.S. (1970). *The Structure of Scientific Revolutions* (2nd ed., enlarged). Chicago: University of Chicago Press.

Ladurie, G. (1966). *The Peasants of Languedoc*. Paris: Alcan.

Laìn Entralgo, P. (1969). *Doctor and Patient*. New York: McGraw-Hill.

Laìn Entralgo, P. (1970). *The Therapy of the Word in Classical Antiquity* (L.J. Rather & J.M. Sharp, Trans.). New Haven: Yale University Press.

Laing, R.D. (1967). *The Politics of Experience*. New York: Ballantine Books.

Laing, R.D. & Esterson, A. (1970). *Sanity, Madness, and the Family*. Harmondsworth: Penguin Books.

Lakatos, I. (1978). *The Methodology of Scientific Research Programmes, Philosophical Papers* (Vol. 1) J. Worrall & G. Currie (Eds.). Cambridge, UK: Cambridge University Press.

Langer, S. (1948). *Philosophy in a New Key: A Study in the Symbolism of Reason, Rite, and Art*. New York: New American Library.

Langlois, S. & Seignebos, C. (1898). *Introduction to the Study of History* (G. Berry, Trans.). London: Duckworth.

Le Grain, M.P. (1869). *Des Anomalies de L'instincte Sexuale et en Particulariment des Inversions du Sens Genitale*. Paris: Carré.

Lerman, H. (1986). *A Mote in Freud's Eye: From Psychoanalysis to the Psychology of Women*. New York: Springer Verlag.

Lerner, H.E. (1974). The hysterical personality: A "woman's disease." *Comprehensive Psychiatry, 15*, 157–164.

Lerner, J.E. (1981). Early origins of envy and devaluation of women: Implications for sex-role stereotypes. In E. Howell & M. Bayes (Eds.), *Women and Mental Health*. New York: Basic Books.

Lesieur, H.R., Blume, S.B. & Zoppa, R.M. (1986). Alcoholism, drug abuse, and gambling. *Alcoholism: Clinical and Experimental Research, 10*, 33–38.

Lesieur, H.R. & Heineman, M. (1988). Pathological gambling among youthful multiple substance abusers in a therapeutic community. *British Journal of Addiction, 83*, 765–771.

Levine, M.P. & Troiden, R.R. (1988). The myth of sexual compulsivity. *Journal of Sex Research, 25*(3), 347–363.

Lewin, B. (1990). *Genes IV*, (4th ed.) New York: Oxford University Press.

Lewis, A.J. (1934). The psychopathology of insight. *British Journal of Medical Psychology*, *14*, 332–348.

Lewis, C.I. (1929). *Mind and the World Order: Outline of a Theory of Knowledge.* New York: Dover Publications.

Lidz, T. (1966). Adolf Meyer and the development of American Psychiatry. *American Journal of Psychiatry*, *123*, 320–332.

Linn, E.L. (1977). Verbal auditory hallucinations: mind, self, and society. *Journal of Nervous and Mental Disease*, *164*, 8–17.

Lipowski, Z.J. (1966). Psychopathology as science: its scope and tasks. *Comprehensive Psychiatry*, *7*(3), 175–182.

Lipowski, Z.J. (1981). Holistic-medical foundations of American psychiatry: a bicentennial. *The American Journal of Psychiatry*, *138*(7), 888–895.

Lithman, Y.G. (1983). Feeling good and getting smashed. In M. Freilich (Ed.), *The Pleasures of Anthropology.* New York: Mentor Books.

Lloyd, G.E.R. (Ed.). (1987). *Hippocratic Writings.* (J. Chadwick & W.N. Brown, Trans.). London: Penguin Books.

Lombroso, C. (1911). Crime, Its Causes and Remedies. (H.P. Horton, Trans.). Boston: Little Brown.

Longino, H.E. (1990). *Science as Social Knowledge: Values and Objectivity in Scientific Inquiry.* Princeton: Princeton University Press.

Luborsky, L. (1984). *Principles of Psychoanalytic Psychotherapy.* New York: Basic Books.

Ludmerer, R. (1985). *Learning to Heal: The Development of American Medical Education.* New York: Basic Books.

Luria, A.R. (1960). Verbal regulation of behavior. In M.A.B. Brazier (Ed.), *The Central Nervous System and Behavior* (pp. 26–41). Madison: Madison Printing Co.

Luria, A.R. (1961). *The Role of Speech in the Regulation of Normal and Abnormal Behavior.* New York: Liveright.

Macfarlane, A. (1970). *Witchcraft in Tudor and Stuart England: A Regional and Comparative Study.* New York: Harper & Row.

Mandelbaum, M. (1938). *The Problem of Historical Knowledge.* New York: Liveright.

Mandelbaum, M. (1977). *The Anatomy of Historical Knowledge.* Baltimore: Johns Hopkins University Press.

Margolis, J. (1978). *Persons and Minds: The Prospects of Nonreductive Naturalism.* Dordrecht, Holland: D. Reidel.

Margolis, J. (1984). *Culture and Cultural Entities: Toward a New Unity of Science.* Dordrecht, Holland: D. Reidel.

Margolis, J. (1987). *Science without Unity; Reconciling the Natural and the Human Sciences.* Oxford: Basil Blackwell.

Margolis, J. (1989). *Texts without Referents: Reconciling Science and Narrative.* Oxford: Basil Blackwell.

Margolis, J. (1991). The trouble with schizophrenia. In W.F. Flack, Jr., D.R. Miller & M. Wiener (Eds.), *What Is Schizophrenia?* New York: Springer Verlag.

Marron, H. (1966). *Meaning in History.* Baltimore: Helican Press.

Maslin, A. & Davis, J. (1975). Sex role stereotyping as a factor in mental health standards among counselors-in-training. *Counseling Psychology*, *22*, 87–91.

Masling, J. (Ed.). (1983). *Empirical Studies of Psychoanalytic Theories* (Vol. 1). Hillsdale, NJ: Analytic Press.

Masling, J. (Ed.). (1986). *Empirical Studies of Psychoanalytic Theories* (Vol. 2). Hillsdale, NJ: Analytic Press.

Masson, J.M. (1985). *The Assault on Truth: Freud's Suppression of the Seduction Theory.* New York: Penguin Books.

Maudsley, H. (1886). *Natural Causes and Supernatural Seemings.* London: Kegan Paul.

Maxwell, G. (1962). The ontological status of theoretical entities. In H. Feigl & G. Maxwell (Eds.), *Minnesota Studies in the Philosophy of Science: Volume III. Scientific Explanation, Space, and Time* (pp. 3–27). Minneapolis: University of Minnesota Press.

May, R., Angel, E. & Ellenberger, H. (Eds.) (1958). *Existence: A New Dimension in Psychiatry and Psychology.* New York: Basic Books.

Mayou, R. & Hawton, K. (1968). Psychiatric disorder in the general hospital. *British Journal of Psychiatry, 149,* 172–190.

Mayr, E. (1982). *The Growth of Biological Thought.* Cambridge: Harvard University Press.

Mayr, E. (1988). *Toward a New Philosophy of Biology.* Cambridge: Harvard University Press.

McGuigan, F.J. (1966). Covert oral behavior and auditory hallucinations. *Psychophysiology, 3,* 73–80.

McGuire, M.T. (1986). Phenomenological classification systems: The case of DSM-III. *Perspectives in Biology and Medicine, 30,* 135–147.

McHugh, P.R. & Slavney, P.R. (1983). *The Perspectives of Psychiatry.* Baltimore: Johns Hopkins University Press.

McKee, C. (1991). Breaking the mold: A humanistic approach to nursing practice. In R. McMahon & A. Pearson (Eds.), *Nursing as Therapy* (chap. 8). London: Chapman & Hall.

McKee, J. (1988). Holistic health and the critique of Western medicine. *Social Science and Medicine, 26,* 775–784.

McKegney, F. P. (1982). DSM-III: A definite advance, but the struggle continues. [editorial]. *General Hospital Psychiatry, 4,* 281–282.

McKeown, T. (1979). *The Role of Medicine: Dream, Mirage, or Nemesis?* Princeton: Princeton University Press.

Medawar, P. (1974). Hypothesis and imagination. In P.A. Schilpp (Ed.), *The Philosophy of Karl Popper (The Library of Living Philosophers XIV* (pp. 274–291). La Salle, IL: Open Court.

Medin, D.L. (1989). Concepts and conceptual structure. *American Psychologist, 44,* 1469–1481.

Menninger, K. (1963). Attests and exhibits (pp. 419–492). In K. Menninger, M. Mayman & P. Pruyser, *The Vital Balance: The Life Process in Mental Health and Illness.* New York: Viking.

Menninger, K., Mayman, M. & Pruyser, P. (1963). *The Vital Balance: The Life Process in Mental Health and Illness.* New York: Viking.

Merleau-Ponty, M. (1966). *Phenomenologie der Wahrnehmung.* Berlin: De Gruyter.

Meyer, A. (1950). *The Commonsense Psychiatry of Dr. Adolf Meyer* (see especially 1906 essay, Principles in grouping facts in psychiatry, pp. 590–606). A. Lief (Ed.). New York: McGraw-Hill.

Meyer, A. (1950–1954). *The Collected Papers of Dr. Adolf Meyer* (4 Vols.). E. Winters (Ed.), Baltimore: Johns Hopkins Press.

Meynert, T. (1892). *Psychiatry*. New York: Hafner (1968).

Mezzich, J.E. (1989). An empirical prototypical approach to the definition of psychiatric illness. *British Journal of Psychiatry, 154* (Suppl. 4), 42–46.

Mezzich, J.E., Fabrega, H. & Mezzich, A.C. (1987). On the clinical utility of multiaxial diagnosis. In G.L. Tischler (Ed.), *Diagnosis and Classification in Psychiatry: A Critical Appraisal of DSM-III* (pp. 449–463). Cambridge, UK: Cambridge University Press.

Mezzich, J.E. & Sharfstein, S.S. (1985). Severity of illness and diagnostic formulation: Classifying patients for prospective payment systems. *Hospital and Community Psychiatry, 36*, 770–772.

Mezzich, J.E. & von Cranach, M. (1988). *International Classification in Psychiatry: Unity and Diversity*. Cambridge: Cambridge University Press.

Miles, A. (1988). *Women and Mental Illness*. Sussex: Wheatshean.

Mill, J.S. (1961). *On Liberty*. Reproduced in M. Lerner (Ed.), *Essential Works of John Stuart Mill* (pp. 253–360). New York: Bantam Books.

Mill, J.S. (1974). *System of Logic* (Vols. 1 & 2). J.M. Robson (Ed.). Toronto: University of Toronto Press.

Miller, W.R., Hedrick, K.E. & Taylor, C.A. (1983). Addictive behaviors and life problems before and after behavioral treatment of problem drinkers. *Addictive Behaviors, 8*, 403–412.

Millon, T. (1981). *Disorders of Personality: DSM-III, Axis II*. New York: John Wiley & Sons.

Millon, T. (1987). On the nature of taxonomy in psychopathology. In C.G. Last & M. Hersen (Eds.), *Issues in Diagnostic Research* (pp. 3–85). New York: Plenum.

Millon, T. (1991). Classification in psychopathology: Rationale, alternatives, and standards. *Journal of Abnormal Psychology, 100*, 245–261.

Millon, T. & Klerman, G. (Eds.). (1986). *Contemporary Directions in Psychopathology: Toward the DSM-IV*. New York: Guilford Press.

Minkowski, E. (1970). *Lived Time: Phenomenological and Psychopathological Studies* (N. Metzel, Trans.). Evanston, IL: Northwestern University Press.

Mintz, S. & Alpert, M. (1972). Imagery vividness, reality-testing, and schizophrenic hallucinations. *Journal of Abnormal Psychology, 19*, 310–316.

Minuchin, S. (1974). *Families and Family Therapy*. Cambridge: Harvard University Press.

Mirowski, J. & Ross, C.E. (1989). Psychiatric diagnosis as reified measurement. *Journal of Health and Social Behavior, 30*, 11–25.

Mishara, A. (in press). *Phenomenology and the Unconscious: The Problem of the Unconscious in the Phenomenological and Existential Traditions: E. Husserl, V. von Weizsaecker, L. Binswanger*. The Hague: Kluwer Academic Publishers.

Mitchell, J. (1974). *Psychoanalysis and Feminism*. New York: Vintage Books.

Mitchell, J.E. & Goff, G. (1984). Bulimia in male patients. *Psychosomatics, 25*, 909–913.

Mitchell, J.E., Hatsukami, D., Eckert, E.D. & Pyle, R.L. (1985). Characteristics of 275 patients with bulimia. *American Journal of Psychiatry, 142*, 482—485.

Mitchell, S.W. (1877). *Fat and Blood, or How to Make Them*. Philadelphia: J.B. Lippincott.

Mitchell, S.W. (1894). Address before the 50th annual meeting of the American Medico-Psychological Association, held in Philadelphia, May 16th, 1894. *Journal of Nervous and Mental Disease, 21*, 413—437.

Möller, H.J. & Zerssen, D. von (1981). Depressive symptomatok in stationärem behandlungsablauf von 280 schizophrenen patienten. *Pharmacopsychiatry, 14*, 172—179.

Montagne, M. (1988). The metaphorical nature of drugs and drug taking. *Social Science and Medicine, 26*, 417—424.

Mora, G. (1980). Three American historians of psychiatry. In E. Wallace & L. Pressley (Eds.), *Essays in the History of Psychiatry* (pp. 1—21). Columbia, SC: R. L. Bryan.

Mora, G. (in press-a). Middle Ages. In E. Wallace & J. Gach (Eds.), *Handbook of the History of Psychiatry*. New Haven: Yale University Press.

Mora, G. (in press-b). Renaissance psychiatry. In E. Wallace & J. Gach (Eds.), *Handbook of the History of Psychiatry*. New Haven: Yale University Press.

Mora, G. & Brand, J. (1970). *Psychiatry and Its History: Methodological Problems in Research*. Springfield, IL: Charles C. Thomas.

Morgagni, G.B. (1761). *De Sedibus, et Causis Morborum per Anatomen Indagatis Libri Quinque* (2 vols.). Typog: Remondiniana.

Mott, R.H., Small, J.F. & Anderson, J.M. (1965). Comparative study of hallucinations. *Archives of General Psychiatry, 12*, 595—601.

Mullan, M.J. & Murray, R.M. (1989). The impact of molecular genetics on our understanding of the psychoses. *British Journal of Psychiatry, 154*, 591—595.

Müller-Suur, H. (1958). Die schizophrenen symptome und der eindruck des schizophrenene. *Fortschrift Neurologie und Psychiatrie, 26*, 140—150.

Müller-Suur, H. (1961). Das sogenannte praecoxgefühl. *Fortschrift Neurologie und Psychiatrie, 29*, 145—152.

Musto, D. (1978). History and the psychiatrist. *American Journal of Psychiatry, 135* (supplement), 22—26.

Musto, D.F. (1973). *The American Disease: Origins of Narcotic Control*. New Haven: Yale University Press.

Nagel, E. (1949). The meaning of reduction in the natural sciences. In R. Stauffer (Ed.), *Science and Civilization*. Madison: University of Wisconsin Press.

Nagel, E. (1961). *The Structure of Science*. New York: Harcourt Brace.

National Committee for Mental Hygiene (1918). *Statistical Manual for the Use of Institutions for the Insane*. Washington, DC: National Committee for Mental Hygiene.

Neisser, U. (1967). *Cognitive Psychology*. New York: Appleton-Century-Crofts.

Neurath, O. (1959). Protocol sentences. In A.J. Ayer (Ed.), *Logical Positivism* (F. Schick, Trans.). Glencoe, IL: Free Press.

Novey, S. (1968). *The Second Look: The Reconstruction of Personal History in Psychiatry and Psychoanalysis*. Baltimore: Johns Hopkins Press.

Oakes, G. (1988). *Weber and Rickert: Concept Formation in the Cultural Sciences*. Cambridge: MIT Press.

Oakeshott, M. (1933). *Experience and Its Modes*. Cambridge, UK: Cambridge University Press.

O'Neal, P., Robins, L., King, L. & Schaefer, J. (1962) Parental deviance and the genesis of sociopathic personality. *American Journal of Psychiatry, 118*, 1114–1124.

Oppenheim, A.L. (1977). *Ancient Mesopotamia: Portrait of a Dead Civilization*. Chicago: University of Chicago Press.

Orford, J. (1978). Hypersexuality: Implications for a theory of dependence. *British Journal of Addiction, 73*, 299–310.

Overall, J.E. & Hollister, L.E. (1982). Decision rules for phenomenological classification of psychiatric patients. *Journal of Consulting and Clinical Psychology, 50*, 535–545.

Owen, M. & Mullan, M. (1990). Molecular genetic studies of manic depression and schizophrenia. *Trends in Neuroscience, 13*, 29–31.

Pagel, W. (1958). *Paracelsus: An Introduction to Philosophical Medicine in the Era of the Renaissance*. New York: S. Karger.

Panzetta, A.F. (1974). Toward a scientific psychiatric nosology: Conceptual and pragmatic issues. *Archives of General Psychiatry, 30*, 154–161.

Paracelsus (1531). *The Invisible Diseases*. Basel, n.p..

Pardes, H., Kaufmann, C., Pincus, H. & West, A. (1989). Genetics and psychiatry: Past discoveries, current dilemmas, and future directions. *American Journal of Psychiatry, 146*, 435–443.

Pellegrino, E.O. & Thomasma, D.C. (1981). *A Philosophical Basis of Medical Practice*. Oxford: Oxford University Press.

Penfield, W. & Perot, P. (1963). The brain's record of auditory and visual experience. *Brain, 86*, 595–696.

Penfold, P.S. & Walker, G.A. (1983). *Women and the Psychiatric Paradox*. Montreal: Eden.

Perry, H.S. (1982). *Psychiatrist of America: The Life of Harry Stack Sullivan*. Cambridge: Belknap Press of Harvard University.

Perry, J. & Cooper, S. (1989). An empirical study of defense mechanisms. *Archives of General Psychiatry, 46*, 441–452.

Peterfreund, E. (1983). *The Process of Psychoanalytic Therapy: Models and Strategies*. Hillsdale, NJ: Analytic Press.

Peveler, R. & Fairburn, C. (1990). Eating disorders in women who abuse alcohol. *British Journal of Addiction, 85*, 1633–1638.

Pfohl, B. & Andreasen, N.C. (1978). Development of classification systems in psychiatry. *Comprehensive Psychiatry, 19*, 197–207.

Piaget, J. (1954). *The Construction of Reality in the Child* (M. Cook, Trans.). New York: Basic Books.

Pichot, P. (1978). Psychopathic behaviour: A historical overview. In R.D. Hare & D.S. Shalling (Eds.), *Psychopathic Behaviour: Approaches to Research* (pp. 55–70). Chichester, UK: John Wiley & Sons.

Pick, D. (1989). *Faces of Degeneration: A European Disorder c. 1845–1918*. Cambridge: Cambridge University Press.

Pincus, H.A., Frances, A., Davis, W.W., First, M.B. & Widiger, T.A. (1992). DSM-IV and new diagnostic categories: Holding the line on proliferation. *American Journal of Psychiatry, 149*, 112–117.

Pinel, P. (1798). *Nosographie Philosophique*. Paris: Alcan.

Pinel, P. (1801). *A Treatise on Insanity* (D. Davis, Trans.). Sheffield, UK: W. Todd.

Popkin, M.K., Tucker, G., Caine, E., Folstein, M. & Grant, I. (1989). The fate of organic mental disorders in DSM-IV: A progress report. *Psychosomatics, 30,* 438–441.

Popper, K.R. (1957). The aim of science. *Ratio, 1,* 24–35.

Popper, K.R. (1963). *Conjectures and Refutations: The Growth of Scientific Knowledge.* London: Routledge & Kegan Paul.

Popper, K.R. (1965). *The Logic of Scientific Discovery.* New York: Harper & Row.

Popper, K.R. (1968). *Conjectures and Refutations: The Growth of Scientific Knowledge.* New York: Harper & Row.

Popper, K.R. (1976). *Logik der Forschung.* 3 Aufl. Tübingen: J.C.B. Mohr.

Popper, K.R. & Eccles, J. (1981). *The Self and Its Brain.* New York: Springer Verlag.

Posey, T.B. & Losch, M.E. (1983). Auditory hallucinations of hearing voices in 375 normal subjects. *Imagination, Cognition, and Personality, 2,* 99–113.

Pottash, A.L.C., Jonas, J.M., Gold, M.S. & Cocores, J.A. (1986). Phenomenologic link between substance abuse and eating disorders. *Society of Neuroscience Abstracts, 12,* 940.

Putnam, H. (1975a). Is semantics possible? In *Philosophical Papers* (Vol. 2). Cambridge: Cambridge University Press.

Putnam, H. (1975b). The meaning of "meaning." In *Philosophical Papers* (Vol. 2). Cambridge: Cambridge University Press.

Pyle, R.L., Mitchell, J.E., Eckert, E.D., Halvorson, P.A., Neuman, P.A. & Goff, G. M. (1983). The incidence of bulimia in freshman college students. *International Journal of Eating Disorders, 2,* 75–85.

Quine, W.V. (1969). Epistemology naturalized. In *Ontological Relativity and Other Essays.* New York: Columbia University Press.

Quine, W.V.O. (1953). *From a Logical Point of View.* Cambridge: Harvard University Press.

Rainer, J.D. (1972). The contributions of genetics to problems of nosology and their interrelationship in psychiatry. *International Journal of Mental Health, 1,* 28–41.

Ramirez, L.F., McCormick, R.A., Russo, A.M. & Taber, J.I. (1983). Patterns of substance abuse in pathological gamblers undergoing treatment. *Addictive Behaviors, 8,* 425–528.

Rawlinson, M. (Issue Ed.) (1987). Michael Foucault and the philosophy of medicine. *Journal of Medicine and Philosophy, 12,* 309–411.

Read, K. (1965). *The High Valley.* New York: Columbia University Press.

Read, K. (1986). *Return to the High Valley: Coming Full Circle.* Berkeley: University of California Press.

Reil, C.J. (1803). *Rhapsodien über die Anwendung der psychischen Cur-Methoden auf Geisteszerrüttengen.* Halle: Curt.

Reiss, B. (1974). New view points on the female homosexual. In V. Franks & V. Burkle (Eds.), *Women and Therapy.* New York: Brunner/Mazel.

Reiss, D., Plomin, R. & Hetherington, E. (1991). Genetics and psychiatry: An unheralded window on the environment. *American Journal of Psychiatry, 148,* 283–291.

Report of the Regents of the Lunatic Asylum to the Legislature of South Carolina. (1853). Columbia, SC: State Printing Office.

Rescher, N. (1969/1970). Lawfulness as mind-dependent. In N. Rescher (Ed.), *Essays in Honor of Carl G. Hempel* (pp. 178–197). Dordrecht, Holland: D. Reidel.

Ricoeur, P. (1981). The hermeneutical function of distanciation. In J.B. Thompson (Ed. & Trans.), *Hermeneutics and the Human Sciences: Essays on Language, Action, and Interpretation.* Cambridge: Cambridge University Press.

Rieff, P. (1959). *Freud: The Mind of the Moralist.* New York: Viking.

Rieff, P. (1968). *The Triumph of the Therapeutic: Use of Faith after Freud.* New York: Harper & Row.

Ritchie, K. (1989). The little woman meets son of DSM-III. *Journal of Medicine and Philosophy, 14,* 695–708.

Rivera-Tovar, A.D. & Frank, E. (1990). Late luteal phase dysphoric disorder in young women. *American Journal of Psychiatry, 147,* 1634–1636.

Roberts, G. (1990). Schizophrenia: The cellular biology of a functional psychosis. *Trends in Neuroscience, 13,* 207–211.

Robins, E. & Guze, S.B. (1970). Establishment of diagnostic validity in psychiatric illness: Its application to schizophrenia. *American Journal of Psychiatry, 126,* 107–111.

Robins, L. & Barrett, J. (1989). Preface. In L. Robbins & J. Barrett (Eds.), *The Validity of Psychiatric Diagnosis.* New York: Raven Press.

Robins, L.N. (1989). Diagnostic grammar and assessment: Translating criteria into questions. *Psychological Medicine, 19,* 57–68.

Robinson, P.H. & Holden, N.L. (1986). Bulimia nervosa in the male: A report of nine cases. *Psychological Medicine, 16,* 795–803.

Rohde, E. (1925). *Psyche: The Cult of Souls and Belief in Immortality Among the Greeks* (W.B. Hillis, Trans.). London: Routledge & Kegan Paul.

Rosen, G. (1968). *Madness in Society.* Chicago: University of Chicago Press.

Rosenberg, C. (1962). *The Cholera Years.* Chicago: University of Chicago Press.

Rosenberg, C. (1967). *The Trial of the Assassin Guiteau.* Philadelphia: University of Pennsylvania Press.

Rosenhan, D.L. (1973). On being sane in insane places. *Journal of Science, 179,* 250–258.

Rosenthal, B.G. (1971). *The Changes of Man.* New York: Basic Books.

Roth, E.M. & Shoben, E.J. (1983). The effect of context on the structure of categories. *Cognitive Psychology, 15,* 346–378.

Roth, M. & Kroll, J. (1968). *The Reality of Mental Illness.* Cambridge, UK: Cambridge University Press.

Rothman, D. (1971). *The Discovery of the Asylum: Social Order and Disorder in the New Republic.* Boston: Little Brown.

Rümke, H.C. (1958). Die klinische differenzierung innerhalb der gruppe der schizophrenien. *Nervenarzt, 29,* 49–53.

Runyan, W.M. (1984). *Life Histories and Psychobiography.* Oxford: Oxford University Press.

Rush, B. (1812). *Medical Inquiries and Observations upon the Diseases of the Mind.* Philadelphia: Kimber & Richardson.

Sadler, J.Z. (1992). Eidetic and empirical research: A hermeneutic complementarity. In M. Spitzer, F. Uehlein, M.A. Schwartz & C. Mundt (Eds.), *Phenomenology, Language and Schizophrenia* (pp. 103–114). New York: Springer Verlag.

Sadler, J.Z. & Hulgus, Y.F. (1990). Knowing, valuing, acting: Clues to revising the biopsychosocial model. *Comprehensive Psychiatry, 31,* 185—195.

Sadler, J.Z. & Hulgus, Y.F. (1991). Clinical controversy and the domains of scientific evidence. *Family Process, 30,* 21—36.

Salmon, W. (1984). *Scientific Explanation and the Causal Structure of the World.* Princeton: Princeton University Press.

Salmon, W.C. (1989). Four decades of scientific explanation. In P. Kitcher & W. Salmon (Eds.), *Scientific Explanation* (pp. 3—219). Minneapolis: University of Minnesota Press.

Sarton (1952). *A History of Science* (Vol. 1). Cambridge: Harvard University Press.

Sarton (1959). *A History of Science* (Vol. 2). Cambridge: Harvard University Press.

Sartre, J.P. (1956). *Being and Nothingness* (H. Barnes, Trans.). New York: Philosophical Library.

Sartre, J.P.(1966). *Being and Nothingness: A Phenomenological Essay on Ontology* (H. Barnes, Trans.). New York: Washington Square Press.

Scaff, L.A. (1989). *Fleeing the Iron Cage: Culture, Politics, and Modernity in the Thought of Max Weber.* Berkeley: University of California Press.

Schafer, R. (1978). *Language and Insight: The Sigmund Freud Memorial Lectures 1975—1976,* University College, London. New Haven: Yale University Press.

Schaffner, K.F. (1967). Approaches to reduction. *Philosophy of Science, 34,* 137—147.

Schaffner, K.F. (1974a). The peripherality of reductionism in the development of molecular biology. *Journal of the History of Biology, 7,* 111—139.

Schaffner, K.F. (1974b). The unity of science and theory construction in molecular biology. In R.J. Seeger & R.S. Cohen (Eds.), *Philosophical Foundations of Science: Proceedings of Section L, 1969. American Association for the Advancement of Science.* Dordrecht, Holland: D. Reidel.

Schaffner, K.F. (1977). Reduction, reductionism, values and progress in the biomedical sciences. In R. Colodny (Ed.), *Pittsburgh Series in the Philosophy of Science* (Vol. 5, pp. 143—171). Pittsburgh: University of Pittsburgh Press.

Schaffner, K.F. (1980). Theory structure in the biomedical sciences. *Journal of Medicine and Philosophy, 5,* 57—97.

Schaffner, K.F. (1984). Reductionism in biology: Prospects and problems. In E. Sober (Ed.), *Conceptual Issues in Evolutionary Biology: An Anthology.* Cambridge: MIT Press.

Schaffner, K.F. (1986). Exemplar reasoning about biological models and diseases: A relation between the philosophy of medicine and philosophy of science. *Journal of Medicine and Philosophy, 11,* 63—80.

Schaffner, K.F. (1993). *Discovery and Explanation in Biology and Medicine.* Chicago: University of Chicago Press.

Schaffner, K.F. (in press). Philosophy of medicine. In M. Salmon (Ed.), *Philosophy of Science: An Introduction.* Englewood Cliffs, NJ: Prentice-Hall.

Scheffler, I. (1967). *Science and Subjectivity.* Indianapolis: Bobbs-Merrill.

Schlick, M. (1959). The foundation of knowledge. In A.J. Ayer (Ed.), *Logical Positivism* (D. Rynin, Trans.). Glencoe, IL: Free Press.

Schneider, J.A. & Agras, W.S. (1987). Bulimia in males: A matched comparison with females. *International Journal of Eating Disorders, 6,* 235—242.

Schneider, K. (1959). *Klinische Psychopathologie.* Stüttgart: Thieme.

Schröder, P. (1915). Von den halluzinationen. *Monatsschrift für Psychiatrie und Neurologie*, *37*, 1—11.

Schütz, A. (1962). Common-Sense and Scientific Interpretation of Human Action. In *Collected Papers I: The Problem of Social Reality* (pp. 3—47). The Hague: Martinus Nijhoff.

Schwartz, M.A. & Wiggins, O.P. (1985). Science, humanism, and the nature of medical practice: A phenomenological view. *Perspectives in Biology and Medicine*, *28*, 331—361.

Schwartz, M.A. & Wiggins, O.P. (1986). Logical empiricism and psychiatric classification. *Comprehensive Psychiatry*, *27*, 101—114.

Schwartz, M.A. & Wiggins, O.P. (1987a). Diagnosis and ideal types: A contribution to psychiatric classification. *Comprehensive Psychiatry*, *28*, 277—291.

Schwartz, M.A. & Wiggins, O.P. (1987b). Typifications: The first step for clinical diagnosis in psychiatry. *Journal of Nervous and Mental Disease*, *175*, 65—77.

Schwartz, M.A. & Wiggins, O.P. (1988). Perspectivism and the methods of psychiatry. *Comprehensive Psychiatry*, *29*, 237—251.

Schwartz, M.A. & Wiggins, O.P. (1991) Research into personality disorders: The alternatives of dimensions and ideal types. *Journal of Personality Disorders*, *5*, 66—81.

Schwartz, M.A., Wiggins, O.P. & Norko, M.A. (1989). Prototypes, ideal types, and personality disorders: The return to classical psychiatry. *Journal of Personality Disorders*, *3*, 1—9.

Sedgwick, P. (1973). Illness——mental and otherwise. In *The Hastings Center Studies* (Vol. I, no. 3, pp. 19—40). Hastings-on-Hudson, NY: Institute of Society, Ethics, and the Life Sciences.

Sedman, G. (1966). "Inner voices": Phenomenological and clinical aspects. *British Journal of Psychiatry*, *112*, 485—490.

Seebohm, T. (1962). *Die Bedingungen der Moeglichkeit der Transcendental-Philosophie*. Bonn: Bouvier.

Seldin, D.W. (1977). The medical model: Biomedical science as the basis of medicine. In *Beyond Tomorrow: Trends and Prospects in Biomedical Science, 75th Anniversary Conference* (pp. 31—40). New York: Rockefeller University.

Semelaigne, A. (1869). *Études Historiques de L'Alienation Mentale dans L'Antiquité*. Paris: Osselin.

Shapere, D. (1974). Scientific theories and their domains. In F. Suppe (Ed.), *The Structure of Scientific Theories* (pp. 518—565). Urbana: University of Illinois Press.

Shapere, D. (1985). Observation and the scientified enterprise. In P. Achinstein & O. Hannaway (Eds.), *Observation, Experiment, and Hypothesis in Modern Physical Science*. Cambridge: MIT Press.

Shaw, E.D. (1986). Political terrorists: Dangers of diagnosis and an alternative to the psychopathology model. *Journal of Law and Psychiatry*, *8*, 359—368.

Sherif, M. & Cantril, H. (1947). *The Psychology of Ego-Involvements*. New York: McGraw-Hill.

Sherman, J.A. (1980). Therapist attitudes and sex-role stereotyping. In A.M. Brodsky & R.T. Hare-Mustin (Eds.), *Women and Psychotherapy: An Assessment of Research and Practice*. New York: Guilford Press.

Sherrington, R., Brynjolfsson, J. Petursson, H., Pottee, M., Dudleston, K., Barraclough, B., Wasmuth, J., Dobbs, M. & Guerling, H. (1988). Localization of a susceptibility locus for schizophrenia on chromosome 5. *Nature, 336,* 164–167.

Shuman, D.W. (1989). The Diagnostic and Statistical Manual of Mental Disorders in the courts. *Bulletin of the American Academy of Psychiatry and Law, 17,* 25–32.

Siegel, R. (1973). *Galen on Psychology, Psychopathology, and Function and Diseases of the Nervous System.* Basel: S. Karger.

Siegel, S. (1956). *Nonparametric Statistics for the Social Sciences.* New York: McGraw-Hill.

Sigerist, H. (1943). *Civilization and Disease.* Chicago: University of Chicago Press.

Sigerist, H. (1951). *A History of Medicine* (Vol. 1). Oxford: Oxford University Press.

Sigerist, H. (1961). *A History of Medicine* (Vol. 2). Oxford: Oxford University Press.

Silverman, D., Gartrell, N., Aronson, M., Steer, M. & Edbril, S. (1983). In search of the biopsychosocial perspective: an experiment with beginning medical students. *American Journal of Psychiatry, 140,* 1154–1158.

Simon, B. (1978). *Mind and Madness in Ancient Greece: The Classical Roots of Modern Psychiatry.* Ithaca, NY: Cornell University Press.

Skodol, A.E. & Spitzer, R.L. (1982). DSM-III: Rationale, basic concepts, and some differences from ICD-9. *Acta Psychiatrica Scandinavica, 66,* 271–281.

Slade, P.D. (1976). Toward a theory of auditory hallucinations: An outline of an hypothetical four-factor model. *British Journal of Social and Clinical Psychology, 15,* 415–423.

Smith, E.E. & Medin, D.L. (1981). *Categories and Concepts.* Cambridge: Harvard University Press.

Spanos, N.P. (1978). Witchcraft in histories of psychiatry: A critical analysis and an alternative conceptualization. *Psychological Bulletin, 85,* 417–439.

Spanos, N.P. (1985). Witchcraft and social history: An essay review. *Journal of the History of the Behavioral Sciences, 21,* 60–66.

Spence, D.P. (1982). Narrative Truth and Historical Truth: Meaning and Interpretation in Psychoanalysis. New York: W.W. Norton.

Spiegelberg, H. (1972). *Phenomenology in Psychology and Psychiatry: A Historical Introduction.* Evanston, IL: Northwestern University Press.

Spiro, H.M. (1986). *Doctors, Patients, and Placebos.* New Haven: Yale University Press.

Spiro, M. (1965). Religious systems as culturally constructed defense mechanisms. In M. Spiro (Ed.), *Context and Meaning in Cultural Anthropology* (pp. 100–113). Glencoe, IL: Free Press.

Spitzer, M. (1988). Psychiatry, philosophy, and the problem of description. In M. Spitzer, F.A. Uehlein & G. Oepen (Eds.), *Psychopathology and Philosophy.* Berlin: Springer Verlag.

Spitzer, M. (1989). *Was ist Wahn? Untersuchungen zum Wahnproblem.* Berlin: Springer Verlag.

Spitzer, M. (1990). On defining delusions. *Comprehensive Psychiatry, 31,* 377–397.

Spitzer, M. (in press). *Hallucinations.* New York: John Wiley & Sons.

Spitzer, M. & Maher, B. (1990). *Philosophy and Psychopathology.* Heidelberg: Springer Verlag.

Spitzer, M., Uehlein, F. & Oepen, G. (Eds.). (1988). *Psychopathology and Philosophy.* New York: Springer Verlag.

Spitzer, R.L. (1980). Introduction. *Diagnostic and Statistical Manual of Mental Disorders* (3rd ed., rev., pp. 1–12). Washington, DC: American Psychiatric Association Press.

Spitzer, R.L. (1987). Introduction. *Diagnostic and Statistical Manual of Mental Disorders* (3rd ed., rev., pp. xvii–xxvii). Washington, DC: American Psychiatric Press.

Spitzer, R.L. (1989). Discussion comments to a paper by R. Blashfield. In J. Barrett & L. Robins (Eds.), *The Validity of Psychiatric Diagnosis.* New York: Raven Press.

Spitzer, R.L. & Williams, J.B.W. (1988a). Basic principles in the development of DSM-III. In J.E. Mezzich & M. von Cranach (Eds.), International Classification in Psychiatry: Unity and Diversity. Cambridge, UK: Cambridge University Press.

Spitzer, R.L. & Williams, J.B.W. (1988b). The revision of DSM-III: Process and changes. In J.E. Messich & M. von Cranach (Eds.), *International Classification in Psychiatry: Unity and Diversity.* Cambridge, UK: Cambridge University Press.

Spitzer, R.L., Williams, J.B.W., First, M. & Kendler, K. (1989). A proposal for DSM-IV: Solving the "organic/nonorganic" problem. *Journal of Neuropsychiatry, 1,* 126–127.

Spitzer, R.L., Williams, J.B.W., Gillon, M. & First, M. (1990). *SCID: Structured Clinical Interview for DSM-III-R.* Washington, DC: American Psychiatric Press.

Stannard, D. (1980). *Shrinking History: On Freud and the Failure of Psychohistory.* Oxford: Oxford University Press.

Stanton, A. & Schwartz, M. (1954). *The Mental Hospital.* New York: Basic Books.

Starr, P. (1982). *The Social Transformation of American Medicine.* New York: Basic Books.

Stengel, E. (1959). Classification of mental disorders. *Bulletin of the World Health Organization, 21,* 601–663.

Stephens, G.L. & Graham, G. (1991). *Introspective Self-Identification and Disturbances of Self-Consciousness.* Paper presented at the meeting of the Society for Philosophy and Psychology. San Francisco, CA.

Stephens, G.L. & Graham, G. (in press). Mind and mine. In G. Graham & G.L. Stephens (Eds.), *Philosophical Psychopathology.* Cambridge: MIT Press.

Stern, S.L., Dixon, K.N., Nemzer, E., Lake, M.D., Sansone, R.A., Smeltzer, D.J., Lantz, S. & Schrier, S.S. (1984). Affective disorder in the families of women with normal weight bulimia. *American Journal of Psychiatry, 141,* 1224–1227.

Stich, S. (1983). *From Folk Psychology to Cognitive Science: The Case Against Belief.* Cambridge: MIT Press.

Stocking, G.W. (1968). *Race, Culture, and Evolution: Essays in the History of Anthropology.* Chicago: University of Chicago Press.

Stone, M.H. (1980). *The Borderline Syndromes.* New York: McGraw-Hill.

Stone, M.H. (1987). Homosexuality in patients with borderline personality disorder. *American Journal of Psychiatry, 144,* 1622–1623.

Straus, E. (1930). *Geschehnis und Erlebnis.* Berlin: Springer Verlag. [English translation: Event and experience. In *Man, Time and World: Two Contributions to Anthropological Psychology* (D. Moss, Trans.) Pittsburgh: Duquesne University Press (1982).]

Straus, E. (1949). *Anesthesiology and Hallucinations* (pp. 139–169). [Reprinted in R. May, E. Angel & H. Ellenberger (Eds.) (1958). *Existence.* New York: Basic Books.]

Straus, E. (1966). The upright posture. *Phenomenological Psychiatry.* New York: Basic Books.

Strauss, J.S. (1969). Hallucinations and delusions as points on continua function: Rating scale evidence. *Archives of General Psychiatry, 31,* 581–586.

Strauss, J.S. & Carpenter, W.T. (1981). *Schizophrenia.* New York: Plenum.

Strawson, P.F. (1962). Freedom and resentment. *Proceedings of the British Academy, 48,* 187–211.

Stricker, G. (1977). Implications of research for psychotherapeutic treatment of women. *American Psychologist, 32,* 14–22.

Strober, M. (1981). The significance of bulimia in juvenile anorexia nervosa: An exploration of possible etiological factors. *International Journal of Eating Disorders, 1,* 28–43.

Styron, W. (1990). *Darkness Visible: A Memoir of Madness.* New York: Random House.

Swerdlow, N. & Koob, G. (1987). Dopamine, schizophrenia, mania, and depression: Toward a unified hypothesis of cortico-striato-pallido-thalamic function. *Behavioral and Brain Sciences, 10,* 197–245.

Switz, W. (Trans. & commentary). (1978). *The Sacred Disease.* In G.E.R. Lloyd (Ed.), *Hippocratic Writings.* Baltimore: Penguin Books.

Szasz, T.S. (1960). The myth of mental illness. *American Psychologist, 15,* 113–118.

Szasz, T.S. (1961). *The Myth of Mental Illness.* New York: Harper & Row.

Szasz, T.S. (1970a). *Ideology and Insanity.* New York: Doubleday.

Szasz, T.S. (1970b). *The Manufacture of Madness.* New York: Harper & Row.

Szasz, T.S. (1972). *The Myth of Mental Illness.* Herts: Paladin.

Szasz, T.S. (1974). *Ceremonial Chemistry.* Garden City, NJ: Anchor Press.

Taube, C., Lee, E.S. & Forthofer, R.N. (1984). Diagnosis-related groups for mental disorders, alcoholism, and drug abuse: Evaluation and alternatives. *Hospital and Community Psychiatry, 35,* 452–455.

Taylor, C. (1976). Responsibility for self. In A. Rorty (Ed.), *The Identities of Persons.* Berkeley: University of California Press.

Taylor, M.A. (1987). DSM-III organic mental disorders. In G.L. Tischler (Ed.), *Diagnosis and Classification in Psychiatry: A Critical Appraisal of DSM-III.* Cambridge, UK: Cambridge University Press.

Taylor, S.E. & Fiske, S.T. (1975). Point of view and perceptions of causality. *Journal of Personality and Social Psychology, 32,* 439–445.

Tellenbach, H. (1987a). Die räumlichkeit des melancholischen I: über veraender-ungen des raumerlebens in der melancholie. [Reprinted in *Psychiatrie als geistige Medizin* (pp. 13–24). München: Verlag für angewandte Wissenschaften.]

Tellenbach, H. (1987b). Hermeneutische Akte in der Psychiatrie (pp. 229–233). [Reprinted in *Psychiatrie als Geistige Medizin.* München: Verlag für angewandte Wissenschaften.]

Tellenbach, H. (1987c). Martin Buber's Einfluss auf die anthropologische Wende in der Medizin. [Reprinted in *Psychiatrie als Geistige Medizin* (pp. 265–270). München: Verlag für angewandte Wissenschaften.]

Temkin, O. (1973). *Galenism: The Rise and Decline of a Medical Philosophy*. Ithaca, NY: Cornell University Press.

Temkin, O. (1977). *The Double Face of Janus and Other Essays in the History of Medicine*. Baltimore: Johns Hopkins University Press.

Thompson, E.P. (1963). *The English Working Class*. London: Routledge & Kegan Paul.

Thompson, R.F. (1967). *Foundations of Physiological Psychology*. New York: Harper & Row.

Tighe, J. (in press). A history of forensic psychiatry in America. In E. Wallace & J. Gach (Eds.), *Handbook of the History of Psychiatry*. New Haven: Yale University Press.

Timmerman, M.G., Wells, L.A. & Chen, S. (1990). Bulimia nervosa and associated alcohol abuse among secondary school students. *Journal of the American Academy of Child and Adolescent Psychiatry, 29*, 118–122.

Tischler, G.L. (1987). *Diagnosis and Classification in Psychiatry: A Critical Appraisal of DSM-III*. Cambridge, UK: Cambridge University Press.

Torrey, E.F. (1973). *The Mind Game: Witchdoctors and Psychiatrists*. New York: Bantam Books.

Torrey, E.F. (1975). *The Death of Psychiatry*. New York: Penguin Books.

Toulmin, S. (Special Issue Ed.) (1977). Mental health. *Journal of Medicine and Philosophy, 2*, 191–304.

Toulmin, S. (1980). Agent and patient in psychiatry. *International Journal of Law and Psychiatry, 3*, 267–278.

Trotter, T. (1807). *A View of the Nervous Temperament*. Newcastle: Edward Walker.

Turk, D.C., Meichenbaum, D. & Genest, M. (1983). *Pain and Behavioral Medicine: A Cognitive-Behavioral Perspective*. New York: Guilford Press.

Turner, M.B. (1967). *Philosophy and the Science of Behavior*. New York: Appleton-Century-Crofts.

Uehlein, F.A. (1992). Eidos and variation in Husserl's phenomenology. In M. Spitzer, F. Uehlein, M.A. Schwartz & C. Mundt (Eds.), *Phenomenology, Language, and Schizophrenia* (pp. 88–102). New York: Springer Verlag.

Urmson, J.O. (1950). On grading. *Mind, 59*, 145–169.

Vaillant, G.E. (1975). Sociopathy as a human process: A viewpoint. *Archives of General Psychiatry, 32*, 178–183.

Vaillant, G.E. (1985). An empirically derived hierarchy of adaptive mechanisms and its usefulness as a potential diagnostic axis. *Acta Psychiatrica Scandinavica, 71* (Suppl. 319), pp. 171–180.

Vaillant, G.E. & Schnurr, P. (1988). What is a case? A 45-year study of psychiatric impairment within a college sample selected for mental health. *Archives of General Psychiatry, 45*, 313–319.

van Fraassen, B. (1989). *Laws and Symmetry*. Oxford: Clarendon.

van Goor-Lambo, G., Orley, J., Poustka, F. & Rutter, M. (1990). Classification of abnormal psychosocial situations: Preliminary report of a revision of a WHO scheme. *Journal of Child Psychology and Psychiatry, 31*, 229–241.

Vernon, J.A. (1963). *Inside the Black Room*. New York: Potter.

Viesselman, J.O. & Roig, M. (1985). Depression and suicidality in eating disorders. *Journal of Clinical Psychiatry, 46*, 118–124.

Virchow, R. (1859). *Cellular Pathology* (2nd ed.). (F. Chance, Trans.). New York: Dorsey (1971).

von Haller, A. (1952). De partibius corporis human: Sensibilitous et irritabilitous. *Comments of the Society of Reg. Sciences of Gotting, 2,* 114—158.

von Ranke, L. (1821). Wilhelm von Humboldt on the historian's task. In G. Iggers & K. Moltke (Eds. & Trans.), *Ranke's Theory and Practice of History.* Indianapolis: Bobbs-Merrill.

von Ranke, L. (1874). *Sammtlicke Werke* (Vol. 33). Leipzig: Franz Deuticke.

von Weizsaecker, V. (1957). Biologischer akt, symptom und krankheit. [Reprinted in V. v. Wiezsaecker & Wyss, D. *Zwischen Medizin und Philosophie.* Göttingen: Vandenhöck & Ruprecht.

von Weizsaecker, V. (1968). *Theorie der Einheit von Wahrnehmen und Bewegen* (4th ed.). Stüttgart: Thieme.

von Wright, G.H. (1971). *Explanation and Understanding.* Ithaca, NY: Cornell University Press.

von Wright, G.H. (1987). *Wittgenstein.* Minneapolis: University of Minnesota Press.

Walker, L.E.A. (1987). Inadequacies of the masochistic personality disorder diagnosis for women. *Journal of Personality Disorders, 1,* 183—189.

Wallace, E. (1980a). Essay: Review of D. Stannard's *Shrinking History. Clio Medica, 17,* 247—252.

Wallace, E. (1980b). Freud and cultural evolutionism. In E. Wallace & L. Pressley (Eds.), *Essays in the History of Psychiatry* (pp. 182—202). Columbia, SC: R.L. Bryan for South Carolina Department of Mental Health.

Wallace, E. (1983a). *Dynamic Psychiatry in Theory and Practice.* Philadelphia: Lea & Febiger.

Wallace, E. (1983b). *Freud and Anthropology: A History and Reappraisal* (Monograph 55). New York: International Universities Press.

Wallace, E. (1983c). Reflections on the relationship between psychoanalysis and Christianity. *Pastoral Psychology, 31,* 215—243.

Wallace, E. (1984). Freud and religion: A history and reappraisal. *Psychoanalytic Study of Society, 10,* 113—162.

Wallace, E. (1985). *Historiography and Causation in Psychoanalysis: An Essay on Psychoanalytic and Historical Epistemology.* Hillsdale, NJ: Analytic Press.

Wallace, E. (1986). Determinism, possibility, and ethics. *Journal of the American Psychoanalytic Association, 34,* 933—974.

Wallace, E. (1988a). Mind-body: Monistic dual-aspect interactionism. *Journal of Nervous and Mental Disease, 176,* 4—21.

Wallace, E. (1988b). Philosophy of Psychiatry: General issues. *Current Opinion in Psychiatry, 1,* 617—623.

Wallace, E. (1988c). What is truth? Some philosophical contributions to psychiatric issues. *American Journal of Psychiatry, 145,* 137—147.

Wallace, E. (1989a). Letter to the Editor. *American Journal of Psychiatry, 146,* 132.

Wallace, E. (1989b). Philosophy of psychiatry II. *Current Opinion in Psychiatry, 2,* 667—675.

Wallace, E. (1989c). Pitfalls of a one-sided image of science: Adolf Grünbaum's *Foundations of Psychoanalysis. Journal of the American Psychoanalytic Association, 37,* 493—529.

Wallace, E. (1989d). Toward a phenomenological and minimally theoretical psychoanalysis. *Annual of Psychoanalysis*, *17*, 17–69.

Wallace, E. (1990a). Mind-body and the future of psychiatry. *Journal of Medicine and Philosophy*, *15*, 41–73.

Wallace, E. (1990b). Psychiatry and religion: Toward a dialogue and public philosophy. *Psychiatry and the Humanities*, *11*, 195–222.

Wallace, E. (1991). Psychoanalytic perspectives on religion. *International Review of Psychoanalysis*, *18*, 265–278.

Wallace, E. (1992a). Freud and the mind-body problem. In T. Gelfand & S. Kerr (Ed.), *Freud and the History of Psychoanalysis* (pp. 17-69). Hillsdale, NJ: Analytic Press.

Wallace, E. (1992b). Psychiatry: The healing amphibian. In D. Browning & I Evison (Eds.), *Does Psychiatry Need a Public Philosophy?* (pp. 74–120). Chicago: Nelson/ Hall.

Wallace, E. (in press-a). The meaning of 'mental health.' In W. Reich (Ed.), *The Encyclopedia of Bioethics*, Revised Edition. New York: Macmillan.

Wallace, E. (in press-b). Psychiatry's sickness and its biological cure. *Psychiatry*.

Wallace, E. & Pressley, L.C. (Eds.) (1980). *Essays in the History of Psychiatry: A 10th Anniversary Supplemtary Volume to the Psychiatric Forum*. Columbia, SC: William. S. Hall Psychiatric Institute.

Wallerstein, R. (1986a). Psychoanalysis as science. *Psychoanalytic Quarterly*, *55*, 414–451.

Wallerstein, R. (1986b). The transformation of thought that the nuclear age requires: Can we achieve it? *Psychoanalytic Inquiry*, *6*, 303–312.

Walsh, W. (1958). *Philosophy and History: An Introduction*. New York: Harper & Brothers.

Walsh, W. (1969). Positivist and idealist approaches to history. In R. Nash (Ed.), *Ideas in History* (Vol. 2). New York: E.P. Dutton.

Warner, R. (1978). The diagnosis of antisocial and hysterical personality disorders. *Journal of Nervous and Mental Disease*, *166*, 839–845.

Webb, L., DiClemente, C., Johnstone, E., Sanders, J. & Perley, R. (Eds.). (1981). *DSM-III Training Guide, for Use with the American Psychiatric Association's Diagnostic and Statistical Manual of Mental Disorders* (3rd ed.). New York: Brunner/Mazel.

Weber, M. (1949). *The Methodology of the Social Sciences*. E.A. Shils & H.A. Finch (Eds. & Trans.). Glencoe, IL: Free Press.

Weimer, W.B. (1977). A conceptual framework for cognitive psychology: Motor theories of the mind. In R. Shaw & J. Bransford (Eds.), *Perceiving, Acting, and Knowing*. Hillsdale, NJ: Lawrence Erlbaum.

Weinberger, D. (1987). Implications of normal brain development for the patho-genesis of schizophrenia. *Archives of General Psychiatry*, *44*, 660–669.

Weiner, D. (1979). The apprenticeship of Philippe Pinel: A new document, "observations of Citizen Pussin on the insane." *American Journal of Psychiatry*, *136*, 1128–1134.

Weiner, D. (1990). Mind and body in the clinic: Alexander Crichton, Philippe Pinel and the birth of psychiatry (pp. 331–405). In G.S. Rousseau (Ed.), *Mind and Body in the Enlightenment*. Los Angeles: University of California Press.

Weiner, H. (1986). Die geschichte der psychosomatischen medizin und das Leib-Seele problem in der medizin. *Psychosomatik, 36,* 361—391.

Weiss, J. & Sampson, H. (1986). *The Psychoanalytic Process: Theory, Clinical Observation and Empirical Research.* New York: Guilford Press.

Weiss, S. & Ebert, M. (1983). Psychological and behavioral characteristics of normal-weight bulimics and normal-weight controls. *Psychosomatic Medicine, 45,* 293—303.

Weitbrecht, J.H. (1957). Zur frage der spezifität psychopathologischer symptome. *Fortschr Neurol Psychiatr, 25,* 41—56.

Wernicke, C. (1894—1900). *Grundriss der Psychiatrie der Klinischen Vorlesun Gen.* Leipzig: Thieme.

Wernicke, C. (1906). *Grundri der Psychiatrie in Klinischen Vorlesungen* (2nd ed.). Leipzig: Thieme.

Weyer, J. (1906). De praestigius daemonicum (On the trickery of demons). 1563. Dr. J. Weyer and the Witch Mania. In C. Singer (Ed.), *Studies in the History and Method of Science.* Oxford: Oxford University Press.

White, K.L. (1988). Introductory essay. In K.L. White (Ed.), *The Task of Medicine: Dialogue at Wickenburg* (pp. 1—96). Menlo Park, CA: Henry J. Kaiser Foundation.

Widiger, T.A., Frances, A.J., Pincus, H.A. & Davis, W.W. (1990). DSM-IV literature reviews: Rationale, process, and limitations. *Journal of Psychopathology and Behavioral Assessment, 12,* 189—202.

Widiger, T.A., Frances, A.J., Pincus, H.A., Davis, W.W. & First, M.B. (1991). Toward an empirical classification for the DSM-IV. *Journal of Abnormal Psychology, 100,* 280—288.

Wiggins, O.P. & Schwartz, M.A. (1991). Research into personality disorders: The alternatives of dimensions and ideal types. *Journal of Personality Disorders, 5,* 69—81.

Wiggins, O.P., Schwartz, M.A. & Northoff, G. (1990). Toward a Husserlian phenomenology of the initial stages of schizophrenia. In M. Spitzer & B. Maher (Eds.), *Philosophy and Psychopathology* (pp. 21—34). New York: Springer Verlag.

Wilkes, K.V. (1988). *Real People.* Oxford: Oxford University Press.

Williams, G. & Nesse, R. (1991). The dawn of Darwinian medicine. *Quarterly Review of Biology, 66,* 1—22.

Williams, J.B.W. (1985a). The multiaxial system of DSM-III: Where did it come from and where should it go? I. Its origins and critiques. *Archives of General Psychiatry, 42,* 175—180.

Williams, J.B.W. (1985b). The multiaxial system of DSM-III: Where did it come from and where should it go? II. Empirical studies, innovations, and recommendations. *Archives of General Psychiatry, 42,* 181—186.

Williams, J.B.W. & Spitzer, R.L. (1983). The issue of sex bias in DSM-III: A critique of "a woman's view of DSM-III" by Marcie Kaplan. *American Psychologist, 38,* 793—798.

Williams, J.B.W., Spitzer, R.L. & Skodol, A.E. (1985). DSM-III in residency training: Results of a national survey. *American Journal of Psychiatry, 142,* 755— 758.

Willis, T. (1667). *De Morbis Convulsivis.* London: n.p.

Willis, T. (1672). *De Anima Brutorum.* Oxonii: R. Daris.

Windelband, W. (1980). History and natural science (G. Oakes, Trans. & introduction). *History and Theory, 19,* 165—185.

Wittgenstein, L. (1958). *Philosophical Investigations* (2nd ed., G.E.M. Anscombe, Trans.). Oxford: Basil Blackwell.

Wolowitz, H. (1972). Hysterical character and feminine identity. In J. Bardwick (Ed.), *Readings on the Psychology of Women*. New York: Harper & Row.

World Health Organization (1967). *Manual of the International Statistical Classification of Diseases, Injuries and Causes of Death (ICD-8)*. Geneva: World Health Organization.

World Health Organization (1973). *Report of the International Pilot Study of Schizophrenia*. Geneva: World Health Organization.

World Health Organization (1978). *International Classification of Diseases* (9th rev. ed.). Geneva: World Health Organization.

World Health Organization (1991). *Mental Disorders: Glossary and Guide to the Classification in Accordance with the 10th Revision of the International Classifications of Diseases—Draft*. Geneva: World Health Organization.

Wu, J. Siegel, B., Haier, R. & Buchsbaum, M. (1990). Testing the Swerdlow-Koob model of schizophrenia pathophysiology using positron emission tomography. *Behavioral and Brain Sciences, 13*, 169–170.

Wulach, J.P. (1983). Diagnosing the DSM-III antisocial personality disorder. *Professional Psychology: Research and Practice, 14*, 330–340.

Wynne, L.C. (1987). A preliminary proposal for strengthening the multiaxial approach of DSM-III. In G. Tischler (Ed.), *Diagnosis and Classification in Psychiatry: A Critical Appraisal of DSM-III*. New York: Cambridge University Press.

Wyrsch, J. (1946). Über die intuition bei der Erkennuung des schizophrenien. *Schweiz Medizin Wochenschrift, 46*, 1173–1176.

Young, R.M. (1985). *Darwin's Metaphor: Nature's Place in Victorian Culture*. Cambridge, UK: Cambridge University Press.

Zilboorg, G. (1935). *The Medical Man and the Witch during the Renaissance*. Baltimore: Johns Hopkins Press.

Zilboorg, G. & Henry, G.W. (1941). *A History of Medical Psychology*. New York: W. W. Norton.

Zimmerman, M. & Spitzer, R. (1989). Melancholia from DSM-III to DSM-III-R. *American Journal of Psychiatry, 146*, 19–28.

Zinsser, H. (1935). *Rats, Lice, and History*. Boston: Little Brown.

Zohar, J. & Insel T.R. (1987). Obsessive-compulsive disorder: Psychobiological approaches to diagnosis, treatment and pathophysiology. *Biological Psychiatry, 22*, 667–687.

Zubin, J. (Ed.). (1961). *Field Studies in the Mental Disorders*. New York: Grune & Stratton.

Zubin, J. (1977). But is it good for science? *Clinical Psychologist, 31*, 5–7.

Zucker, K. (1928). Experimentelles über sinnestäuschungen. *Archiv für Psychiatrie, 83*, 706–754.

Index

morbidity, 23
Morel, B., 67–69
mortality, 23
mouches volantes, 337n
mourning, 157
movement disorders, 285
multiaxial system, 2, 111, 143,
    235, 270, 273, 274
multicausality, 71
multiple personality disorder, 188,
    200, 203, 204. *See also*
    Dissociative Disorders
multiple sclerosis, 247
Multiple Subjectivity Disorder,
    203
Munro, J., 64
Musto, D., 26
mutual concealment, 138, 139,
    141
mythology, 19, 39

Nagel, E., 288
narcissism, 240
Narcissistic Personality Disorder,
    133, 145
National Institutes of Mental Health
    (NIMH), 37, 38
natural
    attitude, 131, 157, 334n
    laws, 32
    selection, 226
neural
    network, 282
    processing, 296
neurasthenia, 34, 54, 62, 75
neurobiological referents, 12
neuroses, 56, 61, 100, 322, 326,
    328
neurosis, 44, 56, 76, 120, 151, 157
neurotic depression, 223
New York State Commission in
    Lunacy, 75
New York State Psychiatric
    Institute, 35
nihilism, 35
NIMH. *See* National Institutes of
    Mental Health

nomological
    invariance, 109
    regularity, 120
    universals, 115
noisy and idle, as diagnosis, 75
nomothetic/idiographic distinction,
    264, 266, 270, 273
nomothetic science
    clinical activity and, 269
    complementarity of, 46, 74, 273, 274
    DSM-III and, 268, 269, 273, 274
    historical investigation and, 21
    limits of, 70, 86, 264–266
    Windelband on, 264–266
nonnaturals, the, 51
normality, 50, 151
normativism, 234
Nosographie Philosophique, 64
nosology, 12, 270
nosology, psychiatric, history of, 39
nosology of context, 10, 269, 270,
    273, 275–277
nucleus accumbens, 285
nursing ethics, 102

objectivity, 13, 131, 194, 239,
    318, 323
object relations theory, 194, 196,
    303
objects, intentional, 196
observables, 71, 92
observation, level of, 274
*Observation on the Nature, Kinds,
    Causes and Prevention of
    Insanity*, 62
obsessive thoughts, 192
obsessive-compulsive disorders,
    102
oedipal desires, 338n
oligophrenia, 319
operational
    criteria of application, 120
    definitions, 2, 5, 104, 108, 121, 318,
    335
operationalism, 119. *See also*
    operationism
operationism, 111, 319, 321

Library of Congress Cataloging-in-Publication Data

Philosophical perspectives on psychiatric diagnostic classification /
  edited by John Z. Sadler, Osborne P. Wiggins, and Michael A.
  Schwartz.
    p. cm. — (The Johns Hopkins series in psychiatry and
neuroscience)
    Includes bibliographical references and index.
    ISBN 0-8018-4637-4 (hc : alk. paper) ISBN 0-8018-4770-2 (pbk : alk. paper)
    1. Mental illness—Classification. 2. Diagnostic and statistical
manual of mental disorders. I. Sadler, John Z., 1953–
II. Wiggins, Osborne P., 1943– . III. Schwartz, Michael A., 1944–
IV. Series.
    [DNLM: 1. Mental Disorders—classification. 2. Mental Disorders—
diagnosis. 3. Philosophy, Medical. WM 141 P568 1993]
RC455.2.C4P48 1993
616.89'0012—dc20
DNLM/DLC
for Library of Congress   93-15949